PIMLICO

108

THE SHARP END

John Ellis was born in Bradford and educated at the Universities of Sussex and Manchester. He was a lecturer in the latter's Department of Military Studies before becoming a full-time writer. His books include *The Social History of the Machine Gun* (also in Pimlico); *Eye-Deep in Hell*, an account of trench life in the Great War; *Cassino, The Hollow Victory*; and *Brute Force: Allied Strategy and Tactics in the Second World War*.

THE SHARP END

The Fighting Man in World War II

JOHN ELLIS

PIMLICO

PIMLICO
An imprint of Random House
20 Vauxhall Bridge Road, London SW1V 2SA

Random House Australia (Pty) Ltd
20 Alfred Street, Milsons Point Sydney
New South Wales 2061, Australia

Random House New Zealand Ltd
18 Poland Road, Glenfield
Auckland 10, New Zealand

Random House South Africa (Pty) Ltd
PO Box 337, Bergvlei, South Africa

Random House UK Ltd Reg. No. 954009

First published by David & Charles 1980
Revised edition published by Windrow & Greene 1990
Pimlico edition 1993

3 5 7 9 10 8 6 4 2

Printed and bound in Great Britain by
Mackays of Chatham PLC, Chatham, Kent

ISBN 0-7126-5891-2

Photograph Credits: *Imperial War Museum, London* pp. 193,
195–99, 202–10, 214–20, 223 top, 224.
US National Archives, Washington DC pp. 194, 200, 201, 211–13,
221, 223 bottom.

Contents

The Sharp End of War

We few, we happy few, we band of brothers;
For he today that sheds his blood with me
Shall be my brother; be he ne'er so vile
This day shall gentle his condition:
And gentlemen in England, now a-bed
Shall think themselves accursed they were not here,
And hold their manhoods cheap whiles any speaks
That fought with us upon Saint Crispin's day.
SHAKESPEARE, *King Henry V*

There's one thing you men can say when it's all
over and you're home once more. You can thank God
that twenty years from now when you're sitting by
the fireside with your grandson on your knee, and he
asks you what you did in the war, you won't have to
shift him to the other knee, cough and say,
'I shovelled crap in Louisiana'.
GENERAL PATTON, 1944

Ever since your victory at Alamein, you have nightly
pitched your moving tents a day's march nearer home.
In days to come when people ask you what you did in
the Second World War, it will be enough to say:
I marched with the Eighth Army.
GENERAL MONTGOMERY, 1943

It is only the complete absence of an enemy
that makes a soldier feel heroic.
CAPTAIN P. COCHRANE

I went where I was told to go, and did what I was
told to do, but no more. I was scared shitless just
about all the time.
PRIVATE FIRST CLASS JAMES JONES

I
Induction and Training

It must be so – it's wrong to doubt
The voluntary system's best.
Your conscript, when you've dug him out,
Has not the Happy Warrior's zest.
Because it seemed the thing to do
I joined with other volunteers
But – well I don't mind telling you
I didn't reckon for three years.
Though we observe the Higher Law
And though we have our quarrel just,
Were I permitted to withdraw
You wouldn't see my arse for dust.
ANON, 1917

So many things happen here that we cannot
explain, or that we cannot prepare for, that our
outward attitude is wary, and tough, and often
comical. We are scared easily. A blast on a whistle
sends us running; the word 'ten-Shun!' stops us
from breathing; the sight of the Sergeant makes
us tremble. The boys who were scared of dying,
and those who weren't, see now that it will be a
long time before they have an opportunity to do
any dying; they are now scared of sergeants,
commissioned officers, KP, and humiliation
before their fellow men.
AMERICAN TRAINEE, 1943

Absurd to think that Liberty, the splendid
Nude of our dreams, the intercessory saint
For us to judgement, needs to be defended
By sick fatigue-men brimming with complaint
And misery, who bear till all is ended
Every imaginable pattern of restraint.
JOHN MANIFOLD, 1941

9

World War II was by far the most sophisticated military conflict to that date. At every level soldiers were required to display much more technical expertise and individual initiative than had ever been the case before. Weapons were more complex, from the light machine gun, through the howitzer, to the tank, while small unit tactics laid a quite new emphasis upon dispersal, mutual support and a flexible responsiveness to the demands of the local situation. The skills and imagination expected of a rifleman in 1944 would have reduced most nineteenth-century soldiers to bewildered inaction. Yet this war was fought almost entirely by non-professionals, by men conscripted from civilian life and thrown into battle after only three months or so of training. The main purpose of this book is to show how well they performed in the vilest imaginable conditions, but first it is necessary to get some idea of how well prepared they were for the ordeal that awaited them.

In one respect, in both the British and American armies, considerable advances were made over previous attempts at large-scale mobilisation. One of the most worrying lessons of World War I had been the number of men at the front obviously unsuitable for combat because of innate psychological deficiencies. From the very outset of the next war it was decided to weed such men out as early as possible rather than waste time and money training them only to have them break down on their first contact with the enemy and so endanger the lives of their comrades and the cohesion of their unit.[1] When the inductees were first medically examined therefore, an attempt, albeit cursory, was made to assess their psychological stability and where this was obviously suspect, particularly on the evidence of their previous medical history, they were either rejected outright or assigned to non-combat formations. Of the 5.5 million men examined by the British army, some 2.5 per cent were rejected outright for psychiatric reasons – a full 12 per cent of the total number of rejections. The Americans were even more cautious. They rejected an amazing 10 per cent of all those examined for these reasons alone, which meant that 32 per cent of all rejections, or around 2 million young men, were solely on psychiatric grounds. This figure caused considerable alarm in both military and civilian circles, though one is entitled to wonder whether, had the tests been anything like exhaustive, anyone would have been deemed adequate combat material. One American psychiatrist recalled that 'my examinational procedure consisted of four rapid-fire questions. "How do you feel?", "Have you ever been sick?", "Are you nervous?", "How do you think you will get along in the Army?"' [2] For other medical men this would have constituted a lengthy cross-examination and they limited themselves to that old military favourite, 'Do you like girls?'

The British were more loath to reject men outright and from early in the war set up special units to absorb those of limited intelligence or emotional stability, known generally as 'dullards'. Many of these were drafted into the Pioneer Corps, responsible for heavy labouring duties both in England and overseas. They constituted the unarmed companies of the Corps and can fairly claim to have got the rough end of the stick. In Italy they were often used as porters to carry supplies to the front and bring stretchers back. An observer officer of the 46th Division, at Monte Camino, wrote: 'They provided bearers for positions well forward of Monastery Hill. During the battle they worked for 72 hours without sleep or rest until towards the end they worked . . . like robots . . . They were all on the wrong side of thirty.' [3] In north-west Europe they often found themselves doing fairly skilled work that in other specialised formations, RASC or REME for example, would have entitled them to special trade rates of pay, but these they never received. Some companies, like the 295th at Calais, were not even provided with the oilskins and leather jerkins that were standard issue for the Sappers and such like.

One category of men who did not find it any easier than in previous wars to stay out of the front line were those with religious objections to military service. In the United Kingdom 60,000 men claimed exemption on these grounds, of whom 3,500 were granted it unconditionally, 29,000 were required to work in agriculture, 15,000 to perform non-combatant duties in the army and the rest had their claims dismissed. Under the terms of the US Selective Training and Service Act of September 1940, provision was made for an alternative service for conscientious objectors, administered by the Civilian Public Service. Little information seems to be available about the remote agricultural and forestry camps that were set up to employ these men, but conditions there were often harsh. In fact, of the 75,000 or so men who registered as objectors, a mere 0.13 per cent of the total number of males registered under the Act, only 12,000 were sent to these camps. An equal number actually went to prison and the rest were drafted into the army, some for only non-combatant duties.

Ironically, however, though it can fairly be claimed that the mass of soldiers in the Allied armies in World War II were of a higher average quality than in any other previous war,[4] the combat formations, the men who did the toughest job of all, benefited least from this increased selectivity. In the American army, for example, official sources make it quite clear that these units, especially the infantry, never consistently got men of the best calibre. The inductees were divided into four categories according to educational background and vague criteria of leadership and initiative, and it was found throughout the war that the rifle battalions always had a far higher percentage of Groups III and IV men than did the rear-echelon formations. To some extent this was unavoidable in that great pains were taken to ensure that a man with civilian skills, and thus more likely to be in a higher category, was assigned to the appropriate specialised branch in the army. Unfortunately this meant that the infantry became the last resort for all men with no obvious skills. This negative aspect of the recruitment of combat soldiers was underlined by the almost complete lack of any checks on the physical resilience of those shunted off to the line battalions. As the official history remarks:

> General service men were assigned to units irrespective of finer physical gradations, largely on the basis of occupational skill. Consequently the question whether, in a given unit, a man would engage in hand-to-hand fighting, march long distances on foot, carry a heavy pack, or go without sleep and food counted very little in his original assignment.[5]

The effect of this is brought home by the fact that in one sample of 6,000 infantrymen examined in November 1943, the average height was only 5ft 7.7in whereas the average height in the army as a whole was 5ft 8.4in. The implications this had for strength and stamina in general are fairly clear.

Certain senior officers were very aware of the dangers of such a system and efforts were made to improve the quality of those assigned to the infantry, with particular regard to the creation of effective NCOs and junior officers. A Physical Profile Plan was introduced by which physique was supposed to count in its own right as a positive qualification for serving in the fighting battalions. High-quality men from other branches, notably Aviation cadets, Army Special Training Program men, and some who had served for more than one year in the Zone of the Interior, were drafted into the infantry and sent overseas as replacements. Approximately 200,000 men were recruited in this way and it did have positive results, evidenced by a definite decline in the number of complaints about the quality of the replacements. Nevertheless, these changes came too late to dramatically alter the composition of the ground forces, the bulk of whose fighting soldiers had already been assigned in the great drafts of 1942 and 1943. In short, the 'poor bloody infantry' once again merited their bleak sobriquet. As always, they had the hardest job to do and yet were regarded as amongst the lowest orders in the military hierarchy. However, it is quite clear that the generals and administrators had better luck than they deserved. Though they chose their actual warriors almost with indifference, these latter proved to be men who could hold their heads high in the company of the most exalted professionals.

It cannot really be claimed that the training they received had a great deal to do with this. It was of two basic types: that for the individual destined to be a replacement, and that for men organised into divisions that had not yet gone overseas. The latter lasted much longer, as the men had not only to master their weapons but also had to take part in company, divisional and corps exercises as their officers familiarised themselves with the manifold problems of command. Even so as the war went on the time allotted was reduced, in the American army, from 52 to 37 weeks. Replacements on the other hand only went through a 3-month course and, towards the end of the war when there was an acute shortage of front-line troops, some American infantrymen arriving in north-west Europe had received only 6 weeks training.

In all the armies individual training had three main purposes: to rid the conscript of civilian preconceptions about his 'rights' and personal freedom; to familiarise him with the weapons that he was likely to have to operate, mainly the rifle, mortar and machine gun; and to give him some experience of the noise and confusion of actual combat. Armies succeeded best in the first of these tasks, not least because it was in that area that they had had the most practice. From the first moment he joined up the recruit was constantly made aware that his only role as an individual was to obey orders and sublimate his personality to the better functioning of the unit as a whole. When Jim Lucas arrived at the Marine 'boot camp' on Parris Island, he and his fellows were from the first only addressed as 'you people'. 'I had never realised that membership of the human race could be made to sound so trivial and repulsive.'[6]

American academics who were sucked into the military and themselves had to undergo this basic training were very aware of its
purposes. One wrote:

> The essential fact about induction, reception-center, and basic train-
> ing experience is the knifing-off of past experience. Nothing in one's
> past seems relevant unless, possibly, a capacity for adaptation and the
> ability to assume a new role. Those who are unable to do so fall readily
> into the psychoneurotic category and may get medical discharges . . .
> The sense of being thrust into a completely alien role and some feeling
> of personal degradation is common to a large number of recruits.[7]

Another who summarised the basic purposes of his induction to
military life made quite explicit the authorities' attempts to de-
humanise the recruit and force him to realise that he was nothing
but a rather inconsequential cog in the larger machine. He became

> . . . aware of the rudiments of military life by actual participation. The
> use of his time is scheduled for him by the staff of the induction center.
> The first thing that he must learn is that there is a time for everything.
> When this time is, and how much is allowed, is determined by the
> institution and not by the recruit. The second thing he must learn is
> that how this is to be used is defined by the institution, except the rare
> 'free time'. Third, the institution defines how the task allotted to a
> given time is to be accomplished. Fourth, the recruit learns that he
> does everything in formation, that is, with his group. In short, the
> recruit is no longer an individual, with the right of personal choices,
> alternatives and decisions. Instead, he is, in informal army usage, 'a
> body'. This 'body' must be trained to act without question or hesi-
> tation to institutional stimuli. The loss of choice and initiative de-
> velops in him a sense of dependency on the institution for decisions.[8]

A British recruit made just the same point about this sense of
dependency when he remarked that 'the Army has two opposite
effects on a man. It makes him more concerned about the personal
petty comforts which he no longer takes for granted: and it makes
him less competent to secure them. He develops a fatalistic
streak.'[9] Other British soldiers were depressedly aware of the way
the army was slowly succeeding in eroding their individuality and
reducing their personal horizons so that they lost interest in anything but the most trivial, day-to-day details. One wrote:

> To thrive on a few encouraging words from an unthinking oaf in
> authority, to delight in a cup of bad tea and a cigarette snatched

between parades, to laugh inordinately at clumsy humour or to be moved almost to tears by another's misfortunes – these were not the natural preoccupations of a mature and fairly experienced mind, yet in all those years of army life they were mine. I was wholly lost in that life, following it with all I had of capacity to experience.[10]

Another appalled recruit gave the following account of his barrack-mates:

> We have spent every evening of the past fortnight on our hands and knees scraping our bedroom floor with razor blades until it is absolutely white! Why? Partly because we were told that the floors were not clean enough, but chiefly because of all this damned competition. One room starts doing something for the weekly inspection, and the next room does it or goes one better. I am not exaggerating when I say that we now have to take our shoes off outside the room and walk about inside in our socks. We are provided with floor-polishers called 'bumpers'. The handle of ours has been scraped with a razor blade till it looks like a bleached bone, and a special pair of woollen gloves has to be worn by anyone who touches it. We have a bucket in the room for rubbish: it has now been burnished so brightly that if you even put cigarette ash into it everybody screams. We unscrew all the handles and latches on the windows before polishing them, also the bit of metal around the keyhole and the door-knob. I have really wondered sometimes if I am not going mad.[11]

Of course, all this suited the army perfectly. One American infantryman gave a graphic resumé of the basic purpose of the 'orientation' aspect of military training, showing just why it was necessary to inculcate into men this slavish deference to the whims and fancies of their superiors:

> Everything the civilian soldier learned and was taught from the moment of his induction was one more delicate step along the path of the soldier evolving towards the acceptance of his death. The idea that his death, under certain circumstances, is correct and right. The training, the discipline, the daily humiliations, the privileges of 'brutish' sergeants, the living en masse like schools of fish, are all directed towards breaking down the sense of sanctity of the physical person, and towards hardening the awareness that a soldier is the chattel (hopefully a proud chattel, but a chattel all the same) of the society he serves and was born a member of. And is therefore as dispensable as the ships and tanks and guns and ammo he himself serves and dispenses. Those are the terms of the contract he has made – or, rather, that the state has handed him to sign.[12]

Yet one must be careful not to succumb to a too paranoidal view of the military's efforts in this direction. Whilst this was certainly the broad thrust of induction and training, in fact the individuals who operated the system were never themselves so untramelled by hidebound procedures, rituals and petty formalism that they could distance themselves sufficiently to cynically produce an army of mindless, yet mechanically perfect robots. But they too were products of just the same training, just the same blind obedience to the interests of the institution as a whole, and the instruction they gave suffered accordingly. The form of doing things was deemed preeminent and efforts to prepare men for the shock of combat often degenerated into catechismic parrottings, militarily valid only in terms of a Pharisaic deference to the 'book' and the 'manual'. A Marine at the Quantico camp wrote:

> Today we pitched tents in the rain, for practice, going through a most ridiculous rigmarole in doing so. No-one knew exactly how to do it – the thing is done so rarely – but all the instructors and officers had read up hastily so we managed to get it all completed sufficiently well in the end. These little farces are taken seriously, since they are prescribed, and they pervade all military life. [13]

Those concerned with weapons instruction in the British army received many complaints from participants and observers about the way in which such instruction was often reduced to virtual gibberish, a time-honoured incantation rather than any attempt to actually explain the workings and use of a particular weapon. One sergeant complained:

> Much of the material crammed up from technical hand-books is delivered as monotonous sing-song catalogues and the class is expected to remember an explanation given verbatim. Any departure from the wording or the order in which it is given, even though the answer may be perfectly correct, is as wrong as the wildest guess ... [Another sergeant had] known instructors when interrupted by a question go back to the point at which they stopped in order to recite again ... [The 'naming of parts' became sacrosanct and, according to another trainee] there appeared to be a tendency among instructors to regard the names of parts with the same awe as a child regards his catechism. [14]

According to another American trainee:

> It is during basic training that conformity is carried to its extreme . . .
> Basic training programs adhere strictly to the Army's set of field
> manuals, which are revised as experience proves necessary . . . Com-
> bat veterans who have been returned to instruct trainees complained
> that they were unable to teach their battlefield knowledge if it con-
> flicted with the field manual . . . This emphasis upon uniformity of
> method tends to become exaggerated, and 'by the numbers' is a stock
> joke. It was found necessary to revise the bayonet manual when, in the
> North African campaign, men were observed bayoneting 'by the num-
> bers' to their own disadvantage.[15]

Some efforts were made to improve the situation. Professor
Valentine, cited above, was in charge of British efforts to improve
the quality of basic infantry training, though it is doubtful that he
was able to achieve much during the war itself. The Americans
made a particular effort to de-emphasise the more obvious aspects
of 'spit and polish' or 'chicken' and the chief of staff reported with
some satisfaction, in late 1942, that of the 472 hours of basic
training only 20 hours were devoted to close-order drill. Both
armies also paid increasing attention to combat simulation, and
basic training came to include short courses in which men were
exposed, as nearly as possible, to the conditions they would encounter on the battlefield. The British set up battle schools which
gave a 3-week course in which the recruit, to quote one trainee:

> . . . was put through the 'tough' things. Clawing through wire with a
> machine gun firing a couple of feet above their heads. Crawling upside
> down along a seemingly endless pole of scaffolding, while instructors
> threw sticks of gelignite. Panting uphill with bursting eardrums and
> thumping hearts to lunge with bayonets at straw-filled sacks. Bursting
> through the 'haunted house' with tommy guns blazing at dummy
> figures which sprang without warning from doorways, floors and
> ceilings.[16]

The very first of these courses rather went overboard in that the
War Office tried to base them upon 'hate' training, emphasising
the brutality of the enemy and attempting to brutalise the trainees
by taking them on visits to slaughterhouses and liberally strewing
the blood therefrom around the actual assault courses. This experiment, in 1942, was not deemed a success and was abandoned
after the first attempt. American courses differed little from that
described above. The vogue term was 'battle inoculation', which

comprised an infiltration course, in which men crawled through barbed wire under live overhead fire; a close combat course consisting of an advance down lanes studded with surprise targets and punctuated by bursts of live fire and explosions; a village fighting course to duplicate the conditions of street-fighting; an overhead artillery fire course; and a 3-day period of field exercises to test the men's performance at squad, platoon and company level.

But to the end the only really effective combat training was that received on the battlefield itself. Replacements only got to know their job properly when they were absorbed into a real front-line platoon, whilst battalions and divisions, trained *en bloc*, never functioned to full effect until they had actually been at the sharp end for some months. There they abandoned such of the 'book' that was not pertinent and evolved procedures related to real life, and these procedures were in turn passed on to the constant flow of replacements. The truth of this is demonstrated by the universally poor performance of Allied units at the beginning of the war when regular or freshly raised divisions, both trained according to largely theoretical precepts, first encountered the enemy. British defeats in France and Belgium, Norway, Malaya, Burma, Hong Kong, the Western Desert, were so comprehensive as to require little further elaboration (see Chapter 6). The Americans, moreover, did little better in the first months of their war and the unpreparedness of the troops had much to do with their failures. Certain units broke completely at Kesserine, in Tunisia, simply because they had not really known what to expect and were fired only by a naïve faith that it would be 'all right on the night'. An American officer drew attention to the nebulousness of his unit's self-confidence:

> We never really thought we were hot in camp. We always thought that out in the theater they would do it better – the sentry would never daydream, the communications would always work and our units would always be where and when they were supposed to be – we could see a hundred flaws in everything we did, a hundred ways in which an alert enemy could beat us by capitalising on our errors. Sometimes we made big talk about what our unit could do in action but we always knew it was just that.[17]

Their fears were justified, and it was not only in Tunisia that American troops' training was shown to be less than adequate. The early stages of the Pacific campaign included many incidents that boded ill for its future conduct. During the invasion of Attu in the Aleutians in May 1943, the 7th US Division went completely to pieces in this its first experience of combat. On New Georgia, in July, certain units were quite unable to cope with Japanese scare tactics and more than a few men were killed by their comrades firing blindly into the night and throwing grenades at an enemy that was not even there. Just the same thing happened on Hollandia when a portion of the 24th US Division was charged with guarding General Eichelberger's headquarters. From 10 pm these men

. . . carried on a terrific war. Tracer bullets from all directions made fireworks in the camp. Automatic rifles were fired and grenades were thrown. Troops on the inside and on the outside thought they were being attacked by the Japanese . . . [In fact] the Battle of Brinkman's Plantation was . . . a battle among Americans. A master-sergeant was killed and a number of troops were wounded. It was a disgraceful exhibition.[18]

In fact, even though divisions and battalions, as organic units, improved immensely during the remainder of the war, the inadequate training of the individual replacement continued to be a problem. In one official questionnaire to a sample of veteran officers from four divisions in the Pacific and Italy, asking what factors they thought were important in explaining poor combat performance, 22 per cent of officers in the former theatre and 24 per cent in the latter named 'inadequate training of our troops for combat'. In Italy, the enlisted men felt just the same way. Out of 1,000 infantry and artillerymen interviewed as they came out of the line at Cassino, fully two-thirds of them averred that training in such things as finding and handling mines and booby-traps, the nature of enemy weapons, enemy tactics, enemy defences, and what to do for trench-foot had been completely inadequate. Even in north-west Europe, in the last twelve months of the war, there were adverse comments by both the Americans and their Allies. General Bradley listed the most common shortcomings of raw troops, notably 'reliance on rumour and exaggerated reports, failure to support manoeuvering elements by fire, and a tendency to withdraw under high explosive fire rather than to advance out of it'.[19] A British staff sergeant of the 1st Royal Ulster Rifles commented on certain American units he encountered in March 1945:

It appeared that the American infantrymen were not trained in 'battle noises'. They seemed to drop to the ground and fire wherever shots were heard close by . . . One thing I did notice. The Americans will bunch, whereas we will go up two sides of a road. It was purely a matter of lack of experience. They were shouting at each other and firing at nothing. They're still doing it in Vietnam.[20]

Be that as it may, it cannot be stressed too highly that what has been said above reflects only on the adequacy of the training received by the combat soldiers, and not upon their innate ability or resilience. What follows will show just what an example of sheer guts and endurance was given by all Allied fighting troops when they eventually found themselves, however unprepared, at the sharp end.

2
The Physical Setting

The world wasn't made in a day,
And Eve didn't ride in a bus,
But most of the world's in a sandbag,
And the rest of it's plastered on us.

SOLDIERS' DOGGEREL, 1916

THE BATTLE

Helmet and rifle, pack and overcoat
Marched through a forest. Somewhere up ahead
Guns thudded. Like the circle of a throat
The night on every side was turning red.

They halted and they dug. They sank like moles
Into the clammy earth between the trees.
And soon the sentries, standing in their holes,
Felt the first snow. Their feet began to freeze.

At dawn the first shell landed with a crack.
Then shells and bullets swept the icy woods.
This lasted many days. The snow was black.
The corpses stiffened in their scarlet hoods.

Most clearly of that battle I remember
The tiredness in eyes, how hands looked thin
Around a cigarette, and the bright ember
Would pulse with all the life there was within.

PRIVATE FIRST CLASS LOUIS SIMPSON, 1945

And every night, dig . . . Dig in case the bombs
drop. Dig for discipline. Dig to save your skins.
Dig through sand. Dig, if necessary, through
rock. Dig for bloody victory.

LIEUTENANT N. McCALLUM, 1942

Climate and Terrain

World War II was a truly global conflict. The fighting ranged across the whole of northern Africa, from Ethiopia to Algeria, across the Pacific from New Guinea to Japan, throughout much of south-east Asia, and covered the bulk of Europe. Allied troops fought in all these theatres and their experiences involved a remarkable diversity of terrain and climate. Moreover, in almost all these places, the physical setting was inimical to what we should regard as normal human existence. This is very clear with regard to the rain forests of New Guinea, the coral catacombs of the central Pacific or the arid wastes of the Western Desert; what must also be stressed is that even in Europe the situation at the front often beggared description. In Italy, Holland and Germany rain and cold produced conditions of appalling severity. For the western city-dweller weather is at worst an inconvenience, but away from the amenities of urban life it can become a scourge, even in Europe. Be it in Italian mountains, a German forest or a ruptured canal system in Holland, mere day-to-day existence became a terrible ordeal.

In terms of false expectations, Italy was undoubtedly the most unpleasant surprise to troops who served there. Wet, cold and raw, it was the very antithesis of the 'sunny' Italy of the tourist handbills. The Fifth and Eighth Armies had to put up with two Italian winters and it would be difficult to decide which was the worst. The first was appalling with its drenching rain and freezing temperatures, but in many respects conditions the next year were just as bad. The Allied offensive had ground to a halt in the Apennines and the troops were left exposed to the full rigours of winter in the mountains. The weather was warm and settled until the end of September but then history began to repeat itself with a vengeance. There were heavy showers from 20 September and during October it hardly let up at all, raining continuously for twenty days. November was little better and there was extensive flooding. In December the temperature fell further and the snows started, only beginning to clear over two months later. Between December and March the temperature fell below zero on at least fifteen nights each month. The weather was 'the worst . . . in Italy for twenty years. Rain fell almost continuously, and in the mountains it turned to sleet. The men holding them were still in summer kit. One night [on Monte Fuso] a rifleman of the 1st Battalion [the

Rifle Brigade] died of exposure. Twelve others were carried down the mountain.'[1] An officer of the 3rd Welsh Guards, on Battaglia Ridge, wrote: 'The rain filled the slit-trenches, and a slit-trench was the only place where a man could find shelter from shell fire. He was permanently soaked to the skin, and permanently in danger. He spent his day in the bleak surroundings of stunted, decapitated trees, hundreds of waterlogged shell holes, unburied corpses of American and German soldiers, sopping blankets and discarded ration tins.'[2] At about this time Lieutenant H. L. Bond (36th US Division) was fortunate to be hospitalised with dysentry and he recalled later: 'I lay in my bed listening to the rain and thinking of the wretched men, my friends now, back there on the mountain getting soaked and shelled. I knew for certain that the worst part of the war was not the shooting or the shelling – although that had been bad enough – but the weather, snow, sleet and rain, and the prolonged physical misery which accompanied them.'[3]

Even so, conditions in Italy were not uniquely bad. Rain was a problem in many theatres. Even in Tunisia it was a marked feature of winter. It fell almost continuously in December 1942 and the following January, and was one of the reasons why the Allied dash to Tunis became bogged down and permitted the arrival of strong German reinforcements. In north-west Europe, too, the last autumn and winter of the war were uniformly bad. Luckily for the invading forces the rain held off completely until 19 August, but from then on it was a persistent misery. In October in Moselle, for example, there was double the average rainfall for that month. In the Reichswald, in January and February 1945, the attacking British troops had to put up with nineteen consecutive days of heavy rain which turned the roads and paths into a quagmire. Further north, conditions were made even worse by the Germans' systematic destruction of the Dutch and Belgian sea defences and irrigation systems. From November 1944 to the following January, the Canadian forces found themselves on the Waal and Maas rivers and, though they fought no major battle, the damp, the penetrating cold, rain and flooded ground made life intolerable. It was fearsomely cold. A British journalist visited this sector where 'the searching east winds numbed mind and body. Men, chattering with cold, their feet numb from exposure and their sodden clothing stiff as a board, dashed forward under terrible fire to win a few more yards.'[4] Conditions in much of the American line were just as bad and, in the Hürtgen Forest, were possibly even more brutal than in the Reichswald. The official US history is not given to purple prose but even it admits that the battle here was 'attrition unrelieved. Overcoats soaked with moisture and caked with freezing mud became too heavy for the men to wear. Seeping rain turned radios into useless impedimenta. So choked with debris was the floor of the forest that men broke under the sheer physical strain of moving supplies forward and evacuating the wounded.'[5] Conditions in the Ardennes, at the turn of the year, were no better. Even when the immediate danger of the German offensive had passed, casualties remained high. In January, the 30th US Division was losing 100 men a day from illnesses attributable to the snow and cold. In places foxholes had to be blasted out with explosives:

> It was the meanest winter in thirty-eight years. The weather was consistently bleak, the ground was covered with a thick blanket of coarse snow. The sharp wind blew in from the north and whipped up angry flurries, like tiny fragments of broken glass, that pierced the faces of the GIs. It was 5° below zero in St. Vith, 7° below at Wiltz, a steady zero at Bastogne. Where the bulldozers had flattened the snow, the ground was a solid sheet of ice . . . Illnesses like flu and trench foot caused by the merciless weather almost equalled combat casualties . . . Virtually the entire army had to live outdoors because the below-zero temperature froze and broke the water systems, heating installations and the sewers.[6]

And the mud that came with the rains and returned again with the thaw, had a horror all its own. Mud in fact is a motif of the whole war for, as on the Western Front between 1914 and 1918, extremes of temperature, incessant movement of men and vehicles, and unending artillery barrages all combined to turn fields and roads into cloying morasses. Observers in all theatres spoke of the uniqueness of their own particular brand of mud. Writing of a visit to France in early 1940, Anthony Gibbs observed: 'The Flanders mud is something which has no parallel on any other portion of the earth's crust. It combines the general characteristics of cow dung with a marked hygroscopic quality, so that the more you mess about with it, the messier it gets.'[7] Captain John Horsfall (1st Royal Irish Fusiliers) was equally impressed by the mud in Tunisia which 'had powers of adherence that I have never found elsewhere. A witch's brew of its own, the grey clay soil disintegrated rapidly when wet into a composition like glue mixed with baking powder . . . Only half an hour of rain was needed to achieve this devilish result.'[8] Which prompted Lieutenant J. M. Austin-Smith (12th [HAC] Regiment, Royal Horse Artillery) to write in a letter home: 'You can't get away from it. I am literally covered from head to foot in mud. Everything one touches is mud, including knife and fork, driving wheel, the cooker, everything.'[9]

In Italy, too, the interminable rain had the usual effect. The Welsh Guards officer already cited went on to insist that

> . . . the greatest enemy by far was the mud. The mud could not be cleared. As there was only one track, in use by one hundred and fifty mules and one hundred men night after night, its surface became a knee-deep glutinous morass, which only a month of unbroken sunshine would dry out. Once the surface had been liquified, a mule's spindly leg, digging deeply in with each step, was a sure way of making the quagmire almost bottomless. It was at its worst after a spell of dry weather, which only dried the mud into a yet stickier consistency and made it necessary with each step to lift the foot out of the ground, instead of merely from it.[10]

The 2nd Royal Scots were operating in the Sintria Valley in October 1944, when the rains came. Dry steam beds suddenly became 'roaring cataracts. Mule trains were held up and some of the animals drowned. In places the mud was so deep that many of the Jocks stuck fast. It was not unknown for a man to be pulled out by his comrades while his boots remained in the adhesive grip of what the Jocks called "Tally glaur".'[11] Captain John Guest, an artilleryman, made a particular effort to make clear to those back home the omnipresence of the mud:

> The ground for fifty yards outside is MUD – six inches deep, glistening, sticky, holding pools of water. Great excavations in the mud, leaving miniature alps of mud, show where other tents have been pitched in the mud, and moved on account of the mud to other places in the mud. The cumulative pyschological effect of mud is an experience which cannot be described . . . My men stand in the gunpits stamping their feet in the wet, their heads sunk in the collars of their greatcoats. When they speak to you they roll their eyes up because it makes their necks cold to raise their heads. Everyone walks with their arms out to help them keep their balance.[12]

In fact, in Italy, mud had an enormous bearing on the whole conduct of the campaign. After the assault on the Gothic Line, in August 1944, the Allies had hoped to press through the Lombardy Plain behind a fast-moving armoured spearhead. In the event they could only repeat the previous pattern of costly grinding infantry assaults. Weather and terrain had the last word. As Field-Marshal Alexander reported: 'The whole area is nothing but a reclaimed swamp – and not wholly reclaimed in some parts . . . Even in the best drained areas the soil remembers its marshy origins and when rained on forms the richest mud known to the Italian theatre.'[13]

North-west Europe had its mud, too, though here the problem was somewhat alleviated by better roads and more of them. In some sectors, moreover, it was kept at bay because there was so much flood-water. Even so, it is still an important motif of the soldiers' memoirs. An English regimental history noted that in Holland, in October 1944, 'everywhere there was to be mud, bogging the tanks, so deeply sometimes that even the recovery vehicles could not pull them out, putrefying anything that came in contact with it, seeping into the tank tents at night, making every-body cold and dirty and miserable from dawn until dusk.'[14] Bill Mauldin (45th US Division) wrote: 'Mud . . . is a curse which seems to save itself for war. I'm sure Europe never got this muddy during peacetime. I'm equally sure that no mud in the world is so deep or sticky or wet as European mud. It doesn't even have an honest color like ordinary mud.'[15]

Nor did better weather mean an end to all problems. Without doubt it made an enormous difference to the troops' living con-ditions, and sunshine and dry dugouts had an immediate impact on morale. But dried-out mud does not simply disappear. As Geoffrey Cox (2nd New Zealand Division) observed in Italy, in the last weeks of the war, it turned 'overnight to the white powder which is the dust of Italy, finer and more irritating than any dust the desert ever saw.'[16] Just the same thing happened in Tunisia and Normandy, and if mud had made life extremely unpleasant, dust made it positively dangerous. Columns of lorries and ar-moured vehicles raised great clouds of it as they passed and these became automatic targets for enemy fighters or artillery. As like as not by the time the attack came the convoy would have passed, and the main sufferers would be the infantry or other units actually dug in in that area.

Of course, in no theatre was exposure to the elements an un-relieved ordeal. Few men spent all their time outdoors and there were periods of good weather. The Italian summers were very pleasant, and after the Normandy invasion the weather was warm and settled until the end of September. Around the Mediterranean

conditions could be holiday-like. On Crete, a soldier of the 23rd
New Zealand Battalion wrote: 'Weather fine, am very happy and in
the best of health . . . Went down to the sea for a swim. All we do is
eat oranges and swim. Having a marvellous time. God! I am as fit as
a fiddle – a real box of birds.'[17] In Libya and Egypt, too, the
climate was generally very healthy. Though the sun was very hot,
most men soon got used to it and there were only a negligible
number of sunstroke cases. Many fewer, in fact, than the authorities had feared. On the whole the men were bronzed and fit, and
in this respect at least much better off than those in other theatres.

But there were drawbacks. Whilst the days were hot, the temperature plummeted at night, and during the winter months an icy
wind often blew up, against which the usual provision of two
blankets was less than adequate. In the desert itself, the heat could
also be a problem, as one journalist found out.

> The heat, it must be admitted, was not an unhealthy dry heat . . . But
> the sun was a burning metallic monster in a cloudless blue sky under
> which you perspired until the moisture dripped from nose, chin and
> elbows, and turned your shirt or shorts black and clinging. And the
> sand – the sand that blew about nearly all the time and penetrated your
> throat and eyes and truck carburettor – caked itself upon the sweaty
> wetness of your face and whole head and turned you into an all-khaki
> figure.[18]

From time to time, the sand was blown up by a hot desert wind, the
khamsin, of which the Arabs said, 'When the Khamsin blows, even
murder is justified', and occasionally it erupted into a fully-fledged
sand storm.

> Anyone who has not been in a sand storm cannot visualise how
> annoying and uncomfortable it can be. On this occasion far away in the
> distance could be seen a wall of sandy dust about one hundred feet high
> coming towards us. It struck us with terrific force and fine sand got
> into everything, including the hair, eyes, ears, and throat. It turned
> day into night while it lasted and afterwards came torrential rain – a
> truly unpleasant experience.[19]

And even unrelieved good weather could become a curse when
combined with the featurelessness of the landscape, for the Western Desert is thousands of square miles of nothing. Places marked
on the map, except along the coastal road, are merely cartographi-

cal abstractions. (Even El Alamein was nothing more than a tiny railway station.) Everything is flat. Features grandiloquently described as 'ridges' would anywhere else be almost imperceptible rises or dips. The ground is either sand, or extensive stretches of fossil-rich limestone scattered with loose slabs of rock. There is no vegetation except a scrub called camel's thorn which is nourished by the dew from the sea. Beyond this there is nothing for the eye and mind to focus upon, except such trivial distinctions as the different types of sand. 'There's gritty sand, good for travelling on; finer sand, where the trucks get bogged; or the seemingly firm surface shows a shibble of dark shingle, a sign of softness underneath. Some of the low-lying areas have perfectly flat pans of hard-baked sand-mud . . .'[20] Such a monotonous landscape eventually forced men into a spiritual vacuum. Private R. L. Crimp (2nd Rifle Brigade) soon began to feel this and noted in his diary:

> Just lately I've been feeling a bit browned off. There's a sort of psychological complaint some chaps get after long exposure on the Blue called 'desert weariness', though I can hardly claim to have reached that yet. But for months now we've been cut off from nearly every aspect of civilised life, and every day has been cast in the same monotonous mould. The desert, omnipresent, so saturates consciousness that it makes the mind as sterile as itself. It's only now that you realise how much you normally live through your senses. Here there's nothing for them.[21]

But of all the trials endemic to that part of the world undoubtedly the most abhorrent was the flies. Almost all writers who served in the African theatre have commented upon them. An official history called them a 'pertinacious, sticky, pestilential horror'.[22] Captain Peter Cochrane (2nd Queen's Own Cameron Highlanders) was unfortunately aware where many of them came from. 'The smell of human dung as well made us indignant. "It spoils yer dinner," complained Matthews, who had the wisdom not to think of the provenance of the flies paddling in the melted fat which constituted his bully beef. For flies there were, it seemed in millions.'[23] But it was not just human excrement that attracted them. The body itself was quite sufficiently enticing. R. L. Crimp noticed that

> . . . the Egyptian sort are militant in the extreme . . . imbued with a frenzied determination to settle on human flesh . . . Soon after sunrise they arrive in hordes from nowhere, then plague us with malign

persistence all through the day, swarming and buzzing round, trying
desperately to land on our faces, in our eyes, ears and nostrils, on our
arms, hands, knees and necks. And once settled they bite hard. Desert
sores, oases of succulence, draw them like magnets.[24]

Worst of all perhaps they were irresistibly attracted to food, and
eating was always a one-handed job, the other being used to try and
keep the flies from actually settling on the plate. This usually
proved impossible and every mouthful included the odd fly. Nothing could keep them away, though the strictest hygiene regulations
were enforced. Private E. Day (51st Highland Division) noted one
tactic that proved a double-edged weapon. 'The flies in this part of
the country seem to be even worse than those in Egypt. The only
way to keep them off is to take your boots and socks off. We haven't
decided yet which is the lesser of the two evils.'[25]

More than any other, the Eighth Army seemed doomed to be
plagued by flies, and even after the move to Italy they were still a
very prevalent pest. For many soldiers the benefits of summer were
almost offset by the swarms of flies it brought in its wake.
S. Phipps (3rd Coldstream Guards) visited a battalion headquarters that 'was swarming with hibernating flies . . . Our plates of
food became black and "murmerous haunts" as the flies descended
in hundreds from the rafters.'[26] Lieutenant D. Grant (41st Royal
Marine Commando) found a meal at Bruccoli to be an equally
trying experience:

> The table was set and the food was served with a semblance of de-
> corum, but it proved impossible to eat with the same civility. We were
> attacked by flies as soon as we sat down. They crawled thickly over the
> table, sipped the gravy in our plates, balanced on the rims of the mugs
> and fell off to drown in tea . . . We were forced at last to hang our
> camouflage veils over our heads for protection and, leaning forward,
> enclose ourselves and our food in miniature tents.[27]

In the Pacific and the Far East, one insect problem far outweighed any other – the mosquito, not so much because of its
actual attentions but because of the malaria that came in its wake.
Essentially a medical problem, this is dealt with in Chapter 5. But
other insects were far from negligible enemies. On Guam, in the
Marianas, the savage fighting upset the ecological balance. Flies
there were normally kept under control by the numerous frogs, but
so many bred in the thousands of Japanese corpses that littered the
island that the frogs were completely glutted. Nor were man-made

measures to combat the insects uniformly successful. The history of the Makin campaign, in November 1943, talks of the need for absolute silence in the front lines and notes that insect repellants did succeed in 'making slapping unnecessary . . . On the other hand, [they] were so strong that they led some of the enemy directly to a target through pitch darkness.'[28]

But the Eastern theatre involved more than individual annoyances, however unpleasant. Here it was more a question of a totally implacable environment where everything combined to make life an absolute misery. Everything was carried to extremes – rain, for example. In New Guinea, at the southern end of the Pacific theatre, 170in of rain fell in 1943. On Leyte in the Philippines, invaded in October 1944, 35in of rain fell in the first 40 days, coming down continuously and turning everything into a sea of mud. Corporal Conroy, a Marine, described conditions on Guadalcanal in 1943:

> You go to sleep in a dry foxhole . . . and it would be dry and hot, and sweat would be pouring down your boots. You'd wake up in the middle of the night . . . and your foxhole would be full of water up to your neck . . . Hell, you'd get wet one day and you'd stay wet the next three days if you were in the jungle . . . In that underbrush so thick you needed a knife to cut your way through, you would be wet day after day. It rained every day so far as I can remember. After a while the skin of your hands became puckered, as though you'd been washing clothes all day.[29]

In Arakan, on the Malayan seaboard, the monsoon season lasts from April to October, in which six months about 200in of rain fall. From May it is almost continuous, beating down with amazing violence. On 5 November 1943, as the 14th Indian Division was moving up for an offensive, 13in of rain fell in one day.[30] In Burma, at the very end of the war, the monsoon was in full spate:

> Units became isolated by water . . . Maps became useless since the water blotted out the natural geography. Men went out on patrol by boat or swam from island to island, floating their personal effects and cigarettes before them in their bush hats. Non-swimmers were helped with bamboo poles. Supplies became short. One unit was reduced to wearing Japanese army boots and smoking captured Japanese cigarettes, while doctors were forced to use Japanese syringes for inoculations.[31]

An officer of the 10th Gloucestershire Regiment, who took part in the 36th Division's march with Stilwell the previous year, wrote home: 'We had a damned awful time in the monsoon, either in blistering heat or drowned out. We were advancing through eight-foot high elephant grass all the time, always above our knees in water and generally waist deep. The leeches were multitudinous and gave us no rest.'[32]

The sort of conditions that are produced by such an extreme climate almost beggar description. Numerous observers have tried to do full justice to New Guinea. An Australian journalist referred to 'the moist and stifling Papuan jungle with its carpet of swamp-ooze and rotting stumps and leaves and its perpetual stench of vegetable decay . . . this Serborian bog of trees, and strangling vines and crazy foliage that shut out the sunlight'.[33] In the reeking nipa and mangrove swamps, where much of the fighting was carried on, conditions were even worse, men having to live and move in 'a stinking jumble of twisted, slime-covered roots and muddy soup'.[34] But every part of New Guinea had its own torments. In the interior are the precipitous, razor-backed ridges of the Owen Stanley Mountains that run right across the island and these had to be traversed by those trying to get from one coast to the other. The most famous route was the Kokoda Trail, a nightmarish switchback never to be forgotten by those who had to use it. In places the mountain-sides were so steep that steps had to be hacked out and laid over with logs. One hill had 1,700 such steps, each one 2in high. An Australian private, B. Findlay, wrote home to describe one journey on the trail:

Some of the old units are so thin that you would be shocked to see them. This trip is a physical nightmare . . . Yesterday we were twelve hours on the track and most of us were 'out on our feet', but we had to keep going . . . You spend four hours rising 2000 feet painfully step by step with your heart pounding in your throat, resting every hundred feet of rise. And then when you reach the top it is only fifteen feet wide, and you immediately begin to descend 2,000 feet. This is dangerous, as well as painful, because you get 'laughing knees', and only your prop stick in front of you keeps you from falling headlong. The farther down you go the weaker your knees become, but you don't lie down and die, as you feel like doing; you keep resting and going on and on . . . The first night out we tried to rest in a shelter of bushes many thousands of feet up, but none of us could manage sleep. Next day we were caught in a fierce storm, and staggered and slipped through it for two long hours. When we rested we lay out in puddles in the pouring rain, panting and steaming and wet through in the fullest sense of the

words. But you had to keep going. Everything was wet and heavier
now . . . At nightfall we staggered into a ramshackle native grass hut.
It had no sides and the rain was driving in on us the whole time . . . At
an altitude of 4,000 feet I lay on the bare ground in wet clothes. It was
bitterly cold. As soon as we settled down the native rats started. One of
them ran across my face and scratched my nostril with his sharp claws.
They kept running over my body, and when I dozed off, they started
nibbling at my hair.[35]

That, it must be emphasised, was a typical journey across the
Kokoda Trail. And though New Guinea was arguably the foulest
area in which any troops fought in World War II, it was nevertheless a nice distinction. Private First Class W. F. Connolly (77th
US Division) fought on Guam, where even the first few yards
marching made one think that the jungle had a vindictive mind of
its own:

The distance across the island is not far, as the crow flies, but unluckily
we can't fly. The nearest I came to flying was while descending the
slippery side of a mountain in a sitting position. After advancing a few
yards you find that the handle of the machine gun on your shoulder,
your pack and shovel, canteens, knife and machete all stick out at right
angles and are as tenacious in their grip on the surrounding under-
brush as a dozen grappling hooks. Straining, sweating and swearing
avails you nothing so you decide on a full-blooded lunge – success
crowns your efforts as all the entangling encumbrances decide to give
up the struggle simultaneously. Just before you hit the ground a low
swinging vine breaks your fall by looping itself under your chin,
almost decapitating you and snapping your helmet 15 yards to the rear,
narrowly missing your lieutenant's head . . . You untangle your
equipment, retrieve your helmet and move on. The flies, the mos-
quitos have discovered your route of march . . . and regard us as
nothing but walking blood banks. We continue to push on . . . [36]

It was not just long marches that were such a hardship. Simply
existing in the line was ordeal enough. General Eichelberger was
very aware of the misery of the US troops facing the Japanese
perimeter at Buna, on New Guinea. For weeks past 'no-one could
remember when he had been dry. The feet, arms, stomachs,
chests, armpits of my soldiers were hideous with jungle rot. The
sun appeared when the skies wrung themselves out briefly, and
steam rose like grey smoke in the dark undergrowth. Then the
soldiers themselves steamed and sweated in their heavy jungle
suits.'[37] These suits were made of a porous material but, by what

Eichelberger admits as 'a well-meant but serious error', he had had them dyed a mottled green to aid concealment and the dye had closed all the breathing holes in the cloth.

Other islands in roughly the same latitude as New Guinea, notably the Bismarck Archipelago and the Solomons, shared just the same appalling climate. Regarding the campaign in New Britain, begun on Boxing Day 1943, one historian of the Pacific War recalled the 'swamps, neck-deep or worse. Then another fortified ridge, another unknown valley. And always the rain and the mud, torrid heat and teeming insect life, the stink of rotten jungle and rotting dead; malaria burning the body and fungus infection eating away the feet.'[38] At Guadalcanal in the Solomons the first invasion was by the 1st Marine Division, and as they moved off the beaches their general impression was one of foul decay. 'No air stirs here, and the hot humidity is beyond the imagining of anyone who has not lived in it. Rot lies everywhere just under the exotic lushness. The ground is porous with decaying vegetation, emitting a sour, unpleasant odour . . . Dampness, thick and heavy, is everywhere . . . [The rain is] unbelievably torrential in season, never ceasing altogether for more than a few days at a time.'[39] Private First Class James Jones (25th US Division) fought there and later tried to exorcise his experiences in novel form:

> The moist humidity was so overpowering, and hung in the air so heavily, that it seemed more like a material object than a weather condition. It brought the sweat starting from every pore at the slightest exertion. And unable to evaporate in it, the sweat ran down over their bodies soaking everything to saturation. When it had saturated their clothing, it ran down into their shoes, filling them, so that they sloshed along in their own sweat as if they had just come out of wading a river. The sun blazed down on them . . . heating their helmets to such temperatures that the steel shells actually burned their hands.[40]

Another notorious island in the Solomons was Pavavu. In late 1944 it was the home of the 1st Marine Division, and even though they were not actually fighting there the conditions drove men almost to breaking point. A plague of rats added to the usual miseries of this part of the world. The Divisional History tells the story of one Marine who ran out of his tent in the middle of the night and started kicking and punching a tree, screaming, 'I hate you, godammit, I hate you!' The only response from the other tents was a weary 'Hit it once for me'.

In the Central Pacific area, containing the Carolines, the Marshalls, the Marianas, Iwo Jima and Okinawa, conditions were nothing like so fearsome. The Marianas, in particular, were noted for their balmy climate, and the health of the soldiers was generally good. But the physical characteristics of all these islands had their own drawbacks. Very many of them were small coral atolls which the Japanese had turned into a deadly honeycomb of interlocked bunkers and firing positions. Of one such island in the Marshalls, Kwajalein, an operational report ventured that 'the entire island looked as though it had been picked up 20,000 feet and then dropped.'[41] But even the climate was not uniformly favourable. A *Time* reporter, Robert Martin, wrote: 'Pelelieu is a horrible place. The heat is stifling and rain falls intermittently – the muggy rain that brings no relief, only greater misery. The coral rocks soak up the heat during the day and it is only slightly cooler at night. Marines . . . wilted on Pelelieu. By the 4th day there were as many casualties from heat prostration as from wounds.'[42]

Similar conditions were encountered in the Philippines, though the actual terrain was much more jungle-like. On Leyte, in December 1944, 'the heat, humidity, uphill fighting, and the constant fever pitch of the men caused scores to keel over from heat exhaustion. They were evacuated to the aid station in a draw several hundred yards to the rear, splashed with cold water and laid in the shade. After resting a while, they doggedly returned to the lines to continue the fight. The battalion c.o. said that the men were soaking wet from sweat all the time.'[43] But the Philippines also had problems all their own. On Mindanao one of the greatest obstacles were the impenetrable thickets of hemp. Referring to the push from Mintal to Calinan, General Eichelberger stressed that 'it is difficult to make clear to Americans, who are used to honest elms, maples, oaks, butternuts and hickories, the tanglewild which results when cultivated abaca is allowed to run loose for five years. Branches join one another; only specks of sunlight get through. Every hour of the day is dusk.'[44] On Luzon, agricultural practice was again the main problem, though here it was a matter of flooded rice-fields, streams and fish-ponds which greatly slowed up the progress of the troops as they came ashore.

For British and Indian troops on the south-east Asian mainland, ordinary day-to-day existence could be almost as grim as that in the rain forests of the south-west Pacific. The incredible precipitation over Arakan, and to a slightly lesser degree over Burma, has already been noted. Heat was another torment. In Malaya, for example, there is no seasonal variation and the daily temperature is a constant 90°F during the day, falling only 20 degrees at night. The humidity is especially oppressive. An Australian journalist described the closely packed forest of cedar trees with their lattice-work of great coiling vines where 'it was as dim as a cathedral and only occasionally did a spear of sunlight pierce the green gloom. There was a sickly moisture about it and the sour smell of swamp ooze and rotting vegetation . . . Damp, soggy heat seemed to roll through its defiles in strangling, invisible clouds.'[45]

In Burma there was more diversity of climate and terrain. Even in the worst regions the climate could be very pleasant at times, and in the hill stations to the north it was often so. But the fighting soldier was rarely allowed to make much of these interludes and most of his time was spent in the least hospitable zones, the bulk of the actual campaigning being undertaken during the monsoon season. The Assam front, around Kohima and Imphal, was the scene of bitter fighting between March and May 1944. This was just before the monsoon season but even so the going was very tough. As on New Guinea and elsewhere, a march was a killing test of stamina and endurance. During the Kohima battle, Captain Horner (Royal Norfolk Regiment) was with a unit pushing through from Jhotsoma to Khonoma:

> . . . to anyone who hasn't soldiered in Assam, the physical hammering one takes is difficult to understand. The heat, the humidity, the altitude, and the slope of almost every foot of ground, combine to knock the hell out of the stoutest constitution. You gasp for air which doesn't seem to come, you drag your legs upwards till they seem reduced to the strength of matchsticks, you wipe the salt sweat out of your eyes. Then you feel your heart pounding so violently you think it must burst its cage; it sounds as loud as a drum, even above the swearing and cursing going on around you.[46]

Digging In

As far as the ordinary infantryman was concerned, the two world wars had more in common than is usually appreciated. It might be argued that the diversity of terrain and climate, of flora and fauna, encountered in the far-flung theatres of World War II offered experiences quite unknown to the 'poor bloody infantry' of World

War I. Yet in all these theatres, as on the Western Front, there was a common bedrock of suffering. For the men in the line the most exotic climes were soon reduced to certain bare essentials – sweat, shivering, dirt, rock, stench and blood – and always there was the infantryman's consistently intimate relationship with the very ground upon which he trod, with clay and sand, earth and rock.

Above all, perhaps, the two world wars have in common the shovel and the entrenching tool. From 1914 onwards the paramount fact in war was firepower of such intensity that only in holes in the ground could the front-line soldier even begin to feel relatively secure. Armoured vehicles briefly robbed defensive tactics of their supremacy, but by 1941 at the latest the anti-tank gun, the mine, and a little later the bazooka/PIAT/*Panzerfaust*, had done much to restore the balance. Attacking remained a hazardous and *slow* procedure, only to be undertaken when absolutely necessary and with the maximum of fire support. The war of movement remains something of a chimera in World War II. It presupposes surprise, confusion, or the enemy's pusillanimity as in France in 1940, Russia in 1941, the great British reverses before Alamein, on the tracks of Patton's armour in 1944 or Slim's in Burma in 1945. But far more typical of this war are the sieges at Kohima, Imphal, Keren, Knightsbridge Box, Bastogne, Stalingrad, Cassino, Aachen; the agonising slog through the Reichswald and the Hürt-gen Forest; the men pinned on the beaches at Pelelieu, Tarawa, Iwo Jima, Dieppe, Salerno and Anzio; the nightmarish rain-forests of Arakan, New Guinea or Guadalcanal; First Army chipping away at Tunisian *djebels*, or ridges, and Fifth and Eighth Armies crawling up Italy like, in Churchill's memorable phrase 'bugs up a trouser leg'. Thus, though World War II never had trench systems as static or elaborate as those on the Western Front, the individual soldier nevertheless spent much of his time burrowing into the ground. The only notable difference, and even this was not universally true, was that between 1939 and 1945 the troops did not spend much time in the same hole. More fluid tactics and a sound grasp of the basic principles of fire and movement meant that constant progress was made. But if defensive firepower was no longer sufficiently predominant as to make only the most trivial gains possible, it was still quite enough to make progress agonisingly slow and to necessitate constant retrenchment after each desperate bound. Even when troops were not themselves on the defensive, actual advances across the battlefield were sporadic and slow, each attack a frenetic spasm in the troglodyte routine. In the front line at least 90 per cent of the infantryman's time was spent under cover either on the defensive, often under bombardment, awaiting an enemy attack, or nerving himself up to the prospect of going forward.

The first British campaign of 1939–40 seemed to presage a rather less violent repeat of World War I. During the months of the *sitzkrieg*, especially on the frontiers near the Maginot Line, British and French troops sat around in sophisticated trench systems, waiting for the enemy to make the first move. A triple line of defences had been constructed, consisting of the Ligne de Contact in front, the Ligne de Receuil and, hopefully, the Ligne d'Arrêt. Life was not particularly dangerous but spirits were very low during that first winter because of the appalling weather. The Gordon Highlanders' historian had this to say of the experiences of the 1st Battalion: 'Only those who were in France and Belgium at the time can appreciate the depressing conditions of the winter of 1939–40. Heavy rains were followed by frost and snow, thaw and frost again. To keep the new defences in repair often seemed a hopeless task.'[47] One of the few cheering events during this period was that the Highland regiments were authorised, on 17 December, to abandon the kilt. In fact, as is well known, when the German offensive did begin in May 1940, the ensuing campaign bore no resemblance at all to the previous war, and will always remain a classic example of war of movement. Unfortunately, from the Allied point of view, most of the movement was in reverse.

In North Africa, despite the remarkable strategic fluidity of the operations, digging in always remained a basic ploy. This applied right across the continent. In the campaign in Eritrea, in late 1940, the fighting often bogged down into old-fashioned siege warfare. Around the fort at Gaballat, in November, the men of Slim's force operated within a 7-mile perimeter. They lived in *tukls*, small grass shelters, or, when within range of the enemy, in shallow trenches dug out of the rocky soil which they buttressed with rock walls and roofed over with branches and earth. In the Western Desert, the British and Commonwealth forces rarely found themselves engaged in this kind of static warfare, although the boot was more than once on the other foot. The tactical ineptitude that marked the middle years of British generalship – the era of the double-barrelled name and the half-cocked offensive – led at one stage to a suicidal reliance on the so-called 'box', a defensive perimeter stuck

in the middle of nowhere and usually garrisonned by a mixed force
of infantry, tanks and artillery. One of the most famous of these
was the Knightsbridge Box where between 27 May and 14 June
1942 the defenders, under constant attack by artillery and armour,
could only crouch in their dugouts and take the occasional opportunity to loose off a few shots. But there were countless other such
defensive positions and the larger 'boxes' were merely desert fighting writ large. Digging in sand or rock was a constant front-line
activity, particularly at night when forward troops had to protect
themselves against possible surprise attack. These leaguers of
armour and infantry remind one of the Roman *castra*, the invari-
able precaution against night attack.

The care with which they were constructed varied enormously.
A South African unit history notes that during the Crusader tank
battles

> . . . a single battalion would perhaps defend a square whose sides were
> 1,000 yards and more in length. Here was no solid British square such
> as met the . . . [Dervishes] in the Sudan in Kitchener's day: the
> Crusader square looked quite deserted. Each man dug a slit trench for
> himself; to reach his nearest companion he might have to scramble ten
> yards. Indeed, to picture a company position on one side of a battalion
> box one would have to imagine a soldier standing at the door of every
> second shop along a street perhaps twelve blocks long . . . The Bat-
> talion were to dig perimeters like this at least once a day, often three
> times in a day – until . . . the withdrawal to Gazala in mid-February,
> 1942.[48]

At other times units knew that they were to occupy a position for at
least some days and then their defences would be more elaborate.
In his autobiographical novel, Lieutenant D. Billany described
one such position in mid-1942:

> When I first joined the battalion, it had just moved in, and was all on
> the surface. We pitched our bivouacs at night like ordinary tents. The
> digging began. Every day there was less of us on the surface, more
> underneath. The first task was to dig pits from which the Bren guns
> could be fired, and a narrow slit trench for every two riflemen. When
> these fighting positions were complete, we went on to dig 'bivvy-
> holes', in which we lived and slept. These holes, usually six feet square,
> went as deep as the digger's patience; probably four feet: and the
> bivouac sheets were stretched flat over the top and camouflaged with
> nets and sand . . . Each section position was a warren of underground
> dens and holes for stores. Everything went below the surface. Return-

ing from other parts of the Company area to my platoon, I had no visible sign to guide me, unless any of the men were working up on top.[49]

Terrain was also an important limitation on the intricacy of one's defences. Most of the 'high' ground, the notorious Ruweisat Ridge for example, was very rocky and digging in was almost impossible. Instead, stone parapets were built and were referred to as 'sangars', from the Hindustani word *sunga*, salvaged from the vocabulary of the North West Frontier and the chronic warfare against the Pathans and others. Captain George Green (5th Seaforth Highlanders) was trapped on such ground during Alamein, just as the German artillery was beginning to find its range:

That was when the real trouble began. The ground was like iron, and it was almost impossible to dig down more than two feet without striking solid limestone. We couldn't get down at all. For the next five hours my group just lay as the shells came over, heavily and accurately. They were dead on range. All this time we were trying to dig. It was the worst ever . . . I never got my head right down: it was just level with the surface . . . In the afternoon we found some Italian trenches 50 yards behind us – we'd never had our heads up far enough to see them before – and after that it wasn't too bad.[50]

Even after Alamein, during the hectic pursuit of Rommel's forces, it was rarely safe to discount their capacity to hit back. Lieutenant Neil McCallum (51st Highland Division) remembered such times in a splendid summary of the reality of desert warfare:

A shabby, gritty landscape. The sweat oozes and trickles all day. This is war, one kind of war, sweat and tiredness and no water till evening and cigarettes made of dirt. The pain of muscles, not wounded, but twisted from the weight of rifles, automatic guns, heavy equipment. The abrasion of the skin by a sand-paste of desert and sweat. The thud of feet on the sand 94 times every minute, 50 minutes an hour . . . And every night dig . . . Dig in case the bombs drop. Dig for discipline. Dig to save your skins. Dig through sand. Dig, if necessary, through rock. Dig for bloody victory.[51]

The fighting in Tunisia was of a different kind to that in the open desert. For the First Army, later to be joined by the Eighth, the war in Africa was a siege on a huge scale in which they tried to dislodge the Germans from the rocky ridges around Tunis and push through to the coast. These ridges were what counted rather than towns or road junctions, possession of which was almost irrelevant if one did not also occupy the high ground overlooking them, for as long as the enemy held this they could observe one's own movements and bring down artillery and mortar fire at will. This then was the essence of the Tunisian campaign, either attacking the enemy's dug in positions or oneself hanging on grimly to some bare hill-top that only reluctantly yielded any adequate cover. A journalist with the First Army, A. B. Austin, described this bleak terrain:

> From north to south, whether you were among cork forests or grain-lands, or scrub or pinewoods, the hills of Tunisia had one thing in common – their curious tortured tops. Their peaks or ridges would either be carved with rocky whorls or curves, or would stick up in knife-edges like the comb of a cock, or would be studded with pinnacles like the jagged spine of a brontosaurus . . . Soon we understood that the whole future of the Tunisian campaign lay in them.[52]

For weeks on end the troops concentrated on consolidating their positions, hacking into the rocks and thin sub-soil to carve out adequate slit-trenches to sleep in or to protect machine-gun and mortar posts. In many respects conditions were not as grim as they were to become on the European mainland. The tempo of the fighting was slower and there was no persistent dispute of key features at close quarters. Troops were not subjected to the strain of being constantly under fire from mortars and small arms. One private of the Rifle Brigade, trapped in the miseries of Italy, remembered Tunisia almost with regret and spoke of 'a gentleman's war [where] everyone packed up when the sun went down'.[53] His memories are perhaps a little too fond. Even when not actually under fire the strain of manning forward positions was quite considerable. A unit had to be alert twenty-four hours a day in case the enemy should decide to attack, and even in relatively calm periods no one knew for sure that an artillery barrage was not imminent or that one's own company or battalion might not be ordered forward. On most nights all weapons had to be manned, the mortars loaded with flares, and only half the men of the sections could sleep at any one time. The rest were either behind the Brens or as much as a quarter of a mile forward, on picket duty. The 1st US Division, for example, had to follow this kind of routine, as well as actually go into action, for three to five weeks at a stretch. Even when they were pulled back for a week or ten days of rest they spent up to half the time travelling back and forth in lorries.

After the fall of Tunis, in May 1943, the bulk of First and Eighth Armies were sent to Sicily and thence to Italy where they spent two years, and above all two winters, grinding away at endless river crossings and mountain assaults. But progress was extremely slow and, more perhaps than than in any other theatre, the Allies spent much of their time dug in, living amongst the rocks and wallowing in filthy holes in the ground. In winter this existence went on for weeks at a time. Of course battalions were not actually at the front proper for this length of time – as in World War I a rotational system was adopted by which units were regularly pulled out for periods of rest. Optimally, a unit would spend five to seven days in the line and the same period in reserve or resting; but the system only worked in this way for part of the time. At other periods, particularly in the US army, weeks went by without units getting more than a few hundred yards from the front.

Actually getting to the forward positions could itself be quite an ordeal, involving not only a long march but also a punishing climb of several hundred feet, in the pitch darkness and burdened down with arms and equipment. Because of the chronic shortage of fighting troops, artillery and armoured formations often had to serve in this way as ordinary infantry. Captain John Guest, in charge of an anti-aircraft battery, undertook such duties in December 1944. 'Most of the time we were on mountain tops at a height of more than 3,000 feet; it practically never stopped raining, and our only communication with the world was by mule, or oxen and sleigh, even for water. The worst part was the occupation of the positions – the gruelling march up in the dark with packs, ammunition, brens, mortars, rations. Men fainted from exhaustion.'[54]

The 'worst part' perhaps, but simply existing on these bleak mountains was no joke. Monte Cassino and its environs was particularly notorious. Lieutenant E. D. Smith (1/9th Gurkhas) wrote in his diary of a spell below Point 593:

Time seems to have stopped; it is as if we have been condemned to live forever in a cold, damp hell on earth, each of us obtaining but meagre shelter behind rocks or in holes in the ground. Each night we pray that the following morning will bring a change in the weather, a respite from the rain and snow and the endless vigil that is never a quiet one as the whine and crump of the gun and mortar continue by day and night. As day succeeds day the anxiety about the next attack has changed into a desperate longing to do anything rather than sit here for ever undergoing an ordeal that tests minds and bodies alike.[55]

But things had been just as bad before Cassino and would be just as bad again. In the Bernhard Line, an American Corps commander wrote: 'It has rained for two days, and is due to rain for two more say the meteorologists. In addition, it is cold as hell . . . I don't see how our men stand what they do.'[56] On Monte Camino, Flanders veterans of 1917 might have felt themselves in a time warp. Lieutenant D. Helme (3rd Coldstream Guards) wrote: 'After the first couple of days we had to stretch groundsheets and gas capes to catch rainwater for drinking. No chance of shaving, as any cut would have become infected; but I had a good wash in a shell hole. Men's hands and feet were rather swollen after the rain and exposure . . . Had only one blanket each . . . and had to sleep two or three together to keep warm.'[57]

Anzio was something of a variation to the usual Italian theme. As usual, the troops were dug in, in filthy weather, under constant bombardment, but this time they were trapped in a narrow beachhead rather than up in the mountains. That they were there at all was largely the fault of dilatory commanders who had failed to appreciate the opportunities open to them after the original unopposed landing in January 1944. Little attempt was made to push inland and the Germans were allowed time to muster forces for a series of determined counter-attacks. None of these succeeded in pushing the Allies back into the sea but they did produce a bitter stalemate which lasted for four months. Wynford Vaughan-Thomas was a journalist there and he made the appropriate comparisons with earlier campaigns.

> As the months passed this front line took on all the character of the Somme or Ypres in 1916. For the first and the only time in World War II the soldiers had to think in terms of communicating trenches, barbed wire in no-man's land and the rest of the grim paraphanalia of *All Quiet on the Western Front*. 'You've got to stay,' one British brigadier insisted to his men. 'You've just got to dig, dig, dig your way to safety.'[58]

He perhaps exaggerates the uniqueness of the conditions at Anzio, but there is no doubt that the basic comparison is valid. The following account by an American replacement for the 3rd Division could well have been written by any doughboy arriving in France in 1918:

> The bottom was squashy. It wasn't a very big hole, about chest deep. Part of it was boarded over . . . All through the night there were flares

going up from the Jerry lines . . . I was scared. It was just plain hell all through the day, and the nights were worse. The hole got about six inches of water, and you couldn't do anything but try to bale it out with your helmet. We wrapped shelter halves and blankets around us but they didn't do much good. They got soaked with rain and then you sat on a piece of wood or something and shivered and cussed . . . You couldn't get out of the hole once the sun came up, or even show the top of your head . . . Jerry threw in a lot of artillery and mortars. The best thing to do was to pull in your head and pray. Some of that big stuff would cave in the side of a wet foxhole like it was sand, and a couple of the boys got buried right in their hole fifty yards away from me. We had two or three casualties every day, mostly from artillery and mortars. If you got it at night you were lucky, because they could get you out right away. God help you if you got hit in the daytime.[59]

Elsewhere in Italy the positions the men occupied were not trench lines as such. The most forward were a series of alarm posts which were occupied only at dawn and dusk, always viewed as the most likely times for the enemy to attack. At these hours everyone had to stand to by their weapons, though the majority of men were some yards behind these outposts, sheltered in slit-trenches, dug-outs or sangars. Slit-trenches offered the worst accommodation of all. An American officer has outlined some of the difficulties:

We could not go very deep, but we were able to make a trench long and wide enough for two of us to lie out flat on the bottom and be protected. It could not have been more than a foot and a half deep. We put the pup-tent canvas over the top to keep the rain out, but this left only about six inches of space for us to move in . . . The rain fell incessantly and even before we tried to settle down to get some sleep, the lower blankets were soaked through. Both my messenger and I were wet to the skin . . . Sometime after midnight the rain stopped, but water, running down the slope to our position, kept trickling into our trench. There was no way at all of keeping warm except by lying close to the messenger who was in the trench with me, and we shared what heat was in our bodies by pressing them close together.[60]

Dugouts were usually occupied by company officers and wireless operators. Captain Cochrane remembered a spell perched upon Point 593 in the Cassino sector:

Officers should be in amongst their men, but the platoon commanders had to hole up in their command posts and could only get round their sections after dark . . . There was nothing much to do in daytime but to chat and after three weeks of this troglodyte life Owens [the CSM] and I knew each other even better . . . Night time was when we were active, rotating platoons and sections . . . two [platoons] forward, one back. We had a couple of little wireless sets to give some communication between each platoon and its forward sections, and a telephone line . . .[61]

Such accommodation was hardly commodious. After Cassino had fallen, Cochrane was able to revisit this dugout and he discovered that it measured 4ft by 5ft and allowed 3ft of headroom. In that – nothing more than a reasonable sized cupboard resting on its back – two men lived for three weeks. Sangars, already mentioned in the context of the Western Desert, were equally numerous in Tunisia and Italy. Like dugouts they were only constructed some distance behind the front outposts. Guthrie Wilson described one such:

> As it is impossible to dig rock that is as resistant as steel, we have no trenches, but sangars are, for comfort, more than a substitute . . . [They are] beehive dwellings of rock . . . We have erected roofs reinforced by sandbags and screw pickets. The sangar that I share with [two others] . . . was three inches deep in slime when we took possession of it, but we have since cleaned it out, filched a tarpaulin, and so are fairly comfortable. It is neither shell-proof nor mortar-proof, of course, but it is at least relatively waterproof. We do not fight from sangars. When we are on duty we occupy posts on the forward slope where the natural protection of giant shoulders of rock serves in place of the slit trench to which we are accustomed.[62]

In such surroundings, usually cursed by the most appalling weather, men rotted for days, sometimes weeks at a time. Spirits only lightened when it was at last time to make one's way back down the mountain. When the relief unit arrived they were given information about enemy positions and patterns of behaviour and, in some sectors, were made to sign for any equipment which was to be left in the position. This latter procedure was very reminiscent of the World War I system of trench-stores, introduced so that troops should not be burdened down more than was absolutely necessary. But the journey back to the reserve positions was no light-hearted jog. The going was probably still as treacherous as on the way up and the journey was habitually made in pitch darkness. Moreover, after their long stint in the line, men were utterly exhausted, having had to exist on three or four hours sleep a day, sometimes not even that, their nerves continually stretched to breaking point by the patrols, stand to's and bombardments.

E. D. Smith's diary gives a chilling description of such a march down, after six weeks in the line:

> The distance was probably less than five miles, but for most of the battalion, the men had hardly walked at all for six weeks. Men were cramped, unfit, mentally exhausted, without any will power. Even though the ordeal was nearly over, the fact did not seem to be understood . . . Never will I forget that nightmare of a march. Officers, British and Gurkha, shouted at, scolded, cajoled, assisted men as they collapsed. At times we had no alternative but to strike soldiers who just gave up interest in anything, including a desire to live.[63]

The harsh physical environment of Italy imbues descriptions of combat there with heightened dramatic impact. The terrain of north-west Europe presented a much drearier and anonymous picture, in which hedgerows, canals, rivers and forests are the most significant features. But this does not mean that the life of the front-line soldier could not be equally grim. As in Italy, the Allied armies relied to a great extent on the infantry battalions and they too spent much of their time dug in, sheltering from the enemy's artillery, mortars and machine guns. Nobody has ever produced a better summary of the rifleman's day-to-day existence in this theatre than Bill Mauldin. His remarks are addressed to those sitting comfortably back at home wondering why the boys at the front were making such heavy going of the final campaigns:

> Dig a hole in your back yard while it is raining. Sit in the hole while the water climbs up round your ankles. Pour cold mud down your shirt collar. Sit there for forty-eight hours, and, so there is no danger of your dozing off, imagine that a guy is sneaking around waiting for a chance to club you on the head or set your house on fire. Get out of the hole, fill a suitcase full of rocks, pick it up, put a shotgun in your other hand, and walk on the muddiest road you can find. Fall flat on your face every few minutes, as you imagine big meteors streaking down to sock you . . . Snoop around until you find a bull. Try to figure out a way to sneak around him without letting him see you. When he does see you, run like hell all the way back to your hole in the back yard, drop the suitcase and shotgun, and get in. If you repeat this performance every three days for several months you may begin to understand why an infantryman gets out of breath. But you still won't understand how he feels when things get tough.[64]

Things were no different for the British and Canadian troops, many of whom were surprised at the static nature of the fighting.

Sergeant H. Green (10th Highland Light Infantry) recalled his experiences in the precarious Odon Bridgehead, in the first month of the invasion. 'Was it but a week ago that digging a slit trench was considered more work than it was worth? Now, the shovel had become a mighty weapon of war, a treasure to be hoarded carefully, lest it be snatched up by some pilferer; being without a shovel left one feeling as naked as a man in Piccadilly without his trousers.'[65] An artillery officer of the 59th Division wrote home to his parents: 'Talk about the BLA [British Liberation Army] – its the BDA – the Bloody Destruction Army. This stabilised front area is just like Flanders must have been – every building a pile of rubble, every field a showpiece of a soldier's desire to get underground, if he's stopping five minutes.'[66]

The quality of life below ground differed enormously. In reserve positions or quiet sectors it was often possible to undertake quite elaborate home improvements and the whole exercise took on something of a boy scouts' outing. Captain John Watney (GHQ Liaison Regiment) was constantly at the front during the Caen fighting, but on most nights he was able to return to positions in the rear. There

> . . . our slit trenches became deeper, safer, and more luxurious day by day. We found . . . an outlet for our creative imagination; we would collect together to discuss the laying of a beam or the building of steps; instead of being satisfied with the single slit-trench, the fastidious built themselves the L-shaped trench, which, when covered by sandbags, gave the body lying along one of the arms of the L complete protection . . . [One saw] homely touches of nostalgic humour; shelves were built on which were placed photographs of the girls we had left behind; jars of roses appeared; steps were brushed in the morning; flowers were planted on the roofs of shelters, and names were given to them.[67]

But one should not be misled. More often than not the terrain, the climate and the enemy would not permit such self-indulgence. In the winter, from Holland to the Saar, men lived not in comfortable hobbit-like burrows, but in crude holes, puddles writ large. Private William Biles (4th Wiltshire Regiment) had to lead such an existence for weeks on end:

> We went back up on the hill and were there in slit trenches for weeks. Never moved out of them. Never washed or shaved, or took our boots off. Had to walk back at night-time to pick up food and take it back to

our trenches. All this time, constantly shelled day and night, 88s mostly. Time and time again, I prayed, lying in the bottom of a trench. Never saw a German once. Thinking mostly about the next shelling. Hearing blokes scream and cry, when trenches around were hit. Used empty food tins to make water in; had to dash to nearest empty trench for other, trousers unbuttoned in advance. Eventually relieved and went to another field. Three days rest, cleaned up a bit, back up the line. Senior NCO shot himself in foot, decided he'd had enough.[68]

Further south, the Americans fared no better. All along the front their divisions ran into inimical terrain, filthy weather and an enemy, well dug in, determined to resist almost to the last man. The Hürtgen Forest, for example

. . . was agony, and there was no glory in it except the glory of courageous men . . . Foxholes were . . . miserable but they were covered, because tree bursts are deadly and every barrage was a deluge of fragmentation from the tops of the neat little firs . . . The Infantry advanced with its battle packs, and it dug in and buttoned up, and then the artillery raked the line so that there were many times when the Infantry's bed rolls could not be brought up to them. Rolls were brought up to a certain point, but the Infantry could not go back for them because to leave the shelter was insane. So the Infantry slept as it fought – if it slept at all – without blankets, and the nights were long and wet and cold.[69]

One of the best descriptions of winter warfare, and one which must have caught the censors in charitable mood, was given to a BBC correspondent by Captain Athol Stewart, a Canadian infantry officer trying to survive in the flooded Dutch lowlands:

Do *you* know what it's like? Of course you don't. You have never slept in a hole in the ground which you have dug while someone tried to kill you . . . a hole dug as deep as you can as quick as you can . . . It is an open grave, and yet graves don't fill up with water. They don't harbour wasps or mosquitoes, and you don't feel the cold, clammy wet that goes into your marrow.

At night the infantryman gets some boards, or tin, or an old door and puts it over one end of his slit trench; then he shovels on top of it as much dirt as he can scrape up near by. He sleeps with his head under this, not to keep out the rain, but to protect his head and chest from airbursts. Did I say sleeps? Let us say, collapses. You see, the infantryman must be awake for one-half the night. The reason is that one half of the troops are on watch and the other half are resting, washing, shaving, writing letters, eating, or cleaning weapons; that is if he is not being shot at, shelled, mortared, or counter-attacked or if he is not too much exhausted to do it.

When he is mortared or shelled he is deathly afraid and in the day-time he chain-smokes, curses, or prays, all of this lying on his belly with his hands under his chest to lessen the pain from the blast. If it is at night, smoking is taboo . . . A trench is dug just wide enough for the shoulders, as long as the body and as deep as there is time. It may be occupied for two hours or two weeks. The next time you are near some muddy fields after a rain take a look in a ditch. That is where your man lives.[70]

In Malaya and Burma, digging in was not such a constant preoccupation. The very denseness of the terrain meant that only when one was in very close contact with the enemy was it necessary to take precautions against his firepower. For long periods, par-ticularly in north-west Burma in 1943 and 1944, the soldiers were simply waiting for the Japanese to make the next move, and were able to shelter in tents or makeshift buildings. But when contact was finally made, war in the Far East was just as much a sub-terranean exercise as elsewhere. In the debacles of 1941 the troops were constantly setting up hasty rearguard positions to try and stem the enemy advance. All such attempts were in vain, largely because the Japanese simply surged round them, but also because it was virtually impossible to make viable strong-points. In Malaya, for example, the 11th Division was told at one stage to dig in around Jitra but the ground was so waterlogged after two days rain that slit-trenches simply collapsed as soon as they were dug. Moreover, the troops were so utterly exhausted after their efforts that they were almost incapable of fighting.

Much of the later Burmese fighting did become fundamentally a matter of digging in. Because of the terrain, combat was often little more than siege warfare. Nowhere was this more true than in Assam during the epic battles of Kohima and Imphal in mid-1944, both of which became bloody positional engagements as the Japanese vainly tried to squeeze out the Allied garrisons. Conditions at Kohima acquired a frightfulness that has rarely been paralleled. Major John Nettlefield (Royal Artillery) recalled Kohima Ridge: 'The place stank. The ground everywhere was ploughed up with shell-fire and human remains lay rotting as the battle raged over them . . . Men retched as they dug in . . . The stink hung in the air and permeated one's clothes and hair.'[71] An officer of the Royal Welch Fusiliers saw the Kohima peri-meter for the first time at a fairly late stage, when the fighting had more and more come to resemble old-fashioned trench warfare. In his first stint in the line, he and his men had to crawl

> . . . through the shallow, muddy communication trenches to take over
> the forward dugouts and foxholes . . . The most lasting impression of
> all was caused by the stench of decaying bodies, half-buried or lying in
> the open between the lines. In some of the slit trenches, rotting bodies
> of Japanese were used to form the protective parapet . . . Space was so
> limited that dugouts, latrines, cookhouses and graves were all close
> together. It was almost impossible to dig anywhere without uncover-
> ing a grave or a latrine.[72]

The dead were always a problem in this kind of fighting. Around
Imphal at Sangshak, a small hill-station, the 50th Indian Parachute Brigade made a stand against the Japanese. The earth was
only three feet deep before shovels came up against an impenetrable barrier of rock. Not only did this make it difficult to scoop
out adequate trenches but it also meant that every shell or bomb
that landed tended to disinter a corpse.

But it is not only these two sieges that demonstrate the importance of the spade in the Fourteenth Army's theatre. Elsewhere
there is constant reference to the desert term 'box', and this form of
static perimeter was a common Allied tactic, particularly where
their troops were uncertain of their ability to match Japanese
competence in the jungle. One of the most famous of such defences
was the so-called Admin. Box, held by the 7th Division, in Arakan.
Once again the British had been cut off by the mobile Japanese but
this time they had been ordered to stand, whatever the con-
sequences, rather than try to cut their way out. The battle lasted
for three weeks and the gallantry of the troops in the Box, as well as
the timely concentration of the 26th Division and part of the 5th,
resulted in the total defeat of General Hanaya's offensive. Brigadier A. F. Hely was one of those trapped in the Box and he
especially remembered the terror of the nights, as men strained
their ears and eyes to try and pick out the Japanese they knew
were crawling all around them. He shared a foxhole with General
Messervy, in the Command Post which was

> . . . [like] just so many slit trenches among thousands, with nothing to
> distinguish it from the others. Everywhere men stood to in pairs, to
> watch each other as well as the enemy, so that if one fell asleep from
> sheer exhaustion the other could kick him awake. One weak link, one
> man asleep, could have meant the throats cut of every single soul in the
> trenches around him. The tension . . . was terrific. Parties of up to a

hundred Japs would creep down every night. You never knew where
they would strike next. You only knew that anything that moved in the
shadowy moonlight was hostile, and you shot it. Everybody had to
fight for his own particular life from time to time. When the Japs came
at you nobody could come to your aid. You had to fight it out yourself.
That was understood.[73]

But the Japanese, too, were great diggers and, as will be seen in
the next chapter, nowhere was this more true than in the Pacific
theatre. There, the tactic most commonly associated with them,
the human-wave attack, was in fact not very common. Much more
usual was fanatical defence to the last man, the soldiers cooped up
in impenetrable and often invisible bunkers. Either way, however,
whether to repulse a Japanese assault or minimise the effect of his
machine guns and mortars, the Americans and Australians were
themselves constantly forced to dig. The foxhole was a *sine qua non*
of survival. In places the Allied defences became almost as elaborate as the Japanese. On the Owen Stanleys, in New Guinea, both
sides dug in along the ridges and on Imita Ridge, for example, the
Australians lived in wood-lined trenches which connected the
various weapons' pits. A few yards in front of the latter were trip-
wires liberally festooned with empty ration cans. In later island
invasions this kind of stalemate was avoided wherever possible,
though it was always deemed essential for troops to dig in at night.
On Guam, General Bruce, of the 77th US Division, felt that
during the day the troops could afford to push on through the
jungle without paying too much attention to their flanks. 'I emphasised the lack of vision in woods or jungle precluded the ordinary concept of fighting in the open. In brief, my idea . . . was to
push boldly forward and then take up strong all-round defence at
night.'[74] It did not always prove possible to properly combine
offence and defence in this way. On Okinawa, many units that were
successfully advancing were caught out by the swift onset of darkness and were attacked by the Japanese at twilight as they were
actually digging in. On other occasions no advance at all was
possible, and the troops remained trapped in their soggy slit-
trenches. This happened to the 96th US Division during the
investment of Conical Hill. Heavy rain was falling continually and
one officer tendered the following terse report when asked what
progress had been made during one day's operations: 'Those on
the forward slopes slid down. Those on the reverse slopes slid
back. Otherwise, no change.'[75]

On other islands the problem was not so much that the foxholes collapsed but that it was almost impossible to dig down deep enough in the first place. A soldier in the 77th Division, again on Guam, described the problems caused by the nature of the ground there:

> Just before dark we reached a large clearing where we'll dig for the night. Our places are assigned to us and I've drawn a lovely spot, about fifteen yards from the edge of the jungle. The first five inches of mud makes pretty tough digging but underneath there's a layer of coral and limestone rock. Frenzied hammering with the pick does nothing but wear down the pick and scatter white powder around the hole to make it stand out as though spotlighted.[76]

The history of the 305th Infantry Regiment also stressed the immense labour involved in digging in this kind of terrain:

> Digging in had a much greater significance than those two words would indicate. It meant coming into an area as the evening sun settled beyond the horizon, covered with sweat and grime, tired of everything but living. It meant digging a hole which wasn't a hole at all, but merely a rectangular depression big enough for one to lie in and deep enough to prevent one's being seen. This unique and vital excavation was done with a short shovel just large enough to plant one's feet upon and a pick with a handle so short one almost had to be either a midget or a contortionist to swing it.[77]

The regimental narrative of the 1st Marines reserved particular execration for Pelelieu where the ground

> . . . was the worst ever encountered by the regiment in three Pacific campaigns. Along its centre the rocky spine was heaved up in a contorted mass of decayed coral, strewn with rubble, crags, ridges and gulches thrown together in a confusing maze . . . It was impossible to dig in: the best men could do was pile a little coral or wood debris round their positions. The jagged rock slashed their shoes and clothes, and tore their bodies every time they hit the deck for safety.[78]

3
Combat: Infantry

They lived in a world which is as different from
this known world of ours as though they belonged
to another race of men inhabiting another planet.

PHILIP GIBBS, WAR CORRESPONDENT, 1916

The rifleman fights without promise of either
reward or relief. Behind every river there's
another hill – and behind that hill, another river.
After weeks or months in the line only a wound
can offer him the comfort of safety, shelter and
a bed. Those who are left to fight, fight on,
evading death but knowing that with each day of
evasion they have exhausted one more chance for
survival. Sooner or later, unless victory comes
this chase must end on the litter or in the grave.

GENERAL OMAR BRADLEY

Already these men moved in another world, in
the world of absorption in the fight and in personal
survival which started just across the river.

CAPTAIN GEOFFREY COX

No man, however he may talk, has the remotest
idea of what an ordinary infantry soldier endures.

SERGEANT H. GREEN

One of the most notable, and most overlooked, features of the Allied armies was the great divide between the front-line troops and the majority of men who existed simply to keep the former in action. This raises many important issues,[1] but the relevant one here is that the experiences of the combat soldier have largely been lost amongst the mass of reminiscences of those for whom the war was merely foreign travel tempered by excessive regimentation. The popular memory of World War II owes more to fond allusions to foreign climes, sunshine, good health and periodic binges than to any real conception of conditions at the front. For only a minority of men ever knew what these could be like – what had been the common experience on the Western Front between 1914 and 1918, was the exception to the rule in most of the theatres of the last war. True, they were a very self-conscious minority, and they bequeathed a literature often just as powerful as that of the Great War veterans, yet this has not impinged upon the popular consciousness in anything like the same way. This is not because the respective ordeals were not equally appalling, but because so few of those who returned home in 1945, let alone those who had never been abroad, had more than an inkling of how grim things could be. In the inter-war years the experience of the trenches had become a genuinely national trauma; in the years since V-J Day only those who were actually at the front have ever really known what it was like. World War I gave us *Journey's End*, World War II *South Pacific*; yet there was much more to the latter conflict than a lack of dames in a Pacific base area. It has already been seen in what conditions men had to exist for weeks at a time. Now is the time to see how they fought and died. If the story lacks the stark simplicity of whole battalions mown down by a handful of machine guns, it is nevertheless a record of appalling suffering, and endurance beyond the limits of hope itself.

Patrols

Of course, no troops were engaged in large-scale attacks all the time, yet even when the lines were fairly static units were not allowed merely to stay in their trenches and dugouts and await further orders. In all theatres great reliance was placed upon patrol activity. By and large patrols were a necessary evil; intelligence had to be gleaned about the actual whereabouts of the enemy, his strength and his intentions. Even if the patrols could not themselves assess the situation, they were usually required to bring back prisoners who might, wittingly or unwittingly, divulge some useful information. Such, for example, was the case in Burma in the long months between the Allied arrival in Assam and the great Japanese offensive of 1944. In fact, from the previous December, this was almost the only kind of offensive activity undertaken by the British and Indians. But this does not mean that life was easy. The patrols were of two types, either half-a-dozen men led by an NCO and supposed only to reconnoitre the ground, or a platoon-sized group, sometimes taking a mortar along, with orders to attack Japanese forward positions or to set an ambush to take prisoners. In either case the going was extremely tough, favoured routes being elephant tracks or dry river beds, and men were given special training and acclimatisation before they were deemed up to it. Around Imphal special forward patrol bases were set up, each with a garrison of a hundred men or so. These were hidden away in the jungle and consisted of a cluster of *basha* huts made of bamboo and leaves surrounded by a network of slit-trenches. In these bases and out on actual patrol the lowering stillness of the thick jungle was most unnerving. It even became the practice not to post sentries at night because they became so jumpy that the slightest unaccountable noise, usually made by animals, could provoke wild reactions and a hail of wasted bullets. On one occasion the whole of the 17th Division stood to for several hours all because of a few wandering ponies.

In the Pacific the Americans were rarely out of touch with the Japanese for very long and the tiny island battlefields meant that the lines were too close together for patrol activity to have much significance. This was not always so, however. On Okinawa, a larger island and one where the Japanese had decided to dig in inland rather than try to defend the beaches, it was some time before the main strongholds were pinpointed and for a time American efforts were concentrated around numerous little groups of apprehensive scouts pushed ahead of the rather puzzled battalions.

In North Africa the experiences of First and Eighth Armies differed considerably. In the desert the two sides were usually some miles apart and patrolling was done by armoured cars, light tanks or a few trucks of infantry that blundered about until they ran into what was assumed to be the enemy. These methods were at best haphazard and a key feature of the desert war was the chronic lack of knowledge about the enemy's, or indeed one's own, dispositions. In Tunisia this was rarely the problem. The basic German strategy here was positional, simply to buy time before an inevitable withdrawal, and the Allies were soon aware just which *djebels* were occupied by the enemy. Even so it was deemed necessary to send out constant patrols, and while many of these did fulfil a useful military function, one cannot help detecting echos of the old World War I philosophy of 'dominating no man's land' – sending men forward for no other reason than that the Germans too probably had patrols out. As in Burma, there was a distinction between reconnaissance patrols and those on a larger scale. The latter were rather akin to the trench raids of the previous war, either a dozen men heavily armed with tommy guns and grenades setting out to lay an ambush or attack an outpost located by an earlier patrol, or a fighting patrol of up to fifty men which was to burst into a German position and make off with a few prisoners. It was not unknown for the larger groups to be out for two or three days.

In Europe, too, psychological motives seem to have been just as important as reasons of intelligence. 'Keeping the men up to the mark' and 'giving the enemy no rest' were a common rationale for constant patrol activity. Accounts of such ventures during the 'phoney war' in France and Belgium might well be taken from a volume of Western Front memoirs. Lieutenant Orr Ewing (7th Argyll and Sutherland Highlanders) remembered crawling about in no man's land and bumping into a German patrol, at which point the enemy 'withdrew and we heard them talking on the other side of the stream. As it was then our time to return we made our way back to our own wire'.[2] Of a similar venture, Lieutenant M. Shephard (5th Gloucester Regiment) wrote: 'It was in the accepted tradition of patrolling. Cap comforters were worn, faces were blacked, grenades were fastened to webbing belts by the hand levers, and ammunition was readily available.'[3]

It is debatable whether the front-line soldiers benefited from being 'kept on their toes' in this manner. There is certainly no doubt that patrols were a horribly nerve-wracking experience. In Italy, British forward companies would send out one fighting patrol of about fifteen men each night, and a soldier could expect to take part in such a venture once every nine or ten days. Things were much worse for the company officers, who had to lead one of these patrols at least every alternate night. Most of them were forced to survive on no more than four hours sleep in every twenty-four, and that taken in odd snatches. One soldier has emphasised how little the unending strain was appreciated back home:

> Since the time . . . the Press was first able to announce, reluctantly and with an undercurrent of disapproval, that 'all is quiet on the Italian Front. Military operations are limited to patrol activity', patrol warfare has been waged with a pitiless ruthlessness that perhaps would satisfy the recumbent fireside sadists . . . rather than the most gory of large-scale attacks. Swift and noiseless thrusts in the dark; unpremeditated death by an unknown hand from a quarter uncertain; silent attack and counter-attack without ceasing – these are the pigments one must use to paint the picture of patrol warfare. [4]

An officer of the Rifle Brigade has left this description of one such patrol in Italy, which amply brings out the acute tensions of all such enterprises:

> There was first the problem of finding your way in the dark, of not making a noise, of not showing up against the moon or the skyline, and of distinguishing between bushes and enemy sentries. There was much creeping forward, much stopping to listen, many false alarms. And then, when something was found, there was the further reconnaissance, the little tactical plan, to gain more information or to try to grab a prisoner. On the return there was still a chance of being lost, of meeting an enemy patrol, of stepping on a mine, or of the coughers and stone-kickers giving away the path of the patrol, and then when our lines were reached there was always the chance that some trigger-happy sentry of our own might fire off into the darkness into the patrol. It was often after a hard day's fighting that an officer would be called upon to take out a patrol to harass the enemy or destroy an abandoned tank or (and this is the hardest of all) for a prisoner, or just to find out how far the enemy have gone. Riflemen were sometimes so tired that they would fall asleep at each pause of the patrol. [5]

Patrols were frequent in north-west Europe, too, particularly during the long winter when the opposing lines congealed. They were also just as unpopular. As Major Brodie (5th Black Watch) recalled, 'the very word "patrol" could send shivers down people's backs'. [6] In this theatre even commandos were called upon to man the line like ordinary infantry. Lieutenant D. Grant (41st Royal Marine Commando) found himself posted near Salenelles where his unit was supposed to deny the use of the village to the enemy, even though it was not actually within the Allied defences. 'The fighting went on all the time . . . and it was our purpose to dominate this no man's land . . . We would be warned that a patrol would be going out at dusk or dawn, and, if it was at dusk, we would see the small file of men, wearing cap comforters above their blackened faces, moving up the path into the wood.' As in Burma, a patrol base had been established, centred upon 'deep caverns supported by corrugated iron, timber and sods' and from this the small groups venture forth. But it was an unpopular mode of warfare, even amongst commandos. 'We hated these raids; it seemed better to us to let sleeping dogs lie.'[7]

Approach to Battle

Unpleasant as it was for the front-line troops, patrol warfare was never regarded by the generals as anything more than an unfortunate lull. The overriding objective was always to attack the enemy, to smash his military forces rather than to simply contain them. Defensive actions were numerous – Crete, Tobruk, Port Moresby, Imphal, Bastogne – but the essential aim of the Allied forces was to liberate conquered territory, to drive the Axis out of North Africa, the Pacific, south-east Asia, Italy and north-west Europe and, if necessary, to assault the Axis countries themselves. Combat was essentially a matter of attacking. At company, battalion, even divisional level this was not always apparent. Months were spent dug in in front of the enemy lines, while local enemy offensives often seemed to necessitate two steps back for every one forward. But it was *reculer pour mieux sauter*. No matter how tortuous their progress, the Allies gradually crept forward. Vast armadas of troopships were launched, men were dropped from the sky, complex artillery timetables were drawn up, armies and corps were trained and equipped for Operation This or That, start lines were designated and targets set, and at the sharp end each individual soldier had to nerve himself once again for his ultimate task, to advance under fire and wrest a few more yards of ground from the enemy.

But first it was necessary to try and stack the odds in the attacker's favour. This always involved some sort of concentration of troops around a particular area for, even when a front was well established, it was never held in such force that the men there could simply leap out of their slit-trenches and press forward. The main point had to be reinforced and adequate reserves provided. But the scale on which this was done varied enormously. Amphibious operations were the ones in which troops were brought the greatest distances and were also the greatest organisational headache. The landings in North Africa, Italy and Normandy each involved many thousands of men, and in the Pacific the whole campaign consisted of a long series of island assaults by the US Army and Marine Corps. Throughout the war over 400,000 British Army and Air Force personnel took part in such landings, while over 3 million Americans were trained for amphibious operations. Crewing the assault and landing craft alone absorbed large numbers of men. By the end of 1944 the British had deployed 13,000 Royal Marines for this purpose as well as 5,500 men from the RNVR and 43,500 ratings. They, and a much larger number of Americans, were responsible for 45,000 vessels and 56,000 landing craft that were built between 1943 and the end of hostilities.[8]

For the assault troops such landings involved two very different types of craft. The bulk of the voyage was made aboard a troop transport or Landing Ships Infantry (LSI) on which the men had minimal accommodation.[9] Luckily such voyages were generally short; the ships were grossly overcrowded and the atmosphere in the men's holds, which were nothing but a steel jungle of tiered bunks or hammocks, soon became utterly foul. Lance Corporal W. Robson (1st Queen's Own Royal West Kent Regiment) wrote home:

> Living between decks is as noisy, as crowded, and as uncomfortable as living in a fairground. The fairground analogy is heightened by the fact that very occasionally a loudspeaker tinnily emits a Sousa, *Land of Hope and Glory* or *It's a Long Way to Tipperary* usually in that order. But worse than anything else is the horrible humid atmosphere . . . Kit is stuffed into racks and if one piece is moved usually a lot more clatters down about your ears.[10]

Captain Howard-Stepney (2nd Coldstream Guards) described equally unpleasant conditions during the voyage to North Africa for Operation Torch:

> There was just room for everyone to sit down, provided that they were not wearing greatcoats or equipment, while at night hammocks were hung from every conceivable projection and tables and floors were covered with sleeping bodies . . . There were no port-holes to open and air entered through the open hatch above. At night, when the ship was darkened, this had to be closed down, and as there was no alternative means of ventilation, the atmosphere soon became unendurable . . . Arrangements for those who succumbed to sea-sick-

ness consisted of 40-gallon drums which slid about the decks with unpleasant splashings.[11]

Food was poor to execrable and had to be queued for, often for hours on end, while liquor and other comforts were virtually non-existent. Sometimes, notably in the Pacific, these trips became a terrible ordeal. Prior to the attack on Guam, in July 1944, the 3rd Marine Division spent seven such weeks at sea, most of them in very bad weather.

Once the ships were close to the shore the troops transferred to the Landing Craft Infantry (LCI) that had hung from the davits of the mother ship. Even if under enemy fire this procedure was agonisingly slow as the soldiers, weighed down with equipment, shuffled along the narrow passageways, each man's weapons and equipment being checked by the officers before he left the ship. Sometimes they climbed into the landing craft before these were lowered the forty feet into the sea. Other landings demanded that they scramble down netting and fall or jump into craft already afloat. Either exercise could be perilous. Private First-Class N. Mailer (112th Cavalry) was obliged to use the former method during the assault on Leyte;

The davit machinery was complicated and a portion of it hung over the water. When a man was harnessed into a pack and web belt and carried a rifle and two bandoliers and several grenades, a bayonet and a helmet, he felt as though he had a tourniquet over both shoulders and across his chest. It was hard to breathe and his limbs kept falling asleep. Climbing along the beam which led out to the landing craft became an adventure not unlike walking a tightrope while wearing a suit of armour.[12]

Once under way, however, simply getting aboard began to seem the least of one's travails. The journey to the shore, no matter how short, could be a nightmare for anyone without a long familiarity with small boats. Often craft were unloaded prematurely from their mother ship and, because they had to hit the beach in pre-arranged waves they had to spend long minutes sailing round in circles or darting about trying to find the right wave. Jack Belden, an American war correspondent, went ashore with the leading wave at Sicily:

Our dash towards the unseen shore became a nightmare of sickness, pain and fear. The boat had gathered speed now and we were begin-

ning to bound from one wave crest to the next with a distinct shock.
There were no thwarts, no seats of any kind in the boat; only the deck
itself to sit on, and the steep, high hull of the boat to lean against. The
motion of the boat threw us all against one another . . . It rolled us
against iron pipes, smashed us against coils of wire, and jammed us on
top of one another, compounding us with metal, water and vomit.[13]

Seasickness is still treated as something of a joke, but it was a real
military concern. The problem was not so much the sensations
caused by the movement of the troop transports but the gut-
wrenching nausea that affected everyone in the landing craft. R.
McKinlay (Royal Naval Commandos) said of the D-Day landings,
'It wasn't too bad for us sailors, but I think one of the main reasons
why Normandy was such a great success was that the soldiers
would rather have fought thousands of Germans than go back into
those boats and be sea-sick again.'[14] Ceaseless vomiting and retch-
ing as well as the dizziness and disorientation caused by the erratic
behaviour of the skyline, could render the soldiers virtually helpless when they actually staggered off the landing ramps.

Considerable research went into the development of seasickness
pills. A combination of hyoscine and benzedrine was used for the
Torch landings, and the later Canadian 'pink pill' was made of a
similar compound. The Americans relied on a tablet made of
sodium amatyl, scopolamine and atropine. All these were tested
during two special exercises prior to D-Day, in January and
March. Unfortunately, contrary to reasonable expectation, on
both occasions the sea was absolutely calm. In the event it is
difficult to say whether the pills were of much military significance.
Certainly there were occasions on which the cure was almost as
deleterious as the illness. Ernie Pyle remembered the run-up to
Omaha Beach with men of the 29th US Division when 'capsules
had been issued to us with our battle kits. Well, we took the first
two and they almost killed us. The capsules had a strong sleeping
powder in them, and by noon we were in a drugged stupor . . .
They constricted our throats, made our mouths bone-dry and
dilated the pupils of our eyes until we could hardly see'.[15] For
once, perhaps, the more prosaic British approach to such problems
was the more sensible. While the Americans set great store by their
so-called Motion Sickness Preventative, the British, as a last resort, fell back on brown, greaseproof paper bags designated by the
War Department as Bags, Vomit For the Use Of.

Once the troops had actually reached the shore, the situation varied enormously from landing to landing. In North Africa, Sicily, Salerno and Anzio, resistance at the water-line was slight. The same was true at Okinawa where the American practice of bombarding the coast with massive concentrations of bombs and naval gunfire had finally persuaded the Japanese to make their main defence inland. In Normandy, only one of the five D-Day beachheads was ever in danger of being squeezed out, while the later landings in southern France were completely unopposed. But the lack of an enemy did not always mean a safe landing. Rough seas or surf could be a problem, as at Algiers where 94 per cent of the first wave of landing craft were lost. Western Task Force, in Morocco, lost 35 per cent – and that in the calmest surf for almost seventy years. Indeed, it was fortunate that the Torch landings were made against such light opposition, for Allied amphibious technique was at a rudimentary stage. A serious error was the amount of equipment each soldier carried. Colonel Macnamara, the Quartermaster for II US Corps, declared: 'The enlisted men were physically overburdened . . . [The rations], bandoliers of ammunition, the clothing, gas masks, weapons and other incidentals weighed . . . 132lbs a man. This was simply 110lbs too many for a combat soldier to carry and enough to make anyone utterly useless.'[16] On top of this each man also carried two barracks bags, at that time infuriating burdens in that they couldn't be slung over the shoulder because of the pack and roll on the back, and if carried in each hand they made balance extremely precarious. Only later did anyone think to add a handle. Not surprisingly, many men who fell over into the waves or stepped into unexpectedly deep water were drowned. Though they had been supplied with life jackets, these proved insufficiently buoyant to support a man carrying this amount of equipment.

Similar problems were encountered during the early Pacific campaigns. On Guam reefs prevented the landing craft getting right up to the beach. This necessitated

. . . a long wade to the beach, searching for footing on the treacherous coral bottom, [the men] wrestling with their equipment, sometimes to their necks in water. The men were top heavy with equipment: the average soldier was burdened with a steel helmet, gas mask, light pack, life belt, rifle and bayonet, grenade loader, ammunition, rations, a pouch of hand grenades, two canteens of water and a machete. Heavy weapons company men carried most of this equipment and in addition part of a mortar or heavy machine gun.[17]

In later operations, both in the Pacific and European theatres, the troops took only the barest essentials ashore with them, leaving the bulk of their equipment to be brought to the beaches at a later date. In theory this was not supposed to take more than two or three days, but in fact it was often weeks before a soldier's kit caught up with him. Even if it did arrive on the beaches fairly quickly soldiers commonly discovered, on locating their battalion's dump, that their bags had been slashed open with a razor blade and all personal possessions and decent clothing removed. Moreover, the lack of heavy personal equipment did not always make the landing much easier. Just keeping one's footing could be quite enough of a problem. A Marine, Peter Bowman, described the procedure for struggling through the surf from boat to beach:

> Men on the right hand side of the landing craft disembark over the front corner of the ramp and step off to the right oblique, while those on the opposite side move similarly to the left. The coxswain keeps the engines turning in order to prevent the boat turning sideways . . . Draw in your breath. Hold your piece at high port. Keep moving. Churn through the foam. Don't try to run or the drag of the waves will upset your balance. Proceed diagonally through the swirling surf with feet wide apart.[18]

On Iwo Jima the boats actually went straight onto the beach, but even here the landing was no easier. An American journalist went in with the leading waves:

> Tough as the Japanese were, the heavy seas were tougher. The prevailing winds reversed themselves during the first ten days . . . so that the beachhead was exposed to the sullen fury of the Pacific Ocean. Because Iwo Jima is a volcano rising straight out of the sea, there is no shallow water. The box-shaped landing craft were tossed about like egg-crates caught on the crest of a spring flood. Unprotected by breakwaters or coral reefs, the boats were swamped by six-foot breakers as soon as their bows rammed into the volcanic sand. The boats floundered, sank, and were spewn along the shore to form twisted barricades of debris.[19]

Once the men were ashore, conditions varied enormously from landing to landing. Except for Omaha Beach in Normandy, where one American officer was reduced to the despairing exhortation, 'We're getting killed on the beaches – let's go inshore and get killed,' Pacific landings were usually the worst. The terrain itself and the Japanese habit of defending the coast-line in force combined to make the establishment of the beachhead extremely hazardous. On Iwo Jima any forward movement not only brought down heavy Japanese fire but had to be made through deep, cloying volcanic ash in which men stepped up to their knees. A Marine officer wrote that no previous landing had matched 'the ghastliness that hung over the Iwo beachhead. Nothing any of us had ever known could compare with the utter anguish, frustration and constant inner battle to maintain some semblance of sanity, clarity of mind and power of speech. Everybody tells me they felt as I did'.[20] In fact, few of the Pacific landings were easy. On Hollandia the major beaches led straight into deep marshes from which there were hardly any exits for vehicles or men. The western peninsula of Pelelieu, like much of the rest of the island, was a mass of decayed coral, judged by the 1st Marine Division to be the worst ground ever encountered in their Pacific campaigns. 'Casualties were higher for the simple reason it was impossible to get under the ground away from the Japanese mortar barrages. Each blast hurled chunks of coral in all directions, multiplying many times the fragmentation effect of every shell.'[21]

A yet more hazardous way of getting troops within striking distance of the enemy was to drop them out of the sky, either as paratroops or glider-borne infantry. The former have attracted most popular attention but glider assault was equally, if not more, important, notably in Sicily, Arnhem and the Chindits' Operation Thursday in Burma. As with amphibious operations, early experiments were less than propitious. In Tunisia for example, in November 1942, British paratroopers were dropped on Souk el Arba. Though they did succeed in capturing their main objective, Beja, there were many unnecessary casualties because it was not realised that the more rarified air of this part of the world meant that they needed to jump from a greater height than in England. The worst shambles was the invasion of Sicily (Operation Husky) in July 1943, when both types of airborne troops were used. British glider units were among the first sent in, but the pilots of the Dakota tugs seem to have panicked somewhat and of the 144 gliders, 69 came down in the sea, others were scattered all over the southern coastline, and only 12 came down in the actual drop-zone. Over 600 unnecessary casualties were sustained, 326 of these being men drowned. Many American casualties were equally unnecessary. The 504th Airborne Regiment had 23 transport aircraft shot down by their own artillery and another 70 were badly damaged. The same thing happened two days later when British troops were flown in to seize the Primasole Bridge: 126 Dakotas were used, but only 39 of these dropped their men within a mile of the target; many of the others were shot down by Allied ships or dropped their human cargos miles out to sea.

Co-ordination improved a great deal in the following months and there were no repetitions of the Sicily disasters. But even in the best circumstances airborne approach was not the ideal way to go into battle. As with amphibious landings, purely physical constraints could be demoralising. Air-sickness was a serious problem, especially in gliders, where the normal instability of aircraft was complicated by a continuous to-and-fro movement as the glider repeatedly pulled against the slack of the towing hawser. Most men were sick on most trips and the floor of the glider was soon awash with vomit. After the formation of the 6th US Airlanding Brigade, the commander and 19 volunteers made 12 flights on which they took different types of air-sickness remedies. All 20 men threw up every single time. Nausea was not the only demand of nature that caused problems. Huw Wheldon took part in the D-Day glider assault and, after a flight which felt like being 'in a very old railway carriage being yanked across the sky', his overwhelming desire on reaching the ground was to relieve himself. As he looked around him he realised that what he had taken to be the setting up of a hasty defence perimeter was in fact the whole complement of the glider urinating.[22] It is perhaps not surprising that the flow of volunteers for airborne units began to dry up. The Americans had to conscript their glider troops from an early date, despite the inducement of an extra $50 a month. By 1944 the British were simply turning whole line battalions – the 2nd Oxford and Buckinghamshire Light Infantry and the 10th Essex Regiment for example – into paratroops. The reluctance of the British soldier is particularly understandable as throughout the war the authorities refused to follow the American example and provide a reserve parachute. Bulkiness was one reason given, though the fact that silk parachutes cost £20 each leads one to suspect Treasury interference. Many lives were needlessly lost until commonsense finally prevailed in 1950.

Neither of these approaches to battle, however, was the usual way for an infantryman to go into combat. Even in the Pacific, after a beachhead had been consolidated, there were still weeks of fighting ahead to liberate the island completely. Then, as in other theatres, ground fighting reverted to its usual form. Before the attack, start lines were designated for each unit, and the most common way forward to these jumping-off points was on foot. If a unit came from the reserve areas part of the journey might be made in trucks, but the last mile or so was normally covered under the soldiers' own steam. They tended to move at night, ready for an attack at first light, and just getting to the start line might involve much arduous labour. Night usually meant total blackness, making it very difficult to keep sight of the man in front and to find one's footing on treacherous rocky or jungle trails. In late November 1942 the Americans were preparing an attack on Buna Village in New Guinea, and the 2nd Battalion of the 126th Infantry Regiment was one unit moving up to the start lines.

> They moved slowly. There was no trail. It was hard for the men to find one another in the darkness, because they had no white cloth for arm-bands, not even cloth from underwear, for they had by then no underwear. Each man grasped the shoulder of the man in front and shuffled forward, the only guide the telephone wire leading to the jumping-off point and the whispered advice of men in foxholes along the way. They moved forward with fixed bayonets, not yet permitted to fire.[23]

Captain Ralph Ingersoll took part in a night march in Tunisia, prior to an attack on Guettar, and his greatest problem was coping with the great mass of miscellaneous equipment he was supposed to distribute about his person:

> Within a hundred and fifty yards I was panting, and I do not remember really ceasing to pant, and breathing simply and normally again, until well after the battle was underway next morning. That was the way it was in the beginning of a march; everyone was so busy that time and space were lost completely, and there was only the ludicrous motion of tripping and stumbling on, batting oneself in the head with a rifle or the barrel of a mortar and trying to stick things down in overfilled pockets and take hitches in belts.[24]

Towards the end of the war, notably in Europe, more sophisticated methods of getting men forward were developed. River crossings were one area of improvement. Great use was made of amphibious tractors such as DUKWs and 'Weasels', which allowed the troops to get across fairly quickly and with reasonable protection against water and small-arms fire. But this was not always the case. The Americans, in particular, had several disas-

trous experiences with river assaults. The 36th US Division made
the notorious crossing of the Rapido in January 1944 using standard 24-men rubber craft and M2 assault boats – simple flat-
bottomed plywood scows. The former were difficult to paddle,
hard to steer and easy to capsize in a swiftly flowing stream.
Moreover, they made attractive targets and could be sunk by the
tiniest shell fragment. The second type were very heavy and were
usually brought to the water's edge by truck. This proved impossible at the Rapido and many of the assault troops were utterly
exhausted when they actually attacked, having carried the boats for
several miles over waterlogged ground. The 5th US Division fared
nearly as badly during the crossing of the Sauer in February 1945.
Though the current was fierce and swollen only small inflatable
Luftwaffe dinghies were available, and fewer than ten men from
each assault regiment reached the far shore. But at least they had
boats of a kind. In the same month the 29th US Division was sent
across the equally swollen Roer on foot. The night

> . . . was as cloudy and damp and chill as February weather can be.
> Many of the men had gotten soaked to the skin in wading through the
> waist- and neck-deep water of the canals and trenches and along the
> banks of the flooded river. A few of the shorter men had gone over their
> heads as they stepped into holes they could not see. Equipment and
> supplies had become soaked and heavy, and in many cases useless . . .
> The men had no way to dry themselves [and] were forced to huddle
> together in the mud-and-water filled trenches, shivering, shaking and
> praying.[25]

During the crossing of the river Wurm, in the previous October,
the 30th US Division adopted a rather unsatisfactory compromise.
Because the river was not as deep as expected, it was decided not to
bring up any boats. Instead each man was told to find a large piece
of wood, throw it into the water and, hopefully, stroll across.

In non-amphibious assaults the most useful development was
that of the armoured personnel carrier. From quite early in the war
infantry had become accustomed to riding on tanks, though this
was more in the interests of speed than for the protection afforded.
General Patton was particularly keen on this tactic but, though
it was frequently used, his and other troops were less than
enthusiastic as a tank is a very unstable platform and offers remarkably few useful points on which to grip. A slightly less *ad hoc*
device was the 'Kangaroo', though even this was something of

an improvisation. Many Sherman tanks had had their turrets removed and 25-pounder guns installed as a way of producing 'instant' self-propelled artillery; in Italy and north-west Europe many of these conversions had the guns removed completely and makeshift seats installed. Such vehicles never actually charged the enemy positions but they did permit soldiers to get across much of the fire-zone with virtual immunity against grenades and bullets. They played a prominent role in August 1944 during an attack towards Caen by the Canadian 2nd Division and the 51st (Highland); in the following December in an attack on Blerick, across the Maas, by the 15th (Scottish) Division; and in the Roermond Triangle in January 1945 during operations of the 52nd (Lowland) Division. One of the most systematic uses of these armoured personnel carriers was in Italy, in April 1945, when a so-called 'Kangaroo Army' was formed to spearhead penetration into the Argenta Gap. Each infantry company had its own allotment of 8 Kangaroos, though these actually belonged to an armoured regiment, and each was supplied with reserve ammunition and 48 hours rations. The battalion headquarters also had 8 carriers, 2 of which were for medical purposes and 2 for reserve ammunition. The whole force was under the command of the 2nd Armoured Brigade and operated in close co-ordination with armoured squadrons and assorted flail, bulldozer and flamethrower tanks.

Bombardment

Once troops had actually reached their jump-off points it might in fact be some time before they were given the command to move forward. In the meantime, just as in most periods of static warfare, they could expect at least some attention from enemy artillery. In the European theatres, in particular, artillery was a vitally important weapon on both sides, sometimes used on a scale that rivalled the great barrages of World War I. Here we are only concerned with the effects of artillery fire on Allied troops; the experiences of Allied gunners will be dealt with in the next chapter. Nevertheless, it is worth pointing out that even the fire of their own gunners could be a painful experience for the Allied infantry, simply due to the sheer noise. Alastair Bothwick (5th Seaforth Highlanders) attempted to describe the stupefying wall of sound that assailed the troops waiting to go forward on the first day of Alamein:

A barrage, even if it is not one's first, is a difficult thing to write about. It cannot be taken apart and described in detail, and in the mass, it is so overwhelming that no broad picture of it can possibly be convincing. The noise is unbelievable . . . When some hundreds of guns are firing at once, the high shrill sound [of a single 25-pounder] grows, until the whole sky is screaming; and when the first shells land, the earth shakes, clouds of dust and smoke arise, and the immense crash drowns the approach of the shells which follow. The infantryman is a fly inside a drum; and only occasionally, when for a few seconds the guns seem to draw breath, can we hear the twanging of harps which heralds the next salvo. The uproar swells and fades and swells again, deafeningly, numbing the brain.[26]

Even larger barrages presaged major operations in Italy and north-west Europe. In May 1944, before the fourth assault on Cassino, the entire artillery of Eighth and Fifth Armies was used. The latter expended 170,000 rounds within 4 hours. A Polish platoon commander wrote: 'Apart from 1,100 pieces of artillery there were the mortars and anti-tank guns blazing away – the noise deafened us . . . I for one felt that if it went on for long I would go mad.'[27] At the Battle of the Senio, in April 1945, the 2nd New Zealand Division used as many guns as the entire Eighth Army at Alamein. A New Zealander has drawn attention to the weird contrast between the deafening din and the absence of any comparable visual effect.

The whole eastern horizon was solid with sound. Overhead shells raced, with all their multitudinous sounds: 25pdrs slithering or tearing past like a long curtain being ripped in two, the 4.5 and 5.5 churning their way through the air, as if they were whole trains being driven at speed, invisibly over our heads, and hurtling down on the bank. Sometimes the noise would seem to get harsher, as if the sky were a vast steel shutter, being hauled down on the enemy . . . It seemed impossible that all this noise could come from something invisible and you looked as if expecting to see the hazed sky streaked and torn by passing shells, as artists show them in comic cartoons. But there was nothing there but the haze and the encircling planes . . . In all honesty it was not nearly as vivid a sight as most descriptions of war would have you believe.[28]

But neither the sight nor the sound of a barrage from one's own guns were anything compared to the effect of enemy artillery on one's own ranks. Sound was often pretty much irrelevant, in fact, for when many types of a shell landed very close one never even heard the whine or whistle, simply a momentary whishing sound and then the noise of the explosion. If it landed too close one never heard anything at all. Nor should one imagine infantrymen advancing through numerous little eruptions of dirt and rock, as portrayed in many films. In Europe and the jungle most casualties from artillery fire were caused by shells exploding in tree-tops and scattering their fragments over a very wide area. In Africa, of course, the cinematic vision is fairly near the mark, and because the shells did actually hit the ground the fragmentation effect was considerably lessened – as long, that is, as they did not hit bare rock. Then, and this was notably the case in Tunisia and Italy, the impact of the shell would throw out hundreds of little chips of rock that were just as deadly as flying fragments of steel. In Italy, Ernie Pyle estimated that upwards of 15 per cent of one American battalion's casualties were caused in this manner. A similar effect from coral on Pelelieu has already been mentioned, and this is only one example of what might happen on any of the coral atolls of the Central Pacific.

But perhaps the worst effect of a bombardment was the dreadful mental strain imposed on even those who escaped unscathed. 'Shell shock' was always a very imprecise term in World War I, and by 1942 had completely given way to such terms as 'battle fatigue' or 'combat exhaustion'. The imprecision of the latter terms was in fact justified in that psychological breakdown in battle could be the result of a whole variety of factors (see Chapter 6). Yet the former term does reflect a basic truth – that of all the components of modern warfare, artillery and high explosives were the most terrifying, the ones that made men feel utterly dwarfed by the material holocaust around them. Private Louis Simpson (101st US Airborne Division) wrote:

Being shelled is the real work of an infantry soldier, which no one talks about. Everyone has his own way of going about it. In general, it means lying face down and contracting your body into as small a space as possible. In novels you read about soldiers, at such moments, fouling themselves. The opposite is true. As all your parts are contracting, you are more likely to be constipated. [29]

And, from an officer of the 1st Scots Guards in Tunisia:

How I hate shells. I have seen strong, courageous men reduced to whimpering wrecks, crying like children . . . And when one has nothing to do, the fumes and dust and echoed cries of 'stretcher bearer!'

strain one's nerves almost to breaking point. Yet if one goes to ground how incredibly hard it is to get into the open again to do a job of work. I would sooner have a thousand bullets or even dive bombers than a day's shelling.[30]

An American survey found that breakdown in combat often *was* shell shock pure and simple, and it was noted that out of one sample of 115 consecutive patients, 105 of them were suffering from a form of acute anxiety largely resulting from exposure to a nearby explosion. Numerous personal accounts stress the terror engendered by such an experience. The noise alone was bad enough. As Guthrie Wilson recalled: 'The first shell landed unexpectedly. We heard the scream of its approach (you hear it for how long? Perhaps one hundredth of a second) and the vast confusing disintegration as it smashed into the ground. It was for all the world as though some gigantic crate of glass were pitched from a mile above earth onto a roadway of concrete flagstones.'[31] Even stray shells would seem inexorably bound towards the very spot on which one cowered. Private S. Bagnall (5th East Lancashire Regiment) was moving forward with his company when they heard the whine of an approaching shell.

> We hit the earth with one thud where we had stood. I could feel the exact spot in the small of my defenceless back (I wish to God we had packs on, I thought, I wish to God we had packs on not because they're any *use* but it feels better) where the pointed nose of the shell would pierce skin and gristle and bone and explode the charge that would make me feel as if I had a splitting headache all over for a fiftieth of a second before I was spread minutely over the earth and hung up in trees. I held my breath and tried to press deeper into the earth and tensed every muscle as though by sheer will power I could abate the force of that disintegrating shock, cheat death, defy God (O God have mercy on me, please, please, *please* dear God, don't let me die!).[32]

Captain M. Howard (3rd Coldstream Guards) has described the mental disintegration that could follow a number of such near misses.

> The first shell arrived. Where it landed I am not quite sure. There was just a sudden whistle and a crash so loud and so near that I was not conscious of it as noise at all, but as force, as violence, as air suddenly expanding in a great annihilating wave. Everything was dark with dust and cordite fumes, and there followed that sinister silence when all the world is still and you feel suddenly released from the panic-stricken

fluttering inside your ribs which a second before was stilled, gripped in a stupefying paralysis . . . Then came another whistle, growing louder horribly quickly, culminating again in the crash that could be felt and not heard, in that instant of blind personal paralysis when all thought and feeling, even fear, is frozen, blotted out as vision is momentarily eclipsed by a wink. Then the release of breathing, the release of fear, the release of the bird under the ribs . . . [The gun fired again and I] pressed closer, impossibly closer, to the ground, fixing my eyes on some silly little detail – a blade of grass, a stone, a struggling ant – concentrating desperately on that until the paralysis, the shutter descended and reduced me to something out of all semblance of a man.[33]

If it is possible, this feeling of helplessness was sometimes intensified by the fact that the bombardment came from one's own side. There are not many documented cases of troops being hit by their own artillery, but it was unhappily quite common for them to be subjected to attacks from their own bombers. E. D. Smith was present during the bombing of Cassino, prior to one assault, and the volume of bombs rivalled the most intense barrage. 'After a few minutes I felt like shouting that's enough; but it went on and on until our eardrums were bursting and our senses befuddled.' But what was worse was that 'several bombs fell on my company and I found myself shouting curses at the planes'.[34] This was far from being an isolated instance and the use of aircraft, notably bombers, in a tactical support role was always a considerable hazard for the troops supposedly being supported. In January 1941, in Eritrea, General Savory's 11th Indian Brigade was strafed by the RAF, though there were few casualties. In November 1941, during the Crusader battles, the 1st Essex Regiment was hit by bombs that were meant to fall on the escarpment they were attacking and forty casualties were incurred. Towards the end of the Sicily campaign, the 2nd US Armoured Division was twice strafed by American fighter-bombers. During the battles of Cassino, in fact, there were several serious blunders. One flight of bombers during the third assault dropped their load on Venafro, ten miles away from the target, destroying the Eighth Army commander's caravan, much of 4th Indian Division's 'B' Echelon and a Moroccan military hospital. There were over 150 casualties.

But the worst errors were those during the first few months of the north-west Europe campaign. In July, on the first day of the Cobra offensive, the Eighth US Air Force bombed the US VII Corps, killing 111 soldiers and wounding 400 more. The British and Canadians were no luckier. On 7 August, prior to Operation

Totalise, this same outfit jettisoned several bomb loads on the 51st (Highland) Division, killing 60 men and wounding a further 300. On the 14th, RAF bombers supporting Operation Tractable struck instead at Canadian and Polish concentrations; in the Regiment de la Chaudière over 400 men were killed and wounded. The Ninth US Air Force performed no better; by the end of 1944 the GIs were referring to it as 'the American Luftwaffe'. Two lapses were especially notable. In October it was called upon to strike against the pill-boxes of the West Wall, around Aachen, but not one aircraft actually hit the target. One even failed to hit the right country and flattened Genk, a Belgian mining village, causing 80 casualties. During the Battle of the Bulge its planes bombed Malmédy, then held by the 30th US Division, and killed numerous infantrymen and civilians in a series of raids which went on for three days. The 30th Division had more cause than most to distrust their own aircrews; between Normandy and the Ardennes they were attacked in error no fewer than thirteen times.

Attack

Nothing of what has been said so far, however, should divert our attention from the basic theme of combat in World War II, the infantry attack across more or less open ground. These attacks were usually presaged by bombardments, and often supported by tanks, while the cardinal principle of fire and movement always meant that those troops moving forward at any one time were covered by their own rifles, mortars, light and medium machine guns. Nevertheless, the essential point remains – at some time or other infantrymen had to advance under enemy fire and put their life on the line; not as a once in a lifetime act of bravado, but simply as a matter of course, again and again, even when it was obvious that the odds were heavily stacked against them. The history of the 1st Gordon Highlanders in north-west Europe is typical of British, Commonwealth and American units throughout the war. During that campaign they fought a total of thirty-six major actions and in all but two of them they were attacking.

This has always been the foot soldiers' lot and in essence there was little new about World War II, from Tunis to Tarawa, from Burma to Berlin. Sometimes, indeed, history seemed simply to be repeating itself. Mention has already been made of the extent to which troops had to dig in and exist in foul conditions reminiscent of World War I. The fighting itself often revived such memories, not only on a strategic level where the huge artillery bombardments before Alamein or the crossing of the Senio in Italy, the war of attrition around Caen, or the dour slogging matches in Italy, the Saar or the Scheldt estuary were little different from operations on the Western Front, but also from the worm's eye viewpoint. Many soldiers could have been miraculously whisked away to join a battalion on the Somme or in the Argonne Forest and hardly have noticed any difference.

When the 1st Division attacked Grich el Oued towards the end of the Tunisian campaign they found a complete German trench system stretching for over four miles and which fell only after bitter hand-to-hand fighting. At Anzio, after the Germans had begun to counter-attack, the beachhead turned into a maze of trenches and dugouts that looked no different from the wasteland of Passchendaele. A regimental history was moved to rare eloquence in attempting to describe the fighting in this sector:

The [1st] London Irish now moved to the western flank – into the Wadis – those muddy death traps into which complete sub-units of men, tortured by lack of sleep, would vanish from the ken of commanding officers . . . In the Wadis there was a continuous draining of strength by casualties from mortaring and shelling and 'disappearances' on reconnaissance and on patrol. Another complete company disappeared, having stumbled by night into enemy held territory, and was swallowed up. Unknown and heterogeneous reinforcements had to be absorbed in the heat of battle and there was constant reorganisation and 're-squadding'. There had by this time been an 80 per cent change-over in personnel since January.[35]

In north-west Europe, too, this kind of bloody trench warfare was all too common. In the Scheldt estuary, in late 1944, the British and Canadians had more than their fill of it. The War Diary of the Regina Rifle Regiment described life in the Breskens Pocket:

The past few days have seen some of the fiercest fighting since D-Day. Lobbing grenades at an enemy ten yards away and continued attempts at infiltration have kept everyone on the jump. Ammunition has been used up in unbelievable quantities, men throwing as many as twenty-five grenades each a night. Artillery laid 2,000 shells on our front alone in ninety minutes . . . and our own Mortar Platoon expended 1,064 rounds of H.E. in three hours.[36]

In all theatres, in fact, the comparison with World War I is much
more far-reaching than might be supposed. In both wars, for
example, it was the Allies that had to attack the enemy. More
importantly, and perhaps contrary to popular imagination, such
attacks were rarely deep thrusts right through the enemy lines or
round his flanks and rear but rather head-on assaults against
heavily fortified defence networks. The war in Africa and Europe
was built around 'Lines' – Buerat, Mareth, Gustav, Gothic, Siegfried – and fortified high ground – Keren, Longstop, Camino,
Cassino, Verrières Ridge, Mont Pinçon. The Pacific war was basically an affair of fortified strongholds – Death Valley, Purple Heart
Ridge (Saipan), the Ibdi and Mokmer Caves and the Sump (Biak),
Ormoc Valley (Leyte), Mount Suribachi (Iwo Jima), Mount
Shuri, Sugar Loaf, Kunishi Ridge (Okinawa) – that the American
forces had to storm and clear out to the last man. As mentioned in
Chapter 2, World War II was not a war of movement, except on the
rare occasions when the enemy was in retreat; it was a bloody
slogging match in which mobility was only occasionally of real
significance. Indeed, except for its importance in the lines of
communication and the fact that it enabled guns to be self-
propelled, the internal combustion engine was not a major consideration in the ground war. In the last analysis, men and the
weapons that they could carry with them were what counted.
Artillery and tanks had an important part to play (see Chapter 4)
but they hardly ever sufficed in themselves to carry an important
network of enemy strong-points.

Such defences were usually a combination of natural features
and the enemy's ingenuity and industry. The Germans even had a
special department, the Todt Organisation, to work on the more
elaborate defence lines, notably the Gothic, the Siegfried and the
Atlantic Wall. But the troops themselves, and their engineer units,
often erected elaborate defences by combining deep bunkers,
trenches, minefields, booby traps, machine guns firing on fixed
lines and hull-down tanks into virtually impregnable bastions.

The African campaigns bore more resemblance than most to the
war of movement that had been forecast by certain military pun-
dits of the twenties and thirties. Even so, in the Western Desert as
well as in Tunisia, the Allies were often forced to attack quite
formidable entrenchments. Such was the case during the Crusader
battles when an attack was launched on the Omars, between Bir
Sidi Omar and Halfaya, where the Germans had a series of heavily

fortified strong-points surrounded by extensive minefields. Somewhat later, Captain Robbie Faure (3rd Coldstream Guards) saw
many survivors of an attack prior to the fall of Tobruk, as they
came straggling back to the Knightsbridge Box. As they 'began to
come in it was obvious that something was wrong. All that night
they came dribbling in, small parties of British and Indians, badly
shaken, many of them, with tales of lying on rocky ledges where
you couldn't dig and they shelled you to pieces until you couldn't
stand it any longer and put your hands up and they took you
away'.[37] El Alamein, too, was a head-on assault against prepared
positions, and every major battle thereafter involved frontal attacks
against German entrenchments on ground of their own choosing.
R. L. Crimp was present during an attack on the Pimples, at Bou
Kernine, in April 1943:

> Men have begun drifting back in small groups, most of them badly
> shaken. They talk of crawling up sheer precipices to find every level
> expanse swept by machine gun fire; of wounded rolling all the way to
> the bottom; of tripwire mines and booby-traps on handgrip ledges; of
> areas automatically illuminated on approach by flares and bulbs, im-
> mediately drawing fire; of premature rifle shots from stumbling men,
> supposed to have given the game away; and of walls and caves and all
> sorts of cunning defensive devices on the summit, piled round with the
> dead of previous assaults.[38]

In Italy almost every attack was of this nature as Kesselring
slowly withdrew northwards, using the countless mountain ridges
and rivers as the basis for yet another dour defensive battle. The
ruggedness of the mountain terrain has already been emphasised as
well as the difficulties of merely moving up, let alone staging
an attack. But the rivers too could be formidable obstacles. For
example on the Senio, never more than 15yd across, the Germans
dug into the 30ft high flood-banks on either side, first defending
the forward bank and then pulling back to the far side, blowing
their small bridges behind them. On other occasions they used
flood-water itself by breaching river banks and irrigation works at
selected points – a tactic used at Cassino, for instance.

Flooding was also extensively used in north-west Europe, as in
the Roer Valley where the Ninth US Army had to fight across
miles of completely waterlogged ground. Much of Holland, too,
was put under water. The Germans dug into the dykes, breached
them at selected points, and zeroed their artillery and machine

guns upon the few roads left above the water, along which the Allies would have to attack.

But water was far from being the only basis for dogged defence. Immediately after D-Day the Allies ran into the Normandy *bocage*, a maze of narrow, sunken roads and high, thick, almost impenetrable hedgerows dividing the myriads of small fields. In these hedges the Germans stationed small groups of machine gunners and anti-tank crews who remained invisible until one was almost on top of them. Major Cooke (8th Royal Scots) afterwards spoke of the 'furtive type of *bocage* warfare' and went on:

> I can see again the earth banks, the green hedgerows, the white dust of Normandy, and I can feel again the hush and quiet, the grim and threatening quiet, that broods over a front-line position. The men, their faces strained, speak in tired, low voices, almost fearful of breaking a spell . . . Over it all runs the memory of an enemy who is seldom seen but often heard. As soon as darkness fell we could hear the crackle of a Spandau or the *burrp-burrp* of a machine-pistol as the Boche once again began his night's work. During the day the crash of a sniper's rifle or the sudden mounting crescendo of mortar bombs, preceded by the unearthly groan of the rocket projector, caused dozing men to stare at each other and bolt to their slit trenches, holding themselves rigid while the smash of bombs tore through the air . . . The Churchill tanks . . . crawled up every morning to support the forward companies, and Boche snipers lay awaiting them; their Bazookas . . . can pierce a Churchill turret at about forty yards . . . The Boche showed individual determination and fieldcraft of the highest order. The constant firing, now from the front, now from the flank, now from the rear . . . [was meant] to draw answering fire and thus reveal our positions. At Estry I believe the enemy held their ground . . . with the minimum of men and the maximum of weapons – and they used those weapons as often as possible.[39]

Elsewhere in Normandy, villages and towns were made the focal points for defence. At Brest the 29th US Division had to eliminate an estimated 79–80 strong-points, and a divisional action report noted that 'all pillboxes were mutually supporting and the coordinated system of tunnels made underground communication possible. It was a difficult system to breach; the pillboxes were constructed to withstand the heaviest artillery fire. As a result it was necessary to attack each pillbox, each strongpoint individually . . .'[40] Around Caen, many small woods, ridges, villages, as well as the town itself, were incorporated into a fearsome interlocking network. By this time the Germans had evolved a fairly standardised defensive lay-out, consisting of three belts of fortified posts which might stretch back up to ten miles behind the front line. First came the Battle Outposts. These were regarded as expendable but had to be manned as long as humanly possible. All useful natural features were incorporated and were supplemented by camouflaged weapons pits and dugouts. Trenches connected the Posts laterally and vertically so that they could be reinforced or their garrisons make good their escape. Machine guns were the main weapons used, though all likely targets were pinpointed so that mortar and artillery fire could be swiftly brought down from the rear. Behind these was another defensive belt known as the Advance Position. Here there was a more extravagant use of wire entanglements and minefields, and the infantry were accompanied by large numbers of tanks, self-propelled guns and mortars. They might be called upon to sit tight and hold their ground or to launch a counter-attack if the situation in the first line seemed to warrant it. In either case they were expected never to retreat. Finally the Germans had a more flexible defence line known as the Main Position. This included vital bits of high ground for observing artillery and mortar fire, and the reserve troops were stationed here, as well as the larger tanks, artillery and mortar batteries.

On the German frontier the Germans opted for an age-old type of defence, the construction of a supposedly impregnable wall, though here concrete replaced more traditional materials. A major part of it, running from Luxembourg to just south of Arnhem, was known as the West Wall. One major assault against it was centred upon Aachen, though the city was ringed with numerous interlocking concrete bunkers. American commanders seemed to think there was something old-fashioned about such a mode of warfare, and they also underestimated the abilities of the garrison – middle-aged German soldiers with abdominal complaints who were contemptuously referred to as 'stomach battalions'. In such strong positions, however, the quality of the troops was of little importance. As an infantryman of the 3rd US Armoured Division remarked: 'I don't care if the guy behind that gun is a syphilitic prick who's a hundred years old – he's still sitting behind eight foot of concrete and he's still got enough fingers to press triggers and shoot bullets.'[41] Even when the wall was breached the war was far from over. Within Germany forests constituted one of the bastions, and the Allies suffered terribly clearing such areas as the Reichswald and the Hürtgen Forest. Sergeant Mack Morris (4th US Division) fought in Hürtgen and he called it a green monument to the Wehrmacht's defence and the First Army's power . . . Hürtgen had its roads and firebreaks. The firebreaks were only wide enough to allow two jeeps to pass, and they were mined and interdicted by machinegun fire. In one break there was a teller mine every eight paces for three miles. In another there were more than 500 mines in the narrow break. One stretch of road held 300 teller mines, each one with a pull device in addition to the regular detonator . . . Hürtgen had its roads and they were blocked. The German did well by his abatis, his roadblocks cut from trees. Sometimes he felled 200 trees across a road, cutting them down so they interlocked as they fell. Then he mined and booby trapped them. Finally he registered his artillery on them, and his mortars, and at the sound of men clearing them he opened fire. The [strongpoints] were screened by barbed wire in concertina strands . . . [and were] themselves log-and-earth bunkers six feet underground . . . They were constructed carefully, and inside them were neat bunks built of forest wood, and the walls of the bunkers were panelled with wood. These sheltered the defenders. Outside the bunkers were the defensive positions.[42]

But it was the Japanese who were the most assiduous diggers of all. In the Pacific particularly, though they lacked many of the Germans' material advantages such as concrete, millions of mines, and tank turrets set into their own emplacements, they were more than capable of establishing very elaborate defensive networks made up of numerous bunkers and one-man dugouts, carefully sited to give the most effective crossfire and mutual support. This point is worth stressing if only because certain re-creations of war against the Japanese have pictured their tactics as nothing more than a series of suicidal infantry onslaughts. These certainly happened, as the following description by Major McCarthy (7th US Division) shows. He was on Saipan, in July 1944, when the Japanese suddenly erupted from the jungle. 'It was like the movie stampede staged in the old wild west movies. We were the cameramen. The Japs kept coming and coming and didn't stop. It didn't make any difference if you shot one, five more would take his place. We would be in foxholes looking up, as I said, like those cameramen used to be. The Japs ran right over us.'[43] But these were far from typical tactics. On the whole this kind of charge was born of despair, when a particular unit or garrison realised that the only alternative was death or defeat. Usually they preferred to dig rather than to hurl themselves into ululating oblivion. They were always ready, even eager, to die but most preferred to sell their lives as expensively as possible, dealing out death from some inaccessible cave or invisible bunker.

The style of Pacific warfare became apparent from the very first when American and Australian troops came up against the Japanese positions in New Guinea. A typical confrontation was across the Kokoda Trail itself, at Eora Creek, where a 7-day battle had to be fought to force a way through. Facing the men of the Australian 16th Brigade was a central keep some 300yd across from which radiated machine-gun pits, most of them revetted and roofed over with thick logs. This position, dug into a ridge, completely dominated the trail below and had to be subdued to allow the Australians to push through to the coast. So the attackers, who clung 'like leeches to the sharp slope, often in a cold, driving rain, could not move by day from their pits or even light twigs to make hot tea, without drawing fire. Their only food was dehydrated emergency ration, eaten dry and cold; their only water was the little they could catch in their rubber capes or such from the roots of the "water tree".' [44] They only broke through when the bulk of the defenders withdrew leaving only a small rearguard behind. The main defensive effort was made at Buna and Sananda, on the northern coast, where the Japanese were told to hold out or perish in the attempt. An Australian journalist described the fortifications there:

> Cocoanut trees, up to a foot in diameter, cut into logs and interlaced with boughs, vines and earth-filling, formed the roofs of whole clusters of strongposts. Infantry fire made no impression on them, and as they rose very little above the level of the ground or the swamps, 25pdr. shells failed to wreck them . . . In these squalid underground chambers, only a few feet square, [the defenders] had a field of fire covering every approach. Through a bewildering maze of zig-zag trenches, came their food, their reliefs and their ammunition. It was a section of the Somme front of 1916 . . . but in a much more unwholesome setting. [45]

Similar conditions were met on Biak, an island off the north-west coast of New Guinea. The defences were made of innumerable caves, some like small, dark hallways, others as deep and extensive as five-storey buildings and with numerous connecting galleries and passages. One of the most important of these was known as the Sump and various methods were used to kill the tenacious defenders. Flamethrowers were tried but could not penetrate far enough into the long, winding cavern to be effective, while the liquid fire often flashed back off unseen internal walls. Then a search was made for crevices and gullies that led down into the caves and hundreds of gallons of petrol were poured into them before being ignited. The resultant explosions indicated that underground explosions had been touched off. Finally, an 850lb charge of TNT was lowered down the main entrance with a winch and detonated electrically. True to style the few surviving Japanese suddenly emerged from the Sump in a final *banzai* charge. Over a hundred of them were mown down for the loss of only one American life.

Elsewhere the story was just the same. On New Georgia

> The Japanese had spent months on fortifications which had to be knocked out one by one. Usually these strongholds were called pill-boxes and were constructed of coconut logs and coral blocks. Some of the stronger built pill-boxes were two storeys deep. If they were bombed or shelled the Japanese would drop through a trap door into the lower level, about fifteen feet underground. Pill-boxes of this type will stand anything but a direct hit. [46]

On New Britain, the Marines faced particularly heavy resistance at a spot they came to call Suicide Creek. A Marine combat correspondent, Sergeant A. C. Bordages, heard the story later from survivors. As so often:

> The Marines didn't know the creek was a moat before an enemy strongpoint . . . Only snipers shot at the Marine scouts who crossed the creek, feeling their way through the thickets. More Marines followed . . . The jungle exploded in their faces. They hit the deck, trying to deploy in the bullet-lashed brush and strike back. Marines died there, firing blindly, cursing because they couldn't see the men who were killing them . . . All day . . . Marine detachments felt for a gap or a soft spot in the enemy's positions . . . They'd be blasted by invisible machine guns and leave a few more Marines dead in the brush as they fell back across the creek. Then they'd do it all over again.
>
> There was nothing else they could do. There is no other way to fight a jungle battle – not in such terrain, when the enemy is dug in and your orders are to advance. You don't know where the enemy is. His pillboxes are so camouflaged that you can usually find them only when they fire on you. So, you push out scouts . . . then patrols from different directions until they too draw fire. Thus you locate the enemy. Then you have to take the emplacements, the pillboxes, one by one in desperate little battles. [47]

During the next stage of the Pacific campaign, the Japanese based their hopes on throwing the Americans back from the beaches and it was here that they placed the bulk of their firepower.

On the Gilberts and Marshalls this is hardly surprising as these are largely elongated coral atolls offering little opportunity for defence in depth. This tactic was retained however in the Marianas, although these islands are much more substantial volcanic outgrowths. Even so, the Americans were still faced with considerable obstacles, either on the beaches themselves or further inland where enemy survivors had managed to escape to pre-prepared positions. On Makin, in the Gilberts, special tactics had to be evolved to flush out the numerous bunkers. A 27th Infantry Division document explained the procedure:

> To knock out these emplacements, an 8-man squad would crawl to within about 15 yards of it and then take up station around it according to available cover. The B.A.R. man and his assistant would cover the main entrance. Two men armed with grenades would make ready on both flanks of the shelter. They would rush the pit and heave grenades into it, then without stopping dash to the other side and blast the entrance with several more grenades. The other men did not fire unless essential. Once the grenades exploded the B.A.R. man and his assistant would follow up with bayonets. Two other men would inspect with bayonets ready. The other four would lay back ready to fire.[48]

On Peleliu, according to another Marine combat correspondent, Sergeant W. F. Conway, the basic tactics lacked this sophistication. There 'Jap-infested caves are dug at staggered levels through solid coral and limestone which ran through hundreds of yards of Peleliu's treacherous hills and ravines . . . Throughout the campaign hundreds and thousands of tons of explosives were thrown at the hills to level them and seal the caves.'[49]

In the Philippines, both Leyte and Luzon had to be meticulously searched to uncover and destroy the numerous Japanese strong-points. In March 1945 the 1st Cavalry Division, on Luzon, attacked the Shimbu defences – well-hidden, underground strongholds tunnelled down deep into the steep, rocky heights, each with four or five entrances protected with rocks and sandbags and each covered by well-sited machine guns and artillery. These had to be knocked out on an individual basis, with flamethrowers and explosives, and in one 2-day period the Division knocked out 137 caves, sealing off in the process 446 connecting tunnels. Napalm was also used extensively and, prior to an attack by the 43rd Division in early May, 250,000 gallons were dropped within three days.

Iwo Jima offered few naturally strong positions, but the Japanese soon remedied this by constructing their own. They combined the strange, gravelly volcanic ash that covered most of the island with cement to make a particularly tough kind of concrete. Artillery, mortars and anti-tank guns were placed in emplacements protected by four- to eight-feet walls from which they were trundled out through armour-plated doors, or fired through narrow embrasures barely above ground level. They also dug deep. Entire hills were scooped out to be rebuilt from within, while long tunnels were pushed through, connecting command posts and strong-points. The Wilderness, protecting Motoyama Airfield No 2, and stormed by the 3rd Marine Division, was reckoned by certain authorities to be 'perhaps the most intensively fortified small area ever encountered in battle'.[50] In another area, 800 pillboxes and 3 miles of tunnels were uncovered within an area of only 8 square miles. During the assault on Mount Surabachi, the 28th Regiment was engaged for three days in an almost

> . . . foot-by-foot crawl with mortars, artillery, rockets, machine guns, and grenades making us hug every rock and shell-hole. Rock slides were tumbled down on our heads by the Japs, and also as a result of our own naval gunfire . . . Each pill-box was a separate problem, an intricately designed fortress that had to be smashed into ruins . . . The walls of many began with 2-foot-thick concrete blocks, laced with iron rails. Then came ten to twelve feet of rocks, piled with dirt and the dirty ashes of Iwo . . . Single entranceways, which were tiny, long holes, and one or two casemate openings were protected against direct hits or flying shrapnel by concrete abutments. The whole structure might look from the outside like a mound rising a few feet above the surrounding ground.[51]

On Okinawa, the Japanese made very little effort to defend the shoreline and for the first few days American patrols were able to roam almost at will over the island. But the strongholds were there and soon proved to be as intractable as on any other island. There were plenty of natural strong-points, as in the cave-riddled heights of Mount Yae Take, in the Motobu peninsula, and here the Japanese operated in small groups, based around Hotchkiss and Nambu machine guns, and moved from cave to cave, emerging to fire upon an American column and then slipping back inside to avoid the counterfire. A common ploy was to let the first platoon of a company column file past and then to open fire on what was normally the company commander and his headquarters section. Elsewhere they simply dug in in the usual manner. On Kunishi Ridge, General del Valle of the Marines neatly summed up the problems this posed. After an assault by the 7th Regiment he observed: 'The situation was one of those tactical oddities of this peculiar warfare. We were *on* the ridge. The Japs were *in* it, both on the forward and reverse slopes.'[52] Another intractable feature was known as the Escarpment and here the 307th Regiment (77th Division) had a bitter struggle, even in the so-called 'mopping up' stage:

On May 3rd, the 1st Battalion made some headway in clearing the escarpment and started on the reverse slope. The centre of the battalion line . . . was cleaned out in a terrible hand grenade battle. The men were throwing hand grenades as fast as they could carry them from the human supply chain at the base of the north cliff. The top of the escarpment was swept clear, and the grenading continued to the reverse slope. The enemy replied in kind and added hundreds of mortar shells. Our men could not obtain an advantage in any way. Officers of the battalion said later that the men would come back to the northern side of the ridge weeping and swearing that they would not go back into the fight. 'Yet in five minutes time, those men would be back here tossing grenades as fast as they could pull the pins,' one platoon leader explained.[53]

This type of warfare was the rule not only in the defensive Pacific battles but also in the Burmese campaigns. Even during the offensive into Assam, at the sieges of Imphal and Kohima, the Japanese did not rely upon frenzied assaults but rather tried to slowly tighten the noose, digging in upon the high ground and gradually edging in from ridge to ridge. Conversely, the British could not simply wait for the attackers to hurl themselves against their machine guns but were forced to attack themselves, to recapture the high ground upon which the Japanese had established their artillery, mortars and machine guns.

Though Japanese defences in this theatre were not as elaborate as on most Pacific islands they were still very tough nuts to crack. Perhaps the most obdurate example of all was a large bunker known as Sugar Five near Donbaik, in Arakan. It was almost completely invisible, as the defenders had hollowed out a small mound, via a dry watercourse, without disturbing a leaf or twig, and it was some time before the 14th Indian Division even discovered the source of the mysterious machine-gun fire that was holding them up. Even then the battle was hardly finished. 'Between 16 January and 18 March four attempts were made to break through the position . . . involving battalions from the Royal In-

niskilling Fusiliers, the 7th Rajputs, the 1st Punjab Regiment, the
17th Dogras, the Lincolnshire Regiment, the Royal Welch Fusiliers . . . and the Royal Scots. Altogether it must have claimed
directly and indirectly a thousand lives.'[54] Eventually artillery was
dug in within eighty yards of the bunker but it was never ascer-
tained whether this would have been the answer, for the whole
division was shortly driven back by a Japanese counter-offensive.
Elsewhere, effective tactics were slowly evolved. In Assam, some
bunkers were destroyed by men creeping forward with grenades or
flamethrowers, and phosphorus smoke grenades were widely used
to cover the infantry approach. On other occasions a small patrol
might be sent forward to draw enemy fire and thus pinpoint their
position. A number of Bren guns would then concentrate upon the
apertures from one side whilst the patrol charged in from the other
and actually got on top of the bunker.[55] At other times it was
simply a vicious slogging match as battalions tried to prise the
Japanese from their bunkers almost with their bare hands. The
following report by a newly arrived officer, Lieutenant K. W.
Cooper (2nd Border Regiment), of a conversation with his
sergeant vividly gives the flavour of ridge-top warfare. The
sergeant is referring to battles in front of Imphal, in early 1944:

> One particular fight which seemed indelibly stamped on the sergeant's
> memory, he referred to as 'that fukkin' duffy on Nippon Hill' . . .
> When the Japs overran it, the Battalion had spent five or six days on
> piecemeal attacks, using platoons . . . Finally a series of company
> assaults had been launched, all with the same outcome – bloody
> repulse. The enemy had dug themselves in like moles – right in and
> under the summit peak of Nippon Hill. 'By Christ, them little bastards
> can dig. They're underground before our blokes have stopped spitting
> on their bloody 'ands.'. . .
>   Another ferocious 'duffy' had occurred on Scraggy Hill. Many of
> the forward posts had been overrun by the Japs, leaving a no-man's-
> land of not much more than ten or twenty yards. This had made
> digging impossible, and the men nearest the enemy were barely two
> feet underground, until mortar boxes filled with earth were brought up
> at night to provide extra cover . . . Apparently the men in the forward
> position had been relieved every half hour. The strain was that bad.[56]

All this explains the prominent position of engineers in the front
line. The bulk of them, at divisional, corps and army level, were
concerned with the maintenance of armoured and soft-skinned
vehicles as well as such miscellaneous duties as laying on water

supplies, bridge-building and supplying maps.[57] Nevertheless, the plastic nature of World War II, the constant need to dig up, blow up, reconstruct, bridge, demolish, just to be able to move forward at all, meant that many of the divisional engineers, in all the Allied armies, were often in the foremost positions. A staff officer with the New Zealanders in Italy wrote that there it was 'an engineers' war, a war of lifting minefields, building approach roads, filling craters, clearing demolitions and, above all, of building bridges. The Germans' most valuable weapon in Italy was not the field gun or the 'plane or the machine gun but the demolition charge which could block a ravine or blow a bridge and hold up an entire army'.[58] In Italy and Europe, engineers were also responsible for supplying the boats used in river crossings and for putting up temporary pontoon bridges, often still under enemy fire. It was they, too, who had responsibility for the demolition of enemy pillboxes and bunkers. Corporal F. Griffin served with the 3rd US Armoured Division during the assault on the West Wall and it was his company that was called upon to blast a way through one line of pill-boxes:

> When we were in a big hurry, we sometimes only blew up certain ones so that we'd break the chain and they couldn't cover each other even if the Krauts did get back. Lots of these pillboxes weren't manned and we never knew which was which, especially if the infantry bypassed them. That bothered the hell out of us because when we're loaded with tetryl like that and a shell lands anywhere near us there isn't enough left of us even to make a good memory.[59]

In the later Pacific campaigns, engineers and Construction Battalions (the SeaBees) usually landed with the first waves and they were constantly in the thick of things. Not only did they have to help consolidate the beachhead and improve communications, or create them, but they were often up with the leading infantry helping them to reduce the Japanese fortifications. Explosives were frequently used, as in Europe, but so too were armoured bulldozers. On Leyte, when the 77th Division were attacking the Ormoc defences, Captain J. Carruth (302nd Engineer Battalion) lent a hand uncovering Japanese foxholes with his bulldozer blade and then leant from his cab to blast the occupants with a tommy gun. On Luzon, the 25th Division had the job of fighting their way up Highway 5, through what the defenders thought were impregnable fortifications. General Muto, Yamashita's Chief of Staff, recalled: 'The American forces started attacking . . . and kept it up incessantly. Superior . . . bombardment and shelling gradually obliterated the jungle area. Bulldozers accomplished the impossible . . . Our front line troops destroyed bulldozers, tanks and artillery by valiant hand-to-hand fighting. However, the enemy advanced inch by inch, capturing this mountain, taking that hill.'[60]

The other notable combat role of the engineers was the removal of mines. Where Germans were fighting these formed a fundamental part of their defences. In the desert the emphasis was upon anti-tank mines. In front of the German positions at Alamein, for example, Rommel laid 445,000 mines, only 3 per cent of which were anti-personnel devices. The role of the Sappers in clearing paths through the minefields was of fundamental importance to the success of Montgomery's plan. The Sappers were aided by the arrival of 500 new Polish mine-detectors which worked electrically, looking something like vacuum cleaners; but this number was far from sufficient and most engineers had to fall back on the nerve-wracking method of feeling with the fingers or prodding with a bayonet. At Alamein the whole system was highly systematised. A reconnaissance party led the way, followed by three teams of 'gapping men' each of which was responsible for the clearance of the 24ft gap that was thought wide enough for the passage of two tanks abreast.

In Europe, because of the increasing effectiveness and cheapness of anti-tank projectiles, as well as the generally unfavourable terrain, anti-tank mines gave way to anti-personnel. Two types were notorious: the schu-mine, with just a large enough charge to blow off a man's foot; and the 'S' mine, a fiendish device which threw a small charge into the air, at about groin height, before it exploded with an inevitably ghastly effect. Nothing indicates the soldiers' fear of these devices more than this observation, based on a combat interview with Lieutenant Elmer C. Raegor (29th US Division) just after an attack on Gut Hasenfeld, in the Roer Valley. 'At first sound of exploding mines, the Germans would lay down final protective fires with machine guns, mortars and artillery. If the men fell to earth to escape this fire, they might detonate more mines. Some elected to remain erect through intense shell-fire rather than risk falling on a mine.'[61]

But we have far from finished with the infantryman's problems. However formidable, earthworks and minefields were not the only obstacles to his getting to grips with the enemy. For even where German or Japanese defences were not particularly elaborate the sheer volume of firepower ranged against the infantryman was in itself a fearsome barrier. Mortars, grenades, machine guns and rifles were all available in large quantities, each as deadly as the other, though of differing importance in different campaigns.

In North Africa, machine guns figured very prominently, especially in Tunisia where the Germans were from the beginning committed to purely defensive battles. These large-calibre weapons, as one journalist noted, 'were sited on fixed lines and were built deeply into the ground with ample top cover from mortars and artillery'.[62] Another noted how these weapons were the basis of German determination to hang on to the key hill-tops and ridges. 'They knew . . . that, in bad weather at any rate, the only fighting object which can get up a hill is a man, and that the surest and most economical way to stop men climbing hills is to spray them from a long distance with machine gun bullets.'[63] The problem was especially noticeable in the Tunisian campaign because the Allies for a long time lacked adequate fire support of their own, with which they might have forced the Germans to keep their heads down as they dashed across open ground. Because of this, numerous regiments suffered terrible casualties in vain assaults on the enemy strong-points. A typical early repulse was that of the Royal West Kent's attack on Bald Hill, in November 1942, when a battalion lost 161 men, including 6 officers killed outright. The attack on Djebel Mansour in the following February by the 1st Parachute Battalion, turned out to be the First Army's tenth attack against firm opposition at battalion strength or more, and the tenth to fail. A little later that month, the 139th Brigade went forward and all three battalions (2/5th Leicester Regiment, 5th Sherwood Foresters and 16th Durham Light Infantry) suffered catastrophic reverses. An officer serving in this campaign, Captain Peter Cochrane, emphasised how difficult it was to keep men going in such circumstances:

Nearly every attack involves some sort of regrouping or change of line, even down to the lowly level of a platoon. With seasoned troops this can be done without loss of momentum, even if at the moment no-one is actually moving forward, but when the soldiers or their junior leaders are inexperienced and bewildered the pause to regroup can be fatal to success. This is not just due to the fact that if one goes to ground under fire it requires a real effort of will to stand up again; it is also because in all the noise and danger of action one is inclined to think the worst. Any pause, therefore, can be taken by raw troops as a sign that the attack has already failed, where the old sweats will sit tight until the next command reaches them.[64]

Machine guns also had an important role in the European campaigns, and in the first weeks after D-Day one detects more than faint echoes of the *Maximschlacht* on the Western Front – for example in the attack by the 2nd and 3rd Canadian Division on Verrières Ridge during the Caen battles. The Black Watch of Canada attacked Verrières itself, moving uphill through cornfields, under fire from three sides. Their colonel was killed and no more than 60 men reached the summit. Only 15 came back; 342 of their comrades lay where they had fallen. Later attacks were rarely launched with such foolhardy confidence, yet even the most cautious and dispersed assaults could be obliterated in a matter of seconds. Lieutenant D. Pearce (North Nova Scotians) took part in an attack on Bienen in March 1945:

My platoon assaulted in a single extended wave. Ten tumbled down nailed on the instant by fire from two or maybe three machine guns . . . The rest of us rolled or dropped into a shallow ditch, hardly more than a trough six inches deep, at the bottom of a dyke. The Bren-gunners put their weapons to their shoulders but never got a shot away. (I saw them after the battle, both dead, one still holding the aiming position) . . . A rifleman on my left took aim at a German weapon pit, and with a spasm collapsed on my arm. His face turned almost instantly a faint green, and bore a simple smile.[65]

In Italy and north-west Europe, however, other weapons were even more feared than machine guns and mines. Another loathed weapon was the mortar, especially the multiple-barrelled *nebelwerfer*. Almost all memoirs from the European theatres make some mention of these latter, whose psychological effect was just as terrifying as the actual moment of impact. Private L. Uppington (1st Worcester Regiment) remembered one spot where his HQ Company was dug in on one side of a railway crossing and the field kitchen on the other side:

You had to take a chance and dash across for food and dash back again, in between being 'stonked' by mortars, particularly the 'Moaning Minnies', which sounded just like a lot of women sobbing their hearts out. The noise would start in the distance and get louder and louder, almost to a scream, and then down would come six 6-inch mortar bombs.[66]

Private First Class Harry Bealor (70th US Division) also particularly remembered the noise of the Moaning Minnies, though his choice of imagery was a little different:

We could hear it fired in the distance. It made a grating noise like the bark of a seal, or like someone scratching his fingernails across a piece of tin. Then for several seconds, everything would be quiet until it hit. The explosion sounded as though someone struck a match in the Krupp works. You'd think the whole damn mountain had exploded. I've seen guys picked right up off the ground and thrown several feet through the air by the concussion.[67]

Soldiers' fear of weapons seems, in fact, to have been related much more to the noise they made than to their lethality. A study by HQ Army Ground Forces showed that the machine gun was the most dangerous weapon in that 50 per cent of hits from this weapon were fatal. For artillery the figure was only 20 per cent and for mortars even less. Nevertheless, various surveys of troops' attitudes to enemy weapons all showed that other factors were more important in eliciting fear. A survey of 264 British soldiers wounded in North Africa showed that 83 per cent most disliked shell-throwing or dive-bombing weapons, while only 17 per cent said that they most feared small-arms fire. In another study of 461 British troops, 92 per cent named artillery, 4.1 per cent machine guns and 3.5 per cent tanks. American studies painted the same picture. A study of 120 psychiatric casualties in Tunisia showed that fully 98 per cent feared the noisier weapons, 42 per cent naming dive-bombers and 35 per cent artillery, a further 11 per cent citing high-level bombing. The following table, based on an interview with 700 wounded GIs, shows similar findings and also reveals the extent to which soldiers equated the purely psychological effect of weapons with their military efficacy. The figures in Table 1 are based on responses to the questions 'What enemy weapon used against you seemed the most frightening/dangerous to you?'

Despite the contempt shown for them in the table below, rifles were far from negligible weapons, even in the midst of so much concentrated firepower. In the hands of experienced soldiers they could put up a fearsome curtain of fire, as the 6th Highland Light

Table 1: US Soldiers' attitudes to enemy weapons

WEAPON	PERCENTAGE WHO RATED IT MOST	
	FRIGHTENING	DANGEROUS
88mm gun	48	62
Dive Bomber	20	17
Mortar	13	6
Horizontal Bomber	12	5
Light Machine Gun	7	4
Strafing	5	4
Land Mines	2	2
Rifles	0	0
Misc. (inc. Booby Traps, Tanks, Heavy Machine Guns)	4	2

Infantry discovered in Germany, in April 1945, during an attack on Ibbenburen. The town was defended by a group of German officer cadets with no heavy weapons. Even so, armed only with rifles, they accounted for 3 officers and 66 other ranks killed or wounded – heavier casualties than in any other comparable attacks by the battalion under artillery, mortar or machine-gun fire. Rifles featured most prominently of all in the hands of snipers, who were used in large numbers in the hedgerows and forests of France and Germany. In Normandy, according to one eye-witness:

> . . . at night snipers crept through the positions, to open fire in the morning with rifles and machine guns on parties coming up from the rear. Dozens of bloody little battles were fought behind the forward positions. The snipers were everywhere. Officers, their chosen prey, learned to conceal all distinguishing marks, to carry rifles like their men instead of the accustomed pistols, not to carry maps or field glasses, to wear pips on their sleeves instead of conspicuously on their shoulders.[68]

In France, especially, machine guns, mortars, even artillery barrages were directed against persistent marksmen once their position had been pinpointed.

The sniper's other natural habitat was any built-up area, and even where a village or town had been pounded with bombs and shells the heaps of rubble still offered excellent cover. More in fact, for while a building is still standing it is possible to collapse it on the men within, but once it has been demolished even artillery can rarely make much impression. This the Allies found out time and again in the various European theatres. Cassino, Ortona, St Lô, Aachen, Bremen were only the most notorious of countless engagements where the infantry swapped the deadly task of flushing out bunkers and slit-trenches for that of clearing a town house by house, street by street. The ruthlessness with which this type of warfare was carried on, tanks and guns to wipe out individual posts and little quarter given on either side, was a far cry from attitudes at the beginning of the war. The history of the Royal Sussex Regiment recalled that early operations in France, in 1940, were greatly handicapped by the High Command's ban on the loopholing of French buildings, a ban that was not lifted until 20 May. Such restraint was not even considered after the Allies re-entered Europe. A private in the Highland Light Infantry of Canada wrote of the attack on Speldrop, in 1945: 'We began the house- and barn-clearing on the edge of town. Not many prisoners were taken, as if they did not surrender before we started on a house, they never had the opportunity afterwards.'[69] But street-fighting was far from being mere savagery, or even just guts and determination supported by adequate weaponry. Lieutenant Colonel I. L. Reeves (4th King's Shropshire Light Infantry) called it 'the most tiring and trying type of fighting [even] under the best conditions'.[70] A high level of concentration was demanded and there was hardly any let-up in the nerve-wracking suspense of every minute expecting an enemy to pop out of a doorway or window. In Aachen, things were further complicated by the Germans' habit of moving along the sewers and appearing in sectors of the town that the Americans thought they had flushed out. Sophisticated tactics were developed to try and minimise casualties. Major Brodie wrote: 'Street-fighting, like jungle-fighting, presents control problems . . . It is really a science or skill of its own and should be carefully practised beforehand.'[71] Certain techniques were common to most units, as can be seen from the following examples. In Ortona, in December 1944, in a battle which claimed 25 per cent of all Canadian battle casualties in the Italian theatre, tactics were based on groups of three or four men moving through the houses on each side of a street. They assaulted each house from the top floor, using heavy explosives to blow a hole in the party wall, 'mouse-holing' as it was called, and then clearing the house from the top down with grenades and sub-machine guns. A BBC correspondent, Denis Johnston, gave an excellent description of similar tactics in the Rhineland:

[Street-fighting] is a bad misnomer, because the last place you see any sane man is in a street where every yard is usually covered by a well-sited machine gun. It should be called house-to-house fighting, which it literally is. The old hands at the game go through a town keeping inside the houses and using bazookas to knock holes in the dividing walls as they go, and when they come to the end of the block and have to cross the street to the next block they throw out smoke first and cross over under cover of that. They say it's usually better to clear out a house from the top downwards if you can. Break a hole in the roof and get in by an upper floor if possible . . . But of course a lot depends on the type of defence being met with; if it mainly consists of sniping it's best to go slowly and very deliberately, and in small groups. Snipers very often won't fire at a group, when they'll shoot a single man; they're afraid of giving away their position to the men whom they can't hit with their first shots. But if the defence is heavy you've got to keep dispersed, move fast, and keep on moving whatever happens. Many a man has been hit through freezing and bunching when trouble starts. You feel inclined to drop down and bury your head, and the next shot gets you; you want to cluster together for mutual company, and in this way you give them a real target, but all the old hands will tell you to keep your head up and your eyes open and your legs moving, and at all costs keep apart.[72]

Much of what has been said above about weapons is also applicable to the war against the Japanese. As has already been made clear, machine guns and mortars were a vital element in their defensive tactics and every strong-point was liberally supplied with them.[73] Snipers, too, were frequently employed as they could remain concealed in their caves or tree-top positions until the enemy was almost on top of them. Even after they had fired it was usually impossible to ascertain from just where the shot had come. First Sergeant Pasquale Fusco (27th US Division) took part in the campaign on Makin, where snipers were a persistent problem:

Smoking out the snipers that were in the trees was the worst part of it. We couldn't spot them even with glasses and it made our advance very slow. When we moved forward it was as a skirmish line, with each man being covered as he rushed from cover to cover. That meant that every man spent a large part of his time on the ground. If one of our men began to fire rapidly into a tree or ground location, we knew that we had spotted a sniper, and those who could see took up the fire. When we saw no enemy we fired occasional shots into trees that looked likely.[74]

Surprisingly, perhaps, there was even a certain amount of street-fighting, both in the Burma and Pacific campaigns. The 2nd

Marine Division, destined for Saipan, was given special training in these techniques because of heavy fighting expected in the capital town of Garapan. During the liberation of the Philippines, the battle for Manila involving the 37th, 1st Cavalry and 11th Airborne Divisions was as bloody an affair as any similar operation in Europe. It lasted a full month and almost every major structure was turned by the Japanese into a minor fortress. MacArthur had hoped to keep the city intact, but was eventually forced to sanction the unrestricted use of artillery. It was this that turned the scales, though only by dint of killing almost every one of the defenders. In Burma, during Slim's final drive to Rangoon, stiff opposition was encountered in the town of Mekteila. One officer wrote:

> Our own soldiers, for so long conditioned to the mysterious and secretive jungle, were now to engage in the bitterest street-fighting in a man-made environment. The Japs would fight from house-to-house and dug-out to dug-out, from air-raid shelter, culvert and canal, as they above all knew how to fight, selling their lives alone and un-applauded and in a fury of despair to the last man in the last burning hospital bed.[75]

The allusion to the 'mysterious and secretive jungle' raises an important difference between the fighting against the Germans and that against the Japanese. For in the latter campaigns it is fair to speak of an extra dimension of strain not found in the western theatres. Though the fighting here was extremely brutal, it was at least fairly straightforward, and the terrain, though it sometimes seemed implacably hostile, was at least reasonably familiar. As Major G. S. Johns Jr (29th US Division) pointed out, though those organising an attack in Normandy might find it a very complex procedure, 'by the time the order got down to the platoon leaders their part was pretty simple; all they, in turn, had to say was "All right, gang, let's take that next hedgerow".' He goes on to describe a typical infantry assault

> . . . with a machine gun being knocked out here, a man or two being killed or wounded there. Eventually the leader of the stronger force, usually the attackers, may decide that he has weakened his opponents enough to warrant a large concerted assault, preceded by a concentration of all the mortar and artillery support he can get. Or the leader of the weaker force may see that he will be overwhelmed by such an attack and pull back to another position in his rear. Thus goes the battle – a rush, a pause, some creeping, a few isolated shots here and

there, some artillery fire, some mortars, some smoke, more creeping, another pause, dead silence, more firing, a great concentration of fire followed by a concerted rush. Then the whole process starts all over again.[76]

Jungle warfare, however, was carried out in an alien environment, against an enemy whose ability to adapt to that environment, as well as their utterly foreign standards of ethics and chivalry, made them seem like men from another planet. In the Far East, men were not only pitting themselves against bullets, shells and bunkers but also were obliged to try to overcome their fear of the terrain itself and adapt themselves to a completely new kind of warfare. New, that is, to the troops themselves, for the principles of jungle warfare had many parallels in the history of war. Of the fighting at Guadalcanal, Major-General Vandergrift wrote: 'You can go back to history and you will find that only guns have been improved and a few gadgets added such as airplanes and underseas craft. Our men worked all day and fought all night. Their work consisted of improving positions and bringing up supplies.'[77] He went on to compare the campaign to those against the Indians in previous centuries. Towards the end of the Guadalcanal fighting hundreds of Marines were asked about the lessons they had learned in the fighting and all ranks offered their conclusions. Colonel Merritt A. Edson said:

> If I had to train my regiment over again, I would stress small group training and the training of the individual even more than we did . . . There must be training in difficult observation, which is needed in the offense . . . Emphasise scouting and patrolling and really learn it and apply it. In your training put your time and emphasis on the squad and platoon rather than on the company, battalion and regiment . . . In our outfits we adopted the custom of dropping all ranks and titles. We used nicknames for the officers. All ranks used these nicknames for us. We did this because the Nips caught on to names of the officers and would yell or speak in the night. 'This is Captain Joe Smith talking. A Company, withdraw to the next hill.' . . . The captain became 'Silent Lou'. My nickname was 'Red Mike'.

Corporal Joseph S. Stankus volunteered a variety of hints:

> Unnecessary firing gives your position away, and when you give your position away here, you pay for it. It's helpful, in using field glasses in this tropical sun, to cup your hand over the front end in order to keep out the glare. The men in my squad fire low at the base of trees. There

is too much high firing going on. I have observed the Japs often get short of ammunition. They cut bamboo and crack it together to simulate rifle fire to draw our fire. They ain't supermen; they're just tricky bastards.

Corporal Fred Carter noted that 'a Japanese trick to draw our fire was for the hidden Jap to work his bolt back and forth. Men who got sucked in on this, and fired without seeing what they were firing at, generally drew automatic fire from another direction'. Corporal Edward J. Byrne emphasised: 'Get used to weird noises at night. This jungle is not still at night. The land crabs and lizards make a hell of a noise rustling on leaves. And there is a bird here that sounds like a man banging two blocks of wood together. There is another bird that makes a noise like a dog barking.'[78] A Marine combat correspondent at Munda lay stress on the Japanese habit of attacking at night:

The constant roar of artillery and mortars made it impossible to sleep at night. In addition the Japs used night harassing tactics. Most of the night fighting was done with knives and machetes. Muzzle blast from rifle fire at night gave away positions and locations of troops. During the night men rested in foxholes three or four feet deep. Usually there were four men in a foxhole, sometimes less. Japs sneaked in pairs towards the foxholes. One would often jump into the middle of our men and try to stab them. The other stood by to see the outcome. Sometimes, the Japs would jump in the foxhole, and then jump out quickly, hoping our troops would become excited and stab each other. 'They must have springs on their feet,' one soldier said.[79]

The Japanese were very well aware that their opponents had not adapted to the jungle anything like as readily as they had, and many of their tactics were deliberately designed to play upon their sense of uncertainty and fearfulness. On Guam, they almost always attacked at night, trying to infiltrate American lines rather than smash their way through. There was

. . . no standard plan in attempts at infiltration. They used a variety of weapons – mortars, small arms, sabres, even hatchets. Sometimes our first notice of the enemy was a grenade thrown in from the outer darkness. Sometimes an enemy soldier in plain sight would walk slowly towards the American lines; fire from all directions easily knocked him down, but this gave our position away. Sometimes, heavy fire and grenades landed in the defense positions, followed by small enemy groups trying to move in where confusion had been created.[80]

Such tactics could be frighteningly effective. On New Georgia, the 169th Regiment thought its bivouac areas had been penetrated by the Japanese. There was a great deal of confusion as knives were drawn and grenades wildly thrown into the dark. Many Americans stabbed each other. Grenades bounced off trees and exploded amongst the defenders. Some soldiers fired off round after round to no avail. Come morning there was no trace of any Japanese dead or wounded but there were numerous American casualties, 50 per cent of them hit by fragments from the grenades.

The Japanese used identical tactics in Burma, where they were faced with an enemy equally unfamiliar with the jungle. The British referred to these infiltration attacks as 'jitter raids'. In one such the Japanese

> . . . crept up close to the defenders in the dark and then set up an awe-inspiring din. 'O.K. Johnny, cease fire', 'O.K. Bill, stand down', and taunts like 'Come out and fight' in both English and Urdu were accompanied with the firing of Chinese crackers as well as much small arms and mortar fire. All this was done in order to draw fire from the excited defenders and cause them to reveal their positions. When an attack followed, it was a mass rush accompanied by the usual shouts of 'Banzai' and misleading commands in English and Urdu.[81]

Indeed, for units newly arrived on this front, the Japanese did not actually have to do anything to unnerve their opponents. The lowering jungle, and the mere suspicion that the Japanese could not be far away was enough to keep troops in a permanent state of incipient panic. General Messervy, commander of the 7th Indian Division was constantly preoccupied with the problems of his troops' adjustment after their transfer from the Western Desert:

> The fear that there was at first of the Japs in the jungle was partly a feeling that you were being watched all the time, but you didn't know from where. 'Stand to' could be a nerve-racking experience, particularly at dawn, when the mists swirling about made every bush come to life and seem to be moving nearer. In the stark, dead silence, the patter of huge drops of dew from the forest trees sounded like footsteps creeping nearer and nearer. Silence was an absolute essential if you wanted to stay alive, for the slightest noise might give away your position and draw a burst of automatic fire from unseen, lurking Japs . . . All the men slept with wires tied to their big toes to be pulled to awaken them. You dare not speak, dare not even whisper when testing field telephones; it was done by gently blowing into the mouthpiece – three blows for OP, four for Battery, five for FOO, and so on.[82]

The Sharpest End

The question still remains of how the individual soldier felt when it was his turn to go forward and stake his own body, his very existence, in an increasingly unfavourable gamble against the laws of probability. If combat in general was the sharp end, each soldier felt himself at the sharpest end of all. The ordeal was very personal and few clues were given to observers, in fact the setting and staging of an attack might lead to very different impressions. Sometimes the sight could be positively stirring, as on the first day of Alamein when the assault troops moved out of the forward trenches in which they had crouched all night. Captain Grant Murray (5th Seaforth Highlanders) saw the attack forming up, 'a sight that will live for ever in our memories – line upon line of steel-helmeted figures with rifles at the high port, bayonets catching in the moonlight, and over all the wailing of the pipes . . . As they passed they gave us the thumbs-up sign, and we watched them plod towards the enemy line'.[83] But Alamein was exceptional in that the troops were aware that this was *it*, the decisive encounter to push Rommel out of Africa, and they had unparalleled confidence in their leaders and material superiority. The vast majority of attacks were much more localised affairs, where the potential rewards were of little apparent significance and the possibility of success nothing like so clear. This description of an American attack around St Vith, by Private First Class Lester Atwell (87th US Division) gives a more typical picture of the drabness, banality even, of men moving forward into enemy fire:

> There came the long, wild scream and crash of a German 88, and the double line, thin-looking without overcoats, indistinct in the swirling snow, wavered and sank down flat, then struggled up and went on, heads bent against the wind. This was 'jumping off' – this cold, plodding, unwilling, ragged double line plunging up to their knees in snow, stumbling, looking back at the last farmhouse in sight with the Red Cross flag planted in front of it.[84]

As they moved up to the start lines the troops seemed to be locked in a world of their own. A Canadian padre wrote of battalions going forward for an assault on the Gustav Line: 'We used to watch the infantry going up into the line. Single file they trudged along, guns carried anyhow, ammunition slung around them, trousers bagged and down at heels. No war loan posters at home would show them

97

that way. The P.B.I. going into the line.'[85] An artilleryman, S. Berlin (53rd Heavy Field Artillery), saw troops moving forward with the apparent lack of interest of men walking through the factory gates for the early shift, the archetypes of Shakespeare's 'warriors for the working day':

> I stood watching the infantry. Without any show of emotion they got up, picked up their PIAT mortars, their rifles and ammunition, and walked slowly up the road towards the enemy, with the same bored indifference of a man who goes to a work he does not love . . . No hesitation, no rush on the part of anybody. Men move slowly against death, and although the shaft of every stomach was a vacuum of bile and lead no sign was given and I tried to cover my fear.[86]

Another chaplain watched the Seaforth Highlanders of Canada as they prepared for an assault on the Hitler Line in May 1944. 'My boys move in tonight . . . New boys with fear and nerves and anxiety hidden under quick smiles and quick seriousness. Old campaigners with a faraway look. It is the hardest thing to watch without breaking into tears.'[87]

But any observer always remained outside the true experience of combat, and differing visual impressions had little to do with how the troops themselves regarded the ordeal. Many different thoughts were in fact flitting across the men's minds. Some were quite mundane, such as a painful awareness of the weight of the equipment carried. This was not just a problem during amphibious assaults. In the early years of the war, particularly, all troops going into battle had to shoulder a substantial burden. The assault troops at Alamein, for example, wore steel helmets and web equipment, carried a rifle, grenades, Bren magazines, water-bottle and entrenching tool, while two bandoliers of ammunition were crammed in the front pouches and in the back-pack were rations for one day, an emergency ration, mess tin, groundsheet, sacks for conversion to sandbags, and a pick or shovel strapped to the top of the pack. Many also had to carry a Bren gun or parts of mortars and medium machine guns. Even so, things might have been worse. Prior to an attack at Keren by the Cameron Highlanders, in March 1941, it had been suggested that they carry corrugated iron shields as a defence against the small Italian grenades. The prototypes were 5ft long and weighed around 35lb, but luckily the idea was never put into effect. From the start of the Tunisian campaign, at company and battalion level at least, the troops were allowed to leave much of this kit behind. At Oued Zarga, for example, the 78th Division carried no back-packs at all but wrapped a few essential items in their gas capes, which were worn slung from the belt as a kind of makeshift haversack. American troops always divested themselves of as much equipment as possible before going into action, sometimes wearing only the small combat pack, sometimes not even this.[88]

Part at least of any man's mind, however, was concerned with what was going to happen to him when the shooting started. Doubt gnawed at him. How many enemy would there be? Were they determined? Would the attack succeed? Will I know what to do? Will I be able to do it? Will I be hit, will it be agony, will I be killed? As Jack Belden wrote:

> Uncertainty is in the very air which a battle breathes. It lies coiled at the heart of every combat . . . The uncertainty of the enemy's whereabouts, the uncertainty of falsehood, the uncertainty of surprise, the uncertainty of your own troops' actions, the uncertainty of a strange land, the uncertainty of rescue and the uncertainty of confusion itself. So I say the unknown is the first-born son of combat and uncertainty is its other self.[89]

This uncertainty produced conflicting reactions. For some, particularly in their first actions, sheer curiosity predominated. Nowhere was this better exemplified than in the desert where many young men went to war with that same naïve fascination that had taken the 'lost generation' over to France in 1914 and 1915. Lieutenant Keith Douglas (Nottinghamshire Sherwood Rangers Yeomanry) thought of the battle of Alamein

> . . . as an important test, which I was interested in passing. I observed these battles partly as an exhibition – that is to say that I went through them like a visitor from the country going to a great show, or like a child in a factory – a child sees the brightness and efficiency of steel machines and endless belts slapping round and round, without caring or knowing what it's all there for.[90]

Captain Robert Crisp (3rd Royal Tank Regiment) noticed in himself an enormous excitement and beyond this 'the dominating emotion in my mind was an immense curiosity . . . There was an extraordinary inquisitiveness that always possessed me in strange new places and circumstances; but above all there was this curiosity about the immediate future and what would happen in it . . .

what would happen to me'.[91] Neil McCallum felt just the same, at least just before his first battle. 'The shooting, the battle, these things had to be seen. That was personal curiosity. The shooting was not to be missed. Curiosity was stronger than patriotism or politics and one went to the shooting with the speculative interest of a man examining a new microbe under a microscope.'[92]

Robert Crisp also notes that at this stage he was unable to conceive of himself actually being killed, or even hit, and that fear was not uppermost in his mind. Others were not so convinced. Veterans doubted that they could come through once again, having seen so many of their comrades fall around them. Newcomers suddenly realised that this was it, that there was absolutely no intrinsic reason – fair play, justice, even common sense – why they should not be killed. That was why they were here; to kill or be killed. Death was not some out-of-the-ordinary occurrence that came only to the old or those with appallingly bad luck; it was the order of the day, indivisible from what was now their daily work. And they were afraid. Neil McCallum attempted to describe this sense of the pervasiveness, the almost routine nature of death, and the constant fear that goes with it:

> The terror is not in a cloak and dagger thriller. There is nothing of that. I do not believe it is entirely personal either, the fear of personal death. It lies in the fact that this killing is quite impartial; it has the cold indifference of a great organisation, it is an impersonal routine, a job . . . The state of mind that action induces primarily and super-ficially is fear, with peaks of almost hysterical tension. Fear becomes commonplace – like death, an accepted every-day, ever-present condition. War is no longer entirely freakish and uniquely barbaric. It becomes normal and real with the deep reality of a nightmare.[93]

As a Marine combat correspondent on Iwo Jima, Sergeant F. W. Cockrel, observed, the thing he had 'wondered about most of all, along with a lot of others, I suppose, [was] fear. There was no reticence about fear on Iwo. It was a familiar, almost a friendly topic; it was the stuff guys bragged about to each other – how full of it they were, this time or that'.[94]

This sense of the randomness and ubiquity of death was one of the greatest strains on morale. Its role in breakdown will be discussed in Chapter 6, but it must be emphasised here that acute fear was felt not only by the psychiatrically unstable, but was with all men for most of the time. Nor did one ever get used to it. Certainly they learned the tricks of the trade and fractionally increased their chances of staying alive, but no man would claim that combat ever became routine. The rookie improved, of course, insofar as he overcame his first feelings of utter panic and became able to fight on despite his fear. One American soldier spoke of a 'scar tissue forming around the heart' that helped transform the new replacement into a useful fighting man:

> In his first taste of combat a young soldier's hands have to be prised loose from a pole to which he has grabbed on. He is too scared to even whimper. We loosen his fingers one by one. As we loosen each finger, someone has to hold it to make sure he won't use it to grab back on. But within a week that soldier is fighting bravely, killing with as much nobility as one can kill.[95]

But the fear was always there. Two very different methods of analysis produce the same answer in this respect. The US army had its soldiers fill in thousands of questionnaires about various aspects of military life, and one survey of great interest records the answers to the question: 'In general, would you say that battle fighting became more frightening or less frightening the more you saw of it?' The responses were fairly unequivocal, though they show an interesting difference between theatres.[96]

Table 2: Percentage of US infantryman who found combat became more or less frightening

	More frightening	Don't know	Less frightening	Frightening all the time
ENLISTED MEN				
Mediterranean theatre	74	7	7	12
Pacific theatre	34	3	32	31
COMPANY OFFICERS				
Mediterranean theatre	28	3	42	27
Pacific theatre	9	5	65	21

In short, amongst enlisted men, 86 per cent of those in Italy and 65 per cent in the Pacific agreed that combat never got less frightening. The higher figure disagreeing in the Pacific might at first sight seem surprising, but it should be remembered that the first experiences of combat there, where uncertainty and fear of the enemy were much greater, were probably so appalling that any sort of familiarity with that baleful environment must make things seem at least a little easier. Familiarity could never breed contempt but at least it helped to take the edge off the nightmare. In both theatres, however, it should be remembered that 'less frightening' in no way implies 'not frightening'. James Jones emphasised this point when he summed up his entire active service in the following classic encapsulation: 'I went where I was told to go, and I did what I was told to do, but no more. I was scared shitless just about all the time.'[97] But questionnaires are always very dubious things, particularly where men's responses are likely to be conditioned by a strong sense of what they *ought* to feel and say. And nowhere is a man less sure that his mind is his own than in the army.[98] Much more direct is this extract from a splendid novel about the Italian theatre, when the central characters are discussing past battles:

'The thing I have particularly noticed, [said Brent] 'is that one never gets used to it.' . . .
   'That's it!' Mitchinson agrees eagerly. 'By the time I come out from the line I can sleep through a Jerry hate session if it's not landing too close. I'm out for a few days and then, by God, when I go in again I jump six bloody feet when our own guns go off unexpectedly.'
   'Yes, I've found the same thing,' says Donald. 'There's no such thing as becoming inured to it. Everyone starts from scratch each time.'[99]

The answers to another American questionnaire emphasised the prevalence of fear. This time a sample of infantrymen were asked how far such feelings actually impaired their ability in combat: 65 per cent of them, from a division in north-west Europe, in August 1944, admitted that on at least one occasion they had been unable to perform adequately because of extreme fear, whilst 42 per cent admitted that this had happened more than once.[100] Yet another survey tried to discover just what the physical symptoms of fear actually were. The results are tabulated in Table 3, bearing in mind of course that most men admitted to more than one symptom.[101]

Table 3: Incidence of fear symptoms reported by US soldiers

SYMPTOMS	Division A (South Pacific)	Division B (South Pacific)	Division C (Central Pacific)	Division D (Central Pacific)
	2,095 men	1,983 men	1,299 men	643 men
	%	%	%	%
Violent pounding of the heart	84	78	74	68
Sinking feeling in the stomach	69	66	60	57
Shaking or trembling all over	61	54	53	39
Feeling sick at the stomach	55	50	46	39
Cold sweat	56	45	43	39
Feeling weak or faint	49	46	36	34
Feeling stiff	45	44	43	31
Vomiting	27	21	18	8
Losing control of bowels	21	12	9	4
Urinating in pants	10	9	6	3

Clearly, James Jones's assertion that he was 'scared shitless' all the time was not all that far from the literal truth. For what is of interest in the above table, besides the actual clinical data, is that the relative incidence of symptoms admitted to correlates very closely with the 'acceptability' of those symptoms. Stereotypes of 'manliness' and 'guts' can readily accommodate the fact that a man's stomach or heart might betray his nervousness, but they make less allowance for his shitting his pants or wetting himself. If over one-fifth of the men in one division actually admitted that they had fouled themselves, it is a fair assumption that many more actually did so.

Even when the physical symptoms were not so dramatic, almost everyone felt some sort of intense reaction to the prospect of going forward under fire. The following descriptions give a more vivid picture than can any statistical analysis. Alexander Baron (5th Wiltshire Regiment) spoke of 'the strange terror that afflicts the body regardless of his will, a twitching in his calves, a fluttering of the muscles in his cheeks, the breath like a block of expanding ice in his lungs, his stomach contracting, the sickness rising in his throat'.[102] Peter Bowman recalled his feelings prior to leaving the landing craft at Iwo Jima. 'Your mouth is a vacuum and speech is remote and any sound from it would be a turgid groan. Your mind looks at itself and it shrinks away and wonders whether or not to stand bravely or run and hide. Feelings, senses and physical motion are faint and far off, and all existence is a rushing wind in your ear.'[103] A beachmaster at Tarawa, Lieutenant-Commander P. Grogan, gave an example of how a rather trite symptom of fear could manifest itself as an extreme physical reaction:

> It was like being completely suspended, like being under a strong anaesthetic, not asleep, not even in a nightmare, but just having everything stop . . . Our lips were cracked with the dryness of fear and our voices sounded to us like the voices of complete strangers, voices we had never heard before. By the second day men's mouths were literally black with dryness from fear. Not just a few of them, but all of them.[104]

A combat correspondent at Iwo Jima, Private Allen R. Matthews, described very similar symptoms. Immediately after the landing, 'I sat on the side of the [shell] hole near the bottom and my mouth was so dry that the roof hurt when I ran my tongue over it. I swallowed to try and renew the flow of saliva but the only thing I swallowed was my palate which seemed to have grown inches. I retched violently and the saliva began to flow so I swallowed again, retched again and felt better.'[105] In Burma, another symptom of extreme and prolonged fear was noticed. As Lieutenant Tim Carew (3rd Gurkha Rifles) observed: 'In soldiers who have been in battle over a sustained period it is the jaws that one notices first of all: they have been clenched for hours, and when they eventually relax mouths droop open, giving men an almost idiot appearance.'[106]

The very intensity of such reactions was more than many men could cope with and led to numerous cases of mental breakdown. And yet, and here is one of the most remarkable points about modern wars, the majority of men lived with their fear and refused to allow it completely to dominate them. Jack Belden's description of his own battle with fear is comparable to the experiences of countless others:

> I am afraid, to a greater or lesser degree, in every battle. I cannot exactly say that I have overcome my fear, but rather that my fear has never yet overcome me . . . I cannot recall any moment on the battle-field when I was completely panic-stricken and lost my presence of mind. I have had flashes of sheer terror when I heard and saw a bomb hurtling toward me, and I had one second of paralysing fear when I was wounded, but I have never lost the capacity of thinking and coming to a decision.[107]

Different men had different methods of keeping their fear under control. One particularly supercilious cliché that was bandied around the American rear areas and home front was that 'there are no atheists in the fox-holes'. Those who believed this might have been in for a rude shock had they tried to put it to the test. For many men nothing so utterly and completely dissipated their residual religious beliefs as the randomness and pervasiveness of violent death. Nevertheless, others did derive some comfort from prayer. According to one GI, interviewed in hospital, he 'used to pray a lot. You automatically pray to yourself when you're going in . . . [saying things like] "God help me" and "Why are we doing this?"'[108] The ubiquitous American research teams conducted one of their surveys on this very question. In the Pacific theatre, when asked whether prayer helped when the going was tough, 70 per cent of the sample said that it helped a lot as against only 17 per cent who denied that it was any sort of comfort. In the Mediterranean theatre the respective figures were 83 and 8 per cent. These were groups of enlisted men. Interestingly, the company grade officers rated prayer somewhat less. Only 62 per cent of those interviewed in the Pacific felt that it helped a lot, as against 21 per cent who deemed it useless, whilst the respective Mediterranean figures were 57 and 23 per cent.[109]

It would be misleading, however, to claim that this espousal of prayer implied positive, thought-out religious sentiments. It was more an instinctive assertion of one's own individuality in the midst of chaos, an attempt to reach out across the nightmare and find some basic standards of order and reasonableness that might seem to at least favour one's own survival. This assertion of uniqueness, the desperate faith in one's right to survive, also took blatantly pagan forms, in the shape of lucky charms and talismans which were supposed to somehow give one special protection. John Steinbeck, who served as a war correspondent in the Mediterranean, was struck by the number of men who carried such magic pieces, be they rabbits' feet, medallions, stones, coins, rings or small toys:

> Whatever the cause of this reliance on magic amulets, in wartime it is so. And the practice is by no means limited to ignorant or superstitious men. It would seem that in times of great danger and emotional tumult a man has to reach outside himself for help and comfort, and has to have some supra-personal symbol to hold to. It can be anything at all, an old umbrella handle or a religious symbol, but he has to have it.[110]

Most of these charms were gifts or mementoes of civilian life and here lies their significance. They summed up the entire web of a man's relationships, defined him as a social being with an established place in the world rather than just an expendable unit in the military machine. If a man could provide tangible evidence that his existence had a reality beyond his own physical body, he was the more able to reassure himself that he was too important to be simply blown away. A team of American psychiatrists noted the importance in combat of 'certain unrealistic motives and rationalisations which contribute to the soldier's defences in mastering his fear. Among these we noted repeatedly phantasies of invulnerability – "They won't get *me*." Many men actually wear amulets and many men who do not wear them fancy themselves invulnerable, protected either by God or by the Goddess Luck.'[111] And the longer the soldier survived the more likely it was that the charm would take on an intrinsic significance. Each day still alive with the talisman intact increased the feeling that the piece itself was inseparable from continued survival. One had been lucky. The charm itself was the only thing that set one apart from others, therefore it must be that that had somehow propitiated the gods. Captain A. Wilson (141st Regiment, RAC, The Buffs) revealed that objects were not the only such insurance against death:

> When he went into action he thought every time of death. It was quite against logic to suppose that you were destined to survive the war. All the appearance of things was against it . . . [So] when you thought about death, you developed a system of taboos. Some people lived with a lucky charm in their pocket . . . [He] never carried a charm, but he had something else: an obsession that death would come as the reward for what the Greeks called *hubris*. He believed, for instance, that death would come on the first day he didn't think about it. So before going into action he would utter a phrase articulately under his breath: 'Today I may die.' It was a kind of propitiation; and yet he could never quite believe in it, because that would have defeated its purpose.[112]

A strong internal restraint on fear were the stereotypes of masculinity already alluded to. In other words, the fear of showing fear was often more powerful than the fear of death itself. Robert Crisp brought this out well when he explored the reality of his own, well-earned reputation for courage during the disastrous Greek campaign. 'It was . . . [only] later that I knew my courage for what it was – a reaction to the shame I felt at being afraid, a manifestation of an ingrown complex which survived in a reputation for a sort of recklessness which, somehow or other, I had to sustain and exhibit until some more genuine and significant emotion took its place.'[113] Private Ian Kaye (5th Black Watch) was one of those who prayed, but not so much in the interests of his physical safety as for the sake of his self-respect and honour. 'I always prayed to myself. I asked especially for courage, *not* for vain glory, but merely that I might be strong enough to cope with any situation in which I might find myself.'[114] John Watney felt even more strongly that his instincts might lead him to shame himself and his inner struggle against them almost obliterated the original fear of death or maiming:

> But I was a coward; and the thing I feared more than anything in the world was to break up in battle and give way to that cowardice. I made up my mind that as long as I had the strength, never, under any circumstances, would I allow that to happen; I prayed, until a lump came into my throat, to be spared that degradation.[115]

Captain Cochrane was sure that such feelings were the very foundation of discipline in war, that no one would ever have gone forward if their fear of seeming cowards had not been even more disturbing to them than the grim possibilities of battle.

> Cohesion follows as a matter of course, and this is the root of it. Men are inclined to do what their comrades expect them to do or, more accurately, because nobody actually wants to fight, they do what they imagine their comrades expect them to do. Whether this be mutual deception or mutual support it does the trick.[116]

This fear of fear also helps to explain the troops' behaviour towards one another just before they jumped off. Many did not talk at all, but others kept up a steady stream of inconsequential banter and feeble jokes in an effort to take their minds off what lay ahead and to convince others, and thus themselves, that they were not afraid. Keith Douglas was very aware of such a propensity in himself. Before Alamein another officer addressed him

> . . . in a mock serious voice which, so carefully did he maintain it, made it clear that it was an insurance against real seriousness. Although at the time it seemed to me – and I think all of us – that we were behaving with admirable restraint, afterwards I realised how obvious that restraint would have been to anyone who, like a film audience, could have taken a detached view of us . . . [But] John and I continued in this awful vein of banter as we went for a place to put our beds.[117]

Neil McCallum noted a rather cruder ribaldry between the men in his platoon, but he too knew it for what it was. 'This flat music-hall humour is a defence. It has no subtlety and no wit. It is stale and hackneyed. It is the grin, the courage, the guts. It is the last defence of human beings who have become automatons of behaviour.'[118]

'Automatons' is a very appropriate word in this context. For few men remember feeling much fear in actual combat or, indeed, much about any of their feelings and actions. They behaved almost completely automatically, in an emotional vacuum where even time itself seemed to stand still. As Robert Crisp said of his own reactions during the 'Crusader' fighting, 'when the race is begun, or the innings started, the fullness of the moment overwhelms the fear of anticipation. It is so in battle. When mind and body are fully occupied, it is surprising how unfrightened you can be'.[119] Major Brodie observed that in one particularly nasty action in Germany he was 'perfectly calm and not the least frightened or in any doubt about what to do. In the whole action until I was wounded, my head was clear and I was completely self-confident, far more so than during an audit board or a general inspection'.[120] An American, J. Glenn Gray, wrote:

> In mortal danger, numerous soldiers enter into a dazed condition in which all sharpness of consciousness is lost. When in this state . . . they can function like cells in a military organism, doing what is expected of them because it has become automatic. It is astonishing how much of the business of warfare can still be carried on by men who act as automatons, behaving almost as mechanically as the machines they operate.[121]

Men's conscious minds became quite detached from the battle, and whilst they performed perfectly competently, this was purely instinctive. An American sergeant at Salerno, C. E. Kelly, puzzled that there seemed to be 'no rhyme or reason to how the mind of a soldier in battle works. There I was charging into Italy, passing dead men and coming close to drowning in a ditch . . . and all I could think about was whether or not the photos in my wallet had been ruined'.[122] Corporal Tom McQuade (8th Royal Fusiliers) was the battalion's Post Corporal and he recalled another incident at Salerno when, on a bullet-raked beach, a soldier came up to him and asked in a genuinely worried voice, 'Hey, Mac! My stamps have got wet and stuck together; do you think I'll be able to use them on my letters?'[123]

Moreover, it was such trivial, irrelevant details that often remained in the mind afterwards whilst the actual progress of the battle, and one's own role in it, was little more than a dim blur. John Steinbeck discovered this when he attempted to reconstruct the course of a battle:

> When you wake up and think back to the things that happened they are already becoming dreamlike. Then it is not unusual that you are frightened or ill. You try to remember what it was like, and you can't quite manage it. The outlines in your memory are vague. The next day the memory slips farther, until very little is left at all . . . Men in prolonged battle are not normal men. And when afterwards they seem to be reticent – perhaps they don't remember very well. [124]

Private Matthews, on Iwo Jima, confirmed this when he tried to recollect just what had happened to him as he struggled ashore:

> Later that day I thought of the words I had read picturing such an attack and I knew then that the writers had seen too much. For although I had desperately wanted to form a picture of what it was like, what I had come through with was the recollection of my mental prodding and a few snapshots, disconnected in time and space, some of them faded as with age and out of focus and only one or two sharp and clear. [125]

A combat correspondent on Tarawa, Jim Lucas, never was able to recall his feelings during the landing. 'Slowly we moved down the pier. We would drop when a man was hit, freeze when the firing ceased, and then move forward. It is impossible to describe one's feelings. I have tried many times to analyse how I felt . . . Few of us had ever gone through such an experience, and I had, throughout, the suspicion that it wasn't really happening.' [126]

And what, after all, was there that the memory could seize upon and retain in any coherent pattern? From the individual's point of view any battle was simply noise and total confusion, one's own actions and reactions being purely instinctive. Lieutenant Hugh Macrae (4th Seaforth Highlanders) in France in 1940 noted: 'When I look back on that day and try to recollect the thoughts that were passing through my head it seems that in such moments of stress one does not really have thoughts, merely reactions. Everything concerning an individual in battle is immediate, both in time and space, and one's mind reacts instantaneously.' [127] Not only did the automatic nature of one's actions make it difficult to recall them afterwards but it also meant that they were not made, consciously at least, within any context. The tactical shape of the fighting as a whole didn't register on one's mind at all and thus there was nothing on to which the memory could cling. Combat became merely a series of fleeting impressions, with no coherent shape. Andrew Wilson summed up battle as 'mostly a series of unheroic things – little successes, little escapes, long periods of waiting . . . It just went on from day to day, and it was enough that you were still there'.[128] For Captain Ingersoll a battle was simply a series of unrelated flurries of activity. 'Nothing could be more violent than the most violent moments, but these moments were spaced out. Between them were long spells of waiting, walking and wait-ing.'[129] An American correspondent in Italy emphasised the seeming meaningless of it all, even to an observer:

> One never saw masses of men assaulting the enemy. What one ob-served, in apparently unrelated patches, was small, loose bodies of men moving down narrow defiles or over steep inclines, going methodically from position to position between long halts and the only continuous factor was the roaring and crackling of the big guns. One felt baffled at first by the unreality of it all. Unseen groups of men were fighting other men that they rarely saw.[130]

Lieutenant Colin Mitchell (8th Argyll and Sutherland Highland-ers) fought in Italy during the last few months of the war and for him 'it was war as I had somehow expected to find it except that it was so much more concerned with small, somewhat pathetic groups of people. I had thought I would be able to influence events and instead I was dominated by them'.[131] Nat Frankel felt that it was this sense of being dominated by events, the sheer enormity of modern battle as well as its amorphousness that made so many soldiers unable to formulate any coherent memories.

> I've seen veterans just bubbling over with memory, with an actual lust to tell their tales of Armageddon. But once they start, even the most articulate of them fall tongue-tied. What was Iwo Jima like? It was . . . it was . . . it was fucking rough man! I know that, but what was it like? Really . . . really . . . really tough! So the very experience of war, what would seem to be the prerequisite for describing it, precludes any actual, palpable narrative.[132]

This introduces the essential paradox of modern combat; on the one hand the mind-numbing vastness of the whole military effort

and the extreme mental anguish of those risking death time and
again, and yet on the other a pathetic sense of inconsequentiality,
bewilderment and helplessness. You knew it had been 'fucking
rough' but often the impressions that lingered in the mind recalled
nothing so much as black farce. The two following accounts of the
first day at Alamein show, in different ways, just how little idea
troops had of what they were supposed to be doing. Captain
George Green (5th Seaforth Highlanders) was lost for the bulk of
his battalion's attack because of the thick dust raised by the artillery barrage. 'The battalion was still holding direction . . . [but]
we just couldn't see each other. Later on, when daylight came, we
found that the plan had been carried through to the letter – much
to our surprise, I admit . . . A German armoured car . . . belted off
at a tangent, still firing, and disappeared into the smoke. It was that
kind of battle; things kept popping on and off in a casual sort of
way.'[133] Neil McCallum arrived in Africa after Alamein but his
men frequently spoke of it, and his memoirs record the graphic
impressions of one private soldier:

> Everyone was shouting, screaming, swearing, shouting for their
> father, shouting for their mother, I didn't know whether to look at the
> ground or at the sky, someone said look at the ground for spider-mines,
> someone said look at the sky for the flashes, shells were coming all
> ways, the man next to me got hit through the shoulder, he fell down, I
> looked at him and said 'Christ' and then ran on, I didn't know whether
> to be sick or dirty my trousers.[134]

The feeling of aimless helplessness was increased by the fact that
soldiers rarely saw their enemy, even if they knew where he was.
This was especially true in the jungle and an Australian in New
Guinea told of 'the mists creeping over the trees all day, and
sometimes you can't see your hand in front of your face under
cover of the jungle. Most of our chaps haven't seen a Jap . . . My
unit made two attacks on Jap positions. We got to within fifteen
feet of them, but we still couldn't see them'.[135] A correspondent on
Laiana described a battle that was nothing but

> . . . bush, noise, death. Nothing else – no rolling clouds of smoke, nor
> flashes from gun muzzles, nor running men nor shouting. More than
> 10,000 soldiers . . . were locked in a death struggle in positions ex-
> tending about 2,000 yards from flank to flank. Yet at the points of
> contact between the opposing forces one rarely saw six live men
> together at the same time. The jungle drowned the battle like an
> opaque green liquid.[136]

Even if one did see one's enemy, even if, most untypically, one actually came to grips with him, the ensuing struggle had little in common with romantic notions of some knightly duel. A Canadian subaltern of the Winnipeg Grenadiers, in Hong Kong, was caught in a hand-to-hand fight with a Japanese officer, and were it not for the fact that life and death were at stake the picture portrayed would be nothing short of farcical:

> I was able to knock his rifle and bayonet out of the hands of one of the Japs, and with my new weapon managed to run through another of the enemy. Unfortunately I had difficulty withdrawing the blade and while endeavouring to do so I was lucky enough to catch the flash of a sword being raised to strike.
>
> Quite subconsciously I jumped for my assailant, grasping the blade with my right hand, and circling his neck with my left arm, forcing his head against my chest . . . While struggling in this fashion we both lost our footing and rolled down a small slope for about ten feet . . . I managed to regain approximately the same standing advantage I had enjoyed earlier, except that by now we had both lost our grip on the sword. Since my opponent's face was tucked against my chest I endeavoured to turn his head in such a way as to enable me to deliver what I hoped would be a knockout with my fist. Unfortunately, I failed to notice that I had forced his steel helmet down over most of his face and the net result of a terrific uppercut was a sprained thumb for me . . . I had completely forgotten that I carried a pistol up to this moment and in something of a frenzy I endeavoured to reach it . . . Complications arose here for I found after inserting my right forefinger through the trigger guard [that] the cut I had received on this finger when I had first grasped the blade had deprived it of the necessary strength to squeeze the trigger. Still further difficulties arose when I attempted to withdraw the finger and found that the flesh, acting much the same as the barb on a fish-hook, rendered it difficult to remove that finger from the trigger guard. However, I did manage and pressing the pistol the the base of my opponent's neck, finally ended the struggle.[137]

The Cost

Were war an expensive game, 'bathos' and 'farce' might be apt summaries of the ludicrous confusion of combat. But the rules demanded that thousands died, and such words make poor epitaphs. It must never be forgotten that amidst the breathless, sweating, cursing banality of combat there was the ever-present fact of sudden dismemberment, disfigurement and death.

There were countless different ways to go. As often as not you never even knew what had hit you. So it was with snipers, who usually hit you in the head. A medic in the 30th US Division assessed a man's chances of surviving such a wound:

> The sniper's finger presses the trigger and the bullet passes through the helmet, scalp, skull, small blood vessels' membrane into the soft sponginess of the brain substance in the occipital lobe of the cerebral hemisphere. Then you're either paralysed or you're blind or you can't smell anything or your memory is gone or you can't talk or you're bleeding – or you're dead. If a medic picks you up quickly enough, there's a surgeon who can pick out the bullet, tie up the blood vessels, cover up the hole in your head with a tantalum metal plate. Then, slowly, you learn things all over again . . . But if the bullet rips through your medulla region in the back of your head (about twice the size of your thumb) or if it tears through a big blood vessel in the brain – then you're dead buddy.[138]

Men hit in the stomach by bullets were lucky if they died. Such a one was 'the Swede', a big Marine at Cape Gloucester. 'You could hear the bullet hit him in the stomach,' said Platoon Sergeant John M. White. 'He just stood there a minute. He said, "Them dirty bastards!" Then he fell down. He was dead.'[139] The effects of shells were much more variegated than those of bullets. Sometimes they obliterated a man so completely that it was hard to believe he had ever existed. An American captain saw the aftermath of one direct hit on a group of sleeping soldiers. At his feet was the more or less intact body of an American sergeant:

> Immediately beyond it there was a gully shaped like a cup with one side blown out, a cup four or five feet deep. At the bottom and down one side of the gully there was a pile of gray shredded fabric. It had no shape and it was not very big. The whole bottom of the gulley was coated evenly with a gray powder and you would not have noticed the pile of gray shredded fabric except for a foot and a shoe with no body attached to it. This object lay by the edge of the pile. There was no blood whatever. All the blood had been blown out of the man who wore this shoe.[140]

Such obliteration was especially unsettling to other soldiers in that it further undermined their faith in the sanctity of their own existence. That men should be killed was bad enough, that they could be blown to nothing was almost too much to contemplate. Ferd Nauheim (5th US Armoured Division) asked a veteran what happened to the bodies of those killed in combat:

A Grave Registration detail that picks them up, takes them back for burial, establishes identification and so on. They're working around here now someplace. Before you woke up, two of their guys had been poking around looking for the body of some captain that got it here yesterday. Later on they got an empty . . . [rations] box from us. What they found of him went off in that. Must have caught an 88 . . . but good. Just think of that. A guy grows up, maybe makes something of himself, probably got a helluva good education, nice home, wife and kids back home thinking about him, waiting for him, and just because he was in the wrong place at the right time yesterday, all that's left can rattle around in a frigging cardboard box. Jesus Christ, that's something isn't it?[141]

Stephen Berlin always remembered the sheer incredulity of a private of the Worcesters, in north-west Europe, whose mate had gone off to relieve himself:

He was half way across the field when he heard it coming. If he had fallen flat he might have got away with a couple of shrapnel wounds. But he didn't. He turned to run back to the trench. The shell hit him. I'm telling you, IT BLEW HIM TO TINY LITTLE BITS! I've seen things up there, sir, that I never want to describe or remember, but if you can picture a booted foot, a section of the human cranium, a bunch of fingers, a bit of clothing, you can get some idea – it was simply a matter of *little tiny bits*.[142]

At other times, whilst the effect of a shell was less comprehensive, it was even more sickening. Major Johns recalled the wrongest conclusion he ever jumped to:

One shell burst not 25 yards ahead of the Major . . . He ran forward into the smoke and dust, nearly falling over a man who was rolling crazily, half in and half out of the ditch. Johns grabbed him by the arm to help him to his feet, crying, 'Come on, boy, let's go.' The man tried to get up but stumbled awkwardly forward. Only then did Johns look down to see that the soldier had no feet. He was trying valiantly to stand on the stumps of his two legs, where his feet had been sliced cleanly off just at the ankles.[143]

Even armour plate was often little protection against shells, and for a gunner or driver trapped in his seat as a missile smashed through the front compartment even total atomisation would have been preferable to the kinds of wounds received. Peter Elstob (Royal Tank Corps) told of a crewman caught in a Sherman: 'From the knees down [his legs] looked as though a steamroller had crushed them. It was impossible to tell one leg from the other. There was a mass of splintered bone and pulped flesh, ending incongruously in two army boots which didn't seem to belong to the rest at all.'[144]

But death was usually more than the sight of individual soldiers bowled over or mangled. In many battles the horror was compounded by the sheer ubiquity of the carnage. In Italy, in August 1944, the King's Own Yorkshire Light Infantry suffered heavy casualties during German counter-attacks on San Sevino. After forty-eight hours the streets were piled with the dead, and those who later walked through the ruins found that each white-washed wall left standing was covered with British and German blood. After a Canadian attack on Saint Lambert, during the race to seal the Falaise Gap, the dead lay so close as to be almost touching and the stench could be smelt even in light aircraft going overhead. In Purple Heart Valley, in the Cassino sector, not only were the dead thick on the ground, and decomposing quickly, but most of the corpses had had their throats torn out by the packs of wild dogs that roamed the area.

Surprisingly, perhaps, the wounded and the dying were often the least affected by their trauma. In the first hours, at least, nature had its own compensations. Lieutenant Colonel M. Lindsay remembers seeing a soldier hit by a rifle bullet in Normandy who 'was in such agony that after a moment or two he had fainted, the bullet having hit him in the forearm and broken the bone. He is the only man whom I have ever seen in pain from a wound, the shock being normally so great that nothing much is felt for some hours'.[145] This state of shock could produce reactions that seemed quite out of keeping with the severity of the wounds. At one stage in the Normandy campaign, Major Brodie went off with a small party to find a wounded man who supposedly had been missed by the stretcher-bearers. 'Sure enough we found a poor little chap with both legs blown off above the knees, moaning softly and, I remember, he was saying "Oh dear! Oh dear!" The stretcher-bearer shook his head and, I thought, looked pointedly at my revolver.'[146] Many men died without being aware of what happened. Robert Crisp and his men witnessed the death of a man hit in the stomach by shell fragments:

The hoarse breathing stopped. For what seemed a long time nothing happened. Just the silence and the circle of sombre faces behind and the man on the edge of nothingness in front. Then, as some unbidden muscle tensed, his mouth fell open and sucked in a great gasp of air, a last desperate mouthful of life. His body quivered like a decapitated chicken, his eyelids went right up and the pupils swivelled back until only the whites stared at me. The arm under my hand went cool, then cold. There was a long sigh, as though a ghost had passed, rustling, through the gaping mouth. He was dead.[147]

Other men, even though they were aware of what was happening to them, seemed quite resigned to their fate. R. L. Crimp spoke to the men of another platoon after one attack and one of them described the death of his friend. 'We were all sitting on the edge of our slit 'un, making a brew while things were quieter like, when suddenly a mortar bomb plomps down. We all dived, except Bill – he'd caught a bit in the tummy. We couldn't do much for him, and anyway he told us not to bother. He said he knew he'd got his lot, and just stayed quiet.'[148]

Such an account of one man's fatalistic passing from this life can make the tragedy almost acceptable, by keeping it within very human dimensions. But this is not the measure of the sharp end. Battle was not a series of poignant incidents to be expunged by averted eyes or the dab of a handkerchief. It was a slaughterhouse:

The Padre and [the] Sergeant . . . were able to get out to the tanks they had lost . . . in order to identify the dead. In some cases the bodies were indistinguishable from one another, simply a mass of cooked flesh welded together in the great heat; we had to sift through this for identity tags. Each tank told the same story – broken legs, broken arms, open chest wounds, and so on, had trapped many, so that they had burnt alive. The screams I thought I had heard during the action had not been imaginary after all.[149]

After the padres came the grave diggers:

Sure, there were lots of bodies we never identified. You know what a direct hit by a shell does to a guy. Or a mine, or a solid hit with a grenade, even. Sometimes all we have is a leg or a hunk of arm . . . There's only one stink and that's it. You never get used to it, either. As long as you live, you never get used to it.[150]

4
Combat: Artillery and Armour

Armoured vehicles have entered the village. It is
found that they are able to conquer ground but
not hold it. In the narrow streets and alleyways
they have no free field for their fire, and their
movements are hemmed in on all sides. The
terror they have spread amongst us disappears.
We get to know their weak spots. A ferocious
passion for hunting them is growing . . .

GERMAN OFFICER, 1918

It takes twenty minutes for a medium tank to
incinerate; and the flames burn slowly, so figure
it takes ten minutes for a hearty man within to
perish. You wouldn't even be able to struggle
for chances are both exits would be sheeted with
flame and smoke. You would sit, read *Good
Housekeeping*, and die like a dog. Steel coffins
indeed!

PRIVATE FIRST CLASS NAT FRANKEL, 1944

[Our radio picked up] the Commander calmly
directing the battle using cricket parlance . . .
We might have been at Lords . . . wondering
whether the tea break was far away. Suddenly,
across the Squadron Leader's voice came a sharp
ominous click. We'd heard it before. We couldn't
see the tank but we knew what the click meant.
Charlie took over the radio network. The others
obeyed his orders calmly, resolutely, as if it were
the most natural thing in the world for their
comrade to depart suddenly like that – with a click
as adieu.

PRIVATE WILLIAM WOODRUFF, 1944

Infantry were the bedrock of World War II combat, just as they had been for hundreds of years. As Montgomery said, though they were 'the least spectacular arm of the Army, yet without them you cannot win a battle. Indeed, without them you can do nothing. Nothing at all, nothing'. By the same token, however, they themselves could have achieved little without the assistance of other arms. The contribution of the engineers has already been touched upon, and we must now give some attention to the other major formations in the fighting divisions, the artillery and the armour, the men whose job it was to soften up or destroy those enemy positions that baulked the infantry advance. It is important to acknowledge the subsidiary role of both these arms. With artillery the point is fairly obvious, for it has never been regarded as a battle winner in its own right. Assessing the true role of armour in World War II is a more contentious topic and many misconceptions and partisan judgements have to be set aside. Suffice it to say at this point that tanks, whether in Africa, Europe or Asia, were hardly ever able to operate as an autonomous arm. Often they needed the infantry to allow them to advance at all; they always needed them to consolidate whatever gains had been made. Without the 'poor bloody infantry' mere guns, whether artillery or armoured fighting vehicles could do nothing at all.

Artillery

The history of World War I is dominated by artillery. To some writers it was simply 'the war of the guns' and daily life was inseparable from the constant thunder of both sides' barrages. The scale of the artillery was enormous. Throughout, the British army fired off 150 million rounds of all types. In the first two weeks of the Third Battle of Ypres, some 4,283,550 rounds were fired. As a comparison, the Third US Army, during the whole of its campaign in north-west Europe, fired only 5,870,843 rounds. Yet this should not mislead us. Throughout most of World War II artillery was fundamental to the success of large-scale attacks. It was certainly available in prodigious quantities. The British and Canadians had a maximum of 4,500 guns in north-west Europe, whilst one American army alone finished the war with 1,464 pieces of 105mm or larger.[1] The main use of all this firepower was as a prelude to infantry assaults, though again not quite on the scale of World War I. The key difference was not so much the number of guns used in any bombardment as its duration. The massive barrages of 1916 and 1917 sometimes went on for weeks at a time, an indication of the bewildered desperation of the generals, while those of the next war were much shorter. By this time it had been generally realised that guns, in no matter what quantity, could only achieve so much, and that within the first few hours. During this time, however, the concentration and volume of firepower equalled anything on the Western Front.

In 1941, during the assault on Keren, the artillery of only two Indian divisions was at times pouring 10,000 rounds an hour into the Italian citadel. Prior to the Battle of Alamein, the whole of the Eighth Army massed 882 field and medium guns, each of which was to fire some 600 rounds during the first night.[2] The nature of the campaigns in Europe made artillery a *sine qua non* of almost every operation. As has been explained, the Germans relied largely on defensive positions and the assaulting troops only had any chance at all if these defences could be at least partially disrupted.

The list of major barrages is endless, and only a few major examples can be given here. As many as 600 guns were used during the Eighth Army's crossing from Sicily to Italy, in September 1943. In late November of that year, during the crossing of the Sangro, nine regiments of field artillery and three of medium fired 600 rounds per day for three whole days. In the following month, during the Camino battles, the artillery of two corps hurled 1,900 tons of shells at the German positions: '800 guns were in action, ranging in calibre from 3-inch to 8-inch howitzers. In an afternoon performance lasting an hour . . . the 346 pieces in II Corps, fired 22,058 rounds, and continuing their practice till the following afternoon fired a total of 64,000 rounds . . . in 24 hours. In the same period the 303 guns in X Corps fired 89,883 rounds, of which nearly 76,000 rounds were fired by 25-pdrs.'[3] Elsewhere in Italy the story was the same. The 432 guns on the Anzio beachhead were firing 25,000 rounds a day during February 1944. Artillery backed up all of the Cassino battles; 610 pieces were used in one assault, and by the end of March over half a million shells had been fired into the town. During a Fifth Army attack, in May 1944, its 600 guns fired 173,941 rounds in 24 hours. During the first third of July, in the same year, the 34th US Division was using 117 rounds per gun per day, and in one day 715 tons of ammunition were expended. During the assault on the Gothic Line, a few weeks later, the 11th US Division used 24,000 rounds in only three days.

Artillery was just as important in north-west Europe, where each big operation was preceded by massed artillery fire and bomber strikes. In the prelude to Operation Veritable, for example, available artillery comprised 576 field guns, 280 medium, 122 heavy and 72 anti-aircraft.[4] Nor was such prodigal use of this arm limited only to the major offensives. During the Normandy fighting guns were used in large numbers almost every day, often on very localised targets. In the precarious Orne bridgehead, Allied artillery superiority was all that kept the Germans at bay. A gunner officer of the 59th (Staffordshire) Division wrote of this period that sometimes his battery fired:

> 1,000 rounds a gun a day during the battle. This was done for two days running, but has not often occurred, I believe, in the history of war. It was necessary to pour water over the guns the whole time to keep them from melting . . . Definitely, it is superiority of firepower, not accuracy that counts. Troop and battery targets were unheard of . . . I have seen battleships, cruisers, destroyers, super-heavies, mediums, heavy AA, light AA and field guns all pour shells as hard as they can into one field for five minutes.[5]

In the Far East and the Pacific, artillery was in no way as important. Though the Americans used massive air-strikes and naval bombardments as a prelude to their island assaults, neither they nor the British in Burma were able to deploy much artillery proper. The nature of the terrain made movement and concentration very difficult and the density of the jungle, coupled with the resilience of the Japanese fortifications, made anything but a direct hit from a bomb or large naval shell fairly ineffective.[6] One incident on the Tiddim Road, in February 1944, is typical of this kind of warfare. A battalion of Gurkhas was sent in to clear a small concentration of Japanese bunkers and their attack was preceded by a barrage that only lifted at the last moment. A post-action analysis, however, commented that

> . . . although the morale effect of our artillery may have been considerable, both on our own troops and on the Japanese, the material damage was small . . . In spite of a concentration of 684 rounds of 3.7-inch howitzer shell and 670 rounds of 25-pdr shell on a . . . target area of approximately 250 yards square, no material damage was suffered by the bunkers, but a few communication bunkers were damaged. Precise numbers of Japanese dead are not known; two were found by our own troops when occupying the position.[7]

However, the limited role and effectiveness of the gunners did not mean that they got off more lightly than the infantry. The denseness of the jungle and the need to get to very close range forced the artillerymen to take up positions in the very front line. Here they were subject to all the nerve-wracking tensions of jungle warfare as waged by the Japanese. Major B. L. N. Ditmas (129th Regiment Royal Artillery) wrote:

We were not gunners first and foremost . . . we were almost as much infantry as gunners. At the O.P. there was sometimes hand-to-hand fighting. At the gun positions shelling and bombing were always a minor consideration. The threat came from the 'jitter party', operating by night, trying every possible means to locate our positions and infiltrate into them . . . We risked the shell and bomb and concentrated in our gun positions until our perimeters were reduced to the minimum and could be defended by ourselves . . . Sometimes a field regiment, a medium battery and a light AA troop with all their transport occupied a 500-yard square. [8]

Even within such a tight perimeter the strictest precautions had to be taken. Major S. T. Clarke (25th Mountain Regiment Indian Artillery) recalled some fairly extreme examples:

To obviate danger of coughs giving away gun positions, 'coughing piquets' were established some 500 yards away. All notorious coughers were obliged to go there, with the knowledge that any night-prowling Japs were likely to fire on them first. This largely cured the early morning coughing to which the Indians were so prone! Each position was painstakingly camouflaged, fresh greenery being cut each day for the purpose. Short bamboo stakes, called 'punjis', sharpened at both ends and hardened by fire, were stuck in the grass wherever there were gaps in the thick jungle through which the enemy might rush in. The men, who slept in pairs, had a deep cylindrical foxhole each at either end of a shallow double sleeping trench covered by a mosquito net. [9]

Actually getting the guns into position was usually an arduous task in itself, often involving manhandling them up hundreds of feet along steep and narrow trails. Lieutenant Colonel T. W. R. Hill (30th Mountain Regiment Royal Artillery) was supporting 82nd West African Division, during operations in Arakan, when his men had to undertake the following haul to get their guns within range of a network of enemy bunkers:

The only effective means of destroying this target was for one gun to take it on at point-blank range from across the river, which was 95 yards wide at this point . . . If the mules could not go, then the detachment would carry their gun. The route available was a track, hacked through dense bamboo, just wide enough for one man. It led up a boulder-strewn stream descending from a 600 foot hill. Slipping and staggering under their loads, the men struggled up the stream-bed as far as it was possible to go. They were now faced with a gradient of 1 in 1½ up which, having cut toe-holds with their *dahs*, they hoisted the gun. It must be appreciated that apart from their bulk and awkwardness, some gun parts weigh 210lb and are a three- or four-man lift. Up this heart-breaking cliff only one hand could be spared to hold the load, the other was wanted to grasp the bamboos and obtain a purchase to avoid falling backwards and letting the load crash to the bottom . . . A reconnaissance was made . . . and by the time it was finished the detachment had man-handled the assembled gun for 1,000 yards across derelict paddy-fields to the rendezvous.[10]

In the desert, too, artillerymen often found themselves fighting in the very front line, as the last defence against German armoured attacks. Again, terrain supplies one of the major reasons, though in a quite different way. In the Western Desert, British generals became rather hypnotised by its vastness and developed a fixation about the central importance of mobility and fluidity. These were, indeed, important concepts, as Rommel repeatedly showed, but he usually managed to avoid the British mistake of trying to cover too wide an area and splitting the forces into penny packets to do so. In the British scheme of things small mixed columns became the order of the day, most of them with their own complement of artillery who might suddenly find themselves in the thick of a small battle. But there was another important reason for this dispersion of the guns, namely the absence of adequate anti-tank weapons. It soon became clear that only the 25-pounder offered real protection against the German tanks and the divisional allotment soon tended to get split up between the infantry battalions and companies, often having to fight shoulder-to-shoulder with them. Prior to the Battle of Alamein, when concentration once again became the keyword, the history of the Royal Artillery in the desert can almost be written in terms of a series of epic 'last stands' in which doomed regiments and batteries tried to hold off vastly superior *panzer* forces.

There were two such incidents during the Crusader fighting, in November 1941. On the 23rd, the 60th Field Regiment and 4th Royal Horse Artillery held off an attack on elements of the 2nd

Rifle Brigade. Their ammunition almost gone and most of the crews killed or wounded, they were only saved from complete destruction by the timely arrival of British armour in the enemy's flank. Two days later near Sidi Omar, the 1st Field Regiment of the 4th Indian Division was attacked twice by upwards of thirty tanks of which they managed to knock out nineteen and forced the Germans to withdraw. This, in fact, was the last occasion on which the panzers went in alone against positions protected by artillery. In future their attacks were always supported by their own artillery and infantry and the heavier tanks would stand off and try to knock out the guns from a distance. The 4th Indian Division was involved in another fierce duel in the following month, during the Gazala battle, when only the presence of the 25th Field Regiment saved the 7th Brigade from being overrun by enemy tanks. In June of the following year, the most heroic efforts of the gunners were not enough. During Operation Aberdeen the South Nottinghamshire Hussars (107th Royal Horse Artillery) fought virtually to the last man and the last round after being surrounded on a ludicrously exposed position. The same almost happened during the Battle of Alamein, despite the new efforts to concentrate the artillery. On 27 October, a battalion of the Rifle Brigade, with the 239th Anti-Tank Battery and the 76th Anti-Tank Regiment, were cut off on the 'Snipe' position, to the west of Kidney Ridge. At the end of the battle, when they were relieved by fresh infantry, it was estimated that they had accounted for 57 tanks and self-propelled guns. Of their own 19 guns, only 6 could be deemed in anything like working order. In Tunisia, too, the use of artillery often left a great deal to be desired. It was here, in February 1943, that Allied artillery fired over open sights for almost the last time. At Sidi Nsir, the 155th Field Battery, detached with a battalion of the Hampshires far beyond the support of other troops, was overrun by German tanks after a gallant defence.

In Europe, however, this kind of eyeball contact was virtually unknown.[11] By late 1943 the major lessons had been learnt and the whole rationale of the gunners' war was now to maximise the power of a single shoot, switching the guns *en masse* to the most urgent target. War for artillerymen was now largely a matter of technique, usually against an unseen enemy, in which maps, telephones and spotter planes played a vital role. New words entered the vocabulary. The 'stonk' (Standard Regimental Concentration) was officially a 525yd block of fire that could be laid down according to a predetermined template by a regiment's field and medium guns, though in fact the infantry began to use this term for any brief, sudden bombardment. The Time-on-Target, or TOT, was a bombardment so timed that all shells would arrive on the target at exactly the same time (obviously, if all guns *fired* at the same time this would not be the case). The Americans, for no clear reason, referred to this as a 'serenade'. Operation Veritable saw the first use of the 'Pepperpot' barrage in which the artillery proper was supplemented by whatever else was available, in this case, 188 Vickers machine guns, 80 4.2in mortars, 114 Bofors guns, 24 anti-tank guns, 12 rocket launchers and 60 stationary Sherman tanks. In Italy, special 'half-step' fuses were developed that enabled 25-pounders to achieve a high trajectory to clear the mountain tops, but not so high that they would fall too far behind the enemy on the reverse slopes.

But even though artillerymen in Europe rarely found themselves in the front line, it would be foolish to imagine that theirs was a cushy life. For one thing their gun positions were a prime target for the enemy gunners and the threat of being blown to bits was never absent. Nor was day-to-day existence particularly pleasant. Though it hardly ever reached the extremes of the infantryman's life in the Italian, Dutch or German winters, the endless days and nights spent in gun-pits or tents could be physically very uncomfortable and, above all, excruciatingly boring. Ernie Pyle visited an American battery of 155mm howitzers in Sicily:

> The men of the gun crew lived in pup tents a few feet from the gun pit . . . For each two gun crews there was also a larger pyramidal tent, empty except for the straw on the ground. Nobody lived in there, but the ground crews used it for a loafing place in the daytime, when they weren't firing, and for playing poker at night by candlelight. They sat or lay on the ground while they played, since there was no furniture. There was a kitchen truck for each battery . . . The men ate outside, either sitting on their steel helmets in the mud, or standing up with their mess kits resting on a . . . wall . . . Supper was at 4.30, and by 5.30 it was dark. There was nothing to do, no place to go, and even inside the big tents the candlelight wasn't conducive to much fun, so usually the crews were asleep by 8.30.[12]

John Guest wrote home in December 1944 and described his accommodation, as an officer with an AA battery in Italy:

I'm sitting in an I.P. tent at a table covered with a looted tablecloth . . .
now very dirty . . . Under the table is a Valor stove which warms my
knees but not my feet . . . At the end of the tent our two beds are sunk
in a trench beneath the level of the ground. There is a good deal of
shell-fire here. The feet of the beds stand permanently in water . . .
The ground for fifty yards outside is MUD – six inches deep, glistening,
sticky, holding pools of water.[13]

Had he been spirited to Holland at this time only the flatness of the
countryside would have made him know that he had changed scene
at all. Stephen Berlin did spend that winter in Holland and soon
came close to despair:

It looks very much as though we shall be bogged down here for the
winter . . . There is mud and water everywhere; it rains so constantly
that we are confined to our bivvies most of the day; fulfilling as it is to
read and write and draw, one cannot keep up these activities 24 hours a
day. The day is so long. We rise early. The night also is long, light
going at six or thereabouts, and caging us in darkness. The wind rises
at night and drives over the flat land; our home flaps and flounders like
a ship at sea; the tent pegs are wrenched from the sandy earth, and
often it is necessary to dress and go out and fix it. The other night we
woke with the damned thing on top of us.[14]

Armour

At the beginning of the war, in both the British and American
armies, much of their armour was manned by ex-cavalrymen,
entire regiments whose whole tradition was based upon horsed
cavalry action. Both they, and the general public who read of the
'So-and-So' Hussars or Carabiniers, tended to envisage armoured
warfare in terms of deep penetration and hell-for-leather charges
across open ground. Whilst they might admit that defensive firepower had now achieved an unparalleled effectiveness, surely,
they thought, armoured fighting vehicles were virtually immune to
such fire, whilst their tracked wheels must mean that they could go
virtually anywhere. In fact, nothing could be further from the
truth. One of the major lessons of World War II was that tanks
have a limited capability, their role being severely restricted by
mechanical unreliability, unfavourable terrain, and improvements
in weaponry. *Blitzkrieg* might have worked in 1939 and 1940 but
this was largely a psychological victory. Once troops had learnt the
manifold shortcomings of tanks, and were provided with adequate

counter-weapons, they ceased to be overawed by them. For the men in the tanks the heady days of armour slashing through the enemy line were soon over. Their war became much like that of the infantry, less dangerous perhaps, but just the same kind of brutal slogging-match against tough defensive positions.

Before going on to examine the nature of armoured combat itself it should be emphasised that it was not just the enemy that stood in the way of supposedly highly mobile tank operations, but that these inherent defects of the machines severely limited their performance. Some of these were purely mechanical. At the very start of the war it swiftly became apparent that existing designs were not sturdy enough for actual warfare. During exercises in Egypt it was found that trackpins broke at an alarming rate. Over rough going, ie not on roads, units were expending in a few days what would be six months' supply of pins for normal peacetime mileage. Dust was also a great problem as it got sucked into the engine and, even after desert filters had been fitted to all tanks, many of them only had a life of 3,000–5,000 miles. In all theatres, when long journeys were anticipated, it was normal to put as many tanks as possible on huge transporters to save wear and tear. Individual models also had their own defects. The Mark II Matilda had weak steering clutches that would not stand heavy wear, and the turret ring was badly designed so that it was prone to be jammed by shell splinters. The Valentine, although mechanically sound, gave its commander only the most limited vision and was so short that it had an inadequate 'reach' over craters or trenches. The Crusader was notoriously unreliable. Two main faults were responsible for hundreds of breakdowns – a water-pump whose seal soon wore away, and an oil gallery pipe that worked loose and whose repair necessitated the removal of the entire engine. The M3 Grant was also mechanically unsound, whilst the M3 Stuart was equipped with 11in tracks that offered insufficient support on soft ground. It tended to bog down where tanks three or four times as heavy went through with ease. Later models, notably the Sherman and the Churchill, were superior, but throughout the war a large proportion of temporary tank losses were attributable to mechanical failure. For the BEF, breakdown accounted for 75 per cent of all casualties. In Burma the problem was aggravated by the humid climate, and an official REME report noted that 'more equipment has been rendered unserviceable in storage than in actual operations'. The experiences of one unit in Europe tells a similar story. Between 8 and

17 February, the 9th Royal Tank Regiment and the 147th Regiment fought in the Reichswald and suffered 85 tank casualties. Of these, 17 were attributable to enemy action, 13 to turret failure, 3 to clutch failure, 20 to unspecified mechanical breakdown, and 32 to becoming hopelessly bogged down.

This last figure raises another important point, that tanks can be severely hampered by terrain and are rarely able to barge around at will. Even in the desert, supposedly a tank-man's paradise, the going was never consistent; and though it was often hard and fast there were many potential hazards. Sometimes there was only a very thin solid crust over a virtual quicksand. There were many salt-pans and, if it rained, these were swiftly transformed into morasses. The sparse vegetation could also be dangerous as hummocks of sand and large sharp stones tended to form at the base of every camel's thorn and these were quite capable of ripping a track off. In East Africa an assault on Gaballat, in November 1940, was led by ten tanks almost all of which were put out of action by stripping their tracks on sharp stones hidden in the long grass.

In Tunisia and Europe mud was one of the greatest dangers, and the weight of the tank became its own worst enemy. It was not uncommon for them to churn themselves in until only the turret remained visible. In north-west Europe, particularly, the tanks were not helped by their artillery whose barrages often churned the ground up to an extent reminiscent of the godless wilderness of Flanders in 1917. What had been fairly solid, if rather sticky going could be transformed into an impenetrable glutinous porridge by the sheer weight of shells falling on it. Even when the mud froze in deep winter there were considerable snags. Tanks' tracks require something solid on which to get a grip, and ice or snow on the roads could soon reduce them to uncontrollable giant toboggans. The British suffered particularly here, in the regiments equipped with Churchills, because Shermans had rubber-plated tracks which did provide some kind of grip.

Another basic component of a tank is the gun and here too Allied armour revealed fundamental weaknesses. Throughout the war, in fact, their tanks were consistently outgunned both by the German tanks and by their anti-tank guns. German supremacy was established at an early date and throughout the Middle Eastern campaign, except for the brief heyday of the Matilda II in 1940, British armour was unable to decisively get to grips with its counterpart in the Afrika Korps. At this stage it was not so much because of a disparity in tank armament, though the Germans did have a slight edge, but because of the overwhelming superiority of the latter's anti-tank weapons. The notorious '88' needs no elaboration, and the long 50mm gun also outranged most British tanks. Tank versus tank battles were rare because all Rommel needed to do when faced with impetuous and usually isolated British armoured groups was to lure them on to his cunningly emplaced tiers of anti-tank guns. Time and time again the British fell into this trap and time and time again the German gunners simply shot them to pieces. Even Alamein, with Montgomery's carefully marshalled superiority of tanks, was far from a foregone conclusion: 500 tanks were put out of action, and the REME detachments were perhaps the real battle-winners in that they put 300 of them back before the end of the battle.

With the mass appearance of Shermans and Churchills, the Allies were somewhat better protected though neither of these was ever proof against the deadly '88'. Worse still, even though both had equivalent armament to the best enemy tanks in Africa, they were far inferior to the next generation that fought in Europe, notably the Panther and the Tiger. Comparative figures tell their own story. The 75mm Sherman had no frontal penetration at any range against the Panther or Tiger, though the Panther's own improved 75mm could pierce the front of a Sherman at 3,000yd. The Sherman could penetrate the sides of both German tanks at ranges of 3,000 and 1,000yd respectively, though neither of them could tackle the Sherman's flanks at up to 5,000yd. Some Allied units had the up-gunned 76mm Sherman and with this prospects were better, though the advantage still lay with the Germans. This gun could penetrate the front of a Panther turret at 600yd and a Tiger at half the distance. However, the Panther could do likewise at 3,000yd and the Tiger at 1,800. In fact, neither in Italy nor in north-west Europe, did the terrain often allow fighting at such long ranges and the 76mm Sherman was an adequate counter to the Panther or Tiger as long as it got the first shot in. Most Churchills in Europe were equipped with 6-pounder guns and they, like the bulk of the Shermans, were out-classed by their opponents. The following pre-D-Day conversation was recorded by Andrew Wilson, himself a Churchill commander, and it sums up the balance of forces very succinctly:

'What do the Germans have most of?'

'Panthers. The Panther can slice through a Churchill like butter from a mile away.'

'And how does a Churchill get a Panther?'

'It creeps up on it. When it reaches close quarters, the gunner tries to bounce a shot off the underside of the Panther's gun mantlet. If he's lucky, it goes through a piece of thin armour above the driver's head.'

'Has anybody ever done it?'

'Yes. Davis in "C" Squadron. He's back with headquarters now trying to recover his nerve.'

'What's next on the list?'

'Tigers. The Tiger can get you from a mile and a half.'

'And how does a Churchill get a Tiger?'

'It's supposed to get within 200 yards and put a shot through the periscope.'

'Has anyone ever done it?'

'No.'[15]

As if this was not enough, the Germans also devised a new anti-tank weapon, similar to the American bazooka and the British PIAT, known as the *panzerfaust*. Its range was short, but it was eminently portable and very cheap to produce. Even if man and weapon perished after the first shot, as usually happened, the exchange for an Allied tank was most acceptable to the Germans. Had their forces been more cohesive when this weapon first appeared in large numbers it might well have completely nullified the Allies' vast numerical superiority in tanks, even taking into account their greater capacity to pour replacements off the production lines.[16]

For all these reasons, armoured warfare was far from what certain ex-cavalrymen might have imagined. For the most part tanks were unable to engage in concerted, decisive thrusts, but were limited to slow, piecemeal engagements against superior firepower. But the lesson was not learnt overnight, least of all by the British generals. In North Africa, where the terrain seemed eminently suitable for large-scale armoured movement, the tank regiments and battalions were time and again thrown forward in vain attempts to batter their way through Rommel's defensive lines. Unfortunately not only were the tanks badly outgunned but, as with the artillery, they were rarely employed *en masse* and the attacks at regimental or brigade level never had much hope of a decisive breakthrough. Until Alamein, in fact, the whole history of British armoured tactics is dominated by this persistent dissipation of the armour. Regiments and squadrons, on their own or as part of small mixed columns, were dispatched hither and thither

'into the blue' to see what they could find. Of tactics around El
Agheila, in 1941, Captain Roy Farran wrote: 'It was hard to
understand our tactics at that time. We had lost all contact with the
enemy but were doing endless patrols up and down the Tripoli
frontier, using our valuable reserves of tank mileage. The tanks
were required to cover about sixty miles a day to get to and from
their patrol positions.[17] A new word was coined to describe these
endless wanderings around the desert. It was known as 'swanning', defined as follows by the War Diary of the 2nd Welsh
Guards: 'It means roughly to wander over an area known to be a
battlefield, in an unspecified and probably unknown direction, for
an unnecessary and probably illegal purpose – and it is a term in
very general use.'[18] Even when the opposing armies were not in
contact this policy was not very helpful; during the British
offensives or Rommel's own drives towards Egypt, it became little
short of criminal. Again and again commanders found themselves
unable to marshal a sufficiently large force against an Axis *point
d'appui* and were forced to send in almost derisory numbers of
tanks against strong defensive positions. Prior to Montgomery's
arrival, and on occasions afterwards, the armoured units might
well have set The Charge of the Light Brigade to music as their
signature tune.

In the very first battles in the desert the British, with their
heavily armoured Matilda Mk IIs – so-called Infantry Tanks –
were able to charge against the Italian positions with impunity.
The cavalry analogy is appropriate, though the comparison should
be with Cromwell's Ironsides rather than with later hussars or
lancers. Just as the New Model horsemen trotted up to their
opponents with their knees 'close-locked' under their neighbours'
hams, so did the men of the 7th Royal Tank Regiment, line abreast,
lumber up to the enemy at no more than five miles an hour. Two
waves of tanks were used if necessary and there was a heavy
emphasis, again like the Parliamentarians, upon prompt rally after
the attack. The '88', however, completely nullified the Matilda's
battlefield role and from then on the armour was expected to
emulate the example of Frederickian or Napoleonic cavalry, trust-
ing to élan and sheer courage rather than any responsible assess-
ment of the tanks' capabilities. Such was the case during the
murderous Crusader battles in November and December 1941.
On 19 November, Robert Crisp was told of an attack by the 8th
Hussars and

. . . officers told me how they had seen the Hussars charging into the Jerry tanks, sitting on top of their turrets more or less with their whips out. 'It looked like the run-up to the first fence at a point-to-point,' the adjutant described it. This first action was very typical of a number of those early encounters involving cavalry regiments. They had incredible enthusiasm and dash, and sheer exciting courage which was only curbed by the rapidly decreasing stock of dashing officers and tanks. [19]

But the regular cavalry and yeomanry regiments [20] were not the only ones in whom the 'cavalry spirit' still burned strong. The battalions of the Royal Tank Regiment, nominally the protectors of the infantry, were not unused to being thrown forward like cuirassiers of old. This happened to the 6th Royal Tank Regiment on 20 November when they stormed one ridge between Sidi Rezegh and Ed Duda but were knocked out to a man by four 88s as they went for the next escarpment. Crisp took part in a charge by the 3rd Royal Tank Regiment and two other regiments in which 'at the signal to go we tore across the intervening desert in a manner that would have brought great joy to the Earl of Cardigan'. [21] Jake Wardrop (4th Royal Tank Regiment) took part in an action at Sidi Rezegh when Brigadier 'Jock' Campbell mustered a group of tanks around his staff car. 'We chased after him for about half a mile . . . and there they were – a long line of Mark IIIs and 50mm anti-tank guns, so we went to town on them . . . Quite frankly I was not so strong on this charging business, but we went storming in right up to those tanks, firing as we went . . .' [22] The Royal Tank Regiment suffered badly again in June 1942, in a headlong assault during the Gazala battle when the 7th and 42nd were sent forward against strong enemy positions on Sidra Ridge and at the end of the attack only 12 of the original 70 tanks were still operational. Only six weeks later, during Auchinleck's stand at Alamein, the whole of the 23rd Armoured Brigade was hurled into the fray in a desperate attempt to recapture the initiative. A New Zealand observer saw them as they 'thundered past our northern flank at a great pace, a real Balaclava charge'. After repeated efforts to batter their way through different parts of the German line, the brigade could only rally 11 of the 104 tanks that had gone into action. [23]

Montgomery's arrival in Africa, albeit as second choice, did herald a more concentrated use of armour but this by no means meant the end of the headlong frontal assault. During Alamein, for example, the 9th Armoured Brigade were given just the same kind of suicidal task that faced many of their predecessors. The three regiments of the brigade were directed to assault yet another fortified ridge, Aqqaqir, and to maintain the attack no matter what the casualties. These orders were obeyed to the letter and observers yet again drew the comparison with Balaclava and the Light Brigade. Of the 94 tanks which went into action that night, 75 were knocked out. After Alamein, according to Liddell Hart, 'armoured fighting changed its form . . . and the form which . . . took shape persisted not only in Africa but in the campaigns that followed in Europe. It was a more cautious form of action, at slower tempo. Concentrated punches were superseded by what has been aptly described as a process of "incessant sparring with anti-tank screens".'[24] Although true in terms of the overall view, it should not be thought that the old *modus operandi* had been completely abandoned. The efficacy of enemy anti-tank weapons was only grudgingly acknowledged and many commanders, generally British, were at heart advocates of the possibility of decisive armoured breakthroughs if only the terrain were suitable or they could mass sufficient tanks at one point. To the very end of the war tankmen were on occasion hurled against enemy defences with the same kind of blind faith that had characterised infantry attacks in World War I.

In Tunisia both English and American units were often thrown forward in a somewhat cavalier fashion, and even after the fighting on the First Army's front had bogged down in the mountains that ringed Tunis the tanks were used in a manner that suggests sheer desperation. On 9 April 1943, for example, a projected infantry assault on the Fondouk Pass failed to get off the ground and it was decided to use the tanks as a spearhead force rather than the *masse de manoeuvre* once the Pass had been forced. They did break through, though casualties were high, and a squadron commander summed up the mood of dedicated fatalism when he said to his friends, 'Goodbye, we shall all be killed.' For his part he was quite correct. Captain E. W. M. Maitland (16/5th Lancers) gave a vivid picture of his part in the attack:

Then came the orders to charge. At first the advance seemed a bit sticky, so I told the driver to press on. There were no signs of anti-tank guns yet and speed was probably our best chance . . . The ground, though flat, was very rough, and at the speed we were going the tank rocked like a tug in the high sea . . . On we went, engines revving, Browning rattling, guns crashing, being flung backwards and forwards and from side to side, with the wireless blaring and excitement reaching boiling point. A thud as half the turret lid banged down on my fingers . . . We were getting pretty close now and several tanks were in flames . . . but we kept banging away with the big gun. I sheered off to the right to get on the flank of the gun firing frontally at us. I got round to the right of the cactus grove, about four or five hundred yards away, when another gun shot at us . . . I decided to use our own dust as a smokescreen by turning right, then right again, and once more to the right to try to rush the cactus . . . For what seemed ages we rushed away with our thin backs to that gun, which must flash again at any moment, while I bellowed and banged on the microphone.[25]

If anything, American armoured units arrived in Tunisia in an even more aggressive state of mind than the British cavalrymen. Their training at home had consistently stressed the value of shock action and, as one historian has pointed out, 'they honestly believed that a phalanx of armour thrown fast and close locked like horsed cavalry into battle, would continue to smash its way through even the toughest anti-tank defence, reiterating the doctrine of weight and velocity *à l'outrance* without looking too closely at the . . . resurgence of the gun and armour race.'[26] Their first experiences actually seemed to justify such a creed, notably at Oran where they smashed through desultory Vichy resistance with all guns blazing. Contact with the Germans, however, soon changed their mood. Captain Ingersoll wrote an excellent description of the new cautious type of tactics they were obliged to adopt:

Tanks do not rush forward in the mechanised version of the flying wedge . . . They advanced hesitatingly, like diffident fat boys coming across the floor at a party to ask for the next dance, stopping at the slightest excuse, going back, then coming on again, and always apparently seeking the longest way round. When they do have to cross a plain they postpone the evil moment as long as possible by clinging to the slower slopes of the nearest ridge until some invisible force pushes them unhappily into the open. When they follow a road, they zigzag in a series of tangents to it, crossing it occasionally and staying on it only when there is no other way through difficult country. They are timid creatures.[27]

These, in fact, were the basic features of Allied armoured tactics throughout the rest of the war. Caution eventually became the better part of valour. Even so, one should not see this new mood as a purely rational response to the increased power of the defensive. For, in Italy, north-west Europe and the Far East terrain, too, was a big constraint and generally made it impossible for the tanks to engage in mass attacks, even had they so wanted. Normandy *bocage*, Dutch waterways, German forests, Italian vineyards and mountains, Burmese or Pacific jungles, all forced armoured units to operate in dribs and drabs, rarely moving at much more than a snail's pace. Indeed, the whole process was dialectical. For not only did the nature of the ground impose severe restrictions on the tank's mobility, it also enhanced even further the role of the defensive. To the innate power of anti-tank guns, bazookas, artillery or hull-down tanks was added virtual invisibility and endless possibilities for surprise and ambush. The following descriptions of conditions in Italy apply almost equally to other theatres. The historian of the 17/21st Lancers wrote: 'Italy was not to provide the opportunity to use [the armoured division] . . . at its best again. Fighting with an armoured division in Italy was like using a dagger to open a tin; the dagger is blunted and the tin is jagged and twisted.'[28] The account of the Royal Scots Greys' operations elaborates the point:

> No country more unsuitable for tanks could be imagined. The ground that was not practically impassable mountainside was flat, very thickly covered with vineyards, orchards and villages, and intersected by a host of streams, sunken lanes and ditches. The vegetation was most often thickest at the height of a turret top of a tank. The result was that an anti-tank gunner had a longer range of vision that the tank commander, although vision at ground level was often very restricted. The anti-tank gunner could generally see up to about fifty or a hundred yards, farther in the open areas of reclaimed land, whereas the tank commander was lucky if he could see twenty yards.[29]

All this meant that the tanks were remarkably vulnerable. On the face of it, it might seem that armour plating offered tank crews an enormous advantage over the infantry, a smug imperviousness to the normal hazards of the battlefield. This was far from the case. Their armour was little proof against armour-piercing shot or mines, and the nature of the terrain denied them the mobility to take their opponents by surprise or back away swiftly from a dangerous situation. Moreover, where an infantryman could dive for cover when under fire, the tankmen were trapped in mobile dungeons, obliged to keep moving until they were actually hit. Armoured personnel often expressed sympathy for the infantry but in actual fact they rarely met footsloggers who had the slightest desire to change places. Stephen Bagnall wrote:

Tanks are different . . . We didn't like them. I'm talking about the machines of course. We all liked tankmen. We admired them. I would rather have been an infantryman than a tankman any day of the week. It might feel safer inside so long as nothing happens, but you couldn't hope for a pleasant death if anything did happen shut up in a blazing steel room that was rapidly becoming white-hot and filled with an infernal symphony of fireworks as your own ammunition caught fire and added to the horror.[30]

The tankmen themselves were very aware of such possibilities and as the war went on, when left to their own devices, became increasingly cautious, aware that 'swanning' was a thing of the past and each tank must look to its own protection just as carefully as any infantryman patrolling between the lines. On the whole, they ceased to attempt firing on the move. The early 2-pounders had been fitted with shoulder rests and were moved manually within the turret, a direct imitation of naval quick-firing guns, and the tanks themselves were supposed to operate like fast gunboats. This sort of tactic was abandoned and tanks fired only when stationary and where possible from a hull-down position, only showing enough of the turret to allow clearance for the barrel.

But the most drastic tactical reappraisal concerned the tankers' relationship with the infantry. At the beginning of the war the so-called 'cruiser' tanks had been regarded as a virtually autonomous arm, neither owing the infantry their support nor deemed likely to need the latter's protection. In 1941 and 1942, in the Western Desert, many battalions came to view the armoured units with suspicion, accusing them of hanging back and leaving foot soldiers in the lurch. For the most part, however, this was simply an unfortunate by-product of senior commanders' insistence upon strewing the tanks all over the desert in a blindly opportunistic fashion and with little or no regard for other forward troops. Also armour and infantry rarely underwent joint training and thus had little understanding of each other's abilities or problems. After the Cauldron battles Brigadier Fletcher, of the 9th Indian Brigade, commented tartly on their conduct:

There appears to have been a complete misunderstanding between the 22nd Armoured Brigade and Nine Brigade as to the capabilities and tasks of the two brigades. The 22nd Armoured Brigade appears to have thought that a battalion could establish itself in a box in the Desert in a matter of half an hour . . . I consider that infantry who have to operate with tanks should be trained with them. There would not then be this wide divergence of opinion as to the tasks and capabilities of the two parts of a force engaged in any one operation. In the Desert infantry require forty-eight hours in which to establish a box which can stand by itself against an enemy tank attack. In addition, they must be allowed to lay mines. Lack of mutual understanding and of common doctrines extended beyond the failure of tanks and infantry to understand each other.[31]

By 1943, however, not only was the armour more aware of the needs of the infantry and foremost artillery, but it had also realised that the former could provide essential protection from anti-tank guns and, in Europe, *panzerfausts*. In Italy, north-west Europe and the Far East it was finally appreciated that tanks were far from being invulnerable cataphracts, but must at all times be aware that their very survival would often depend on the closest co-operation with the infantry.

As has been noted, certain lessons had already been learnt in Tunisia. In Ingersoll's words, tanks were becoming 'timid creatures' and increasingly saw their role as one of co-operation. On the one hand, they provided fire support for the infantry. One journalist was with US II Corps when they came up against a German-held ridge with

> . . . caves and holes blasted in the cliff face where enemy machine gunners waited . . . But they had a plan for dealing with it. Whenever the forward troops came under heavy fire from one or other of the enemy's nests they plastered its loopholes with tracer bullets as a signal to the tanks and artillery spotters behind them that it was on those particular targets that they wished their own shells to explode.[32]

On the other hand, the first steps were taken to provide infantry cover for the tanks. Even before they reached Tunisia, during the pursuit of Rommel after Alamein, the 7th Armoured Division laid great emphasis upon holding armoured, infantry and artillery units in close combination. The brunt of the attack on enemy anti-tank guns still fell on the armour, but artillery forward observation officers worked in closest concert with squadron commanders during the actual assault, and the infantry were always kept close at hand to exploit local successes. The divisional history records:

> When the half light came, the tanks moved into close range and the rattle of Besas replaced the crack of the tank guns as 'soft' targets presented themselves. At this stage the motor infantry were launched

to complete the work of the tanks by attacking such enemy gun crews as remained in position, finishing off lame ducks, clearing the battlefield and pushing forward patrols to harass the enemy as he withdrew into the darkness.[33]

But it was in Italy that armour/infantry co-operation really began to take hold. The following account, by Brigadier Richard Goodbody, of the 2nd Armoured Brigade's tactics in Italy is an excellent resumé of the new style of fighting that was forced upon the virtually 'blind' armoured units. In any attack

. . . the infantry were senior partners. They first decided how a position should be attacked, and were then given an appropriate number of tanks to support them. The rest of the tanks were responsible for helping and supporting the leading tanks from behind. The infantry scoured all bushes, hedges and ditches to clear out any bazooka-men or snipers who might be in a position to pick off tanks or their commanders at ranges of a hundred yards or less . . . There was no hard and fast rule as to who should lead. It might change as much as three or four times in a mile, depending on the terrain and on whether opposition was likely to be anti-tank or anti-infantry. In this way the best anti-tank tactics possible in the circumstances were superimposed, as it were, on the infantry tactics. Each partner was aware of the difficulties and limitations of the other. If in the event tanks suffered heavy casualties, they saved the lives of many infantrymen and the sacrifice was worthwhile.[34]

Such close co-operation was also the rule in north-west Europe. There were, of course, occasions when the armour moved freely over large distances – the 11th Armoured covered 340 miles in 6 days during the drive to Antwerp, and US units thrust forward at a great pace after the crossing of the Rhine causing one tankman, Lieutenant G. P. Leibman (5th US Armoured Division) to remark, 'All we do is attack and push on, attack and push on. It is France all over again, except this time the flags flying from the houses are not French tricolours, but flags of surrender.'[35] But this only happened when the Germans were retreating in disarray, their line ruptured by *combined* assaults on the ground and from the air. Whenever the Germans chose to stand, terrain and defensive firepower both made it extremely difficult for the armour alone to batter a way through. Right up to the last month of the war in Europe the tanks had to rely on the infantry for protection during an advance.

This protection was necessary from the very beginning of the campaign. The Normandy *bocage* was particularly unsuitable terrain for armour as the German anti-tank crews could remain concealed until the tanks were almost on top of them and needed to cover only the roads as it was down these that the tanks were forced to travel. An officer of the 3rd Scots Guards has described how these problems forced the tankmen to rely almost completely on the infantry for protection:

> We advanced with the infantry right round us, to protect us from bazooka men and snipers, and from hedge to hedge, making each hedge a bound. Each hedge was practically a tank obstacle anyway, as they were always on top of very high earth-banks. As we came through a hedge we made the infantry look first to see if there was a Panther in the next field. If not, we went through into the middle of the field, brought the supporting Troops up to the hedge behind, and then settled down to a quarter of an hour's speculative shooting-up of the next hedge, H.E. into likely looking places, and Besa everywhere, including the tree-tops. All this you must imagine happening under intense mortar fire and very considerable small arms fire . . . coming from all over the place, but from nowhere where you could pinpoint it . . . This may sound a very slow method of advance but it paid time and time again.[36]

This officer also notes that the Scots Guard were more adept at this kind of joint enterprise than other regiments because in the Guards' Armoured Division infantry and armoured components from the same regiment were brigaded together and had practised such techniques for a long time. Be that as it may, the 'ordinary' armoured divisions were not slow to learn the relevant lessons. The history of the Fife and Forfar Yeomanry notes that by the end of 1944

> . . . a sound technique had been evolved for co-operation with infantry . . . [and we] worked fairly continuously with the foot soldiers . . . The technique employed was sufficiently elastic to be varied according to the circumstances. When advancing in open country the leading squadron was 'loose', that is, it was unencumbered by infantry. But the two remaining squadrons each carried a company of infantry on the backs of their tanks. This meant that approximately one section of infantry could be accommodated on each armoured vehicle. The Infantry Battalion Commander . . . had a wireless set on the regimental frequency. The result . . . was that any infantry company commander riding along on his tank could speak to his commanding officer at short notice. As soon as opposition was encountered, generally in a village, a tank squadron carrying its infantry company were brought up to go into action and tackle the enemy. In this way both flexibility

and speed were maintained in clearing up minor opposition and in pressing behind a disorganised enemy.[37]

In this account the emphasis is upon mutual co-operation, but other accounts stress the heavy degree to which the tanks had to depend on the infantry for their own survival. The key factor here, especially during the battle for Germany itself, was the *panzerfaust*. The Fife and Forfar's historian recorded:

How the troops hated the bazooka. Enemy infantry [so] armed . . . could nip swiftly from one position to another, making it often impossible to locate them. So tank machine gunners used a generous proportion of incendiary cartridges. And these, given the slightest encouragement, would start off a fire wherever they landed. That very often discouraged the bazooka boys, and it also led to an impressive looking trail of bush and forest fires and even burning buildings.[38]

Most units adopted such random tactics at times. The history of the 7th Armoured Division tells how

. . . men with bazookas were the chief menace to the armour. They would lie in wait by the roadside or near a roadblock and with one discharge from their cheap single-shooters could immobilise or destroy a tank. Spraying the sides of the road with machine gun fire as the tank moved forward was all the crew could do unless the going permitted the tanks to travel at full speed which greatly reduced the enemy's chance of scoring a hit.[39]

But such tactics were hit-and-miss at best and often the going did not permit the tanks to roar through in such a devil-may-care fashion. The 3/4th County of London Yeomanry, for example, got caught in a forest just across the Rhine, known to all as Bazooka Alley. One officer recalled:

At the end of a forest glade tanks began to bog down. The woods were full of enemy armed with rifles and bazookas who put up a vigorous fight. Owing to the trees, ruts and ditches it was difficult to move forward or backward, and the mist and darkness made it impossible to bring effective fire to bear. In these circumstances it was a moot point whether to stay in one's tank and be hit by a bazooka or get out and be sniped.[40]

In such circumstances, therefore, it was vital to send the infantry in front of the armour to flush out anti-tank guns and bazookas before they could actually get a tank within their sights. The history of the 4/7th Royal Dragoon Guards is candid about the gulf between theory and reality in pre-D-Day armoured doctrine. An operation they undertook on 11 June

> . . . was the first time that we had made an attack with infantry on an objective, planned according to the book, and as such it was a dismal failure. The theory which had been preached for combined tank and infantry attack was that the attack should go in waves, with tanks followed by infantry, followed by more tanks. Experience soon showed that to have tanks leading at all was a mistake; that in close country they must go side by side with the infantry, and in more open country they could give best support from a position slightly in rear or to a flank.[41]

Peter Elstob wrote that, as the campaign progressed, he and his colleagues 'had discovered that in close country an unaccompanied tank was helpless against concealed enemy infantry armed with bazookas . . . Now the tanks carried infantry on their backs who went in to search out the enemy lying in wait for the armour'.[42]

Fortified defensive lines were another severe problem for the armour and they were rarely able to smash their way through without the help of the infantry and the engineers. Their contribution to such an assault was not negligible, however, and used as self-propelled artillery they could play a useful part in knocking out strong-points once they had been pinpointed and isolated. John Foley took part in operations against the Siegfried Line where the numerous pill-boxes were often too tough a nut for unaided infantry. In such cases, after isolating the pill-box with smoke,

> . . . we fired high explosives at the embrasures, and sometimes this was sufficient to persuade the pill-box crew that the war held no future for them. But if not, we had a very effective weapon in the shape of one of the funnies: they called it an AVRE . . . [with] a petard which hurled a dustbin sized charge of high explosive. This usually succeeded in blasting the embrasure wide open and causing the occupants to lose all further interest in the campaign. Yet sometimes it didn't, and then we carried out the third movement of the drill which was to bring up a flame-throwing tank . . . There was no fourth movement to this drill; it wasn't really necessary.[43]

The essential point, however, still remains. Despite all the seeming transformations in the conduct of war in the twentieth century, machines still did not dominate the battlefield. Rather, their seeming invincibility had been negated by other devices, and just as these could be easily handled by ordinary infantrymen so did it fall, as ever, upon other infantry to seek out their opposite numbers and smooth the path of the all too vulnerable tanks. It would be contentious to try and assess the relative importance of armour and infantry in World War II. But what has to be admitted is that the former could not have fulfilled any useful role without the latter. Whether the reverse was also true seems at times open to doubt. Certainly there were many infantry assaults in which the aid of tanks was a hindrance or a pure chimera. Of the former case, an anonymous US infantry officer wrote:

> The best way, even under favourable conditions, to completely immobilise troops in a small area is to put an armoured outfit there too . . . Did you ever try to keep field telephones in operation with tanks all over the place? – Well, I don't recommend it. The resulting confusion made it extremely difficult for either the infantry or the armor to get any real effort started, and time which should have been spent by the commanders in working out their own problems frequently had to be spent in arguing with each other about who would do what, where and when, or why not etc.[44]

The following remarks by an officer of the 3rd Scots Guards, whilst patting his own unit on the back, are pretty damning about the general level of support that infantry units could expect from armour. He is discussing the various lessons learnt from the fighting in late 1944. One of these was that

> . . . the tanks must support the infantry, and not *vice versa. This is where everybody else went wrong.* Tank crews can very easily get into an attitude of mind where they think that, not only does the whole battle depend on them, but that, if they suffer losses, they are so important that they need not go on. Also that once they have captured ground all their responsibilities are ended . . . [But] if you can once convince the infantry that you will see them on to the objective at any cost, that you will not desert them the moment a German tank appears, and that once you have got them there, that you will stay and see that nobody pushes them off, then the battle is as good as won.[45]

Such, then, was the pattern of most armoured fighting in the later years of the war, when the defensive had once again got the measure of the new armoured wonder weapon. It should not be thought, however, that Allied commanders in Europe had given up hope of using massed tanks to make a decisive breach through enemy positions. In both Italy and north-west Europe one detects a constant sense of frustration that the massive Allied numerical superiority in AFVs could not be used to more spectacular advantage. As the two armies crawled up Italy, senior officers looked eagerly to the day when they would break through into the supposed tank country of the Lombardy Plain when once again the armour could be deployed *en masse* in more traditional cavalry manoeuvres. Their impatience led to at least one debacle of the sort that had characterised war in the Western Desert. During the Gothic Line offensive of autumn 1944 the eternal search for a vulnerable *point d'appui* in the German defences came to centre on Point 153 in front of the river Marecchia. It had been hoped that the Germans were badly overstretched in this vicinity, yet when it became apparent to those on the scene that this was far from the case the attack was still ordered in, the Queen's Bays being responsible for taking Point 153 itself. The operation was doomed from the start, the regiment having to advance across more than a mile of open ground into the teeth of German anti-tank guns which had the ranges calculated to a nicety. An anonymous officer of the Bays has left an account of what followed:

> We were ordered to make the attack in the face of the anti-tank screen firing down the line of advance. We knew that we should not get far even if we could spot the guns that had already fired . . . While we waited for the word to go, we looked at the ground we had to advance over. There wasn't a stitch of cover anywhere that a tank could get hull-down behind and fire . . . [We topped the crest and] armour-piercing shot seemed to come from all directions . . . As they halted to fire, to locate the opposition, the tanks were knocked out one by one. Most of them burst into flames immediately. A few were disabled, the turrets jammed or the tank made immobile. As the survivors jumped out, some of them made a dash across the open to get back over the crest . . . but they were almost all mown down by German machine gun fire . . . All but three tanks [ie twenty-four] of the two squadrons that took part in the attack were destroyed, and many gallant officers and men were killed in action that morning.[46]

But perhaps the worst tank slaughter of all was during the great battle for Caen, when Montgomery launched one offensive after another in increasingly desperate attempts to batter his way through and link with the Americans to encircle the bulk of the German forces in France. In these attacks, notably Operations

Goodwood (18–21 July), Totalise (8–11 August) and Tractable (14–16 August), the armour attacked with the infantry but all hopes for a significant penetration rested with the former. Many armoured units suffered heavily in the first of these operations, not least the Fife and Forfar Yeomanry. Lieutenant W. S. Brownlie was a member of this regiment and his diary amply conveys the horror of the occasion as the tanks ran up against numerous concealed anti-tank guns and hull-down Panthers and Tigers:

> I had little idea of what was happening to the rest of the chaps down in front, but tanks were blazing everywhere and the number of burnt and shattered men who kept crawling back through the waist-high corn was frightening. We did what we could for them, but many died or were killed by the shells which were raining down continuously. I ran out of ammo. about midday and replenished from a knocked out tank. By the middle of the afternoon the barrels of the two machine guns were worn out and had to be renewed . . . It was the blackest moment in the history of the Regiment and not a word was said by anyone except in such phrases as 'You know . . . has had it' and so on.[47]

In fact the regiment lost 51 tanks and over 100 men. Total armoured casualties during Goodwood are a matter of some conjecture but it seems unlikely that they were less than 300 tanks written off completely and another 100 requiring attention by the REME. In Operation Tractable the task of forcing a way through the German defences was given to the Canadians: 160 tanks were allocated to the first wave and 90 to the second, the spearhead infantry riding in improvised Kangaroos. Sergeant L. R. Gariépy was in the forefront of what became generally known as 'The Mad Charge':

> We, the crew commanders, knew then that many of us would not make it; it was inconceivable, in view of these tremendous defences. Each of us looked at the other, wondering: How many? Who? . . . The smoke-screen supposed to blind the enemy turned out to be a thick dense mist in the path of our advance, soon supplemented by the dust clouds created by the tremendous bombing; the area was 'vision zero'. Very little could be done to keep direction except by aiming the tank 'at the sun' . . . The only reason why our casualties were not very much higher is that the smog obscured us to them as much as it obscured them to us. Speed, nothing but speed, as on we went, crashing through obstacles at twenty to twenty-five miles per hour, very rough inside a tank going across country, and each hedge hid from four to six anti-tank guns, pointed right at us, waiting . . . We just barged ahead, some

of the tanks appeared to be going on at crazy angles, and in the confusion I did not know who was right and who was wrong; I just kept charging 'at the sun', blasting everything large enough to hide a field gun, and taking a terrible whipping in the turret of the bucking 32-ton monster.[48]

In the Far East, however, not even the most hide-bound traditionalist could have hoped to indulge in such tactics. There the constraints of terrain and the enemy's mode of warfare were absolutely binding. In both Burma and the Pacific armour only had a very limited role, being of necessity relegated to merely supporting the infantry and very dependent on that same infantry for its own protection. As was seen in an earlier chapter, Japanese bunkers were one of the main problems for the Allies and most operations centred round the reduction of such strong-points. Such tanks as there were out East were generally used as mobile artillery to supplement this kind of attack. Not surprisingly, tank versus tank battles were almost unknown and in Burma the Japanese only once tried to bring British armour to battle, when they attacked 'A' Company of the 3rd Carabiniers in the Kabaw Valley in March 1943. They were routed for their pains. Bunker-bashing was the Allied armour's normal function, and an officer of the 7th Light Cavalry noted that 'it was considered great fun to stand literally ten feet away from the slit of a bunker and pump every available round into it, also to run backwards and forwards over the bunker until the whole thing collapsed'.[49] Even more than in Europe, the armour had no autonomous role but was very much responsive to the demands of the infantry. This was equally the case during the great sieges in Assam. At Imphal, after the Japanese's own fortifications had been destroyed, the tanks proved very useful in carrying barbed wire and other stores up to the captured positions and helping the infantry to consolidate them, as well as bringing the wounded back.

Moreover, just as in Europe, the tanks were very dependent on infantry support to protect them from ambush. On Guam, units of the 77th US Division followed their division's Standing Operating Procedure on tank-infantry co-operation:

> The plan called for the attached tank platoon to advance with the support elements of the leading company: one just off the trail on one side, another echeloned twenty or thirty yards to the rear in the brush

on the other side of the trail; the three remaining tanks of the platoon to follow about a hundred yards in the rear. This formation was designed to enable the tanks to support one another if an anti-tank weapon was encountered; to keep the leading tanks out of the centre of the trail; and to widen it for the foot troops. Infantrymen protected each tank from Japanese who might try to rush it with grenades or heavy charges. One moved in front, guiding it round holes and large stumps, and watching for mines. Fundamental in the plan was that foot soldiers should precede the tanks and not merely follow them into action.[50]

W. H. Lawrence, of the *New York Times* described a small action on Okinawa which gave clear proof of the great limitations imposed on armour in this type of warfare. A tank

... moved into battle ... accompanied by a Browning Automatic Rifle team of three men and four riflemen ... Three times this tank went out to fire its 75mm shells and machine gun bullets. Three times the armed infantrymen walked with it, both to shoot at snipers and to protect the tank against satchel charges of explosives that the Japanese try to plant under the treads of our armour ... For the day, this tank and the others that fought beside it, and the infantrymen who tried to move along with them, could count no tangible gain in yards won. To be sure, they had probably killed lots of Japanese. Undoubtedly they had knocked out a few more pillboxes and smashed in the mouths of caves from which the Japanese weapons operated. But our men had fallen too, and our armour had taken a terrific beating. This is war on Okinawa.[51]

Burma was no different. Of operations in 1945, Lieutenant Colonel M. R. Smeeton (Probyn's Horse) wrote:

We knew what the infantry wanted us to do – to go ahead and clean up the mess so that they could advance with the least danger – but they did not always understand, in this very close fighting amongst smoke and trees and burning huts, how blind, ungainly and vulnerable the tanks themselves could feel, in spite of their power, when too far ahead or separated from the infantry. Eventually we worked out a system of very simple signals, and became more and more adept in recognising the direction of fire and spotting the enemy foxholes and bunkers. Like all forms of shooting it was a question of learning where to look and what to look for.[52]

I have dwelt at some length upon the tactical handling of armour in World War II in order to clear up any misconceptions about its use and to emphasise the severe limitations imposed by terrain and defensive weaponry. As with all land operations between 1939 and

1945, the cliché 'war of movement' must be employed carefully, and it should be constantly borne in mind how often, for the armour just as much as for the infantry, battles were simply a brutal slugging match in which gains were measured in terms of yards rather than miles. It still remains to be seen just what this type of warfare meant for the tank crews in terms of their day-to-day existence.

As already hinted, it might seem, at first sight, as though their lot was appreciably better than that of the infantry, in that they had a motorised vehicle to carry them from place to place. The tankers themselves were certainly convinced of this advantage when they passed weary columns of marching infantry, but their mode of transport had, in fact, many inherent drawbacks. Tanks were designed to strike a balance between mobility, firepower and ar-moured protection; designers, therefore, worried about engines, guns and armour before they even spared a thought for facilities for the crewmen themselves. Though one obviously had to fit the latter in somehow, their comfort had always a very low priority. To the end of the war tanks remained noisy and extremely uncomfort-able and generally afforded a poor alternative to moving on foot.

For one thing, their crews were not spared the extremes of climate. Surprisingly, perhaps, they were often very cold because the tank's engine was deemed more important than the men who manned it. In many models the engine was cooled by a fan in the turret and this wafted cold air, rain or snow indiscriminately over the actual motor and those in the bowels of the tank. The Matilda I was notorious for this as was the ubiquitous Sherman in which there was 'always a considerable downdraught going through the commander's cupola, and in a snowstorm this had its disad-vantages. A snowflake which is descending quite happily several feet away from the tank, is suddenly sucked out of the vertical and whipped up against the unhappy commander'.[53] The Cromwell, too, suffered from this defect and more cold air or whatever was sucked through the driver's visor. In the desert, however, this cold air could provide some sort of ventilation and air-conditioning. It was for this reason that although temperatures in stationary tanks often reached alarming levels, the starting of the engine brought speedy relief, and heat stroke, over which many fears had been expressed, was never a problem amongst armoured units.

Lack of space was another problem common to all tanks. Of the Stuart, Roy Farran wrote: 'I think the Light Tank Mark VIB must be the most uncomfortable vehicle ever invented. It is like travelling along on the inside of a sharp cornered rocking horse and it is impossible to move anywhere without skinning your elbows.'[54] The tiny Stuart is rather an extreme example but, in fact later tanks only offered marginally more room to their crews. A Sherman, for example, was 20ft long, 9ft wide and 11ft high. Into that area had to be fitted an engine, petrol tank, breech mechanisms, ammunition and stores, as well as five men, all of whom were performing fairly energetic actions most of the time.[55] Only great familiarity with the interior of the tank enabled one to perform these actions without bumping into a fellow crewman or clouting oneself on one of the innumerable levers, handles and stanchions that projected everywhere with what seemed deliberate bloody-mindedness. Fighting in such vehicles had much in common with playing squash in an 'iron maiden'. The cramped conditions, and the instability of a tank on the move, soon overrode one maxim of pre-war armoured theory. Before 1940 it had been assumed that tank commanders in action would remain inside their turrets, with the hatch down, and observe the battle by looking through a small periscope. This proved impossible in practice and, despite the risk, they found they could only give adequate directions to the crew by standing up in the turret or even sitting on the edge of the open hatch. Peter Elstob recalled that one of the first lessons he had to learn in Normandy was that 'a tank with hatches closed was like a blind monster at the mercy of a fast, sharp-eyed enemy, and that, dangerous as it was for the commander to keep his head out, it was not so dangerous as shutting himself in'.[56] Moreover, no matter what the risks, the commander at least knew that he had the best chance of getting out quickly if the tank was hit, and was somewhat aloof from the claustrophobic confusion beneath his feet. Alan Gilmour (48th Royal Tank Regiment) was a driver in a Churchill in Tunisia and he has given a graphic description of one action that makes even the life of a powder monkey at Trafalgar seem preferable:

With every round fired clouds of dust obscure the driving compartment, and every time the 6-pdr fires two feet above my driving hatch the goggles jump on my nose and I experience the sensation of being hit on the head with a mallet. The roar of the tank's engine is drowned by louder noises so that its behaviour had to be gauged by the instrument panel, and yet I am loathe to take my eyes for an instant from periscope or visor. Dimly the festoon lamps show my co-driver, sweat pouring down his face, eyes glued to the telescopic sight of his gun. In the low padded compartment . . . we crouch, the two of us shapeless figures engulfed in a miasma of smoke and dust through which the facia lights barely penetrate. Behind us in the turret the crew are choking with the fumes of cordite which the fans are powerless to dissipate. Cut off from visible contact with the outside world, the wireless operator, wedged in his seat, cannot possibly know in which direction the vehicle is moving. To all five of us the intercom, our lifeline, relays a bedlam of orders, distortions and cries from another world.[57]

Each crew member had his own problems and it would be hard to say which of their jobs was the least exhausting. The gunner, of course, had fairly long periods when there was nothing to do, though in tanks with a crew of four he usually acted as co-driver as well. And when in action he had to concentrate very hard, trying to observe his targets and the fall of his shots as well as listening to the commander for instructions. As Kenneth Macksey explains:

The introduction of bigger guns firing at higher velocities brought vexatious problems in their train . . . In order to be sure of hitting the enemy, a tank gunner was dependent upon his commander's ability, rather than his own, to detect the target and, above all, to estimate its range. Upon this data he could then align his telescope graticule upon the target and open fire. More often than not, because human error intervened, this resulted in a miss, whereupon the gunner, if he had observed the fall of shot, could make corrections to his aim before firing again; dependent then upon the accuracy of his observations and corrections, not to say his coolness when in action, a hit might be obtained with the second or subsequent shots.[58]

If indeed there was time for such a shot, for once a tank had fired it usually meant that it had declared its position and an enemy tank or anti-tank gun would be frantically trying to zero itself in on the target. Here the role of the loader was crucial as he desperately grabbed a shell, hoping to distinguish between high explosive and armour-piercing, and rammed it into the breech. Robert Crisp described his frenzied actions, though he suggests that the frantic tempo had its own compensations. 'The loader was all right . . . He would be too busy to be scared . . . tugging the next shell out of its bracket, pulling down the ejection lever, whipping in a new shell with enough force to close the breech, bending under to tap the gunner in the "gun ready" signal, and then starting all over again as he heard the shot and saw the recoil next to his face.'[59]

The driver's job was one of almost unrelieved fatigue as he wrestled with two clutches and sluggish controls, bouncing around in his tiny compartment, peering through the slit trying to reconcile what little he could see with the never-ending babble of instructions from the commander. Nor was his job over when the tank arrived in position at night. Some maintenance work was always necessary before he could bed down, and the next morning he had to be first up to ensure that the tank would still start. But the commander's job was no sinecure. In action the mental effort was enormous as he tried to co-ordinate the actions of driver and gunner, assess the stream of information coming through his earphones, and make snap decisions upon the evidence of his own eyes. Nor was simply moving from place to place a mere matter of lounging in his turret like royalty on display. Long drives, whether or not the tanks made much actual ground, could be fearsomely tiring. Pat Hobart of the 3rd Armoured Brigade wrote of the drive to Dunkirk, in 1940: 'I can't recall much of these days except endless driving and a great tiredness . . . and straining tired eyes through the dark to see the vehicle ahead by night, and all the time . . . a lack of knowledge of what was going on, feet aching from hour upon hour of standing in the turret and bruised shoulders, back and chest from the jolting of the cupola ring.'[60] Nor was this merely the psychological shock of defeat. Even during the great advances in north-west Europe sheer fatigue could take most of the satisfaction from knowing that the enemy was on the run. A squadron leader of the 8th King's Royal Irish Hussars wrote of the drive from Caen to Bayeux in late July 1944: 'I have never been so tired. For the last five days I have averaged three hours sleep per night and that inside a tank. During this night march I kept falling down in my turret, and at last handed over to my lance-corporal and slept on the back of the tank.'[61]

Fatigue, in fact, was the most besetting problem for armoured personnel. In this respect they were actually worse off than the infantry, generally being driven even harder and having to get by on remarkably little sleep. In the Western Desert the authorities drew up a report, presented in July 1942, which suggested that tank crews were being pressed too hard, and the facts it put forward would certainly seem to substantiate this conclusion:

The following is a brief outline of the average tank crew's day. The men are awakened at about 0500 hours i.e. before daylight, and get into

their tanks which they drive out of leaguer[62] to battle or patrol positions, which they reach by first light. Battles commonly occur in the
early morning or in the late afternoon or evening . . . It is unusual for
actual fighting to occupy more than three of the daylight hours. The
rest of the time is spent in alert watchfulness or patrolling, and in
waiting for or preparing an attack. It is universally agreed that these
hours of expectancy are much more trying than the actual battle
periods . . . [and] it is not at all uncommon for the crew to remain in
the tank for the whole of the daylight hours. Engine noise and fumes,
gun fumes and the wearing of headphones all day add to fatigue.

   It is usually 2100 hours or later . . . before the opposing tanks
gradually draw apart and finally seek their respective leaguers. This
often necessitates two or three hours night driving . . . On reaching
leaguer they must first refuel, load and stow away ammunition – a
process which requires $1\frac{1}{2}$–2 hours – and must then carry out . . .
general maintenance . . . and distribute rations. It is rarely earlier than
0030 or 0100 hours when the men are at last able to get into their
blankets . . . It is evident that three hours is the maximum sleep that
can be obtained.[63]

Even without saying anything of the mental strain of action, the
report is eloquent testimony to the extreme hardship of the tank
crews' life. This terse statement by an anonymous officer in Libya,
in November 1941, is further indication of the enormous psychological pressures involved:

An action takes it out of a man. A sane man is afraid of being killed; a
man likes a meal. You may have the food aboard, but you may lack the
chance to cook it; as often as not it's army biscuits and jam, spread in
the turret on the move. The machine gun gives off toxic fumes when
fired. That does not help. When a shell bursts near, the turret acts like a
drum – that's how my gunner got concussion; that doesn't help
either.[64]

Even though in Europe the daily distances covered were much
less, the daily routine was just as wearing. The history of the 16/5th
Lancers describes a typical day during the fighting in Italy, when
the regiment was moving towards Perugia, in May 1944. The tanks
had not reached leaguer, or 'harbour' as they called it, until
10.00 pm when orders for the next day were given, a meal was
heated up on the turret floor and, once 'B' Echelon had arrived, the
tanks were replenished and given essential repairs.[65] All this, of
course, was done in complete darkness. At about 1.00 am they
finally bedded down only to have to rise again at 3.30. Similar
routines were followed in north-west Europe, particularly when

the tanks were moving forward to take up the 'slack' left by German withdrawals. A regimental history paints a striking picture of life in Churchill tanks during the Normandy campaign:

> Five men in close proximity, three in the turret and two below in the driving compartment, all in a thick metal oven, soon produced a foul smell, humanity . . . cordite and heat. Noise: the perpetual 'mush' through the earphones twenty-four hours each day, and through it the machinery noises, the engine as a background, with the whine of the turret trainer and the thud and rattle of the guns an accompaniment. The surge of power as the tank rose up to the crest of a bank; the pause at the top while the driver, covered with sweat and dust and unable to see, tried to balance his forty tons before the bone-jarring crash into the field beyond, with every loose thing taking life and crashing round inside the turret . . . After dark was the time for maintenance . . . [and] the guns had to be cleaned and all repairs finished before first light and stand-to. Thanks to the tanks, repairs were not many, but crews could not go on for long without a rest.[66]

An American tankman, Nat Frankel (4th US Armoured Division) has drawn attention to another disadvantage of such periods of continual movement. Pushing off from Fénétrange, in December 1944, his unit was

> . . . pushing so hard we were virtually maniacal. It was as if the entire division were performing in a 'Roadrunner' cartoon, or as if a 33 LP were being played at 78. We didn't even stop to piss. Individual soldiers would squeeze into the turrets and urinate down the sides of the tanks. Sometimes two men were back to back, their cocks bent over a metallic ridge. An odd phenomenon, as if the tanks themselves were running with yellow sweat.[67]

More often, as has already been stressed, the tanks could make little forward progress. Even so, the daily routine remained much the same, whilst being bogged down in front of strong German positions brought its own tribulations. One of the worst was that mortar and artillery fire was so heavy that the crews were obliged to grab what sleep they could in the tanks themselves. This was far from easy. John Foley described the way it was done in his Churchill. Looking at one some years after the war he

> . . . had difficulty in believing we ever managed it . . . But we were helped, of course, by the diminutive size of the ex-jockey . . . [in our crew]. He used to curl up around his seat in a weird, foetus-like attitude. This allowed Crosby and Hunter to let down the backs of

152 COMBAT: ARTILLERY AND ARMOUR

their seats and by drawing their knees up to their waists they were able to lay down. Pickford used to sit on an ammunition bin, wedge his knees against the front of his wireless set, rest the back of his weary head on the two-inch bomb-thrower, and somehow snore. I was the luckiest of all. I had a tiny tip-up seat about the size of a tea-plate. Perched firmly on this, with my feet resting on top of the 75mm gun, I was able to drop my chin on my chest and doze off quite satisfactorily.[68]

In the very worst sectors this kind of thing could drag on for weeks on end. Ferd Nauheim did not join his division until February 1945. He soon found, however, that

. . . every conversation worked its way round to Hürtgen. For seventeen days and nights they had clung to what they had and had captured four towns. The Germans had been thoroughly prepared for the attack. Every road had been targeted in with painstaking care. The roads and woods were filled with mines and booby traps . . . [A veteran said] 'One time we didn't get out of the tanks once for four days. Heavy artillery, 882, mortars, screaming mimis pounding in all around us. You got out of the tank to take a leak and you were a dead duck. We used our damn helmets and dumped them out of the turret.'[69]

Clearly, then, the front-line infantry had little reason to be envious of the tank crews. Few were, but, as Stephen Bagnall has shown above, this was not because of the physical and psychological stress, of which most infantrymen were only dimly aware, but because of the absolute horror of being caught in a burning tank. For this was the real nightmare of tank fighting, the knowledge that one was imprisoned inside a tank and virtually incapable of taking evasive action. In actual fact the infantrymen were little better off – no one can really do much to avoid shells, bombs or bullets – but they got an important psychological fillip from the imagined advantage of being able to crouch, duck, lie prone or dive for cover. In a tank you *knew* that you could do nothing but wait for a shell to strike. 'Were you ever inside a tank when it got hit?' asked Marine Lieutenant Larbey on Tarawa, 'The spot inside the tank where the shell hits turns a bright yellow, like a sunrise.'[70] But only lucky men had the time for that sort of observation. When German armour-piercing shot hit a tank it was more likely to look like a very vivid sunrise. One historian, also a tank commander in Italy, recalled that it only needed 'a glancing blow from an armour-piercing shot . . . [to] gouge metal from the turret side like a finger rubbing along a pat of butter, producing a brief rosy glow on the inside of the turret wall as the steel became white-hot at the point of impact, then cooled'. But this was seen as a let off. The German gunners were very good indeed and the same officer described

> . . . the express-train roar of the near-miss in front of them or behind, and [they] saw the long furrows ploughed up around them as the gunners found the range. To be hit by one of these hurtling solid projectiles meant a terrifying, bone-shattering crash, and the probability that the flash from the disintegrating molten metal would ignite the ninety gallons of petrol or diesel carried in the side tanks, or the charge in one of the high explosive shells which were clipped round the turret walls.[71]

The next moment or so was a terrifying moment for the crew, for those at least who had not been mangled, decapitated or sliced in two by the shell or flying fragments. Even if a tank was only immobilised by a hit, everybody knew that they only had a very short respite before another shell would come ripping through the hull. Peter Elstob's crew soon learnt an important lesson of tank warfare, that 'when a tank was hit by an armour-piercing shell those who were still alive and able to move got out fast before the next one hit it; the whole thing was as unlike a boxing match as it could be, because in a tank battle the first hit was the winning one'.[72] The first or second hit was almost certain to set the tank on fire and it was then that any watching infantry were truly thankful that they had never been assigned to an armoured unit. An American officer who saw many 'brew ups' wrote:

> A tank that is mortally hit belches forth long searing tongues of orange flame from every hatch. As ammunition explodes in the interior, the hull is racked by violent convulsions and sparks erupt from the spout of the barrel like the fireballs of a Roman candle. Silver rivulets of molten aluminium pour from the engine like tears . . . When the inferno subsides, gallons of lubricating oil in the power train and hundreds of pounds of rubber on the tracks and bogey wheels continue to burn, spewing dense clouds of black smoke over the funeral pyre.[73]

Long before this pall of smoke appeared those trapped inside the tank were dead. Andrew Wilson commented sardonically on his own chances of survival in a stricken Churchill. 'But there was one

consolation . . . When the Churchill was hit it caught fire three
times out of five, and it could take up to ten seconds for the fire to
sweep through from the engine compartment to the turret. The
American Sherman caught fire every time, and the flames swept
through in about three seconds . . . The Germans called them
"tommy cookers".'[74] The Allies too showed a grim sense of
humour in this respect; for them the Shermans were 'Ronson
burners' because of that firm's claim that their products always
'light first time'. Nat Frankel fought in Shermans and has explained in detail the mechanics of getting out of an immobilised
tank – and the odds against it:

A tank, you see, had four gas inlets, and each one was filled with high
octane. If any of those four were hit, the whole machine would go
up . . . When that gas got hit, your options were, to say the least,
limited. Oh, we had a fire extinguisher, but that was for overheated
motors; it was useless for an exploded tank. Now, there were two ways
to get out. One was via the turret; the other was through a trapdoor on
the opposite side of the driver from the bow gun. Often the turret
would be inaccessible to anyone inside the tank; if the machine was hit
badly, particularly if it was knocked on its side, the trapdoor would jam
as well. At best you would have ninety seconds to get out that door; if it
jammed you would need fifty of those seconds to push it open. That
would leave forty seconds for three men to squeeze out. Tick, tick, tick,
boom! And what would happen if both the turret and the trapdoor
were inoperative? What would happen is, you'd die! It takes twenty
minutes for a medium tank to incinerate; and the flames burn slowly,
so figure it takes ten minutes for a hearty man within to perish. You
wouldn't even be able to struggle for chances are both exits would be
sheeted with flame and smoke. You would sit, read *Good Housekeeping*,
and die like a dog. Steel coffins indeed![75]

In fact, the intensity of the heat and the hail of exploding ammunition often meant that the end came very quickly. No matter how
it came, however, you were very comprehensively dead. Norman
Lewis (Field Security Police) saw destroyed tanks on the Salerno
beachhead: 'In one case the trapped crew had been broiled in such
a way that a puddle of fat had spread from under the tank and this
was quilted with brilliant flies of all descriptions and colours.'[76]
Stephen Bagnall, as we know, had often seen tanks brewing up.
After all 'there were escape hatches: and they often stuck. Little
blackened dolls about two feet high have been found in tanks. Once
they were men'.[77]

5
Casualties

It is a good thing not to be too squeamish, the
smell of septic limbs and heads is enough to
bowl one over. As usual, a good many deaths, one
had the back of his head off,
another from the nose downwards completely
gone. But it is the multiple wounds that appear
worst, men almost in pieces, the number
intensifies the horror, we get so few slight cases.
REVEREND WALKER, 1916

The wounded were forbidden to moan for aid so
that the Germans would not know the extent of
the losses they had inflicted. The mortar crews
abandoned their weapons, whose muzzle blast
betrayed the location of the foxhole line, and took
up rifles from the dead . . . The 2/11th Infantry
had only two officer survivors in the three rifle
companies and their total casualties numbered
over 300.
CROSSING THE MOSELLE, SEPTEMBER 1944

The surgeon offered me a choice between
amputating both legs and survival, or cutting off
the rotten bits of flesh with odds against its
working. I opted for the latter, but the method
was intensely painful that I would start weeping
an hour or so before his daily treatment.
CAPTAIN P. COCHRANE, 1941

Fatal Statistics

On the Western Front, in World War I, the British armies lost a total of 677,515 men killed, died of wounds or missing, whilst 1,837,613 were wounded. These figures represent 13.4 and 36.4 per cent respectively of the total number of men who served in France and Belgium. During World War II the British Army called up 3,788,000 men, of whom approximately 2¼ million served overseas. Of these 126,734 were killed or died of wounds and 239,575 were wounded – 4.6 and 8.7 per cent respectively. The US Army Ground Forces and US Marine Corps between them utilised the services of around 7½ million men, of whom almost 5 million served overseas. Of these 202,434 men were killed and 641,013 were wounded – 4.0 and 12.8 per cent respectively.[1]

At first sight these casualty rates are grotesquely disproportionate. But one should recall what has already been said about the low proportion of combat troops in World War II armies. On the Western Front the vast majority of serving soldiers were line officers or riflemen and as such were expected to take their turn in the line and be exposed to the full rigours of trench warfare. Thus the percentage of casualties cited above corresponds reasonably well with the percentage of men who actually served at the front. This is in no way true of World War II figures. In the British, American and most Commonwealth armies as many as two-thirds of the troops were involved in activities behind the front line, working in the numerous roles necessary to keep a mechanised army in the field.

In the British army the situation got progressively worse as the war went on. Already, in December 1940, Churchill was complaining to the Secretary of State for War that whilst an infantry division only contained 15,500 men, each one seemed to be absorbing the services of 35,000 soldiers. Deducting the actual divisional troops this left

> . . . a great mass, amounting to 540,000, [which] has now to be explained. We are assured the corps, army, L[ine] of C[ommunication] troops etc. plus the 70,000 security troops justify this enormous demand upon the manhood of the nation . . . Before I can ask the Cabinet to assent to any further call-up from the public, it is necessary that the whole subject shall be thrashed out, and that at least a million are combed out of the fluff and flummery of the fighting troops, and are made to serve effective military purposes.[2]

In Burma, in April 1945, British and Indian L of C troops alone amounted to 117,795 men and a substantial proportion of the remaining 561,512 'operational' troops were involved in support activities at army, corps and divisional level. In north-west Europe, at the end of 1944, the British Second Army numbered 322,000 men and the Canadian First Army 192,000, whilst their parent organisation, 21st Army Group, contained 302,000 L of C troops. This imbalance continued right down to divisional level. In all theatres the normal British infantry division contained 17,000 men but only 4,000 of these, less than a quarter, actually carried a rifle and bayonet.

American sources present the same picture of the ineluctable growth of the armies' 'tail'. At the end of 1942, though the US army as a whole numbered slightly under 5 million men, only 1,917,000 (38.3 per cent) were classified as ground combat troops. During 1943, at the peak of American mobilisation, 2,583,000 extra men were inducted and assigned to various arms and services within the army. Over one-fifth of these went into the USAAF, leaving 1,991,000 ground troops. Of these, 338,700 went into the Infantry, 55,100 into armoured formations, 48,600 into the Tank Destroyers and 111,100 into the Artillery. This totals only 553,000 men or just over one-quarter of the Army Ground Forces called up in that year. As a comparison, it is revealing to note that between them, Military Intelligence, Finance, the Military Police and the Quartermaster and Transportation Corps absorbed 340,400 men. Even taking into account those members of the Medical Corps, Combat Engineers and others who were likely to find themselves in or very near the front line, it is still only possible to speak of, at the most, one million ground combat troops – only 37 per cent of the total induction. Equally significant is the fact that although the army reached a peak total of $7\frac{1}{2}$ million men, this still only involved a net increase of 365,000 combat troops over the 1942 figure. Other types of statistics tell the same story. It was estimated, for example, that each infantry division required, as well as its organic service troops, the labours of a further 25,000 non-divisional troops to keep it in the field. With reference to the war in the Pacific, one source went so far as to compute that about 18 men were needed in the supply services to keep one rifleman firing, even though the riflemen's food and clothing accounted for less than 5 per cent of all military cargoes. When veterans returning to the States in 1945 were asked whether or not they had ever been in combat – and it is

reasonable to expect a great deal of latitude in their interpretation
of what constituted actual combat – only 39 per cent of officers and
37 per cent of enlisted men answered in the affirmative.

In short then, only between a fifth and a quarter of any army's
paper strength was actually involved in the shooting war. But these
were the men who suffered the bulk of the casualties. Unfortunately, there are few hard figures available to substantiate this
point for the British forces. One analysis that does exist can,
however, be taken as fairly typical. In Normandy, in 1944, out of a
sample of over 3,500 battle casualties, the infantry, less than a
quarter of the army as a whole, accounted for just over 71 per cent
of them. American sources are much more detailed on this point.
With regard to the infantry alone, it has been estimated that whilst
these divisions constituted only 10 per cent of the army's total
strength, they accounted for 70 per cent of the battle casualties.
The story was the same in all theatres. In Tunisia, the Infantry
Armor and Field Artillery, between a quarter and a third of the
total army strength, accounted for 80.2 per cent of the total casualties. In north-west Europe, it has been estimated, these formations
sustained 81 per cent of the total battle casualties. The Infantry, as
usual, were particularly hard hit. Though they represented only
20.5 per cent of the total army strength, they accounted for 66.7 per
cent of the total battle casualties. Armoured divisions made up
another 10.6 per cent and airborne units 3.7 per cent. In the
Pacific, the figures have been presented in a slightly different way,
though the message is equally clear. In the south-west Pacific, for
example, the average annual number of wounded per 1,000 overseas strength of each arm was infantry 145.9, armour 48.5, artillery
24.1, and all other arms and services 15.4. The equivalent figures
for the Italian theatre were infantry 274.8, armour 69.2, artillery
72.0 and all others 17.9.

Nor does the contrast between combat troops and others only
apply within the context of the army or corps. In Italy, the Fifth
Army followed the usual pattern; in January 1944, for instance, of
the 180,000 American troops there only 77,000 were actual divisional troops, though it was from these latter that most of the
casualties came. But even within the divisions themselves one
section of the troops suffered most and, though the Infantry made
up only 67 per cent of the division's authorised strength, they
suffered, on average, 92 per cent of its battle casualties. So it was,
too, with the 77th US Division which fought in the Pacific: the

total number of men killed in action throughout the war was 2,132, and 1,854 (86.9 per cent) of these were from the three infantry regiments. A few British unit histories also make this point very clearly. The 15th (Scottish) Division fought in north-west Europe and between 13 September and 15 November 1944, as a whole suffered 2,860 battle casualties, but 2,562 (89.6 per cent) were from the ranks of the nine infantry battalions.

The picture, then, is fairly clear. If World War II casualty figures are to be made comparable to those of the previous war in representing a percentage of men actually exposed to battle conditions, the crude figures will simply not suffice. For the British and American armies, at any rate, they must be multiplied *at least* threefold. This gives us average casualties of up to 13 per cent killed and 32 per cent wounded, remarkably close to the equivalent figures for the Western Front.[3] It must be emphasised that there is no intention here of playing down the slaughter on the Western Front. A totally fair comparison of the respective casualty rates would also necessitate some slight upward adjustment of the World War I percentages, to take account of the men in France and Belgium who never served at the front. In terms of battle casualties the Western Front will always remain a Golgotha of unequalled proportions, but, even so, for the fighting soldier World War II was far from the relatively easy option that the gross figures might seem to suggest. Upwards of one in three of them could expect to eventually become a battle casualty. That is no cakewalk.

A detailed breakdown of World War II casualty figures can be found in Appendix 1, and those with a statistical bent will find plenty of material to occupy them. Certain points thrown up there however are of general interest, and need to be touched upon here. On the whole, the experiences of prisoners of war are outside the scope of this book, but it is worth noting the great disparity between the number of Americans captured by the enemy and the total for the British and Commonwealth forces. Even forgetting exact proportions, the bald figures speak for themselves and offer eloquent testimony to the major defeats in France, Malaya, Hong Kong, Greece, Crete and Tobruk. The US total is 103,918, that for the Commonwealth 353,941, 2.1 and 8.8 per cent respectively of the number of soldiers who served overseas. It is these early defeats that so effect the Commonwealth figures.[4] After 1942, there is little to choose between America's and her Allies' record in this respect. In north-west Europe, for example, between D-Day and the end of the war, American and Anglo-Canadian ratios are almost identical, at 1.8 and 1.4 per cent respectively. Nor did the Americans first meet their enemy as to the manner born; in the first year of the war, in the American defeats in the Philippines, they lost 3,331 Army and 1,542 Marine killed and wounded, whilst the totals for those captured or missing were 30,119 and 1,926. In Tunisia, the American forces lost almost as many men as POWs as the combined total of dead and wounded. Even so, the basic disparity remains, as the following comparison clearly shows. For the war as a whole total American missing and prisoners were only 10.9 per cent of their gross casualties; for the British and their immediate Allies they were 38.21 per cent.

If the Allied casualty figures are broken down further, by individual country, several other features emerge. At first sight the New Zealand casualty statistics seem to indicate a brazen exploitation of these superb soldiers, with 30.8 per cent of their soldiers who served overseas becoming battle casualties as against only 18.9 per cent for the Americans and 21.6 for the British. In fact, this figure of roughly one-third is fairly normal for actual combat troops, and only shows that the New Zealand contingent was too small to include any significant number of service and L of C troops. This seeming disparity is evident in all theatres, though it has to be admitted that at times the gulf was so wide that non-British troops were entitled to wonder whether they were not seeing rather too much of the action. In Italy, in 1944, British battle casualties were 8.9 per 1,000 ration strength, whilst Indian and Canadian were just under 35.0 and New Zealand a staggering 229.2.

American figures allow comparison between their major services, the Army Ground Forces and the Marine Corps. Again, it is probably the lower number of service troops in the latter that explains the differences. The figures for fatalities are in fact very close: 2.7 and 2.9 per cent of the total who served. The gap widens for wounded men, where the proportions are 6.5 and 10.0 per cent. There is also a substantial difference with regard to prisoners of war, who represent 1.9 per cent of the total Army forces and only 0.3 of the Marines. This difference is probably explained by the nature of Pacific combat, in which the Marines were exclusively engaged, and in which the Japanese had absolutely no interest in taking prisoners. Individual Commonwealth figures for prisoners of war are high almost without exception, as each country played its part in the debacles of 1940 and 1941: for the British 35.6 per cent of total losses, for the Australians 47.9, and for the South Africans 53.6. The major exception are the Canadians, for whom POWs and missing were a mere 8.5 per cent of the overall battle casualties. Even taking into account their absence from the first catastrophes, Dieppe notwithstanding, such a figure does seem to indicate a remarkable reluctance to throw in the sponge.

One variation that had nothing to do with nationality or the structure of the ground forces was the differing casualty rates on different fronts. Comparisons here must be tentative at best since it is extremely difficult to find reliable assessments of the numbers of troops who served in the various theatres. One broad conclusion does stand out, however. For both the Americans and their Allies, war in the East proved much less costly, in terms of battle casualties, than did war in Europe. It should be emphasised that this applies to losses in combat only for, as will be seen, the great enemy in this part of the world was not the Japanese but the virtual certainty of contracting some incapacitating disease. And this latter fact helps to explain the low proportion of battle casualties. The Far Eastern theatres were, to adopt economic jargon, very labour extensive in that large reserves were necessary to fill the gaps created by disease; however, only a very small proportion of these men were in action at any one time. Moreover, actual combat, particularly for the Americans and Australians in the Pacific, was in short, sharp bursts as the invasion armadas went from one cluster of islands to another. The fighting itself was brutally severe, but it rarely lasted very long and once it was over large numbers of men went on rest or leave, were assigned to garrison duty, or took to the transport vessels again. Thus the figures for the American Army and Marines in the Pacific show that 2.5 per cent of those who served there were killed and 7.3 per cent wounded. Commonwealth statistics for the Burma campaign, both the initial defeat and the reconquest, give only 1.7 per cent killed and 4.8 wounded.

The percentages in Europe were significantly higher. In Italy the Americans lost 5.4 per cent of their total forces there killed and 18.8 per cent wounded. In the north-west European fighting, the figures are not quite so high. The American figures are 3.5 per cent of the total ETO (European Theatre of Operations) ration strength killed and 11.3 per cent wounded, Anglo-Canadian figures are 3.9 per cent killed and 10.6 per cent wounded. In both cases the explanation lies not so much in any differing severity in combat itself, but in the fact that the fighting in Europe was much more continuous than that in the East and included constant patrol and defensive duties with hardly any prolonged lulls.

But to return to the essential point of these statistics, that most fighting in World War II was done by a remarkably small proportion of troops whose caualties were very high. Let us take a few examples from units in north-west Europe. Throughout the campaign the 50th (Northumbrian) Division suffered 452 officer casualties and 6,002 from other ranks. If we assume that 90 per cent of these casualties were in the nine rifle battalions, and that the division as a whole had an 80 per cent replacement rate, then slightly over 49 per cent of all men who served in these battalions throughout the campaign became battle casualties – a fifty-fifty chance of being hit. The equivalent figure for the 15th (Scottish) Division, based upon the same assumptions, is 58.4 per cent. If we look only at battle fatalities in each division, we find that in the 50th one had a 1 in 10 chance of being killed, and in the 15th a 1 in 9 chance. In some infantry battalions the odds were even worse. In the 6th King's Own Scottish Borderers, men had a 63.9 per cent chance of being hit, whilst 1 in 10 were killed. In the 1st Royal Norfolk Regiment, 66.3 per cent became battle casualties and as many as 1 in 6 were killed, the equivalent figures in the 1st Dorsetshire Regiment being 63.9 per cent and 1 in 7.

If you were an officer, the outlook was even bleaker. Table 4 repeats, in a slightly different form, the information given above but differentiates officer and other ranks casualties.

Table 4: Comparison of British officer and other ranks casualties
in selected units in north-west Europe, 1944-5

UNIT	% HIT		% KILLED	
	Officers	ORS	Officers	ORS
50th (Northumbrian) Division	65.9	50.0	16.5	8.7
15th (Scottish) Division	72.2	62.9	28.7	16.8
6th King's Own Scottish Borderers	67.5	62.5	17.5	8.9
1st Royal Norfolk Regiment	72.1	64.5	17.4	17.0
1st Dorsetshire Regiment	70.6	62.0	25.9	13.2

At the end of the war, the commander of another battalion, the 1st Gordon Highlanders, made a calculation of his own:

> It occurred to me to count the number of officers who had served in the battalion since D-Day. Up to March 27th, the end of the Rhine crossing, it was 102 . . . I found that we had had 55 officers commanding the twelve rifle platoons, and that their average service with the Battalion was thirty-eight days, or five and a half weeks. Of these fifty-three per cent were wounded, twenty-four per cent killed or died of wounds, fifteen per cent invalided, and five per cent had survived.[5]

Other more generalised figures tell the same story. If we take as our control the fact that officers represented between 4 and 5 per cent of an infantry battalion's strength,[6] it will be seen from the following figures that they consistently suffered a disproportionately high number of battle casualties. In Sicily, for example, they represented 10 per cent of the total British killed and 7.7 per cent of the wounded. In Tunisia, 8.5 per cent of the First Army British dead were officers and 6.6 per cent of the wounded. A slightly different figure for mainland Italy tells the same story. Out of a random sample of hospitalised soldiers in 1944, 26.8 per cent of all cases were officer battle casualties whilst only 13.8 per cent were other ranks wounded in combat. The same is true of American figures. Despite the US army's less than perfect showing in Tunisia, their officers were still well to the fore as representing 9.8 per cent of the total casualties in the campaign. A study was made of four US infantry divisions in Italy and here again it was found that officers suffered disproportionately. In this case, a distinction was also made between the various ranks and second lieutenants suffered the heaviest casualties of all; though they accounted for only 0.9 per cent of the division's strength they made up 2.7 per cent of all battle casualties. The study emphasises what a drain on qualified personnel this involved:

> Assuming, for the sake of demonstration, that the full complement of 132 Infantry second lieutenants was present in a division on each day of combat, that there would be no non-battle casualties, and no duplication of battle casualties, the division would lose a full complement of its Infantry second lieutenants in 88 combat days. On the same assumptions, the divisional complement of 99 Infantry captains would require 294 days of battle for 100 per cent casualties.[7]

A final point about officer casualties, which may come as something of a surprise, is that in World War II they tended to be proportionately higher than in World War I. Two British regiments have compiled comparative statistics and both give pretty much the same results. Thus in World War I the Highland Light Infantry lost 1 officer to every 16 other ranks, whilst in the period 1939–45 1 officer fell for every 12 other ranks. Equivalent figures for the Coldstream Guards were 1:20 and 1:12.

Even so, it was not the officers who suffered most heavily of all. And most of the above figures only relate officer casualties to the total enlisted strength of a battalion whereas, even at this basic level, there were quite a few specialist soldiers who were in considerably less danger of becoming casualties. The men who really bore the brunt were the ordinary riflemen in the platoons and squads, and insofar as it is possible to isolate their casualties it seems clear that they were the hardest hit. Few studies have been done on this point but what little evidence there is seems fairly conclusive. The study of the US infantry divisions in Italy, cited above, makes the point fairly clearly. It shows that though the ordinary riflemen made up only 11 per cent of a division's total complement, they accounted for 38 per cent of its casualties. In other words, whilst the casualty rate for second lieutenants was three times greater than their proportion of the roster, that for riflemen was 3.4 times greater. In World War II as in most others it was the 'poor bloody infantry' that did much of the fighting and most of the dying.

Though one hopes that the major points have been made clearly enough, much of the preceding section has something of an actuarial ring about it. Percentages and ratios all too often lose sight of the fact that real people are involved. Let us now examine some actual attacks and offensives to show, on the one hand, just what a few days' battle could mean, and on the other, that even the long-term cumulative figures could understate the extent of the slaughter.[8]

In the Western Desert, though the fighting was hard, casualty rates remained relatively low. At Alamein, for example, 220,476 soldiers took part, of whom 2,350 (1.1 per cent) were killed and 8,950 (4.1 per cent) wounded.[9] But all units were not so lucky. The disastrous effect of faulty armoured tactics has already been discussed, and the infantry too were sometimes recklessly thrown forward. Two such incidents occurred during the deadly Crusader battles. On 20 November 1941, the 2nd Black Watch attacked three German strong-points known as Butch, Jill and Tiger. In under 2 hours they lost 24 officers and 440 men. Two days later, the 24th and 25th New Zealand Battalions attacked around Sidi Rezegh and lost 450 casualties, 120 of them killed, the bulk of which were in the 25th Battalion who gained the dubious distinction of sustaining the highest casualties of any New Zealand battalion in one action in the whole war. On 30 September 1942, the 5th Queen's Regiment made a night attack on Munassib Depression during which one company was decimated and the remaining two completely wiped out. The front-line role of artillery in the pre-Alamein battles made many units' casualties correspondingly severe. One such was the 11th (Honourable Artillery Company) Regiment RHA which between 24 May and 18 July 1942, out of a full complement of 670 men, lost 463 killed, wounded and POWS.

If casualties in the Pacific were in the long run lower than in other theatres, this can hardly be said of the actual battles. One American source has listed all the major American campaigns throughout the war and worked out for each the average casualties per 1,000 men per day. In Italy the highest figure is for the operations in May 1944, with 0.53 per 1,000 killed and 2.31 wounded. The heaviest average in the ETO was during the First US Army's first weeks in Normandy. Figures for deaths are not available but the wounded rate was 3.30 per 1,000. On Iwo Jima the dead and wounded figures are 3.77 and 10.34 per 1,000 respectively, on Eniwetok they are 4.98 and 13.10, and on Tarawa, probably the greatest bloodbath of them all, they are 14.49 and 32.25.[10] The actual numbers are even more striking. On the first day at Iwo Jima, the 4th and 5th Marine Divisions lost over 2,400 men, 600 of them killed. Five weeks later they and the 3rd Marine Division had lost a total of 6,821 men dead and 18,000 wounded in subduing the island. To put it another way, out of 3 divisions 1½ had become casualties. Another Marine division, the 2nd, suffered very heavily on Tarawa. On the first day, 1,500 of the 5,000 assault troops were killed or wounded in securing two small beachheads, neither more than 250yd deep. When the island was secured, four days later, they had lost 1,069 dead and 2,391 wounded. On Okinawa, four divisions, the 1st and 6th Marine and 7th and 96th Infantry, suffered over 30 per cent casualties. The 1st Marine Division, for example, lost 1,115 men killed and 6,745 wounded, whilst the 96th Infantry lost 1,506 killed and 5,912 wounded.[11] Nor did the Australians get off lightly in their share of the Pacific

fighting. For example 1,100 men left Australia with the 126th
Regiment. They fought on New Guinea, in the Buna beachhead
and, when they crossed the river Girua in December 1942 to
answer muster prior to being replaced, a mere 92 men were left.

For sheer, unrelieved suffering, however, nothing equalled the
fighting in Europe. One of the many American army questionnaires was to a sample of riflemen in Italy, and 87 per cent of them
said that they had seen a close friend killed or wounded in action.
The results of individual attacks certainly bear this out. In January
1944, the 36th US Division attacked across the river Rapido and in
two days they lost 143 men killed, 663 wounded and 875 missing,
all of them from the combat soldiers of only two of the three
regiments. On the Anzio beachhead, in February of the same year,
the 2nd Battalion 157th Regiment went into the notorious wadis
with 800 men. A week later only 200 were left and half of these were
themselves battle casualties. In September 1944, the 88th US
Division attacked down the Santerno Valley and in under a fortnight lost 2,105 men killed and wounded. Their Allies fared no
better. In the first three weeks of the Gustav Line offensive, every
Canadian rifle company involved had sustained 50 per cent casualties. In the street-fighting at Ortona in December 1943, a brigade
of the 1st Canadian Division lost 1,372 casualties and a quarter of all
Canadian deaths in Italy occurred in this small town. British battalions suffered particularly heavily during their progress from
Salerno to the Winter Line. Between 9 September and 31 October
1943, the 5th Sherwood Foresters suffered 560 battle casualties,
the 9th Royal Fusiliers 572, and the 5th Hampshire Regiment 448.
On 29 January of the following year the 2nd Sherwood Foresters
sustained some of the heaviest casualties of the whole Anzio fighting. At the end of the day they could muster no more than 8 officers
and 250 other ranks. The commanding officer, the adjutant and all
company commanders were casualties; one company was commanded by an NCO as all the officers had been killed or wounded.
But even these losses were surpassed by those of the 10th Royal
Berkshires in the same beachhead. In early February they bore the
brunt of a big German armoured push and were overwhelmed
where they stood. The final entry in the battalion *War Diary* reads:
'Battalion now consists of battalion H.Q., two sections of C Company, a few carrier and mortar personnel, totalling 40 men in all.'[12]
Attacking the enemy could be a murderous affair. On 7 September
the 8th Royal Fusiliers were ordered to attack Croce, in the Gothic

Line. As they formed up a heavy German barrage fell on them but their pleas for a postponement were ignored. Two companies led the assault and when they actually reached the town one was down to 20 men, the other to 3.

Casualties were often just as heavy in north-west Europe. By early 1945, 47 American regiments, spread over 19 divisions, had sustained 100 to 200 per cent casualties.[13] Some examples from the Third US Army prove the point. By the end of the war the 90th Division had over 35,000 replacements; 5th Division over 30,000; 25th, 79th and 80th Divisions over 25,000; 4th and 6th Armoured Divisions over 20,000. Except for the winter lull, battle casualties were high throughout the campaign.[14] The first weeks in Normandy were very severe. The carnage on Omaha Beach is too well known to require much elaboration. Suffice it to say that the three leading regiments incurred 2,500 casualties in a few hours. Things were no easier off the beaches themselves. The army made a survey of sample companies from 1st, 4th, 9th and 29th US Divisions and came up with depressing results. Between 6 June and 31 July, the rifle companies had lost 59.6 of their original complement of enlisted men and 68.7 per cent of their officers. Equivalent figures for heavy weapons companies were 36.9 and 51.9 per cent. Some units suffered even more heavily. The 12th Regiment, in June alone, lost 76 per cent of its officers and 63 per cent of its enlisted men. An officer who fought with 30th US Division in the battle for St Lô commented:

> The people who do the actual advancing to close with the enemy are the rifle platoons . . . The battles progress no faster than they do. Now the aggregate strength of these 81 platoons is about 3,240 men. I hazard a guess that at least 75 per cent of the total casualties were in the rifle platoons, or a total of about 2,950 [for our Division]. This figure is 90 per cent of the rifle platoon strength.[15]

The killing continued right through the battle for Germany. The 30th Division was also involved in the assault on Aachen and the experiences of one of its replacements are ample testimony to the ferocity of the fighting:

> Private Elmer S. McKay, a nineteen year-old mortarman replacement, recalls arriving in the 30th's lines during a bombing raid . . . 'I lined up with the rest of the replacements. I counted 33 men, which I thought was a rather large number of replacements for an infantry company whose total complement was 190 men plus five officers.' . . .

Little did the scared replacement realise it then, but by the time the battle for Aachen was over, he would be a platoon sergeant himself, the sole survivor of the men who had come with him, in charge of thirty men whose average age was just nineteen.[16]

The ghastliness of the Hürtgen Forest has already been highlighted. The experiences of the 4th US Division were typical:

In thirteen days some companies had run through three and four company commanders. Staff sergeants and sergeants commanded most of the rifle platoons. The few officers still running platoons were either replacements or heavy weapons platoon leaders displaced forward. Most squad leaders were inexperienced privates or privates first class. One company had only twenty-five men, including replacements . . . This was hardly a division: this was a conglomeration . . . [T/5 George Morgan] summed up the campaign and the situation in a few words: 'Then they jump off again and soon there is only a handful of the old men left.'[17]

Further north, the 21st Army Group suffered just as heavily. France, Holland and Germany all took their fearful toll of casualties. By the end of the Normandy battle the 3rd Division, which had landed on D-Day, had suffered 7,100 casualties, 904 of whom had been killed. By the same date, though they had landed later, the 15th (Scottish) Division had lost 5,354 men. Of the 52 officers killed, 43 were from the 9 infantry battalions. A single battalion of the 51st (Highland) Division had lost 44 officers in a mere 7½ weeks fighting. Martin Lindsay commanded the 1st Gordon Highlanders. In early January 'the adjutant showed me the figures of the four rifle companies' casualties since D-Day. They were appalling. Their combined officer strength, at any one time, was 20; their casualties had been 9 killed and 30 wounded. Their combined Other Ranks' strength was 500; their casualties had been 149 killed and 351 wounded, a total of exactly 500'.[18] Much of the fighting in Holland took place in winter when the fighting was reduced to harassment and patrol activity. Over the whole period, therefore, casualties were much lower, though there were several spasms of intensive combat. Probably the most brutal of these was the Scheldt Estuary attack in October. In only 5 days of battle the Canadian Black Watch lost 264 officers and men. The three battalions of the 9th Brigade, in the first week of the offensive, lost 111 of all ranks killed and 422 wounded. In Operation Veritable, the Anglo-Canadian offensive into the Rhineland in February, XXX Corps alone lost 10,000 men in slightly over 4 weeks.

The Reichswald fighting was a part of this operation and there the spearhead division, the 53rd (Welsh), suffered 5,000 casualties in 9 days. These represented half of their total losses in the whole of the north-west European campaign.

The Wounded

In one respect, however, even the combat troops of World War II were decidedly better off than any of their predecessors. By 1939 medicine had made great advances, which were speedily applied to the battlefield and gave the wounded a much greater chance of recovery than had ever been the case before. In the British army between 1914 and 1918, 3.4 per 1,000 officers and 2.3 per 1,000 other ranks died of their wounds each month. In France and Germany, between 1944 and 1945, the respective figures were only 1.5 and 1.0 per 1,000. Even in Burma, a country totally inimical to first-class medicine, the mortality rate among wounded men had been cut to 5 per cent per annum by 1945.

The contrast would be even more striking if the figures took account of the fact that in both wars a large percentage of those classified as dying of their wounds were beyond recall no matter how quickly they might have received medical attention. Amongst those cases not irredeemably moribund the advances in medical and surgical technique had a dramatic impact. In World War I, for example, two-thirds of all belly wounds were fatal; in World War II the proportion was cut to one-third. Moreover, this percentage fell during the course of the war. In 1945 the rate of recovery from such wounds was 75 per cent, though they were still generally fatal in unstable medical situations such as retreats or amongst airborne and commando troops. The mortality rate from chest wounds in World War I was 54 per cent, and that for amputees 70 per cent. In World War II the respective figures were a mere 5.7 and 20 per cent. The medical advances did not only serve to reduce mortality. Less amputations were deemed necessary and, whereas 67 per cent of damaged eyes were lost in World War I hospitals, the corresponding figure in World War II was almost a half. American figures show the same general trend. In the American Civil War, 13.3 per cent of those wounded died soon afterwards; in the Spanish-American War this figure was halved, though it rose again in World War I to just over 8 per cent; during World War II, however, it fell again to only 4.5 per cent.

Three discoveries played the vital role in this advance, all of them to do with medicinal rather than surgical technique. Perhaps the most important of all was penicillin. It is an antibiotic, so called because the action of one type of microbe, in this case *penicillium notatum*, is used to oppose the growth of another. Fleming had noted the effect in 1928 though the discovery could not be utilised until Florey and Chain isolated and tested it at Oxford in the late thirties. The timing was remarkably fortuitous and it became possible to produce the drug in large, relatively inexpensive quantities by 1943 from when it played a crucial part in reducing the chances of post-wounding infection. The microbe used destroys various common and dangerous bacteria, notably streptococci and staphylococci. It also acts upon the spirochaetes of syphilis, no mean advantage in wartime when venereal disease is one of the soldiers' greatest hazards.[19]

Limited amounts of penicillin were used in the Middle East and Tunisia, both by the Americans and the British, but it was first used in large quantities in Sicily. Later, in the Italian and north-west European campaigns, it was almost as common as bandages and blood. It was also used extensively in the Far East, though once again the forgotten Fourteenth Army seem to have had legitimate cause for complaint in that no appreciable quantities arrived until the very end of 1944. For the D-Day invasions, on the other hand, 21st Army Group had a fully organised penicillin programme, with special officers to supervise its administration, so that even during the worst periods on the beachhead the majority of casualties had their first injection within a few hours. By the last year of the war the American army was using 2 million ampoules of penicillin every month. It has been estimated that in this theatre, and this figure is probably generally applicable, the drug saved 12 to 15 per cent of the cases that would otherwise have been fatal. Moreover, in the majority of cases it roughly halved the time spent in hospital.

But penicillin was not the whole answer to infection. Its main use was in combating local sepsis. Against systemic infections, notably streptococcal septicaemias, it was relatively powerless. For these the chemical group of sulphonamides (or sulpha-drugs) were more effective. Again the timing of the original discovery meant that drugs could be relied on to a much larger scale than had ever been possible previously. Domagk in 1932 is the key name, after he had shown that red dye protonsil controlled certain types of infection. The actual mechanics of the process are not without a certain poignancy. The sulphonamides are very similar to a certain acid which bacteria need as a vitamin; they mistake them for the vitamin and poison themselves. By 1943 all American soldiers carried with them a small packet containing twelve sulphonamide tablets and a small amount of powder for smearing on any wound.

The combination of sulphonamides and penicillin gave World War II physicians a range of chemotherapeutic aids that had been completely absent in World War I and which drastically reduced some of the dangers inherent in being wounded. If systemic infection is one of the greatest of these dangers, the other is certainly shock. This brings us to the third major innovation in war medicine – the widespread use of blood transfusion, one of the procedures subsumed under the general heading of resuscitation, by which patients who are badly shocked are treated in an attempt to reverse the remorseless slide towards death. During World War I a prime method was *rechauffement*, simply keeping the patient as warm as possible, though this eventually came to be frowned upon. Another ploy, and this was also much in evidence during World War II, was the injection of a glucose-saline solution to replace blood plasma lost through sweating. But most important of all during World War II was the supply of fresh batches of actual blood plasma – blood without the red corpuscles – used to replace the fluid part of the blood that seeps away through the walls of the capillaries when a man is wounded. In those cases where plasma and corpuscles have escaped through cut blood vessels, whole blood is transfused instead of plasma alone; this being necessary because after a severe wound the heart becomes involved in an inevitably losing battle to maintain blood pressure and keep up a supply of oxygen and glucose to the brain. Some help is given by the automatic contraction of certain blood vessels in the skin – hence the pallor of a shock victim – but this is rarely sufficient. Moreover, the heart's task is made yet more difficult by the thickening of the blood due to loss of plasma, which in turn contributes to the lowered temperature and irregular pulse of the patient. To operate in these circumstances, without first trying to restore a normal blood pressure by transfusion, is to risk death.

The possibility of blood transfusion had been known since at least the turn of the century when the existence of different blood groups was established. A little was done in World War I with on-the-spot donors, but the real breakthrough was the discovery of adequate means of storing blood and this transformed pre-operative resuscitation. Even in 1941 the Americans were still relying on local donors, but they quickly realised what benefits would accrue from the use of refrigerated whole blood and powdered plasma. In the last three years of the war transfusion became a basic technique on all fronts. Special units were set up in all forward medical installations and a constant flow of blood was maintained from England and the United States. On average between 10 and 12 per cent of all wounded men were transfused. In the 21st Army Group there were 17,360 recipients, who received an average of 4.3 pints of blood or plasma each. US consumption was on an equally liberal scale; in the ETO alone the army used 385,231 pints of whole blood and plasma.

All these discoveries greatly improved the chances of those who had to pass through the medical installations. In one respect, however, medical arrangements sometimes fell below the standards achieved on the Western Front. This had nothing to do with the level of medical expertise but was a reflection of the different type of fighting in the two wars. Conditions on the Western Front were indescribably bad but they did offer the troops one advantage, that because trench lines were so static it was possible to set up large and cumbersome casualty clearing stations very near the front line, whilst regimental aid posts were usually in the foremost set of trenches. Though it was a far from easy task to get the wounded back down a water-logged communication trench or across bullet-swept no-man's-land, nevertheless, assuming he was picked up at all, a wounded man could look forward to extensive treatment fairly quickly.

This was not always the case in World War II. The Americans were generally very fortunate. In the Pacific the tiny size of most of the islands they had to assault meant that even in the most savage fighting the casualties could be swiftly brought to the beaches and returned to the ships in empty personnel or vehicle transports.[20] In North Africa and Europe, too, the Americans were able to keep their major medical installations well up to the front and maintain a minimum distance between each link in the medical chain. Even when evacuation was called for, the liberal use of aircraft kept the time spent in transit to a minimum. The British and Commonwealth troops were not always so fortunate. In France and Belgium they were mainly in retreat and it was difficult for the Dressing and Clearing Stations to stay in one place for any length of time. The problems were compounded by a shortage of transport, clogged up roads and vast amounts of bulky medical equipment more appropriate to the static installations of the previous war. It was quite common for casualties to take thirty-six hours to reach a Casualty Clearing Station, and many unnecessary deaths resulted. In the Libyan campaign, congestion was no problem, but the CCSs were still too ponderous to be moved very far. If the advance or retreat was swift, this could mean that wounded men had to travel huge distances to receive suitable attention. An average medical chain at this time could involve successive journeys of 8–12 miles from the Regimental Aid Post to the Advance Dressing Station; 80–90 miles further to the Main Dressing Station; another 80 miles to the Casualty Clearing Station, and anything up to 250 miles more to a General Hospital. All these miles had to be covered in lorries with no suspension worth the name, in extremes of heat or cold, and in constant danger of air attack.

In Burma the situation was even worse. Distances as the crow flies were not of much significance. The impenetrability of the terrain meant that even the shortest journey could take hours, even days, because it was often impossible to rely on anything but stretcher-bearers or impressed native labour. No matter how painstaking and solicitous such porters were, the trek from the front line could be a ghastly experience for the wounded man as his bearers tried to negotiate clinging foliage, hidden obstacles and tortuous inclines. In Burma, in 1942, a casualty could expect to be in transit for as much as 6 weeks before he finally reached a General Hospital. At the siege of Kohima, two years later, the wounded could only be temporarily patched up within the perimeter itself. Then they had to endure a 3-hour journey down a very steep slope, carried by Naga tribesmen, a 43-mile ride by ambulance in torrid heat over an appalling road, and finally a 2-day journey by train. In orthodox offensive operations in this theatre things were made even more difficult by the fact that battalions and brigades were split into small columns, operating fairly independently; it was not, however, feasible to split the major medical units, attached at brigade level and above, into viable independent units. The problems this created were only overcome when air transport became available and the great distances involved became of only marginal significance. By late 1944 normal policy was to set up Advanced Surgical Centres next to the forward airstrips where casualties were given emergency treatment before being taken by light aircraft, flying at tree-top height, to centralised Corps Medical Centres. All expected to be fit within 3 weeks were held there and the rest taken by air ambulance to advance and base hospitals. Air evacuation was soon handling thousands of cases each month and it was not unknown for men to reach base hospitals within 7 hours of being wounded, having also been treated at a dressing station and medical centre.

From the Tunisian campaign onwards, air evacuation also became the norm in the Mediterranean and European theatres. During the advance to the Elbe and Baltic in April 1945 all casualties were flown out, and in north-west Europe as a whole some 100,000 cases were taken out in this way. On the single busiest day 816 men were airlifted for medical treatment.

But even at this late stage of the war there was much more to dealing with casualties than simply loading them into airplanes. The most important and difficult stage was getting the wounded from where they had been hit to where they could receive some preliminary attention, prior to deciding which was the most suitable point in the chain for more extensive treatment.[21] Both the American and British systems adhered to the same basic principles and their chains of evacuation were very similar. The very first person to attend to a casualty might well be the wounded man himself or a comrade, for all soldiers carried field dressings to cover the wound and help staunch the flow of blood. In many attacks, however, soldiers were under strict orders not to tend a fallen comrade but to press on with the advance. If the wounded man could get to his feet he was expected to find his own way back to the Regimental Aid Post (US equivalent is Battalion Aid Station). Different campaigns had different definitions of 'walking wounded'. Medical facilities on New Guinea were totally inadequate and one journalist

> . . . met two wounded men coming out from Kokoda and Deniki – men of the 39th Battalion. One had been shot through the foot, the other through the left eye. The bullet had passed obliquely and shallowly through his skull from just above the cheekbone, and emerged behind the ear. He complained of severe headache, but said the wound itself was not painful. The man with the bullet through his foot was leading him. The pair had walked 113 miles in 16 days. They expected to reach the roadhead in another five.[22]

If the wounded man could not move he had to wait until the stretcher-bearers picked him up. This might take quite a time. In hopefully swift advances stretcher-bearers attached to British companies were often told to keep up with their own unit at all costs and limit themselves to tagging those left behind and offering whatever assistance could be given on the spot. Bearers from succeeding companies or from the RAMC Field Ambulances would actually take the man back to the Aid Post.[23] The Americans always followed this policy. The Medical Corps men actually attached to the company were not stretcher-bearers and their only function was to give such first-aid as was possible, tag the casualties and put them into suitable positions for the litter-bearers who were attached to the division's medical battalion.

At the Aid Post, only emergency treatment was given and the severity of the injury assessed. Then stretcher bearers from the British Field Ambulance, or one of the three American Collecting Companies took the man on to the next stage. Usually four men were assigned to each stretcher. Two were sufficient to lift the load but it was often vital that the patient be kept as stable as possible. Even four were often not enough. In Arakan in late 1942 the going was especially hard, and in one instance it took an NCO and 5 bearers $17\frac{1}{2}$ hours to take 2 walking wounded and a stretcher case from the Aid Post to a Dressing Station only 3 miles away. Nor were such difficulties unique to Burma. During the Italian winters six men were generally needed for each stretcher. It was often four to five miles from the Aid Post to the next stage, all over almost impassable tracks. The 4th Indian Division, at Monte Cassino, found that it had to set up relay posts every 400yd or so. In more favourable terrain the bearers were supplemented by ambulances and jeeps. The advantages of the latter were enormous. Under the best conditions it took 40 bearers $7\frac{1}{2}$ hours to haul 80 casualties over a mile course; 1 jeep, with provision for 3 litters, could do this in about 5 hours.

At the Advanced Dressing Station (US equivalent, Collecting Station) essential emergency treatment was given – transfusions or the finishing of incomplete traumatic amputations for example – and then it was decided how urgent was the need for definitive surgery. If the case was pressing the patient was operated on at the Field Surgical Unit (British) or the Field Hospital Platoon (US). If the operation could wait, he was evacuated further back to the Casualty or Divisional Clearing Stations and from there to various hospitals in the rear.

The field surgical installations were the major organisational innovation of World War II. Pre-war theory had made insufficient allowance for the fluidity of the modern battlefield and both the British and the Americans had entered the war expecting that large semi-permanent hospitals quite near the front would be able to handle most of the surgical casualties. This rarely proved to be the case and subsequent experiments were largely an attempt to develop medical units that were mobile enough to keep up with the battle yet sufficiently well-equipped to offer the best possible attention. In the last analysis the contradiction is insoluble because adequate surgery demands time, and field units attempting to keep up with the fastest advances would never be able to actually perform any operations. Nevertheless, the challenge was more than adequately met and even in the most unfavourable circumstances the doctors managed to strike an excellent balance between swift surgical intervention and reasonably extensive facilities.[24]

Surgery itself did not undergo any dramatic changes. The only area of lively debate was the question of primary suture; at what stage, that is, to stitch up an open wound. The optimum arrangement was deemed to be secondary suture by which the wound was excised in the forward medical units but not stitched up until some time later when the patient was in a more stable environment. But this was only feasible when there were surgical centres fairly close to the fighting, and base hospitals within reasonable reach. In Burma, especially, it became the practice to rely on delayed primary suture by which the wound was sewn up in special forward holding units because the long trip to the base hospitals involved a very high risk of infection. One method that was almost universally abandoned after 1941 was that of letting the wound heal by granulation alone, with or without an evil-smelling plaster. The risk of infection was found to be too great, though in both France and the Middle East thousands of unnecessary cases of chronic toxaemia had already resulted.

But what of the wounds themselves? Basically, World War II was fought with explosive missiles and, whereas in the first two years of World War I approximately 80 per cent of all wounds were caused by gunshot, notably from machine guns, in World War II British battle casualties in all theatres can be broken down as in Table 5.

Table 5: Percentage of British battle wounds cause by different weapons
during the whole war

CAUSAL AGENT	PERCENTAGE OF WOUNDS
Mortar, grenade, aeriel bomb, shell	75
Bullet, anti-tank shell	10
Landmine, booby trap	10
Blast, crush	2
Chemical (phosphorous)	2
Other	1

These are official figures but they do seem to be somewhat at odds with smaller samples of battle casualties, where bullet wounds tend to figure more prominently. As a general rule gunshot wounds (GSW) accounted for between 25 and 30 per cent of all wounds in Africa, Burma and north-west Europe. The overall figures are also somewhat distorted in that they refer only to wounded men; a large proportion of those who later died of their wounds were GSW cases,[25] and it seems fair to assume that such wounds were also a prime cause of instant fatalities. This is supported by certain American figures. In both the Pacific and the Mediterranean it was found that of all those hit by bullets, 23 per cent were killed outright or died of their wounds. The equivalent figure for casualties from artillery fire was 19 per cent, from mortar fire 10 per cent and from grenades 5 per cent. Another sample of over 2,000 men hit made the same point, and also showed that although bullets were the greatest killer, 42 per cent of men hit by machine-gun fire died of their wounds as against 26 per cent of those hit by rifle fire.

Nonetheless, the basic point still remains that the majority of the wounded were not hit by bullets. The rifle by now was a subordinate weapon, mainly used by snipers or to keep the enemy's heads down. The pistol never had been of any use and even the machine gun had lost some of its old battlefield dominance because of the new emphasis upon dispersal and the widespread use of tanks and armoured personnel carriers. Light and heavy machine guns were used to pin the enemy down or deny him assembly points rather than to break up the kind of large-scale offensives that characterised the fighting on the Western Front. The mortar was the new anti-personnel weapon at company and battalion level, whilst artillery had never surrendered the central role it had assumed during the last two years of World War I.

None of this improved the lot of the combat soldier. Despite its high lethality, the bullet was in some ways the least of the evils listed above. The wounds it caused tended to be fairly small and they were also usually sterile, owing to the great heat of the missile and to the fact that its high velocity led to a rending of the clothing, so that scraps of soiled clothing were not carried into the wound. Moreover, bullet wounds generally focused the surgeon's attention on one particular point. Exploding shells, mortar bombs, grenades and mines, on the other hand, often caused multiple injuries, each of them worse than a simple bullet hole as jagged splinters of metal ripped and cartwheeled through tissues, arteries and organs. Internal damage could be devastating, whilst even flesh wounds often involved the removal of whole areas of tissue and muscle. In such cases the best surgery could never make full cosmetic restitution. Nor could it do much for those who had ears, jaws, arms and legs sliced off, and it was an irrelevance to those who were decapitated or cut in two by red-hot chunks of metal.

The bodily location of injuries has been analysed in several Allied samples, and there seems to be a remarkable consistency from theatre to theatre. The main point to emerge is that the whole body was equally at risk. Most men were not, for example, hit in the head or the upper chest. This is not surprising. The effects of explosive missiles were fairly random, whilst even small-arms fire relied on indiscriminate saturation rather than marksmanship. Even when men were under cover, explosive devices had a way of hurling shards of metal into the seemingly most inaccessible regions. By and large, therefore, the wounds were distributed in accordance with the percentage of body area. The head and neck accounted for 10 to 15 per cent of all wounds.[26] A further 50 per cent were to arms, hands, shoulders, chest and abdomen,[27] and a high proportion of these were to arms and hands, doubtless because this is the part of the body that moves about most, and is instinctively used to protect more sensitive portions of the anatomy. The genitalia emerged pretty much unscathed; only an average of 0.6 per cent of wounds were in this area. The rest of the single wounds occurred in the legs and feet, an average of just over 30 per cent. In some instances the high proportion of this kind of wound may be attributable to the prevalence of mines, but overall the correlation is fairly weak. In the 15th Division in north-west Europe, for example, 39 per cent of one lot of casualties were hit in the lower extremities, but in fact only 7 per cent of the division's total casualties in the same period were attributed to mines.

Nor is it possible to make any other convincing generalisations about the connection between type of missile and location of wound. The only conclusion that can be drawn from the available figures (Table 6) is that explosive missiles are more likely to cause head wounds than are bullets, almost certainly because the former are completely random whilst the latter are, in theory at least, aimed low.[28]

Table 6:

Percentage distribution of single wounds by body area and type of missile

	Head and neck		Extremities		Trunk	
	Alamein	N.W. Europe	Alamein	N.W. Europe	Alamein	N.W. Europe
Shell	26	18	48	47	15	12
G.S.W.	13	11	63	62	15	10

A final question is whether different types of troops were likely to suffer different kinds of wounds. Two distinctions that spring to mind are those between armoured troops and infantry, and between officers and men. In the former case, with regard to the site of wound, there was a significant difference in only one respect – that multiple wounds were much more common for tankmen than for foot soldiers. A sample of Normandy casualties shows that 41 per cent of tankmen suffered multiple wounds as against 26 per cent of the infantry. This, of course, accords with common sense, in that explosions in a confined space meant a very concentrated fragmentation, and in most cases red-hot splinters from the armour plating itself were as much of a hazard as the actual missile. As to the type of wound, there was another not unexpected difference between the two arms in that burns were much more common amongst tank crews because of the risks from exploding ammunition and petrol tanks. In fact, it is only surprising that the figures for armoured personnel are as low as they are. At Alamein, for example, burns accounted for 1 per cent of wounds to the 7th Armoured Division's infantry battalions and for 10 per cent of those in the AFVs. Similar proportions were recorded in other theatres, although for a limited period in 1942, when British armour was more than usually outclassed, burns accounted for 27 per cent of all armoured battle casualties in North Africa. The only other noticeable difference between the two arms concerns the wounding agent. Armoured vehicles afford protection against bullets and mortars; thus, whilst 62 per cent of one sample of hospi-

talised infantry wounded had been struck by these weapons, the
figure for armoured troops was only 35 per cent. Even this figure
might seem surprisingly high until it is remembered how many
tankmen were only hit when they were baling out of their disabled
vehicles. Conversely, in this same sample mines and artillery shells
account for 57 per cent of armoured casualties, as against only 34
per cent of the infantry's.

Few figures distinguish between officers and men in any of these
respects, and those that do show few significant variations. By and
large, the indiscriminate nature of modern weaponry meant that all
ranks suffered equally. One tentative conclusion from a north-west
European sample is that officers were slightly less likely to be
struck by small-arms fire and more likely to be injured by mines.
This would seem fairly logical in that officers led attacks and were
thus the most likely to trigger off a concealed mine or booby-trap.
On the whole, however, the only firm conclusion that can be drawn
is that already alluded to, that the officers stood a greater overall
chance of being wounded than the ordinary soldier. For those
involved the exact nature of the wound was doubtless somewhat
academic.

Disease

It might be thought that a discussion of casualty rates and the
effects of modern weaponry would cover most aspects of the medical history of World War II. Yet this is far from the case. In fact
surgery took something of a back seat to more mundane branches
of preventative medicine, and the greatest drain upon manpower
was not the enemy but disease and accidents. This was so not only
in the obviously unhealthy parts of the world; in every theatre
more men fell victim to microbes and viruses than to enemy action.
Only the US army, in the European theater of operations, can
claim to have treated more surgical than ordinary medical cases,
and many of the former were in fact accidental injuries. Everywhere else the enemy was at times no more than a minor irritant.
Although battle casualties amongst front-line troops were awe-
somely high, for the medical authorities they were only a small part
of the job. Whereas the British had 240,000 men wounded, the
RAMC treated 5 million cases of all kinds; the American total
of 640,000 wounded has to be set against a total caseload of
17½ million. The respective ratios are 1:21 and 1:27.

The consequent loss in manpower was enormous, for most of the sickness cases were far from trivial. In Italy, for example, the mean stay in hospital for non-battle casualties was 4 weeks. Even taking into account the fact that wounded men stayed in longer, on average 7 weeks, it is obvious that the vast bulk of man days lost, 413,393,000 by the US army, were not attributable to enemy action.

Table 7 is a breakdown of the British figures and gives the exact details of this gross disproportion between battle and non-battle casualties. The figures for three theatres are shown, expressed in terms of casualties per 1,000 ration strength per annum.

Table 7:
Causes of British army casualties, battle and non-battle, 1941-5

		1941	1942	1943	1944	1945
BATTLE CASUALTIES	Middle East	35	31	22	–	–
	Italy	–	–	64	90	10
	Burma	–	4	14	102	73
NON-BATTLE INJURIES	Middle East	49	48	49	–	–
	Italy	–	–	65	44	53
	Burma	–	33	64	45	61
SICKNESS	Middle East	585	506	442	–	–
	Italy	–	–	575	513	441
	Burma	–	1021	1746	1334	780

The pattern is clear. In the Middle East sickness alone was causing almost twenty times as many casualties as was actual combat, and even accidental injuries were more costly, in one year doubly so. The contrast in Italy is not quite so dramatic, though even here the ratio of wounds to sickness, over the whole period, is about 1:9, whilst only in one year are accidents less costly than wounds. In Burma the disparity is enormous. In 1943 the ratio of battle to non-battle casualties was 1:129, though remarkable progress had been made by the last year of the war when the proportion was cut to 1:7. American figures, aggregated by theatre for the whole war tell the same story. Even discounting men killed in battle, the ratio of battle to non-battle injuries to disease in Italy was 1:1.5:11, whilst in the Pacific it stood at 1:4:20.

The one bright feature of these figures was that medical advances meant that very few soldiers actually died from disease. Amongst British troops in north-west Europe, the death rate from sickness was a mere 0.1 per 1,000, as compared to 4.7 for those killed in action or dying of their wounds. The United States army lost only 0.6 per cent of their troops to disease in World War II, as compared to 10 per cent in the Mexican War, 7.2 per cent of Union troops in the Civil War and 1.3 per cent in World War I. In World War II, in fact, those in the army ran no greater risk of dying from non-battle causes than the civilians at home. The rate for the American army was almost exactly the same as that for the corresponding age-group out of uniform, about 3 per 1,000 per year. The British figures show that soldiers actually stood a better chance, and in 1943 and 1944 the ratio of civilian deaths by disease to army deaths was 1:0.7.

The most common diseases were remarkably uniform from theatre to theatre. In the Middle East, only a few types of complaint ran at more than 20 cases per 1,000 ration strength per year. These were diseases of the digestive system (79 per 1,000 per year), skin diseases (50), dysentery (33), venereal disease (31), malaria (29), inflammation of the tonsils (23) and sandfly fever (21). In Italy, the five most important diseases, in descending order, were malaria, skin diseases, tonsillitis and pharyngitis, venereal disease, and infections of the respiratory tract. In 1943, for example, *each* of these diseases caused more casualties than did enemy action. In north-west Europe, in the first quarter of 1945, the top five were diseases of the ear, nose and throat, of the digestive system, skin complaints, muscular diseases, and venereal disease. For the troops in Burma there lurked an array of exotic illnesses such as scrub typhus, dengue fever or Naga sores. 'Sore' hardly does the latter complaint justice. It was an ulcer caused by inexperienced soldiers tearing off leeches leaving their heads imbedded in the flesh. It would start as a small blister but within a few days grow to the size of a saucer, destroying all the skin and often tendons and muscles as well. The putrefying flesh gave off a vile smell. The most common complaints, however, were much the same as those in more 'civilised' theatres. The five most prevalent were malaria, unidentified pyrexia or fever, dysentery and diarrhoea, venereal disease, and diseases of the digestive system. US figures for the

Pacific show a similar pattern. Malaria was a particular scourge in New Guinea and Guadalcanal. On the former, Australian troops of the 16th Brigade made it a point of honour not to report sick unless their temperature was above 103°, whilst on the latter some American units suffered 75 per cent casualties from this disease alone. Dysentery was so widespread on certain islands that only the most acute cases, those that simply laid down to die, could be excused duty. Many others simply cut away the seat of their trousers and carried on as best they could.

Malaria is perhaps the most consistent of all these diseases. Even in north-west Europe in 1945 it was running at a rate of 1.2 cases per 1,000 men, 4 times the number of 'flu cases, and 24 times those of measles. However, almost all of these cases were men who had suffered a relapse after contracting the disease in more unhealthy parts. In North Africa and Italy, on the other hand, where the disease is endemic, about 50 per cent of the cases were first-time sufferers and many of the others had been re-infected as opposed to just suffering a relapse.

But it was in the Far East that malaria was the greatest problem. In Burma in 1943 the hospital admission rate for malaria alone was 628 cases per 1,000 men, a full 45 times the number of battle casualties. It can fairly be claimed that when the Allied effort in south-east Asia hung on a knife edge, it was the mosquito and not the Japanese that was largely responsible. Luckily, the large contingent of Indian troops in this theatre seemed somewhat less susceptible, though even they suffered 50 per cent malaria casualties in this same year.[29] Even more important, considerable progress was made in combating the disease as the war went on. At first the authorities came close to despair when the Japanese seizure of Java cut off one of the main supplies of quinine, the first effective counter. But the scientists quickly produced two excellent substitutes – atabrine, used by the Americans and Australians, and mepacrine, used by the British. They were very similar. Taken in tablet form they had to be swallowed once or twice a day and both had unpleasant side effects: they tasted extremely bitter and made one retch immediately after swallowing, whilst after any kind of prolonged dosage they gave the skin a permanent yellowish tinge. The troops were very suspicious of them and most subscribed to the inevitable myth that they made one impotent. Early experiments were certainly not encouraging. Vast numbers of pills were issued prior to the invasion of Sicily but many troops refused

to take them either through fear or, as with the veteran Eighth
Army, lofty contempt. One entire division actually refused to draw
its quota until specifically ordered to do so. Many men waded
ashore with the pills shoved in their pockets, without any water-
proof covering, and there were several reports of the sea turning
yellow in places.

Drugs were not the only response to the malaria problem. The
other main tactic was to thwart the carrier itself. Men were supplied with mosquito nets which had to be used all through the
night, and from one hour before sundown to sun-up all troops had
to wear slacks instead of shorts and roll their shirtsleeves down and
keep them buttoned. Repellent cream was also used, which had to
be smeared on every four hours. The first such issue was extremely
unpopular. Made of pyrethum and citronella, it was disgustingly
greasy and men went to great lengths to avoid using it. In 1944 it
was replaced by dimethyl phthalate and other liquids, subsumed
under the popular heading 'skat', and the men were much more
willing to actually use these. Malaria even became a matter of
military discipline. Officers were made responsible for ensuring
that their men adopted all these measures, and the commander of
any unit with an exceptionally high malaria rate could expect to be
replaced or even put on a charge.

By and large the measures worked. The combination of drugs –
by mid-1944 the Fourteenth Army was consuming 12 million
mepacrine tablets every month – and anti-mosquito precautions
reduced the infection rate dramatically. In the Far East it fell from
the peak of 628 cases per 1,000 men to only 128 per 1,000 in the last
months of the war. In Italy, the 76 cases per 1,000 in 1944 were
reduced to only 19 in the following year. Efforts were also made to
ensure that such cases as did occur imposed a minimal drain on
manpower. In Burma, forward malaria treatment centres were set
up as sections of a forward hospital devoted exclusively to malaria
treatment and convalescence, so that the majority of cases did not
have to be evacuated to remote parts of India to free beds for battle
casualties. The measure was also conceived as a way of making men
less likely to deliberately contract malaria to get away from the
front. On average, the time spent away from his unit by a malaria
victim was cut from six months to five weeks.

For other diseases there were no such dramatic breakthroughs
and most continued to exact the same toll throughout the war.
Hygiene was a constant problem in this respect. In the insecurity

of their general situation few troops were prepared to pay much attention to the seemingly petty dictates of regimental MOs and hygiene officers. Wherever men gathered so did refuse and excrement and so, sooner or later, did flies and disease. Flies, as has been seen, were a severe problem in many theatres, and they and other scavengers greatly increased the chances of disease. A US doctor wrote, after the liberation of Kwajalein:

Once the Japs are dead, sanitation becomes the major problem. We bury the filth and the stinking corpses. We dig heads and screen them. From now on flies are enemy number one. We screen the mess tents and the galleys and all refuse containers . . . We fight the rats. We oil the standing water against mosquitoes. The way to fight flies and rats is to starve them out. [30]

The heads, or latrines, were the bane of a hygiene officer's life. On New Guinea, for example, the main cause of dysentery and associated diseases was polluted water which had been fouled by natives or troops who had neither the time nor the inclination to use the latrines. Elsewhere, things were well worked out, in theory at least. In British rear areas deep trench latrines might be used or buckets that were then taken to what were known as Otway pits. In forward areas the incinerator latrine was the preferred method. A petrol tin was used as the receptacle and the accumulated contents were set alight with a little petrol or oil twice daily. Those responsible for such things noted that 'with careful maintenance one of these latrines was shown to last fifteen men for a fortnight'. [31] But such diligence was unusual, particularly in the Middle East. In 1941, the DDMS of Western Desert Force reported testily: 'The general standard of hygiene in the Force is now deplorably low and discipline in this, as in other matters, is very lax.' [32]

A great advance in the fight against flies and other sources of infection was the introduction of DDT (dichlorodiphenyltrichloroethane) in late 1944. The Americans came to rely upon it heavily and attributed much of their later success in combating disease-bearing lice, mosquitoes, flies, fleas etc to the liberal use of DDT sprays. At times the men's uniforms were actually impregnated with the stuff, notably as a safeguard against scrub typhus. In the D-Day landings all troops had typhus injections, but 750,000 impregnated shirts were also issued as a counter to lice. On Saipan liberal spraying with DDT of mosquito-breeding areas reduced an outbreak of dengue fever by 80 per cent in two weeks. In Naples, in 1944, it performed miracles in checking the ravages of a typhus epidemic. However these excellent results had inherent drawbacks. Certain medical officers claimed that the very efficacy of such measures made the troops careless about more mundane hygiene safeguards. The *Official British Medical History* aspired to new heights of 'po-faced' officialese when it complained about complete reliance upon DDT at the expense of more routine precautions: 'To most individuals there is no emotional satisfaction in getting rid of refuse in the approved ways.'[33]

Much of what has been said about illness so far has had to do with tropical, or at least very warm, climates. It should never be forgotten, however, that cold and damp could be an equal menace, and the bleak European winters were the cause of innumerable casualties. The common cold was inevitably present, though only 3 per cent of British troops in Europe actually had to be hospitalised on this account. Exposure was not unknown. In December 1943, in Italy, there were 113 cases among the 78th Division alone, 5 of whom died. In the Hürtgen Forest, 9,000 American troops fell victim to diseases associated with the appalling conditions, notably trench-foot and respiratory diseases.

Trench-foot was probably the most serious of these problems, at least until preventive measures were strictly enforced. The name had been coined during World War I, though the Americans preferred to speak of immersion-foot. Very akin to frostbite, it was the result of getting the feet wet and not being able to dry them for hours or even days on end. The feet went numb, turned purple and, in extreme cases, the nerves died off and gangrene set in. In such circumstances toes, or even the whole foot, had to be amputated.

In 1915 on the Western Front, trench-foot reached a peak of 38 cases per 1,000 men. Nothing in World War II approached this level, partly because a much lower proportion of soldiers were actually stuck at the front and partly because the most energetic measures were taken to forestall it. In the 21st Army Group for example, in the many waterlogged areas, the troops had to wash their feet twice daily with foot soap, apply liberal amounts of foot powder, made of talc, camphor and boric acid, and then put on a dry pair of socks.

At least such was the ideal, for in both north-west Europe and Italy the actual exigencies of the situation often made such pre-

cautions impossible. Between October and November 1943, X
Corps in Italy found that trench-foot was one of the 5 most
common diseases. The experiences of one group of 30 infantrymen
were typical. They had to spend 6 consecutive days on a mountain
top, under enemy observation, unable to light a fire or even take
their boots off. All of them ended up in hospital for at least 6 weeks.
The Americans suffered particularly heavily. Between November
1943 and the following October the monthly incidence of trench-
foot rose from 371 to 1,805 cases. One report went so far as to claim
that 25 per cent of all casualties, battle and non-battle, were attributable to the condition. American equipment did not help.
Until the last year of the war both Fifth and Eighth Armies were
using socks manufactured in the United States that proved far too
thin to cope with the cold or the moisture. The Americans were
also very short of galoshes, and their boots as well as their ordinary
shoes soaked up a great deal of water. Nor were soldiers encouraged to follow the prescribed safeguards when they found
that, if they took their boots off, their feet swelled so much that it
was almost impossible to get them on again.

Things were not much better in north-west Europe. In the week
ending 15 October 1944 there were only 320 cases of trench-foot.
A month later the weekly figure was 5,386. This was the largest
number of cases in this theatre, though the complaint peaked again
in December and mid-January. By April 1945 a total of 44,728 men
had been hospitalised for this reason alone. For it was not simply a
minor irritant but a crippling affliction which could take men out of
the line for good. In December 1944, 4,587 cases were reported in
the Third Army alone, and an army medical report estimated that
95 per cent of these cases would not be returned to duty before
spring. A later analysis showed that in fact 41 per cent of these
cases had been returned to the States as disabled. This was a
serious problem for those worrying about the acute manpower
shortage; what it meant for the men in the line is amply highlighted
by these observations of a combat soldier turned historian when,
during the battle for Aachen, the 30th US Division had many
casualties even during the supposedly quiet periods in reserve:

Many were from trench foot . . . and behind the lines the dressing
stations and field hospitals were full of soldiers whose toes had turned a
dull purple. If they were lucky the medics caught the complaint in time
and they would be put to bed in long lines of cots on which lay soldier
after soldier, their feet sticking out from under the blankets, with a

little ball of cotton wool separating each toe. If they were unlucky their toes would come away with their wet socks when the medics had finally eased them off.[34]

Another great cause of non-battle casualties is perhaps the most overlooked of all. The bald figures have already been mentioned in the discussion of Table 7, but it is worth re-emphasising just how many soldiers were put out of action by injuries sustained off the battlefield. Once again the Eighth Army had a particularly poor record in this respect, and their devil-may-care attitude seems to have led to chronic carelessness. From 1941 to 1943 there were consistently more accidents than battle casualties and in the latter year there were over twice as many.

In all theatres, fractures, burns and head injuries were the most common type of accident. The first and last, respectively 36 and 7 per cent of all incidents, were usually attributable to traffic accidents caused by bad roads, tired or careless drivers and often non-existent lighting. Burns were generally the result of the careless use of petrol. Even when burns suffered in combat reached a peak in North Africa in 1942, there were still more 'domestic' accidents of this type. A prime cause was the *ad hoc* 'desert stove' in which a tin was filled with sand, soaked in petrol and set alight. Accidents were also very common when naked lights were introduced as men were cleaning their clothes with petrol or using it to destroy vermin. Even in the heaviest periods of fighting the ratio of domestic to combat burns was usually between 2 and 3:1.

For the rest, accidents covered the whole gamut of human irresponsibility and bad luck. Some men shot themselves by mistake, some were killed on the assault courses, some fell off mountains, some off sidewalks. Some cut themselves whilst shaving, others blew themselves to bits. A surprisingly rare occurrence was snakebites. Despite the exotic nature of the fauna in Africa and the Far East, only three British soldiers actually died of a reptile bite; less, in fact, than succumbed in Tunisia and Italy after being kicked by a mule. But for sheer bad luck this story of Dugald Rankin of the 8th Indian Division tops them all. He took part in the last major battle of the Italian campaign, on the line of the Senio river in front of Bologna:

The battle took place at night, and was of the greatest severity. Within an hour or two all four company commanders had been killed or wounded. A young regular officer was sent forward to pull a very tricky situation together, and this he did magnificently. By dawn it was all over and our exhausted troops bedded down.

A little later a call came through from Brigade asking our CO to restage the battle of Senio for the Press and cameramen. The Colonel protested vigorously but the call had come from a very high and distant source . . . The officer who had behaved with such gallantry some hours previously was woken and given the glad news. With the utmost difficulty he got the survivors of his company to their feet and went through the charade of throwing bombs at an absent enemy. While supervising this piece of theatre he trod on a Schu mine and blew his leg off . . . The photographs – they looked phoney as hell.[35]

6
Discipline and Morale

Who are these? Why sit they here in twilight?
Wherefore rock they, purgatorial shadows?
Drooping tongues from jaws that slob their relish,
Baring teeth that leer like skulls' teeth wicked?
Stroke on stroke of pain – but what slow panic
Gouged these chasms round their fretted sockets?
And from their hair and through their hands' palms
Misery swelters. Surely we have perished
Sleeping, and walk in hell; but who these hellish?

WILFRED OWEN, 1917

Those men who have seen actual war at first hand,
seeing their buddies killed day after day, trying to
tell themselves that they are different – *they* won't
get it; but knowing deep inside them that they *can*
get it – those guys too know what real weariness
of body, brain and soul can be.

BILL MAULDIN, 1944

It always looks like a muddle. It often is. But the
actual business of fighting is easy enough. You go
in, you come out, you go in again and you keep
on doing it until they break you or you are dead.

7TH HUSSARS OFFICER, 1941

The basis of any army is discipline, unquestioning obedience of the orders of one's superiors. Other factors are of some importance, and will be touched upon in the final chapter, but without discipline there is little chance of persuading men to stoically accept all the horrors of modern warfare. Deference to the commands of superiors has to be automatic and unquestioning, and any signs of democratic thinking or individualism that might threaten such a response must be ruthlessly stamped out. This indeed, as we have seen, is one of the prime objectives of military training. Hopefully, some degree of military expertise will also be imparted, but this is secondary to developing the instinctive feeling that, as far as their inferiors are concerned, officers are omnipotent. This chapter tries to discover how far the various armies succeeded in enforcing discipline, and to what extent its judicious application helped morale; but as a preliminary one must see just what sort of men the officers were and how the other ranks regarded them.

Officers

In the British and American armies officers represented a little over 10 per cent of the total manpower; the US army in April 1945, for example, contained 891,663 officers and 7,376,295 enlisted men. Table 8 shows how this vast force was broken down by rank. I have been unable to find similar figures for the British army though there is no reason to believe that they differed very much.[1]

Table 8: Distribution of ranks in the US army, April 1945

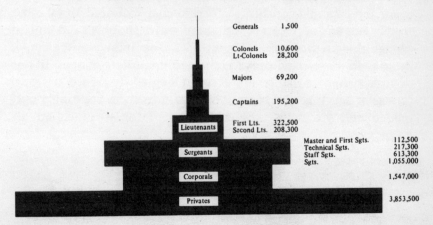

Generals	1,500
Colonels	10,600
Lt-Colonels	28,200
Majors	69,200
Captains	195,200
First Lts.	322,500
Second Lts.	208,300
Master and First Sgts.	112,500
Technical Sgts.	217,300
Staff Sgts.	613,300
Sgts.	1,055,000
Corporals	1,547,000
Privates	3,853,500

The very size of such armies meant that it was impossible for the pre-war regular establishment to supply more than a fraction of the eventual demand for commissioned men. Of the total accession to the US officer corps during the war, only 0.5 per cent were from the regular army, though the 2.3 per cent of National Guardsmen and 2 per cent of World War I veterans might be considered to have a similar background. The vast majority of officers, however, came straight from civilian life, being converted into officers and gentlemen in the American Officer Candidate Schools and the British Officer Cadet Training Units. All in all, some 75 per cent of American officers came direct from civilian life, though many of them served a short period as enlisted men before being selected for officer training.[2] Education seems to have been the prime determinant of whether a man was deemed suitable officer material, though this had obvious class implications in both Britain and the USA in that it was only the better off who had been able to afford to attend grammar or public schools, colleges, or universities. A Commons reply after the war revealed that three samples of 5,000 OCTU candidates consisted of 25 per cent public schoolboys with almost all the others from grant-aided grammar schools.

In the British army, however, even this represented a significant change from pre-war traditions. In 1939 it was found that 84.3 per cent of Sandhurst entrants had been to public school; moreover 40 per cent of these same entrants were themselves the sons of military professionals. At first in World War II the authorities tried to restrict their intake of cadets to this same tiny clique. Selection was purely a matter of a brief interview in which family connections, sporting activities and possession of those nebulous characteristics that constitute a 'decent chap' counted for far more than brains and application. But, haphazard, snobbish and limited though this method was, it is quite clear that many, most even, of the officers so selected proved outstanding leaders of men. In one of his poems, 'Aristocrats', Keith Douglas described his own unease at serving with such noble war horses, so seemingly outmoded and yet whose presence counted for so much on the battlefield.

◀ Walking wounded, Normandy, summer 1944: a sergeant of the Durham
Light Infantry, 50th Division, lights up under a hedgerow; and (*below*)
American wounded await evacuation over the Normandy invasion beaches.

▲ ▼ Among front-line infantry fatigue through exertion, nervous tension
and sheer lack of sleep often became chronic, to the point of halucination;
men became dull and careless, dangerous to themselves and their comrades.
Troops snatched what sleep they could, like these GIs in France; (*below*) one
Tommy in each two-man slit-trench was supposed to stay awake at all times,
while his mate slept.

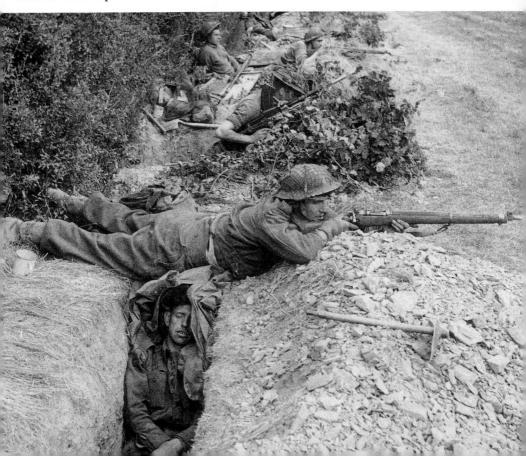

► The face of responsibility: a US Marine captain who distinguished himself in close fighting on Eniwetok atoll in the Marshall Islands, February 1944.

► One more beach, one more battle: a GI on his way to the invasion of the Philippines, October 1944.

◄ 'Street-fighting is a bad misnomer, because the last place you see any sane man is in a street where every yard is usually covered by a well-sited machine gun. It should be called house-to-house fighting. . . . Not many prisoners were taken, as if they did not surrender before we started on a house, they never had the opportunity afterwards.'

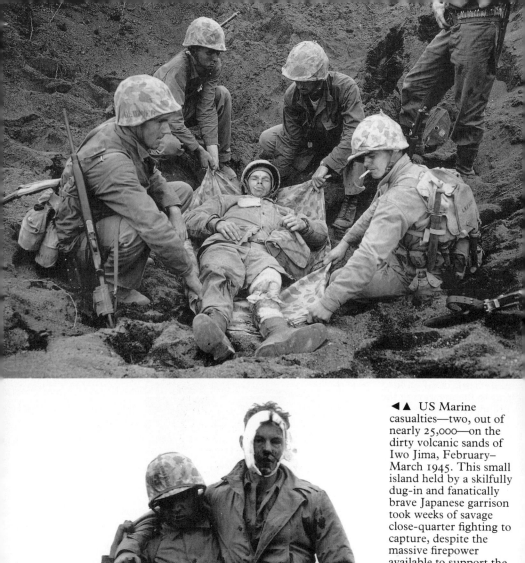

◀▲ US Marine casualties—two, out of nearly 25,000—on the dirty volcanic sands of Iwo Jima, February–March 1945. This small island held by a skilfully dug-in and fanatically brave Japanese garrison took weeks of savage close-quarter fighting to capture, despite the massive firepower available to support the infantry.

▶ A combat-weary Marine manages a grin for the photographer during the liberation of the Philippines, winter 1944–45. This was one of the few episodes of prolonged street-fighting in the Pacific theatre.

▲ British and Canadian troops fought in near-impossible conditions in the flooded polders of Holland in winter 1944–45—'a new form of hell' where '... every assault was a model of tactical insanity'.

◄ Battle fatigue.

► The Ardennes, December 1944: artillery fire is deadly in mature woodland, where 'tree bursts' cause many casualties. GIs, intent on digging themselves into even minimal cover, ignore a dead comrade a few feet away.

◄ Flesh wound.

► Two ways to die in a tank. Tank commanders who went into action exposed in the cupola hatch, for the sake of visibility, often paid the price of this Guards Armoured Division soldier during the drive to relieve Arnhem. (*Below*) Crew trapped inside a burning tank died by fire, or if they were lucky—as apparently in the case of this *Afrikakorps* Panzer crewman—by dismemberment when the stored ammunition detonated.

◀▲ When soldiers came out of the line they craved sleep, dry clothes, hot food, and mail from home. In the closing stages of the European war a chronic shortage of infantry in both British and US Armies made such periods of relief infrequent and brief.

▲▼ Veterans.

▲ ▼ Typical improvised 'concert party' just behind the front lines in North-West Europe. No matter how unsophisticated the entertainment on offer, the sheer relief of being at least temporarily out of danger was an almost ecstatic pleasure. (*Opposite*) US Marines bathe in a bomb-crater on a Japanese airstrip on Okinawa.

◄ Tank commander of US 1st Armored Division, Italy, 1945, resting before one of the final battles.
▲▼ Comradeship. 'Combat soldiers are an exclusive set, and if they want to be that way, it is their privilege.'

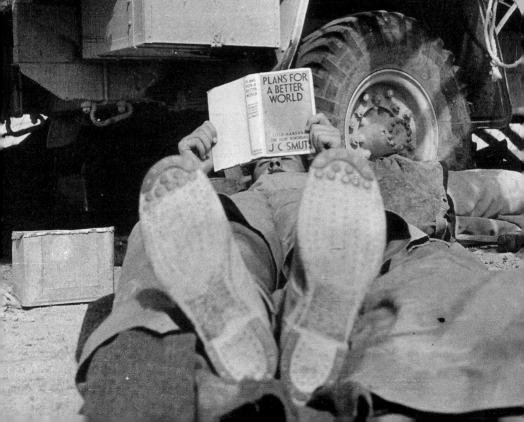

▲ The approach to battle: France, 1944. In the most mechanised armies yet seen, the infantryman still spent much of his war on his feet, loaded like a mule; and from mid-August 1944 the weather was persistently wet.

◄ The Ardennes, winter 1944–45: '. . . the meanest winter in thirty-eight years'. In January the US 30th Division was losing 100 men a day from illnesses attributable to snow and cold; in places the foxholes had to be blasted out with explosives.

▲▶ The face of battle:
Canadian survivors of the
costly Dieppe raid,
August 1942; and (right)
men of No. 4 Commando
land at Newhaven, only
hours after the Dieppe
fighting. The young
Commando, with a leg
ripped off his denims to
allow fast application of a
field dressing, appears to
be still in shock.

◀ The approach to
battle: Operation
'Torch', North Africa,
November 1942. GIs
await their moment of
truth in the landing craft
approaching the invasion
beaches.

▲ ▶ '... A shabby, gritty landscape.' Few areas of the Western Desert resembled the sweeping dunes of Hollywood fiction; most of it looked like a slovenly construction site—or, after the passage of the armies, like a fly-blown garbage dump.

(*Right*) Getting below ground level in the desert could be heartbreaking work: '... the ground was like iron, and it was almost impossible to dig down more than two feet without striking solid limestone.'

(*Opposite*) 'Desert Rat'.

▲ ▼ Advanced Dressing Station, 51st (Highland) Division, El Alamein, October 1942. The availability of penicillin, sulphonamides and transfusable bottled plasma gave the wounded of World War II a greatly improved chance of survival if they were found and treated in time. (*Below*) Very few pictures of Allied dead were accepted into the official archive record, and those that were never passed the censor for publication, for obvious morale reasons. This 8th Army infantryman died when Stukas attacked a routine patrol which happened to be accompanied by an Army photographer.

▲ ▼ The claustrophobia, and excrutiatingly slow movement, of jungle campaigning were exacerbated by constant humid heat and, in monsoon months, incredible rainfall—13 inches were recorded in one day on the Arakan front in November 1943. These Sikh infantry were photographed during the heavy fighting in Assam, March 1944; in this terrain one could step upon an enemy before seeing him. (*Below*) British wounded often had to be left behind during the 'Chindit' operations behind enemy lines in Burma, in full knowledge of their probable fate; these fast-moving columns evading the Japanese hundreds of miles from any help were physically incapable of carrying casualties in litters for any length of time.

◄▼ US Marine .50 cal. machine gun team solidly dug in on Bougainville in the Solomons, winter 1943. (*Below*) One of the concrete-reinforced Japanese bunkers on Tarawa. Some 3,000 tons of ordnance was fired or dropped on to the 290-acre atoll preparatory to the November 1943 assault landing, which still cost the US Marines some 3,400 casualties in 76 hours of fighting. The 2,600 Japanese defenders died almost to a man.

► US Marine machine gunner coming out of the line after nearly three weeks' combat: Cape Gloucester, New Britain, January 1944.

◀▼ Every theatre of war had its own brand of mud, and every soldier was convinced that the mud where he fought, marched and tried to sleep was uniquely miserable. Here a convoy bogs down on the Ledo Road, Burma. (*Below*) US Marine artillerymen in a flooded emplacement on Okinawa.

▶ Heavy artillery fire and air bombardment could reduce towns to a condition recalling the Western Front of 1914–18. This is Cassino, Italy.

▲ The knife-edged rocks of Monte Camino. It was impossible to dig in on these stony ridges; in winter infantrymen existed for weeks at a time in icy, rain-lashed hides of piled rocks, and stone splinters added lethally to the effect of shell- and mortar-fire.

◄ A town reduced to rubble—like San Angelo, Italy—was more difficult to capture from stubborn infantry than one still more or less intact. Largely immune to further bombardment, the dense heaps of masonry provided innumerable hidden, protected defensive positions for men and guns; they had to be found, and taken, one by one.

► Polish troops bring their dead off Monte Cassino, May 1944.

▲ ► The Normandy
bocage country of small
fields, massive overgrown
banks, and sunken lanes
was perfect defensive
terrain for determined
German infantry, anti-
tank teams and mortars.
Troops of the 52nd
(Scottish) Division
advance with supporting
tanks, August 1944, and
come under mortar fire in
a narrow lane.

◄ Cassino, May 1944:
captured German
paratroopers carry out of
the line a Tommy whose
left foot has been blown
off by a mine.

How can I live among this gentle
obsolescent breed of heroes, and not weep?
Unicorns, almost, for they are falling into
two legends in which their stupidity and chivalry
are celebrated. Each, fool and hero, will be an immortal.
The plains were their cricket pitch
and in the mountains the tremendous drop fences
brought down some of the runners. Here then
under the stones and earth they dispose themselves,
I think with their famous unconcern.
It is not gunfire I hear but a hunting horn.

The nonchalant bravery of such officers was often amazing. According to the regimental history of the Scots Guards, an attack on Musaid in June 1941 'was remarkable in several ways. It was across open ground against an unreconnoitred position of unknown strength. The charge was led by the Commanding Officer with rifle and bayonet and smoking a pipe'.[3] R. L. Crimp, in another desperate battle, saw 'the Colonel and the Adjutant . . . having grand sport with borrowed rifles, picking off the crews climbing out of stricken panzers. They vie with each other in choosing their targets, take careful aim, and chalk up their respective "bags" with mock-emulative gusto. You'd think they were out shooting grouse'.[4] During the Sidi Rezeg fighting, the 2nd Black Watch was almost wiped out attacking a German position. A Rhodesian officer who survived recalled:

The enemy held his fire until we were past the wire. And then his machine guns let go. Such of us that survived fell flat to take what cover we could; but our Adjutant, who had been wounded, crawled to where we were lying and got to his feet. 'Isn't this the Black Watch?' he cried. 'Then – charge!' He waved us on with his stick and was instantly killed.[5]

Most of the older regimental officers and a good number of young subalterns were wiped out in the Middle Eastern campaigns but their type lived on. In the County and Guards regiments, especially, the 'old sweats' were constantly amazed at the careless gallantry of young 'chickos' straight from England. Their language and languid deportment seemed from another era. After one Tunisian battle, a newspaper correspondent encountered a group of 17/21st Lancers officers

. . . chattering away as if they had been enjoying a bath after polo: 'Absolute Gilbert and Sullivan. There was the Brigadier with his head stuck out and all the stuff flying around, and there was I sitting down and trembling like an aspen' . . . 'They said, Hold on at all costs, and we were stuck out in front, so we supposed that was where they meant' . . . 'Old George was pooping off at anything and everything' . . . 'I say, wasn't it a shame they beat up that German motor-cyclist? Could have had a bloody good motor-bike if only everybody hadn't shot him to pieces.'[6]

At Anzio was an imperturbable officer whom the Americans dubbed 'Typical Englishman No 1'. According to one correspondent

> . . . the gallant captain was . . . a reservoir of strength and his clipped English and stylised public-school attitude to every situation helped to create the legend that nothing could 'rattle' him. It was impossible to believe that an exploding shell held any menace when the captain remarked in his quiet drawl, 'God, that one landed only a mashie shot away.'[7]

Private Ian Kaye (5th Black Watch) remembered his platoon commander's address before an attack on Hörst, in 1944. '"OK? If we manage to get into the village without a fight, we move in to clear the houses on each side of the road, and once that is done, we dig in like billy-ho! *Right*? Let's go then, lads. Good luck and bloody good hunting!" That was how he approached things. But he was a damned good bloke and he made *you* feel good too.'[8] Captain F. Majdalany (2nd Lancashire Fusiliers) described the arrival of a new officer to join his battalion in Tunisia:

> Sheldon watched him walk away. He'd be all right. The keen young public-schoolboy type. The kind that hero-worship easily and bust themselves for the honour of the house. You could laugh at them. You could be irritated by them. But they won your bloody wars for you. Because they had been bred and conditioned to bust themselves for the house. Boys, admittedly. Childish, innocent, naive, and in need of a captain of the school to hero-worship. But they won your wars for you. The boy had charm, too, Sheldon thought, and charm is one of the most important things for an officer to have.[9]

Such men had provided the backbone of the British Army for 150 years and more, but by 1941 it was futile to think that there would be anywhere near enough of them. They were a vanishing class within British society and such as there were of them were being killed and wounded in large numbers. The authorities fairly quickly realised this and made a concerted effort to broaden their catchment area, so that in 1942 new methods of officer recruitment were introduced, spearheaded by the War Office Selection Boards. Meritocratic criteria were uppermost and each board included a non-regular officer and a psychiatrist. The interviews lasted three days, at an isolated country house, and many psychological tests were used. Some 60,000 officers had been passed by the end of the war, of whom only 12 per cent were subsequently deemed manifestly unsatisfactory – the advantages of the new system were undeniable.[10] Within a few months there was a new feeling that the officer corps was no longer a snobbish élite and applications for commissions rose by 25 per cent over the 1939–41 level. Moreover, to the chagrin of a few Blimpish die-hards, above average gradings at the end of the training course went up by 12 per cent.

The American army had long been more systematic in its selection procedures, though here too questions of economic advantage, as well as family connection, still counted considerably, particularly where the exact nature of one's posting was concerned. Though the system did, by and large, adhere to democratic criteria, it did not completely succeed in finding the best men for the job. The army was quite soon obliged to set up Reclassification Boards to weed out incompetent officers, though it should be noted that many of these were ageing regulars and National Guardsmen who had attained senior positions during the frantic expansion of 1940 and 1941. These Boards examined 6,700 officers, of whom 327 were demoted, 4,123 kicked out, and 2,250 similarly propelled sideways or upstairs.

As in any other group, there were always good officers and bad ones, those who were popular with men and those who were hated. Generalisations about the relations between officers and men are dangerous, but a few basic points seem valid. On the whole, relations were much better in combat units, partly because the officers had an obviously useful role and their men were only too eager to be told what to do in the chaos of action, and partly because the fighting battalions and divisions had a much closer *esprit de corps* than did the amorphous rear-echelon formations. An American survey found that officers in inactive theatres were invariably held in lower esteem by their men, whilst in active theatres the best relations were found in the front-line units.[11] Lieutenant Colonel John Mulgan (Oxford and Buckinghamshire Light Infantry) recalled how, in the fighting units of the Eighth Army, even the most rarified young officers developed a genuine bond with their men:

The young gentlemen of England do their best, of course. They always do their best, particularly in wartime. In peacetime the young gentlemen can be average hell . . . Their ignorance is wide and alarming and their acceptance of a social framework is as instinctive as the act of breathing. In wartime they developed at once the standard virtues – courage and character, and in some hesitating way a sort of kindliness. But all their education held them back from understanding other men; it needed battle and pain and sudden death to bridge the gap that they themselves created . . . There still remains with me a vision of that sun-tried Desert Army, as a model of what men in the ugly business of fighting should attain to; and behind this belief lies a hope that this might remain as a lesson and an ideal.[12]

Two remarks by hospitalised American veterans show how the soldiers' own instinctive suspicions were overriden by the stress of combat. Said one: 'Regardless of the situation, men turn to the officer for leadership, and if he doesn't give it to them then they look to the strongest personality who steps forward and becomes a leader . . .' The other was even more to the point: 'About officers – everybody wants somebody to look up to when he's scared. It makes a lot of difference.'[13]

However, it would not do to romanticise the situation. Even at the front the relations between officers and men often left much to be desired, particularly in units new to combat. In Tunisia, a British correspondent met numerous GIs who 'praised [the British soldier] to the limits of their indecent but graphic vocabulary; but one and all regretted that so many "lords and such folk" were officers, even while they violently stated that they were good officers, and that their own in their view were "jumped up farts" and "nothing but brush salesmen".'[14] On New Guinea, during the first attacks on Buna, Colonel Rogers, the I Corps Intelligence Officer, found that the men 'were receiving far less than adequate rations and there was little discipline or military courtesy . . . When Martin and I visited a regimental combat team . . . it was found that the regimental post was four and a half miles behind the front line. The . . . commander and his staff went forward from this location rarely, if ever.'[15] The situation improved a great deal later in the war as more and more officers became combat veterans, known as such to their men, but in terms of leadership at least the officers were never quite as respected by their men as they thought they were. An interesting insight into this is contained in one of the US army questionnaires. In 1944, samples of men from several infantry divisions were asked what was most important to them, in combat, in making them want to keep going and do well; the officers were asked what they thought these incentives for the men would be. Nineteen per cent of the officers felt that 'leadership and discipline' must be the key factor, but they shared this opinion with a mere 1 per cent of the men.

The further one got to the rear, the more could one speak of real tensions between officers and men. Indeed, they were inevitable to some extent in all units, for the whole point of being an officer was that one was to remain aloof from the other ranks – itself a marvellously contemptuous definition – and the enlisted men. Undue familiarity was to be avoided at all costs, as this might lead the men to question one's orders or even one's right to give them. In the field, the more overt aspects of this isolationism were mitigated by the common sense of suffering, the lack of amenities for anyone, and the manifestly heavy load the officers bore in combat. In some units, and especially in armoured formations where officers and men were in intimate contact, a close bond was formed. As Lieutenant Wilson wrote:

> Looking at his men, [he] sometimes wondered what was his bond with them. It came to this: three months ago he'd taken them over as a stranger. They knew nothing about him and obeyed him only because they had to. Now they'd seen half a dozen battles together, and the troop had come through almost as a whole. They obeyed him because they trusted him.[16]

Nevertheless, though there were strong centripetal forces at work in the front line, there were other influences that had a markedly divisive effect. The whole rationale of the officer corps was based upon a rigid distinction between commissioned and other ranks. An American, M. Brewster Smith, went through an officer training course after a period as an enlisted man and was very aware of what the authorities were trying to do. The course was nothing less than

> . . . an assault on [the candidate's] personality organisation [in which] his previous valuations fail him and in order to find a basis for self-respect, he must adopt new standards or escape from the field . . . New appropriate attitudes are built up and established. The catastrophic experience provides a kind of purgatory, a definite demarcation from the candidate's enlisted incarnation that puts a barrier between the new officer and his enlisted memories. It has some of the characteristics of a conversion experience, or the ordeal of a medieval knight.[17]

A key factor in this process is the buttressing of the officer's self-esteem by overt privilege; better uniforms, pay and quarters, a separate mess, a servant, ready access to transport etc. Some of these privileges were absurdly unfair. A common gripe of GIs already badly starved of leave, was that officers were entitled to furlough pay even for that leave which they were unable to take, whilst the enlisted men simply forfeited the lot. The question of 'sanctions in the Army, wherein the punishment must not degrade the rank is [also] a sore spot of contention. For identical infractions of the same rule the higher rank will actually suffer less – and less proportionately. Officers are rather lenient with one another on courts martial. An NCO will usually be reduced to the grade of private for inefficiency, whereas an officer will be merely transferred.'[18] Nothing shows this better than a poem by Lincoln Kirstein, an American private in Europe, describing an actual incident. An officer came into a French bar in which some privates and noncoms were drinking and proceeded to get ostentatiously drunk. At one point he pulled out his pistol and accidentally shot the *patron*'s wife dead. He was charged only with drinking with enlisted men. The whole question of privilege remained a vital issue to American soldiers throughout the war and complaints about it occurred repeatedly in the reports of the army's research branch, the following being typical examples:

'I consider the Army tradition bigoted and medieval, utterly out of keeping with our democratic ideals.' (India/Burma)
'They treat you like a dumb idiot not able to have an opinion of his own and not able to think for himself.' (Okinawa)
'We are fighting for democratic and free-speaking peoples. The Army has too much class distinction.' (ETO)
'I hate to be treated as a slave; to be called to do things as one calls a dog. Cheap labour.' (Italy)[19]
'The Army officers I know and have been under have always treated the Enlisted Men like slaves and no good.' (ETO)
'The officers have got the idea that the Enlisted Man is just a man to clean up his dirt and take what's left over. That is most of them, not all.' (Italy)
'Officers deserve respect and privileges, but they don't deserve the jeeps, gasoline, whiskey and women that naturally go along.' (Oahu)
'We aren't in the Army to build officers' Paradises. Most of the officers aren't worthy of the uniforms they wear.' (Saipan).[20]

Nor was the British army without its problems in this respect. There, too, the distinction between officers and men was seen as absolutely fundamental to the maintenance of discipline and it tended to be flaunted in front of the men at every available opportunity. Even at the front the position was made quite clear. In one tank unit, near Nijmegen, the officers made their mess in a farmhouse parlour where there was 'a crackle of wood in the stove, a bottle of Bols on the table, and a patter of rain on the blacked out windows'. One officer went out to talk to his men

> . . . who were sitting, half-soaked, in the lee of a truck trying vainly to light a stove to brew tea. It wasn't anybody's fault: there was simply nowhere else for them to go. But suddenly he saw the frightening difference between the officers' war and the men's – how everything, from the award of honours to the warmth of a stove, fell to the officers, while it was taken for granted that the men should bear their part with regimental pride.[21]

Away from the front, distinctions were even more rigid, ordinary soldiers being treated almost as an untouchable Indian caste. The Far Eastern theatre, indeed, offers two remarkable examples of snobbery and rank consciousness. During the battle for Hong Kong a company of the Canadian Royal Rifles were organising themselves for a last stand at Stanley Barracks when they received a telephone call from a senior British officer asking them to resite their reserve platoon position, which was then in the officers' mess. 'I have a definite promise from the Brigadier that no troops will be allowed in the Officers' Mess,' he announced brusquely.[22] A letter to *SEAC*, the forces' paper in that theatre, tells its own story and speaks volumes about army attitudes to rank. An Australian, Private C. Brown wrote:

> With wrath we of this camp learned this morning of a new order to the effect that ex-POWs must salute all Japanese officers. No-one who has not witnessed the countless humiliations and cruelties inflicted on POWs by the Japanese can appreciate the anger and disgust that this order excites in us . . . We Australians suspect that the order emanates from one of the not-yet extinct Poona pukka sahib type, the type that sees something sacrosanct in an officer – any officer.[23]

Officers, of course, were exempt from this injunction. An Australian divisional order gives a splendid lecture on the niceties of etiquette in such circumstances: 'An officer will in no circumstances return the salute of a Japanese but will merely indicate that he has noted the action by a direct and severe look into the eyes of the Japanese concerned.'[24]

Discipline

Whether a more relaxed system of discipline in the army would have contributed to better fighting efficiency is very much a debatable point. In fact, very few attempts were made to introduce a more democratic structure, and those that were might seem to bear out the views of the traditionalists. In Merrill's Marauders, for example, formal signs of rank and discipline were almost entirely absent, and whilst the unit fought exceptionally well, it as good as mutinied in August 1944. It should be noted, however, that their protest was against Stilwell and his staff rather than against their own officers. For the most part discipline was defined and enforced in the old-fashioned manner and it has to be admitted that, whilst most men chafed and grumbled at the myriad petty constraints on their freedom, there were very, very few cases of serious insubordination.

Unfortunately, there seem to be no figures relating to minor offences, for which men were tried by their company or battalion commander who had the authority to fine them or confine them to barracks for not more than twenty-eight days. Drunkenness, returning late from leave, petty insubordination etc were dealt with in this way, but it is not known what proportion of men were actually brought before their COs or what were the most common offences.

More serious crimes went before a court martial, where the accused was tried by officers of other regiments and where the available sanctions ranged from a reprimand, through demotion, confinement with hard labour, penal servitude, all the way to death by hanging. Some figures are available here. In the British army, between September 1939 and August 1945, a total of 211,684 men appeared before courts martial, 127,807 of these in England and only 83,877 abroad.[25] On the face of it the figures seem substantial but, in fact, they are only a small proportion of the total number of soldiers. The actual ratios fluctuate between 6.5 trials per 1,000 men in 1939–40 and 17.5 per 1,000 in 1944–5. In the American army, a total of 30,000 men were convicted and imprisoned by general courts martial, those that dealt with serious offences such as robbery, rape and murder. In the ETO such offences involved only 0.53 per cent of the total number of troops who served in this theatre. The death penalty was used very sparingly, only 102 American soldiers being executed throughout the war. All but one

232

of these, who was shot for desertion, were for crimes that would invoke the death penalty in civilian life also.

The Military Police were one of the main agents in preferring disciplinary charges against ordinary soldiers and the following breakdown of their activities in the 21st Army Group gives some idea of the most common offences. In all 36,366 charges were laid including:[26]

10,363	absence without leave (AWOL)
6,409	offences involving military vehicles
2,792	improper dress
1,249	theft
1,092	drunkenness
72	looting

Clearly AWOL was by far the most pressing problem but this is discussed in more detail later in the chapter. Two of the other categories, vehicles offences and looting, are worthy of elaboration. The first were surprisingly common and were a reflection of the men's frustration with their consistent inability to ever obtain military transport despite the plethora of trucks and jeeps. Thus by far the most common offence was the 'borrowing' of such a vehicle to get around in the rear areas. In big cities the scale of this abuse was remarkable. Just before the Ardennes offensive, in Brussels, an average of seventy jeeps were being reported lost each day. Looting was a bigger problem than the above table might seem to indicate. Charges were rarely brought simply because neither the British nor the American armies had worked out any official policy on the subject. On the whole officers and MPs tended to overlook any but the most brazen 'liberation' of civilian property. One American officer spoke of

. . . The widespread looting of private property which went on not only in enemy Germany but in friendly France. 'How was the looting?' was the first question by a newcomer to a town that our troops had just occupied. Although looting was officially frowned upon, it had powerful group sanction and approximately 80 per cent of my company engaged in it in one form or another. This looting continued for extended periods after order had ostensibly been restored.[27]

Nor was it restricted to civilian property. Vast amounts of military material was seized by soldiers, more likely those working in the rear echelons, while it was in transit. Often this was simply because the soldiers themselves were short. In the Middle East, one soldier witnessed 'a train loaded with Naafi goods destined for the front . . . being ransacked. Scores of squaddies are climbing into the wagons and helping themselves to as many bottles of beer, bars of chocolate and packets of biscuits as they can carry'.[28] In Europe, however, the main motive for this type of theft was to resell the merchandise on the Black Market. In France and Germany, cigarettes brought $2.40 a packet, a chocolate D-Bar $1, a pair of GI shoes $30, and a khaki shirt $20. Lieutenant McCallum remarked that 'a man was a fool if he didn't leave the port of Le Havre with at least $1,000 in his pocket'.[29]

Morale and Combat Fatigue

On the whole discipline held together very well, especially among the front-line troops, and there was never any question of a long-term or widespread collapse of the traditional deference to superiors. Obedience was often grudgingly given but it was almost always forthcoming even, as we have seen, in the face of almost certain death. But it would be idle to think in terms of unthinking machines, snapping to attention with a cheery grin, eager to 'have another crack at the Boche, sir'. Whilst there was no concerted rejection of the hierarchical assumptions that underpinned military organisation, there were numerous examples of soldiers, both individually and collectively, being temporarily unable or unwilling to face up to the strains of combat. Individually, soldiers either deserted or broke down psychologically, whilst collectively they panicked or came to the point of mutiny. It is vital to appreciate the intensity of the strain under which combat soldiers laboured for much of the time. The physical rigours of the front have already been dealt with; what we must focus upon now is the dreadful fatigue and mental tension that these engendered.

Fatigue of itself was a fearsome burden. One is not talking about mere tiredness or the smug yawns at the end of a heavy day, but about that end of the spectrum of fatigue that is usually only of interest to psychiatrists or secret policemen, about sleep deprivation so acute that the mind itself begins to give up the unequal struggle. Examples abound from all theatres. Not surprisingly, men found themselves particularly short of sleep during the endless retreat that constituted the campaign in France and Belgium in 1940. An officer of the Highland Division wrote:

The state of exhaustion these infantrymen were in is almost impossible to describe. For six weeks . . . they had never had the opportunity to rest properly, to get off their clothes or even their boots . . . There were no beds, not even chairs to sit on, no shelter, no proper periods of rest or meal times . . . Men fell asleep standing on their feet so long as they could rest their heads on something, a wall, the parapet of a bridge, the side of a truck.[30]

The War Diary of the 1st Royal Irish Fusiliers wrote of 'a lack of sleep so acute that eyes throbbed and felt as if they had grit in them, so compelling that men went to sleep on their feet, waking with a guilty start that was physically painful'.[31] In the 2nd Gloucester Regiment no one had any sleep for four days and nights and liaison officers had to give orders to other officers individually because at a group conference everyone else immediately fell asleep. Regimental Sergeant Major Pierce kept himself awake on the march by sticking his bayonet in his belt with the point under his chin.

In this campaign physical tiredness was no doubt compounded by the psychological effects of defeat. Nevertheless, such degrees of exhaustion were far from unique to this theatre. In all of them, in fact, many troops were driven to their limits. In Syria, Captain John Verney and his men were trapped on a ridge under enemy bombardment; the position was desperate but no one was 'frightened or even excited. Chiefly we were scorching hot and thirsty and dead tired. I saw men sleeping, literally sleeping, with bullets spattering round them'.[32] By the end of the North African campaign all units were bone weary. As the historian of the Argyllshire Highlanders noted of the 8th Battalion in Tunisia:

The officers and men who had endured the whole campaign were tired to a degree which they did not realise. They were not so much physically tired as mentally exhausted by the nervous strain, for the Battalion had never been more than a few miles from the battle front and had never been given a chance of real relaxation or genuine undisturbed rest for six months.[33]

In Burma and the Pacific things were made even worse by the utterly enervating climate. An American correspondent in Burma wrote of the men, British and American, who were driven to the last extremities during the fighting there:

I cannot find words to describe this weariness of the battlefield. I know that in extreme cases it can cause death. I know that there are hundreds of people who died on the retreat from Burma because, when the rains came and turned the paths into muck, the going became so tough that men, enervated by months of ceaseless resistance, literally and completely were exhausted and lay down on the paths and died.[34]

With regard to American divisions in the Pacific, we have the testimony of the troops themselves, as set out in one of the official surveys. A sample of company officers from two divisions in the South Pacific were asked what factor was the most important in explaining bad combat performances by their men; 72 per cent named 'fatigue of troops from being held in combat too long' as one of the major reasons, whilst another 41 per cent also cited 'lack of endurance due to poor physical condition'. Colonel L. J. Thompson's description of the progressive deterioration of the soldiers on Guadalcanal is equally applicable to numerous other Pacific battlefields:

All of these men lost weight and none of them were pudgy when they landed on the beach. Weight losses in muscular, toughened young adults ran as high as 45lb. Rain, heat, insects, dysentery, malaria all contributed, but the net result was not bloodstream infection, nor gastro-intestinal disease, but a disturbance of the whole organism. A disorder of thinking and living, of even wanting to live. As weeks passed hope left most of the men. Soon they were sure that they were expendable, doomed. Fatigue wore them down, painful aching fatigue that they felt could never be relieved or cured.[35]

The survey mentioned above also included officers in Italy, and they too felt that fatigue and poor physical condition were among the main reasons for inadequate combat performance. Another survey, in the same theatre, was carried out amongst men serving in rifle and heavy-weapons companies. They were asked: 'When you were last on active duty, how many hours of sleep did you average each twenty-four hours?' They answered as follows:[36]

Hours	% giving answer
Less than 2	3
2–4	28
5–6	54
7 plus	13

This, it should be noted, was in April 1945, at a time when the line was fairly static and some degree of rotation with other battalions could be instituted. During prolonged offensive operations, such as Cassino or the Gothic Line, the number of hours of sleep can be at least halved. John Steinbeck was only a war correspondent but he, too, came to know what it meant to be tired almost to the point of physical collapse. One of his later dispatches gives a starkly detailed description of the approach of mental and physical disintegration:

> Your skin feels thick and insensitive. There is a salty taste in your mouth. A hard, painful knot is in your stomach where the food is undigested. Your eyes do not pick up much detail and the sharp outlines of objects are slightly blurred . . . The whole world becomes unreal . . . Gradually your whole body seems to be packed with cotton. All the main nerve trunks are deadened, and out of the battered cortex curious dreamlike thoughts emerge. It is at this time that many men see visions . . . And out of the hammered brain strange memories are jolted loose, scenes and words and people forgotten, but stored in the back of the brain. These may not be important things, but they come back with startling clarity into the awareness that is turning away from reality. And these memories are almost visions.[37]

The campaign in north-west Europe, though it brought final victory, was no less exhausting than any of the earlier slogging matches. By the last month of the campaign, according to one regimental historian:

> Signs of the prolonged strain had already begun to appear. Slower reactions in the individual; a marked increase in cases of 'battle exhaustion'; and a lower standard of battle efficiency – all showed quite clearly that the limit was fast approaching . . . At home there seemed to be widespread impression that resistance ceased on the Rhine; and the sweeping advance across Germany had become just an easy triumphal procession. How far that idea deviated from the truth requires no emphasis.[38]

Bill Mauldin, as usual, got down to the nitty-gritty details of just why the soldiers found it so difficult to get enough sleep:

> One thing is pretty certain if you are in the infantry – you aren't going to be very warm and dry while you sleep. If you haven't thrown away your blankets and shelter half during a march, maybe you can find a guy who has kept his shelter half and the two of you can pitch a pup tent. But pup tents aren't very common around the front. Neither is

sleep for that matter. You do most of your sleeping whilst you march. It's not a very healthy sleep; you might call it a sort of coma . . . You don't feel very good when you wake up, because there is a thick fuzz in your head and a horrible taste in your mouth and you wish you had taken your toothbrush out before you threw your pack away. It's a little better when you lie down, even in the mud. Rocks are better than mud because you can curl yourself around the big rocks, even if you wake up with sore bruises where the little rocks dug into you. When you wake up in the mud your cigarettes are all wet and you have an ache in your joints and a rattle in your chest.[39]

Others too wrote of the effects this chronic lack of sleep had on the soldiers. Lieutenant Ainsworth (2nd Household Cavalry) remembered his first sight of American soldiers in Normandy who, 'being dog tired, did not take the slightest notice of us. If British faces have a reputation for stolidity, then surely those of the Americans are graven. Quite expressionless, sallow with fatigue, one and all masticating gum and silent in their rubber-studded top boots, they padded by . . .'[40] For the men themselves the effects of such fatigue were unnerving. Tankers almost got to the point of hallucinating in some of the long drives across France and Germany. A Grenadier officer of the Guards Armoured Division remembered a night drive to Brussels, one of those ordeals 'where sleep comes over in great waves, at times almost impossible to fight off. The strain of trying to follow the route on the map and pick out the road with only the thin pin-pricks of sidelights to help, brought before one's eyes strange hallucinations of barriers and bridges and herds of cattle that were just not there.'[41] Things were just as bad for the infantry, for whom even the most straightforward activity soon became a mental and physical torture. Major A. D. Parsons (4th Wiltshire Regiment) took part in the assault on Mont Pinçon which was a fight not only with the Germans but with 'the burning sun, the choking dust, our parched throats and empty bellies, the craggy slopes and tangled thickets, the rocky earth and above all our utterly weary bodies'. At one point his company were told to dig in near the summit. 'We were as tired as troops could be, and many of us fell asleep as we were digging positions in the rocky soil, falling headlong, pick in hand, into the half-dug trenches, dead to the "wide".'[42] No other story, perhaps, better conveys the effect of crushing fatigue than the following by an American staff officer. Academy class-mates of his were fighting in the Hürtgen Forest and he used to drive out to meet them when they came out for a brief rest:

We tried to get them to tell us what it was like in the line now. One man said: 'Well, its not too bad until the doughs get so tired that when they are coming out of the line and there is a dead dough from their own outfit lying on his back in their way, they are just too goddam tired to move their feet and they step on the stiff's face because what the hell . . .'[43]

However, as many of these extracts have themselves indicated, physical fatigue was far from the only strain upon the combat soldier. One thing that numerous soldiers refer to is an increasing weariness of the spirit, a slowly dawning and dreadful realisation that there was no way out, that the odds were stacked against the front-line soldier and it was only a matter of time before they got killed or maimed or broke down completely. A British officer in north-west Europe wrote of this continuous mental torment. 'There's only one way to fight it, strength; you must be strong with yourself, with your men, with everything; never weaken; never show that you're afraid. Everybody cracks up in the end of course, but you hope something will have happened by then.'[44] But what if even that hope runs out? For that is what happened to most men who fought through for more than a few months. As early as 1941 an officer of the 7th Hussars gave the following appreciation of armoured warfare in the desert to a group of newcomers from the 2nd Royal Gloucester Hussars: 'It always looks like a muddle. It often is. But the actual business of fighting is easy enough. You go in, you come out, you go in again and you keep doing it until they break you or you are dead.'[45] An infantry officer in the desert remarked how the possibility of death is always uppermost in a soldier's mind. For a while his belief in his own uniqueness seems an adequate guarantee of immunity, plus the fact that he is 'a unit in a homogeneous army, in which it is possible to forget individual fears in the feeling of strength derived from the mass, he is also the individual with greater protection, more certain powers of survival than his fellows. His private magic is good'. But the months go on and his friends fall around him; the laws of probability remorselessly undermine his fragile system of personal magic. 'His own escapes appear more and more miraculous, and the easy-going attitude of chance wears thin. His good luck cannot hold. Sooner or later there will be his shell or his bullet. When he realises this the result may be many things according to the individual.'[46]

For some the reaction was only a kind of dour fatalism. By 1943, Corporal Ralph Pearse (2nd West Yorkshire Regiment) was quite convinced that he could not survive the war. 'Both Sid Wright and I were sure by this time that we couldn't go on coming through battle after battle alive. Like Sid, I'd become a fighting man and nothing else; no hope of anything else but more fighting, until in the end we knew we must be killed. We didn't care much. We knew it was inevitable.'[47] Others felt an increasing sense of alienation in which the grim realities of the present drove out both memories of a more pleasant past and any hope for a better future. The front was a world apart, but for the men stuck there it began to seem the only real world, escape from which was as unthinkable as being teleported to the moon. William Woodruff, at Anzio

. . . concluded that the bunch of boys he'd known bursting with life had never existed. He'd dreamt it. They certainly weren't the same men lying on the earth around him now. These men lying in the mud were a species apart. They didn't belong to that other world. They'd always lived in the mud and filth with their wits scared out of them and that's how they'd end up. It was their lot.[48]

Many Americans too testified to this sense of being walking dead, men without hope or identity outside their own company and their own tiny piece of real estate. For James Jones, the realisation of this was actually essential to his ability as a combat soldier. Unless a man admitted to himself that he was already finished he would spend too much effort trying to stay alive. What he must aim for was a 'final full acceptance of the fact that his name is already written down in the rolls of the already dead . . . He must make compact with himself or with fate that he is lost. Only then can he function as he ought to function under fire. He knows and accepts beforehand that he's dead, although he may still be walking around for a while'.[49] Certainly many GIs did feel that it was only a matter of time. Yet another American survey investigated this point when a sample of Italian veterans were asked 'While you were in combat, did you ever have the feeling that it was just a matter of time until you would get hit?' They answered thus:[50]

	%
Almost always felt that way	26
Usually	13
Sometimes	23
Once in a while	21
Practically never	15
No answer	2

Whether all these men approached their fears with the fatalistic acceptance advocated by James Jones might be doubted. His stance on this question seems a little too self-consciously stoical, to smack of a rather romantic conception of the damned. For most men it was just another strain to intensify their mental anguish. One soldier wrote:

> New officers who come here to take over can't understand a man's feelings after living the way he does over here. A man feels he is downed at times. He feels as long as he is able to keep going he will be kept over here, until he is a physical wreck or until he is buried with four or five more in some dark jungle or scattered over the ground by artillery shells or bombs. No one back home can really understand our feelings. [51]

Reactions to these physical and mental pressures varied. Most men stuck it, but only just. The following judgements by a British and an American observer show one side of the coin. The former, a correspondent in Tunisia, wrote:

> The cheerfulness and good nature of the British soldier in the most trying of conditions is now so much a commonplace that it is no longer noticed. I want to notice it here, with moved admiration. They have endured much in the way of hideous discomfort, but they are as full of goodwill and kindness as if they were enjoying a holiday at Blackpool and wanted to share their good fortune. [52]

The American correspondent wrote:

> I was convinced for all time of the dignity and nobility of common men. I was convinced for all time that common men have a pure and common courage when they fight for what they believe to be a just cause. That which was fine in these men outweighed and made trivial all that was horrible in their plight. I cannot explain it except to say that they were at all times cheerful and helped one another. They never gave up the fight. They never admitted defeat. They never asked for help. [53]

Both these statements were made during the war itself, but it would be wrong to see them as mere propaganda. For both authors they represent the fundamental truth of everything they had so far witnessed. Extensive reading about the front line only serves to reaffirm their judgement, and much more will be said about this sense of spiritual uplift in the final chapter. Nevertheless, simply to accept them at face value would be to miss the point. One must probe beneath the surface and realise on just what extremes of torment men were still able to put a good face. Only then can one appreciate what a miraculous and moving achievement it was. The eulogies just cited are not sentimental hyperbole about unimaginative, cheery souls smiling through a fairly unpleasant experience; they are fitting tributes to men who were often at the very limits of strain and fatigue, men in an agony of the soul, for whom the effort of smiling or thinking of others were gestures of iron self-control and unsurpassed devotion. A magnificent side of the human spirit was revealed, but the iron in these men's souls was forged in hell.

As these two correspondents would have been the first to admit, no one *wanted* to be there. They wanted out, even at the price of being maimed. A continual theme of the men's writings is the desire for a wound that would get them out of the line, preferably serious enough to get them home. A British officer wrote of the early days of the Italian campaign: 'We had not reached the stage of envying someone with a slight wound, enough to ensure a few weeks between sheets in a hospital bed; that came later.'[54] Private Finch (6th Grenadier Guards) was wounded at Monte Camino by a machine-gun bullet that ricocheted off one of his grenades and took a lump out of one of his fingers. As he stared and showed his hand to a mate muttering wonderingly, 'Christ, look at that,' his friend could only answer, 'You lucky bastard! I've been looking for one of those for three years.'[55] An American ETO veteran, interviewed in hospital, said: 'Men in our division gave up all hope of being relieved . . . All the men have hope of getting back but most of the hope is that you'll get hit someplace that won't kill you. That's all they talk about.'[56] A Pacific veteran echoed this when he asserted that 'we feel the only opportunity we will have to get home is to get wounded. There isn't an old man in the unit who has any hope or confidence of being able to enjoy life again'.[57]

A few went so far as to give themselves that wound, usually shooting off a finger or putting a bullet through their foot. Many personal accounts make reference to individuals having done this, but it is very difficult to assess just how common a practice it was. Official figures are very sketchy. According to those for the Second Army, in north-west Europe between 6 June and 30 September 1944 there were 29,860 casualties through battle and injury. Of these only 179 (0.6 per cent) were known to be self-inflicted. It is

possible of course that many self-inflicted wounds went unde-
tected or that officers covered up in what they knew to be aggravated cases, but it seems unlikely that the authorities in the rear
would be fooled as men driven to this extremity rarely made much
effort to ensure that the wound seemed natural. They simply
wanted out and were past caring about the punishment or moral
opprobrium that would attach to an obvious wound in the hand or
foot. Of course, shooting oneself was not the only method. Nat
Frankel records that during the battle of the Belfort Gap, 'one
night I got down on my hands and knees and pleaded with God to
give me trench foot. At the risk of understatement, I'll say that I
needed a rest. The day had been one of continuous shelling, and I
had seen one too many severed heads and far too many frozen,
dangling blood vessels'.[58] The next day he woke up with trench-
foot. Whilst one doubts that many men relied solely on divine
intercession, and is convinced that none were so rewarded, it does
seem likely that more than a few soldiers in Europe deliberately
neglected to look after their feet in the hope of getting a few days
out of the line, even at the cost of amputated toes or feet.

Another, more straightforward way out was to desert. Thousands of men did this. Again one is only talking of a small proportion of men in relation to the army as a whole, but desertion was
still at times a serious problem to the authorities. The situation in
the Middle East, in May 1942, was sufficiently bad for General
Auchinleck to cable London suggesting the immediate reintroduc-
tion of the death penalty for this crime.[59] His appeal was rejected,
in deference both to public opinion and fears that the men's morale
would only slump further. The death penalty was retained in the
American army, though in fact only one soldier was shot for
desertion.[60] This execution however was clearly sanctioned by
General Eisenhower *pour encourager les autres*, at a time when
American desertion figures were reaching alarming proportions.

The relevant figures for the British army, throughout the whole
war, are shown in Table 9.[61]

According to American figures there were 40,000 official deserters, of whom 2,854 were court-martialled and 49 sentenced to
death though, as already mentioned, all but one of these were re-
prieved. This represents a much lower percentage of the total armed
forces than do the British figures, but two points should be
borne in mind. It is probably fair to assume that desertion is much
higher when an army is actually engaged in combat and the

Table 9: Incidence of desertion in the British army 1939-45

PERIOD	TOTAL NUMBER DESERTERS	INCIDENCE (per 1,000 per year)
Oct 1939 - Sept 1940	6,889	4.48
1940 - 1941	22,248	10.05
1941 - 1942	20,834	8.49
1942 - 1943	15,824	5.90
1943 - 1944	16,892	6.19
1944 - 1945	17,663	6.24

American forces were not heavily committed until mid-1943, after which date the British too had approximately 40,000 deserters. Moreover, the American authorities were always loath to brand men as deserters and they applied the term 'Absent Without Leave' (AWOL) to thousands of men who would have been deemed deserters in any other army. James Jones tells us that

> . . . when elements of the First and Third Armies crossed the Seine above and below Paris, and bypassed it in the chase after the Germans, ten thousand men went over the hill and descended on the newly liberated, playtime city. Most of them showed up back at their outfits in a week or two. But the number was so alarming that Eisenhower declared Paris off-limits to American troops.[62]

Another point to be borne in mind, and this applies to both armies, is that deserters, like battle casualties, were mainly infantrymen. Two British samples from the Middle East and north-west Europe show that 81 per cent and 89 per cent of them, respectively, were from the infantry companies. It is necessary, therefore, to multiply the desertion rate by 4 or 5 times to get a realistic ratio. In British combat units then we are talking about a peak desertion rate of around 40 men per 1,000 per year. This represented a serious problem for the high command who were constantly troubled by an acute shortage of combat soldiers. In Europe, particularly, even a shortfall of 3 to 4 per cent could have serious repercussions in the already overstretched battle lines.

Yet even so we are talking about only a tiny proportion of men who succumbed to the strains of fighting in this way. For the average combat soldier it was unthinkable to thus shirk one's responsibilities, not so much because it left one's 'side' in the lurch, but because life would become just that bit worse for one's immediate buddies and mates. Almost invariably the demands of comradeship prevailed over the ever-increasing yearning to get away from the stress of never-ending battle. This is evident in official studies of those who did desert, for these tended to show that a large proportion of deserters had been maladjusted in civilian life. In one American sample of AWOL cases it was found that 60 per cent of them admitted to being truants from school 'at least several times' and 25 per cent 'very often'. The corresponding answers of an average sample of enlisted men showed only 27 and 5 per cent respectively. British studies pointed to several other atypical characteristics. Deserters were usually very young. A sample of 2,000 in north-west Europe showed that 73 per cent of them were under 26 whilst this was true of only 46 per cent of the British Liberation Army as a whole. A Middle Eastern study showed a similar discrepancy, the respective figures being 68 and 24 per cent. It was also found that a high number of deserters showed signs of some psychological deficiency. The north-west European study showed that 57 per cent of the men showed signs of some definite mental disturbance and fully one-third had a long record of this type of illness. In an earlier experiment carried out in England, it was found that 43 per cent of all cases of AWOL involved only 4 per cent of the men, whilst men with substantially below average intelligence were twice as frequent among recurrent absentees as might be expected on the basis of an average army sample.

With the sickening exception of Private Slovik, both armies treated the problem of desertion and cowardice in the face of the enemy remarkably leniently. According to one officer in north-west Europe they 'had been treated as comparatively minor military delinquencies, and the men had had every reason to think that these were not regarded as very serious offences. The maximum paper sentence was three years [penal servitude] and few men actually served six months'.[63] One reason for this was a more enlightened attitude to the psychiatric implications, but there was also the eternal problem of manpower and a reluctance to lose any fit man for the duration. In north-west Europe, in fact, hundreds of sentences were reviewed and approximately 60 per cent were suspended and the men returned to the front. Of these, it might be noted, 82 per cent performed satisfactorily thereafter. Many men did not even go to trial, particularly if their battalion was in the line, and the culprit was caught in time. Captain Horsfall remembered a deserter from his own company in Tunisia. He was tried by his own commanding officer who gave him 14 days field punishment 'or some other entirely illegal sentence, [and told the CSM] to make his life hell . . .'[64]

The final, and most telling, reason for not overrating the extent of desertion in World War II is simply that it was so difficult to accomplish. For men at the front there was just nowhere to go. The Pacific Islands and Burma were virtually desertion-proof just for this reason. Even in Europe much of the countryside was so devastated and denuded of supplies that it was extremely difficult to feed oneself or find somewhere to hide. The sheer size and depth of the armies themselves meant that a deserter had to walk for miles, constantly on his guard, to find a spot not under the scrutiny of ubiquitous military authority. Divisional and corps Military Police were the main obstacle here, but it was not unknown for battalions at the front to take drastic measures of their own. An American officer at Cassino met a young Lieutenant with a drawn pistol who had been posted on the only trail leading away from a forthcoming attack. He said

> . . . he had orders to make everyone stay. Too many men had come down the trail complaining of sickness or minor wounds, so he . . . [was] to stop everyone except the seriously wounded. I had not realised the situation had been quite so bad . . . I did not think I would ever see one of our officers use a gun on one of our own men. It is true that, so far as I know, he never did fire it. But he threatened to.[65]

So far, the methods of getting out of the line have been matters of conscious choice or wishful thinking. However there remains one individual response that was a purely involuntary reaction to the stress of combat – psychiatric breakdown. Many thousands of men were driven to this way out. On average, psychiatric cases represented between 10 and 15 per cent of all battle casualties or, to put it more simply, for every 5 soldiers wounded, another was killed and another became a psychiatric casualty. In fact, the proportions fluctuated wildly from front to front and unit to unit, and the psychiatric component could be anything from 3 to 30 per cent. Statistical analysis is also complicated by the fact that many different types of psychiatric casualty are lumped together in one set of figures so that it is impossible to differentiate between soldiers who broke down because of the unfamiliar nature of military life or because of intolerable domestic or innate personality tensions, and those whose collapse could be attributed to the stress of combat. Suffice it to say that the latter was an identifiable group, and that there were many thousands of them.

The authorities, remembering what had happened on the Western Front in the previous war, were well aware of this. The original term, 'shell shock', was rejected, however, and deliberately euphemistic names such as 'combat fatigue' and 'battle exhaustion' coined. On the one hand, this was meant to allay public opinion, on the other to reassure the soldiers that the condition was nothing to be ashamed of, that it was curable and that they could therefore expect to be returned to duty after a spell of medically supervised rest. Whilst all this was true,[66] and whilst it was valid to dispense with the traumatic phraseology of World War I, one should beware of any complacency about the exact nature of such psychiatric illness. As has been seen, even 'normal' fatigue at the front was a far cry from the lassitude of a civilian ambling off to bed. 'Combat fatigue' was a completely debilitating condition in which the various stresses upon the soldier gradually wore out his ability to cope until the mind finally rebelled and sent out frantic danger signals, such as dizziness, nausea, stomach cramps, profuse sweating, exaggerated jumpiness, headaches, palpitations, a perpetual gnawing in the pit of the stomach, insomnia, nightmares. A report by a team of American psychiatrists gave a list of the stresses at the front and its very matter-of-factness is more chilling than most other more literary descriptions. Fear, in itself an unremitting drain on the soldier's resources, was but one aspect of the problem:

In addition . . . there seem to be other emotions and reactions generally present in many, probably most, [combat] soldiers. These would include (1) the phobic-like reactions to specific types of shellfire, the 88mm shell and the tree burst . . . land mines to engineers, bazooka fire to tank crews; (2) the impotent, angry frustration and resultant anxiety from inactivity, from being pinned down by enemy fire or retreating from a superior force; (3) the fear and anxiety aroused by the mobilisation and expression of the man's own aggressive tendencies; (4) the anxiety incident to distrust of the wisdom of the orders received; (5) the lack of relief and any failure to receive adequate and prompt supply of mail, food, clothing and ammunition; (6) the loneliness of foxhole fighting and the inability to communicate with his group; (7) the anger and resentment toward . . . comrades who let him down, or break the code and toward those in the rear echelons who do not share his dangers and deprivations; (8) the guilt over performance (e.g. killing a young German boy) or in failure of his own performance; (9) the horror and grief (plus the revival of old, hidden and displaced hostilities) incident to seeing buddies wounded, mutilated or killed, with whom he may have to remain for some time afterward; (10) the constant danger and discomforts of being hungry, cold and wet, and the all-pervading physical and mental exhaustion of continuous fighting.[67]

These stresses were working on most front-line soldiers most of the time. Hardly any of them have any equivalent in civilian life and thus they make untoward demands on the soldier's mental resilience such that, in the long run, *any* soldier will break down. This point is crucial. As a proportion of the total number of combat troops who served overseas the battle-exhaustion figures are small, but this is because many men were killed or wounded before they could succumb, whilst the bulk of those intact at the end of the war had not been up front long enough to be finally broken. Soldiers and psychiatrists are unanimous on this point. A young American platoon leader in Europe said: 'We all get the jitters, especially if it lasts long enough. You get jumpy and want to dive into a hole every time you stop running or walking. You get to thinking there might be some pleasure in getting hurt – it would keep you from going nuts.'[68] An American doctor wrote: 'A state of tension and anxiety is so prevalent in the front lines that it must be regarded as a normal reaction in this grossly abnormal situation.'[69] Both the Americans and the British produced studies that showed that the useful life of a front-line soldier was definitely finite. Lieutenant Colonel J. W. Appel and Captain G. W. Beebe stated firmly: 'There is no such thing as "getting used to combat" . . . Each moment of combat imposes a strain so great that men will break down in direct relation to the intensity and duration of their exposure. Thus psychiatric casualties are as inevitable as gunshot and shrapnel wounds in warfare.'[70] They concluded that almost any soldier, should he survive, would break down after between 200 and 240 combat days.[71] The British allowed 400 combat days, around 2 years; this was not meant to impute more resilience in their soldiers but was a reflection of the more frequent rotation of front-line units.

But even if a man did not actually crack up, this did not mean that he was not in a state of constant psychological turmoil, and one that gradually increased as the days wore on. The psychiatric dimension of combat is not to be understood simply as x number of hospitalisations, of a fixed percentage of men who suddenly cracked up, but as a dreadful strain on *all* soldiers, *all* of whom would break in the long run. Breakdown was not something like a broken leg or a bullet wound, but was the final surrender to weeks or months of extreme suffering and tension. An American correspondent described two GIs who had reached the end of the line:

> A couple of big country-looking soldiers in one of the new divisions were standing at the south end of the garden grinding their heads against the wall like little boys having a tantrum. They had the palms of their hands against it, too, and were digging into the mortar with their nails, as if clinging for shelter against a hail of bullets, but there was no shooting going on around them. Some medics were trying to talk the pair into getting into an ambulance, so they could take them to the nice, quiet rear, but the men couldn't or wouldn't budge, or even talk. Instead they continued to grind themselves into the wall, sniffling, now, like little boys who have cried themselves out.[72]

A Canadian officer in north-west Europe, Lieutenant Pearce (North Nova Scotia Regiment), was still unwounded after seven months of almost continuous action. During one attack, however, he was ordered to report to his commanding officer. 'I hadn't any idea, apparently, of how far gone I was emotionally. Instead of furnishing a coherent account, I simply stood in front of him weeping inarticulately, unable to construct a sentence, even to force a single word out of my mouth.'[73]

Such men, temporarily at least, had completely broken down. But almost all their fellows were also at some point along the path that led to this emotional disintegration, all caught up in the same internal conflict that must eventually break them. One of the best academic articles on the subject of combat fatigue was by two psychiatrists who actually went into action with a US infantry battalion in France, and they paint a grim picture of the progressive deterioration of those veterans who were not killed or wounded. During the first few days of combat the men were in a constant state of fear and displayed numerous physical symptoms, such as continually wanting to relieve themselves, intense thirst, loss of appetite and such like. They became totally self-absorbed and many 'became selfish to the point that they took food, blankets, entrenching tools and similar articles from others for their own use'. This soon stopped, however, and after the first days of combat a definite group spirit emerged, as well as an increasing confidence in their performance under fire:

They became familiar with the sounds of their own as contrasted with the enemy's artillery and automatic . . . weapons. From the sound they could determine the caliber of artillery fire . . . thereby knowing when to 'hit the dirt'. Without being conscious of it, they chose paths of approach which afforded concealment and cover, and they constantly watched for snipers in trees and hedges. Smoke and fire discipline at night became automatic . . . Concurrently, the physiologic reactions to danger, referred to above, became modified or controlled to the point that they no longer hindered the soldier in combat.

Within three weeks the soldiers had reached peak efficiency and maintained this level for a further week. But this adaptation to combat was only bought at the price of rigid self-control, a constant damping down of the desire to cower in a foxhole or run to the rear. For a while personal preconceptions of honour and group loyalty sufficed, but after the fourth week the pressures began to tell and 'the first symptom of combat exhaustion made its appearance . . . in most soldiers'. They became tired very easily and sleep had decreasing recuperative value. Discrimination between weapons was lost. The soldier 'became over cautious; he stayed close by or in his slit trench whenever possible; he walked rather than rode in a vehicle, so that he would be able to get cover more readily; and he became a "follower" rather than a leader'.

He also began to be progressively more aware of the absence of close friends, as often as not having himself witnessed their being blown apart or sliced down. He began to see the inevitability of his own death, and to feel utterly helpless, ceasing to believe that his own competence or fortitude would make the slightest difference. After six weeks, more pronounced psychological symptoms began to appear, mainly

. . . a general slowing of mental processes and apathy, [a belief that] as far as they were concerned the situation was one of absolute hopelessness . . . The influence and reassurance of understanding officers and NCOs failed now to arouse these soldiers from their feeling of hopelessness . . . The soldier was slow-witted . . . Memory defects became so extreme that he could not be counted on to relay a verbal order . . . [If such a soldier was not evacuated he] became practically nonreactive both physically and emotionally. He could then be best described as one leading a vegetative existence . . . . He remained almost constantly in or near his slit trench, and during acute actions took little or no part, trembling constantly.

In fact, very many soldiers were not evacuated until they had got beyond this point, either becoming almost catatonic or suffering a final collapse triggered off by an especially brutal incident. This was usually a very near hit or the sight of yet another buddy being killed before one's eyes. Then 'the soldier became disorientated or confused. Often he ran about wildly and aimlessly, with a total disregard for danger, rolled on the ground and cried convulsively'.[74]

All this, remember, is not the description of a handful of exceptional cases. It is what happened, in continuous combat, to almost all the soldiers of an infantry unit who were not killed or wounded. It happened to every nationality, on every front, in every company, battalion and regiment. The only reason units as a whole did not fall apart was that there was a constant flow of replacements, and at any one time most men had not yet reached this crisis point.

But their time would inevitably come. 'You keep on doing it until they break you or you are dead.' Theoretically, every man in a unit was still a fit fighting soldier, yet every one of them was being slowly racked between these grim alternatives. The furthest ones gone were instantly recognisable. The GIs had a term for it, 'the two thousand year stare'. Everyone had seen it. James Jones recalled the look of men who had

> . . . had all, or more, than they can take. The staring eyes, the slack lips, the sleepwalker's stance. I've seen men with that look on their faces. I've had it on my own face. It feels stiff, and the muscles don't want to work right when you try to smile, or show expression, or talk. Mercifully, you're out of it for a while; *un*mercifully, down in the centre of that numbness, though, you know you will have to come back, eventually.[75]

This was in the Pacific, but the stare was universal. Ernie Pyle remembered seeing it in Italy:

> A soldier who has been a long time in the line does have a 'look' in his eyes that anyone who knows about it can discern. It's a look of dullness, eyes that look without seeing, eyes that see without conveying any image to the mind . . . [A look of] exhaustion, lack of sleep, tension for too long, weariness that is too great, fear beyond fear, misery to the point of numbness, a look of surpassing indifference to anything anyone can do. It's a look I dread to see on men.[76]

Ralph Ingersoll saw men coming out of the Hürtgen Forest and they 'did not talk; they just sat across the table or on the edge of your cot and looked at you very straight and unblinking with absolutely no expression in their faces, which were neither tense nor relaxed but completely apathetic. They looked, unblinking, and I can see the colour of their eyes now'.[77] It affected tankers and infantrymen alike. Nat Frankel described his state of mind on the road to Bastogne when

> . . . like most of the 4th, I was numb, in a state of virtual disassociation. There is a condition . . . which we called the two-thousand-year stare. This was the anaesthetised look, the wide, hollow eyes of a man who no longer cares. I wasn't to that state yet, but the numbness was total. I felt almost as if I hadn't actually been in a battle, as if I had just awakened but couldn't get my body to the bathroom to brush my goddam teeth.[78]

Looking back, Frankel is able to use a flippant image, but nobody who has not endured the mental anguish that leads to such reactions should dream of fobbing it off in this way. Combat is torture, and it will reduce you, sooner or later, to a quivering wreck. Many men lasted surprisingly well until their first slight wound or near miss; for a while their personal magic seemed proof against anything. As an anonymous American infantryman put it:

> Before I got hit with fragments, I was confident all right. I thought the others might get hurt but not me. Then a sniper's bullet got me and that shook my confidence right there. I knew my number could be up, too. I got better, came back, and was going on for a while; but I was not as cocky as I used to be. Then some buddies of mine got it, and that wore me down more. 'My number's coming,' I felt it in my stomach and that got me shaky – that or something. Then during a shelling, a blast came near me and I was hit by fragments. It shook me so badly, I thought it was my time now. But I jumped up and tried to shoot or something. I don't know what happened after. I must have blacked out or something. I came too in the hospital, I was shaky and jittery and everything else.[79]

For personal reserves were finite, frighteningly so. The sheer magnitude of the firepower deployed against one, the randomness and ubiquity of the deaths it caused, must inevitably erode belief in one's own sacrosanct destiny. Bill Mauldin wrote of 'those men who have seen actual war at first hand, seeing their buddies killed day after day, trying to tell themselves that they are different – *they* won't get it; but knowing deep inside that they *can* get it – those guys . . . know what real weariness of body, brain and soul can be'.[80] The mind did its best; it desperately tried to suppress the instinctive desire to run, pretended it could flog on regardless, despite acute physical debilitation. But it could not; the well must inevitably run dry. A British soldier wrote of the

> . . . truly terrifying fact that the first time you go into battle you strike the rock and your courage gushes out and you can never strike the rock again except perhaps (but I doubt it) after a long interval, like between wars, and your courage flows at its outset with the fullest force and thereafter diminishes; perhaps if you are very brave it diminishes imperceptibly, but it does diminish as a chord on a piano once struck grows steadily weaker and can never behave otherwise.[81]

Lieutenant Patrick Davies (3rd Gurkhas) made the same point in a different way and underlined just what an achievement it was for men to keep going as long as they did:

> Almost every action of every waking hour in our Battalion was consciously directed towards achieving battle [with the Japanese]. In those battles which we strove to achieve, the price for both success and failure was death. We knew this very well. It seems to me remarkable that a man can so repeatedly overcome his natural fears that he goes through this process time after time . . . I do not believe that one man enjoys war after his initial exposure, should that exposure continue for several weeks. The glamour disperses as the tensions prolong, and it is then that ordinary men come close to the heroic. Anyone can be brave once.[82]

Fred Majdalaney wrote an epitaph to a brother officer which highlighted just this same aspect of true heroism:

> 'He didn't know what fear was,' some idiot wrote in some newspaper. The fool, the bloody fool, that writer. Of course he knew what fear was . . . He knew how to overcome it, that's all. He knew how to bend fear back with the arms of will-power. He wrestled and fought with it like Laocoon with the snakes . . . But fear always grows stronger and the muscles on the arms of will-power begin to ache, they can't bend back fear for ever. The struggle gets harder all the time. Will-power sweats and groans and aches and gasps for breath; the snakes must crush Laocoon in the end . . . 'He didn't know what fear was.' Do they think they honour him by saying that? Can't the idiots see that it was Prometheus walking along that grass verge, with eagles tearing at his liver every inch of the way? Can't they see that the whole point is not that he *didn't* know what fear was but that he *did*?[83]

But the army will not, cannot, make allowance for this aspect of battle. For them a soldier is either fit for combat or not. Until he is maimed, dead or a gibbering wreck he is by definition capable of going forward yet again. And so he must keep on doing until he fits into one of these three incontrovertible categories. An American in Italy recalled one of his fellow officers who was reaching the end of his tether:

> He had been across the Rapido on the second night of the attack. That experience was the climax of nearly four months of heavy fighting, and it did something to him. He seemed to be aware, for the first time, that the best energies of his entire life would be consumed in the fighting. He and men like him would have to give and give and give; perhaps they would have to give so much that never again would they be good for anything, even if they did live through the war . . . [He] kept looking more and more beaten. He was very tough inside, but too much combat can break any man.[84]

The end becomes inevitable. Self-control, no matter how rigid, must break eventually. One's comrades simply watch and wonder, unsure of the exact moment, of the exact form the collapse will take. Their

> . . . thoughts may be summarised in the pithy army expression 'he has had it', implying that the individual concerned has lost his power to conceal his fears. Manifestations of shattered control vary in intensity from reluctance to move into danger at the one end, to a form of paralysis whereunder the subject becomes incapable of moving any muscle of his body. It may be reflected in tears or in adamantine dourness. Or it may end in sheer screaming insanity.[85]

But it will come, in one form or another. That was why men *wanted* to be wounded. This was not a hysterical reaction, but a sober appraisal of the facts. There was no other way out for a soldier who wanted to keep life and sanity intact. The following vignette, in the aftermath of a fierce tank battle in the Western Desert, says it all:

> The MO was waiting for us. He set about treating the four wounded men and evacuating them in his ambulance. While this was going on the Squadron leader came over. He said nothing, but put his hand on my shoulder. It was almost more than I could bear. It signified the end of the action, that strange, unforgettable point where the walls of control collapse. I looked at the wounded men, at Johnson, and

realised for the first time what it meant . . . One of the men was crying, weeping like a small child.

'It's O.K. now,' I said. 'You'll be O.K. soon.'

'It's the relief, sir,' he answered. 'It's such a relief.'

We were all suffering from an intense thirst. The driver gave us water in a mug. I handed it round. I offered it to Johnson first. He didn't need it.[86]

Panic and Mutiny

Armies are more than a simple aggregation of the soldiers that serve in them. They, and more especially the regiments and divisions that constitute them, can be very homogeneous bodies whose traditions and standards of behaviour act as a powerful support to their individual members. Despite their own desire to hide or run, the men feel obliged by an unspoken code to suppress such instincts and abide by assumed norms of courage, honour, duty etc. But this group solidarity can work both ways. Just because the soldiers are in such an enclosed world, and because they force themselves to sublimate their own individuality to the creditable performance of the unit, any *lowering* of morale therein can also spread remarkably quickly. As long as the regiment seems to believe in itself, this can be a sufficient prop to men who, left to themselves, would simply find a hole and stay in it. But should that unitary confidence be lost, then a feeling of panic and despair can swiftly grow, persuading even those that were prepared to stand firm that all is lost. In other words, collective morale is just as important as that of the individual, and the history of World War II abounds with examples of its working for good and ill. The latter effect was less common than the former, but even so there were more than a few examples of individual units, sometimes whole armies, succumbing to mass panic or despair.

Many different factors could cause a collective lowering of morale, some hard to pin down, others clear and straightforward. In some instances, indeed, it is difficult to talk of anything more precise than a general malaise, not related so much to specific circumstances as to a deep disenchantment with the war as a whole. The official British medical history makes an interesting observation about the troops in the Middle East in 1941:

There was a general expectation amongst men in the M.E.F. that they would suffer much the same fate as their fathers, who had been glibly

promised a 'country fit for heroes to live in' and had subsequently
spent many years drawing unemployment benefits . . . Men worried
about their pay and the pay of their dependants; they had no confidence in the help dependants would receive in the event of their own
death in the service of their country, and they frequently pointed to the
vastly superior amenities enjoyed by soldiers from other parts of the
British Empire and by American soldiers.[87]

On the whole, however, such general considerations were not an
important factor in determining soldiers' day-to-day morale. For
those at the front the prospect of combat was such an all-absorbing
reality that the actions and moods of the moment were shaped
within this limited context. The troops' behaviour was determined
largely by the military situation simply because there was little
opportunity to think of much else. Generalised aspirations or folk
memories were of little relevance, at the time, to men caught in the
daily struggle with the imminence of death.

The pressures of the military situation could manifest themselves in various ways. At one end of the spectrum were the fears
generated by unfamiliarity with combat, and a tendency to over-
rate the power of new weapons and the fighting abilities of the
enemy. With regard to weaponry, numerous observers commented on the British soldiers' early helplessness in the face of German
dive-bombers. In the Western Desert, Greece and Crete, whole
groups of men could be reduced to quivering inactivity by the
approach of a single Stuka. An official report on the Greek evacuation noted that the experience there 'had engendered a ludicrous
anxiety regarding the power of aircraft and all areas were infested
with self-appointed critics. Shouts of "sit down" enforced by a
discharge of rifles greeted any movement by day . . . By night
lights could not be used as shouts of "put that light out" followed
by rifle shots greeted any attempt to use sidelights'.[88] A serving
officer made the same point even more forcibly. 'I have never seen
so many men so unashamedly afraid as I saw on the bomb-torn
roads of Greece; and I have not, thank God, ever seen it like that
again.'[89]

As regards fear of the enemy, both British and American troops
conceived a respect for Japanese abilities that at times bordered on
complete military paralysis. In the early campaigns, the front-line
troops felt themselves hopelessly outclassed as jungle fighters and
were inclined to retreat at the drop of a parrot's dinner. Of the
soldiers of the 15th Brigade at Asun and Jitra in the Malayan

campaign, a Japanese general wrote: 'The Indian troops have no fighting spirit . . . They are glad to surrender [and are] relieved to be out of the war.'[90] A report on American units in New Guinea, by Lieutenant Colonel D. Larr, noted that troops did not seem prepared for combat. They refused to move up to actually close with the enemy and stood off, hoping that artillery and aircraft would do their job for them. On several occasions, he was told, soldiers had thrown away their rifles and retreated in panic. In Arakan, in the early stages of the reconquest of Burma, the 14th Indian Division suffered a series of serious reverses and was eventually withdrawn, it being the opinion of one medical officer that the whole division was a psychiatric casualty.

Irrational fears about the enemy's prowess trapped soldiers in a vicious circle. They started off by thinking that any position was by definition untenable, and this soon provoked a precipitate retreat which in turn refuelled the feelings of anxiety and inadequacy so that it soon became almost impossible to make the men stand at all. Moreover, the continental movement back, by day and night, intensified the crushing fatigue and debilitated morale yet more. An officer with the 11th Division in Malaya wrote: 'It can't go on like this. The troops are absolutely dead beat. The only rest they're getting is that of an uneasy coma as they squat in crowded lorries which jerk their way through the night . . . They're bound to crack soon.'[91] Of the retreat to Dunkirk, a company commander of the 2nd Coldstream Guards wrote:

> We did all the tasks we had to do, but I remember little of them. We ate and slept wherever we could, quite irrespective of the hour. I seemed to have lost all sense of time . . . Whenever I woke, I could remember neither time nor place. It took several painful minutes, like a numbed man recovering feeling, before full awareness returned. Over everybody there was an air of heavy fatigue and depression.[92]

During the campaign in the Western Desert, the constant reverses suffered by the Eighth Army and the long retreats to new positions, tried morale almost to breaking point. Both in November 1941 and the middle of the following year, the Allied armies came dangerously close to collapse.

But it was not simply military reverses that could try morale. Even military success was sometimes bought at such a price that the satisfaction of victory was not enough to keep men going. It has already been shown that individual soldiers could only take it for so long before they inevitably cracked. At times whole units fell apart for just the same reasons. Of course, battalions had far greater resilience than an individual soldier because of the constant injection of new blood. Nevertheless, in some cases it is undoubtedly fair to speak of a collective despair, of a unit as a whole becoming so battle-scarred that even the replacements were immediately affected by common feelings of exhaustion and hopelessness. Such group fatalism could have pernicious effects amongst beleaguered garrisons, living and fighting cheek by jowl for weeks on end. Having spoken to men who had visited Imphal during the epic siege, one officer 'was disturbed to know that the morale of the besieged troops was very low. This may well be denied later by those concerned, but it was given to me at the time and I had no reason to doubt it'.[93] Conditions in the Hürtgen Forest were in many ways reminiscent of a close-quarters siege, though in theory at least the boot was on the other foot. In one American regiment, in the 8th US Division, the men proved so loath to advance that the commanders conducted a purge of officers. On one day a battalion and company commander were relieved, followed a little later by three more company commanders, a second battalion commander and one platoon commander who was arrested for refusing to lead his men forward. In at least one company all the officers were either relieved or broke down under the strain.

Divisions and even armies, too, could feel the strain in this way, though the results were never quite so dramatic. Usually it involved just a general air of fatigue and pessimistic fatalism. Hamish Henderson felt he was speaking for the whole of the 51st Highland Division when he wrote a poem entitled 'The Highland Division's Farewell to Sicily'. The chorus runs

> Then fare weel, ye banks o'Sicily,
> Fare ye weel, ye valley an' shaw,
> There's no Jock will mourn the kyles o' ye.
> Puir bliddy bastards are weary.

The 1st US Division, which had fought with the First Army in Tunisia, was pulled out of Sicily at the same time as the Highland Division, partly because they too were becoming almost embittered at their spearhead role in the ceaseless fighting. A saying was current at the time that 'the American Army consists of 1st Division and eight million replacements'. Having borne the brunt of two campaigns, the division as a whole was verging on the insubordinate. Discipline was very lax and at times rules and orders were openly ignored. The commanding officer, General L. C. Allen, seemed unable to do much about it. 'Discouraged by the hard going and left to brood about their fate in Allen's *laisser aller* régime, his men developed too much pride in their past achievements and too much self-pity in their present plight.'[94]

Sometimes it could fairly be said that a whole army had succumbed to this kind of emotional attrition. Towards the end of the Tunisian campaign, one journalist noted of the Eighth Army that they were

> . . . tired and not very interested. Colleagues here a long time confirm that: they say that Tripoli had always been looked on as the goal; and that this is an appendix. The men, they say, have become so involved in battle that they have forgotten about what the war is being fought for. The main worry is about their wives, whom many feel will have grown away from them in these lonely years.[95]

Towards the end of the Burma campaign, too, it was possible to speak of the deterioration of a whole army's morale. A journalist who had marched with the Fourteenth Army wrote shortly after the war:

> Officers were affected no less than the troops and those responsible for the maintenance of morale and efficiency . . . were up against a wave of demoralisation . . . These facts may be hard to accept, but they were found in the monthly intelligence reports submitted by units. Every month saw the same references to the growing depression among the British troops. No attempt was made at the highest level to halt this process.[96]

This malaise among veteran units was also apparent during the European campaigns, most noticeably in Italy where certain battalions had been abroad for years on end and where the fighting was a seemingly endless series of bloody river crossings and mountain assaults. One regimental history declared that by April 1945 'morale was not in an easy state . . . Every man knew that if he survived this next battle, he had probably survived the war'.[97] This raises another important point about group morale, and one that applies equally to the fighting in north-west Europe. Though always reticent where such matters are concerned, many sources dealing with the end of the European campaigns allude to what was generally called 'stickiness' on the part of certain battalions or divisions. Indeed, there were some such allegations in the first weeks of the Normandy fighting, levelled especially at those divisions pulled out of Italy for the new offensive. A combination of war-weariness and a rather condescending sense of superiority, it was charged, led many of these units to proceed with a caution beyond the dictates of mere prudence.[98] Firm evidence for this is lacking, but it is certainly true that by spring 1945 the word could fairly be applied to any unit in Germany or Italy. For all of them had begun to see that the end of the war was near. Death ceased to seem inevitable and men realised that if they could hang on for just a few weeks more, they might actually see their homes again, even remain mentally and physically intact. This resurgence of hope did not make the fighting any easier. To the very end everybody was

> . . . dog tired, and our spirits were sinking lower and lower. Every day seemed to be the same . . . There seemed to be no end to it and little hope . . . Pervading everything . . . was a feeling of endless tiredness and a gloomy sense of growing depression, like a man walking home on a foggy night, who had lost his way, and finds himself floundering weary and aimless, ankle-deep in a muddy bog.[99]

For the new glimmer of hope, paradoxically, intensified the morale problem. A feeling of near despair is hardly the state of mind a commander would welcome in his soldiers, but at least it does bring with it a sense of fatalistic resignation. But when men see that victory is near, their general weariness is compounded with a growing sense of futility. No one ever wanted to be killed in battle, but how much worse to be blindly struck down in the death throes of a beaten enemy. As one officer wrote:

> In my mind . . . the battle was over. There was only the formality of mopping-up to be endured. Having survived a period when survival was subordinate to the immediate task and duty, and when exhilaration in the accomplishment had been supplanted by something near to drudgery, I could find no enthusiasm or sense of purpose in a tomorrow in which death seemed to have become causeless.[100]

In all the Allied armies, then, morale was often at a low ebb. Even so, it is one of the abiding truths of World War II that most men did as they were told to the bitter end. On the whole, authority, a sense of duty and personal pride asserted themselves over any inclination to simply give up. But one should not romanticise the conduct of the fighting troops nor suppose that it reflected innate superhuman qualities that enabled men to keep smiling through or whatever. For this would be a ludicrous misrepresentation of the horrendous strain upon those who had to force themselves forwards in attack after attack. Most men *did* go forward, certainly, but each occasion was a gut-wrenching, nightmarish ordeal. And just because it was such a hard thing to do, it should come as no surprise that on occasion units failed and momentarily panicked or refused to obey orders.

Cold-blooded refusals, by front-line troops at least, were extremely rare. Official accounts are likely to be more than reticent on this point, but none of the other source material leaves the impression that such behaviour was common. Extensive research has only thrown up a handful of examples and all of these barely merit the term mutiny. One is rather speaking of an erosion of confidence in officers which made it impossible for a unit to function effectively. More often than not, this only led to a general air of sullen unco-operativeness, as in the later stages of the Australian army's Pacific campaign when officers and men alike failed to see any real point in their part in the fighting. A brigadier spoke of 'a tendency among all ranks, including officers, to question vigorously the purpose and soundness of operations in the Solomons . . . [It became necessary] to bring to the notice of commanders the dangers of permitting unchallenged discussion on such a contentious subject'.[101] At times, however, this lack of confidence was at a much more intimate level, reflecting on the competence of battalion commanders and the like. After D-Day, for example, one Canadian paratroop battalion went on a three-day hunger strike, protesting against the harsh disciplinary measures of their new commander.[102] In January 1945, officers of one battalion of the 2nd Division, in Burma, asked that their colonel be relieved of his command, because of his seeming inability to make sound decisions. This was granted and it was in fact the third time the unit had made a similar request. Two of the others had been whilst they were actually in action. In the American army there were more dramatic hints about the lack of confidence in officers. A common 'latrine rumour' was that an officer in such-and-such a battalion had been shot by his own men during an attack. The record remains mute on this point, however, and it remains open to question whether it actually happened or whether the rumours were mere wish-fulfilment.[103]

The one authentic mutiny amongst British troops, though it does not reflect overt accusations of incompetence, does denote a particularly insensitive handling of matters by senior officers. The incident in question took place on the Salerno beachhead and involved men from a draft of reinforcements to the 51st (Highland) Division. As the official report shows, the bulk of the men were more than willing to join or rejoin their own formation. In the event, however, they were ordered to another division, and to a man all 700 of them refused to go. They were addressed on the beaches by General McCreery who asked them, amid boos and catcalls, to rethink their refusal. The bulk of them then decided to accept their new postings, but 192 soldiers remained adamant. These latter were immediately shipped off to Constantine and tried as mutineers. All but one of them were convicted and received sentences of between five and twelve years penal servitude, though most of these were suspended and the men posted back to Eighth Army units. To this end they were shipped off *en masse* to Phillippeville and over the next weeks most of them deserted only to be recaptured and sent to prison. They were only pardoned in September 1944 when most rejoined their original units in northwest Europe.

At the time there was considerable bitterness amongst their own division because it was felt that the men had been pilloried for excessive loyalty. In fact, as a later historian has shown, a key reason for their enthusiasm to rejoin the Highland Division was the leaked knowledge that it was due to return to England.[104] Nevertheless, given that this information had become common knowledge, and given that any man would genuinely prefer to serve with his own unit and his own comrades, one is entitled to see the original decision to reallocate the men as somewhat unimaginative, particularly as most of them were Eighth Army veterans with excellent combat records. If an army preaches the virtues of battalion, divisional and army loyalty, it might reasonably be expected not to flout such a concept just to scrape together an amorphous draft of replacements.

On the whole, however, such mass disobedience as there was by combat soldiers was more in the nature of spontaneous panic, engendered by continuous fighting, heavy casualties or the sudden appearance of the enemy in large numbers. Inexperience was a key factor too, and it is very noticeable that the units involved in such incidents were usually fresh to the front, often in their first real battle. This was the case during the *blitzkrieg* that led to the Dunkirk evacuation. Even the regular battalions had only known counter-insurgency campaigning in Palestine, whilst the Territorial battalions and the Guards were without any experience of real war. The problems were intensified by a ponderous and hide-bound High Command as well as the most lamentably inadequate equipment. Once the army realised that it, not to mention its major ally, was outclassed and that no one had any effective military response except endless retreat, it is hardly surprising that there were more than a few instances of blind panic. Official and regimental histories present a Trappist reticence typified by the following tight-lipped admission that, on the beaches themselves, the behaviour of certain units and stragglers presaged a 'threatened collapse of discipline [but this was] averted by senior officers'.[105] Other researchers have unearthed a little more detail, as is shown by the following résumé. Incidents included

> . . . a hotel cellar . . . packed with British, French and Sengalese troops, singing, weeping and screaming drunk; groups of men, deserted by their officers, prowling the town in a mood of savage violence; of a major shot dead through the head by another because it was the only way of preventing him from capsizing an already overloaded rowing boat; a senior officer refusing to leave a foxhole he had dug in the sand; a corporal of the Guards who kept order in his boat, filled with fear-crazed troops, by threatening to shoot the first one who disobeyed him . . . dispirited men [back in England] hurling their rifles from the trains carrying them from Dover.[106]

The compiler of this list makes much of these references in an attempt to debunk the supposed 'myth' of Dunkirk. If such researchers merely wished to set the record straight, their emphasis upon such details as those set out above would be all well and good; but it is quite wrong to mention them in isolation in an attempt to imply that most units behaved in this way. This is simply not the case.[107] Bearing in mind the utter exhaustion and confusion that characterised the Dunkirk beaches, it is hardly surprising that some men broke under the strain. What is surprising is the basic fact that, in the midst of what some would prefer to regard as a 'collapse', someone managed to organise over 1,200 ships and boats to disembark 350,000 soldiers.

Dunkirk was not the only disaster to overtake British arms during the first years of the war. In the Far East, in Malaya and

Burma, defeat was even more thorough-going and few men actually managed to get away. Here, too, there is perhaps more evidence of general defeatism and a tendency for units to break *en masse*. Again, however, inexperience was a basic factor, both since most units were new to any sort of combat and because jungle warfare made the greatest demands of all, placing troops in an unfamiliar environment in which they were usually isolated from all but their immediate comrades. A key bridge in Malaya, at Parit Sulong, was abandoned by men of the Norfolk Regiment because they had been out of touch with battalion headquarters for over twenty-four hours and thought that they were cut off. By the time such units as could make it had fallen back on Singapore, their morale was very low. On 9 February 1942, three Australian battalions of the 22nd Brigade fell back in great confusion after a Japanese attack. Many were almost running and for the rest an observer wrote of 'a file of men walking, staggering, dragging along . . . Some were bootless, some shirtless, and a few had not even trousers . . . They were covered with mud from head to foot, scratched and bleeding, exhausted, beaten'.[108]

In the first Burma campaign demoralisation was even more widespread, largely because the defeated soldiers had no refuge to aim for other than India or China. At times total disintegration was a very real possibility. Of the 17th Indian Division at the bridgehead over the Bilin, Brigadier R. G. Elkin wrote: 'Here there was chaos and confusion, hundreds of men throwing down their arms, equipment and clothing and taking to the water . . . As we crossed the river was a mass of bobbing heads.'[109] At Kawkereik, the 16th Indian Brigade fared even worse. Composed of 1/7th Gurkhas, 1/9th Jats and 4/12th Frontier Force Regiment, none of the battalions had been with the brigade for more than six weeks and in each of them up to half of the recruits had only three months service. The brigade was ordered to halt the advance of the Japanese 55th Division towards Moulmein, but even before contact was made morale was seriously affected by wild rumours about the size of the Japanese force and the subsequent withdrawal was at best precipitate. An official report noted that 'no clear picture of the withdrawal of 1/9 Jats can be painted as it was nothing short of panic'.[110]

American troops, too, in the first months of the Pacific War, sometimes proved inadequate to the undreamt of strains of jungle combat. The pusillanimity of certain officers on New Guinea has already been noted and it is not surprising that this, combined with general inexperience, had a poor effect on the men. During the fighting (by the 32nd US Division) on the Girua river, according to an American commander:

> Stories of inaction and even cowardice of our troops were filtering back. The officers didn't know their jobs. The commanders were too far to the rear. Instead of fighting, there seemed to be an idea that if they waited long enough the Japs would starve to death or quit . . . The troops just did not go. They acted scared to death of Jap snipers. There were cases of men throwing away their machine guns and running in panic. The officers didn't seem to know what to do.[111]

The banzai charge could also be a potent weapon against raw troops. A captain who had served in Luzon remembered one yelling onslaught which had completely unnerved his men. 'His whole company had "taken off", and . . . he too had been tempted to flee. He hadn't. When the Japanese charge had run its course and the attackers had been killed, it turned out that there were just eight of them and only two were armed.'[112]

Whilst jungle warfare accentuated the problems of introducing green troops to actual combat, failures in this respect were not limited to the Far Eastern theatres. In Tunisia, in their first meeting with the Germans, certain American units made a hardly auspicious debut. After a large-scale attack by Rommel on Sbeitla, in February 1943, substantial elements of the 1st US Armoured Division panicked and the whole fate of the campaign hung in the balance until order was restored. One American general, E. N. Harmon, commented bluntly:

> It was the first – and only – time I saw an American army in rout. Jeeps, trucks, wheeled vehicles of every imaginable sort streamed up the road towards us, sometimes jammed two and even three abreast. It was obvious that there was only one thing in the minds of the panic-stricken drivers – to get away from the front, to escape to some place where there was no shooting.[113]

The British made much of this temporary collapse and throughout the campaign many disparaging remarks were made about the quality of American troops. The accusations were somewhat uncalled for, on the one hand because this was an isolated example, and the 1st Division itself fought well for the rest of the war, on the other because the British forces in Africa had not themselves always been paragons of calmness.

In the Sudan in November 1940, during an attack on Metemma, the 1st Essex Regiment broke and fell back in complete confusion. A report was produced by a psychiatrist who found numerous reasons for this sudden collapse. The battalion had been overseas for two years (at that time this seemed an inordinately long tour), there was a long history of 'unhappiness in the officers' mess', many promoted NCOs had been lost to other units, the men had spent much of the last eight months digging defences in very high temperatures. On the day in question an ammunition truck had blown up and a rumour spread that a withdrawal had been ordered. As the men vaccillated, the wounded from another battalion, many with ghastly facial wounds, passed through their ranks and this precipitated a sudden rush to the rear. Some were later found as far as twenty-five miles back. Once reassembled the battalion was moved out of the theatre and there was a wholesale reposting of officers.

The campaign in Greece was hardly one of the most inspiring feats of British arms. The finale took place on Crete and the Dunkirk-style evacuation back to the Middle East was less than orderly. Many men deserted and took to the hills. On 22 April, two platoons of Marines near Maleme disobeyed orders to stand and fell back, ignoring all subsequent commands to return. The beaches became seriously infected with crowds of stragglers and at one point the 22nd New Zealand Battalion had to form a bayonet cordon around the beach to protect the evacuation of those embarking in some semblance of order.

In the Middle East itself, though there seem to be no examples of units actually cracking, it could hardly be claimed that the great British retreats of November 1941 and the following June were highly disciplined affairs. Of the 'Dash to the Wire', or 'November Handicap', as the first of these retreats was variously known, Lieutenant J. Cloudsley-Thompson (4th County of London Yeomanry) recalled:

> The transport vehicles of both South African Brigades stampeded through our lines, stirring up clouds of dust. The head of our own column soon joined in the flight . . . The fitters' truck passed me going flat out, then the . . . breakdown lorry doing a good 45 m.p.h. – it had constantly delayed us in the past because the driver said he could not keep up – and we joined the riot. We crossed an aerodrome, but the ground staff had already fled. Everybody had joined the mad flight. Thousands of lorries were rushing madly across the desert.[114]

In Tunisia, too, British units occasionally failed to fulfil their commanders' expectations. On 21 February 1943, the 2/5th Leicestershire Regiment, a particularly raw and undertrained formation, was attacked in its positions on a ridge in front of Thala and fell back in confusion. Even more serious was the virtual collapse of a whole brigade some weeks later. The 169th Queen's Brigade, comprising three battalions of the Queen's Regiment, entered the line with the Eighth Army on 26 April and two days later was ordered to attack two hills. The attack was repulsed and the ensuing withdrawal quickly degenerated into a stampede. A semi-official history also makes reference to 'a generalised panic which occurred in January 1943, in one brigade. The principal factors which combined to produce this mass reaction were found to be . . . fatigue following three days mortar fire . . . inadequate food supplies; poor selection [of men] . . . heavy losses in officers and NCOs; and the fact that the men had not been long in the theatre.'[115]

Europe, too, saw its share of breakdowns of morale, not least because, even at this stage of the war, the bulk of the troops were going into action for the first time. In Italy, the Salerno landing was the scene of regrettable incidents in both American and British units apart from the meeting already referred to. Norman Lewis was attached to Fifth Army HQ and on 12 September saw a line of American tanks go by, 'making for the battle, and hardly any time passed before they were back, but now there were fewer of them, and the wild erratic manner in which they were driven suggested panic. One stopped nearby, and the crew clambered out and fell into each other's arms weeping'. Two days later the rot had spread much further and Lewis suggests that HQ itself did much to contribute to the generalised panic. Rumours of a German breakthrough flew thick and fast and senior officers began to distribute carbines before themselves taking off into the blue yonder:

> Outright panic now started and spread among the American troops left behind. In the belief that our positions had been infiltrated by German infantry they began to shoot each other . . . Official history will in due time set to work to dress up this part of the action . . . with what dignity it can. What we saw was ineptitude and cowardice spreading down from the command and this resulted in chaos.[116]

The record is not entirely one-sided, however. On 10 September, the 6th Grenadier Guards were sent into attack the notorious tobacco factory but were surprised by an armoured counter-attack which wiped out one platoon. A brigade officer felt after the battle that

> . . . perhaps it is better to gloss over the rest of that day. The morale of the Grenadiers was not high, and it is certain that small parties considered the only plan was to return to the beaches as quickly as possible. On their right some [8th Royal] Fusiliers . . . had a similar idea. By midnight the small roads were full of frightened soldiers, many retiring pell-mell regardless of officers.[117]

In north-west Europe, too, inexperience accounted for many of the failures at battalion or company level, though in some cases veteran units were brought to breaking point by the sheer brutality of the fighting. Some units faltered at the very first. A correspondent on Omaha Beach wrote afterwards that it would be always 'marked in my mind by a line of American soldiers waist deep in water and immobilised by fear. Descending arcs of tracers were entering the water around them, and they could not bring themselves to move. They seemed as permanently fixed in time and space as those Marines in the statue of the flag-raising on Iwo Jima'.[118] Some raw British units fared little better. For most of them the landing was very straightforward and the first real contact with the Germans came a few days later. F. M. Richardson was a field ambulance commander with a Territorial Division and in his brigade

> . . . in a very early brush with the Germans . . . [a] battalion ran away, a scene which no-one who has witnessed it is likely to forget . . . After a short-lived attempt to let the unit pull itself together under a new C.O., it had to be disbanded. So completely had some junior officers' nerves gone to pieces that I once found myself standing alone on a road where I had been chatting to some of them, when one of our own light spotter aircraft flew over us.[119]

For other units, however, it was the strain of the savage fighting rather than the first shock of battle that was the cause of temporary collapse. The British were particularly susceptible during the latter stages of the Normandy battle, after the attrition of Caen. On 11 July, on Hill 112, part of the 5th Duke of Cornwall's Light Infantry had suddenly fallen back in disorder:

They had come running back in panic through the ranks of the [4th] Somersets. A wounded officer of the DCLI had been trying to prevent them; he had been hit in the jaw, so that part of his face had dropped, and he was waving a pistol and trying to shout, making horrible sounds . . . [Some of the Somersets were so badly rattled that one sergeant] had leapt into a sitting position on his slit trench, pointed his rifle down the line of his own men, and shouted that he would shoot the first bastard who moved.[120]

At around the same time an exhausted battalion of the 3rd Division failed to move forward when ordered. As an observer wrote: 'The old sweats had gone to ground when they heard a Spandau, and the young reinforcement, in action for the first time, thought that what his elders and betters did he should do too. Such is the state to which too much hard fighting and mental exhaustion can reduce a fine formation.'[121]

In the American armies it was the first major assaults into Germany that found morale at its lowest ebb. During the battles of the Siegfried Line, the Hürtgen Forest and beyond, there were several cases of whole units being quite incapable of maintaining the momentum of the attack. During the Aachen battle, part of the 30th US Division was violently counterattacked only to be deserted by attached Shermans from the 2nd US Armoured Division who suddenly discovered that they all needed urgent maintenance. Two hours elapsed before they were somehow persuaded to return to the aid of the infantry. Around Pruem, on 17 September 1944, the infantry were the ones to crack. In the 1st Battalion 22nd Infantry (4th US Division), 'enemy shelling so unnerved several officers, including the c.o. of the attached tank platoon, that they had to be evacuated for combat exhaustion . . . [In one company] when Lt. Marcum was wounded, the other officers apparently lost all control. Men began to get back individually and in small groups'.[122] In November of that year things got even worse. The problems of the 8th US Division in the Hürtgen Forest and the wholesale dismissal of officers necessary to get men moving at all have already been mentioned. At about the same time, the 28th US Division was trying to break through to Schmidt and had endured three days of merciless shelling that led to a crisis that spelled 'a threat to the very existence of the division'. Company commanders in one battalion, 2nd/112th Infantry, reported that 'their men's nerves were shattered, that they had to order some to eat, and that many cried unashamedly when told to remain in their foxholes.'

Then came a temporary lull in the shelling, but when it started again the men

> . . . already groggy to the point of insensibility could stand no more. Panic-ridden, men of one company grabbed wildly at their equipment and broke for the rear . . . The impulse to run was contagious. Once the men got going, they would not stop. The reserve company too pulled out . . . Few doubted that the Germans were close on their heels. Pushing, shoving, strewing equipment, the men raced wild-eyed through Vossenack . . . The battalion staff tried frantically to stem the retreat. It was an impossible task. Most men thought only of some nebulous place of refuge called 'the rear'. By 1030 the officers had nevertheless established the semblance of a line running through the village . . . but in the line there were no more than 70 men.[123]

Schmidt was indeed a name of ill-omen for the American army. It was not taken until the following year and even then there was a temporary crisis of morale. This time the 78th US Division were in the lead and at one point, as the 310th Regiment was passing through the 309th, they were caught by vicious automatic cross-fire. The official history tersely records that 'as the men went to ground, commanders temporarily lost control'.[124] The men could not in fact be rallied until the following day.

7
Relaxation

Ah, how one loves life when one has almost lost
it . . . When danger is, for a moment, at a distance
from us, what pleasure there is, with every limb
utterly relaxed, to absorb oneself completely in
the sweet sensation of being *alive*.

PRIVATE P. LINTIER, 1915

To a foot soldier war is almost entirely physical.
That is why some men, when they think about
war, fall silent. Language seems to falsify physical
experience and betray those who have
experienced it absolutely – the dead.

PRIVATE FIRST CLASS L. SIMPSON

It was unbelievably good to sit quiet. No mud,
dust, shell holes, dead cows, smells. It was good
to lie back and know you were alive; good to
shave, eat, sleep – above all to sleep.

SERGEANT J. W. FRASER, 1944

The fundamental role of the front-line soldier was to kill or be killed. This alone was his *raison d'être* and everything his commanders did was aimed at maximising his ability to do this, and very little else. Prodigious amounts of energy and money were spent in ensuring that the sharp end remained as finely honed as possible, and the constant supply of weapons, ammunition, and replacements retained the highest priority. But even the most hardened general realised that there were physical and psychological constraints upon the continued effectiveness of the individual soldier and that some sort of allowance had to be made for his inability to function like a machine. This was not necessarily construed as an obligation upon the authorities or even as a reward to the men, but simply as a means of ensuring that the spring did not irreparably wind down. And the armies' provision for the physical and emotional well-being of the troops always reveals a minimalist philosophy in striking contrast to their largesse with munitions and suchlike. As far as relaxation was concerned, everything was reduced to the bare essentials, just enough to get by on. Food intake was calorifically sound yet gastronomically vapid; pay scales allowed just enough to avoid creating an army of social lepers; the little vices of life were allowed for – alcohol, cigarettes, women – but in such a penny-pinching or mealy-mouthed manner that was supposed to be gratification of sorts became purely mechanical tokenism, a finally frustrating travesty of the 'real life' equivalents.

Ration Scales and Chow Lines

Whilst it might seem a little extreme to look for much sensual pleasure in eating, it is certainly true that the British army, in the first years of the war at least, seemed bent on reducing its solid rations to calorific content alone, with absolutely no regard for taste, texture or variety. In France and Belgium, in 1940, the situation was bearable because the static nature of most of the campaign meant that hot food was readily available, whilst the wealth of the countryside gave plenty of opportunity for unit kitchens and individual soldiers to supplement their rations with fresh meat, vegetables and dairy produce. In the Middle East, however, conditions were the exact reverse. For the front-line troops especially, it proved very difficult to get hold of anything but the most basic necessities. For anyone who fought there an

everlasting memory will be the staple diet of bully and biscuit.
These two items are a *leitmotif* of the whole Western Desert Force
and Eighth Army campaign. The historian of the 7th Armoured
Division relates that

> . . . for the first year of the war in the Desert it was very difficult for
> anyone to adhere to the time-honoured custom of the British Army of
> making issues of food from a ration scale. Although these scales exis-
> ted, they were quite valueless because the food simply did not exist. At
> one period the troops were issued with as much as eight ounces of jam
> and eight ounces of rice per day in order to produce a reasonably
> balanced diet. During the first campaign it was not unusual to have
> bully beef for all three meals each day – fried for breakfast, cold for
> lunch and stewed for supper.[1]

Things did not change appreciably in the next two years. The
authorities did try to vary the diet somewhat, but few of their
innovations reached the front lines. A tank officer in Libya in
November 1941 said: 'A man likes a meal. You may have the food
aboard, but you may lack the chance to cook it; as often as not it's
Army biscuits and jam, spread in the turret on the move.'[2] Tank
crews usually got some kind of hot meal before they bedded down
for the night but this was almost certainly bully beef or perhaps a
tin of meat and vegetable stew. In April 1942, an infantryman
noted in his diary that 'rations are very poor these days. For
breakfast, a slice of bread and bacon; for lunch, half a slice of bread
and tinned pilchards; for dinner, meat stew and potatoes, rice and
prunes'.[3] Later in the year Lieutenant McCallum was complaining of

> . . . a diet which had been mainly bully beef, biscuits, rice and tea.
> Even if one added the etceteras, the morning porridge, the sausage, the
> olio-margarine, the occasional 'meat and vegetable' compound which
> took the place of bully, the menu was hardly elaborate. The staples
> were bully (half a tin per man per day), biscuits (a little over a packet
> which contained a dozen), rice and tea. There had been no bread, ever.
> There had been none of those delicacies which the home papers tell us
> we have enjoyed.[4]

Even in 1943 the story was much the same. E. T. C. Gordine
(Royal Engineers) recalled desert rations at this time being 'scarce,
tinned and dehydrated'.[5] In fact, even dehydrated food was not
common at the front. The following day's meals for the 3rd Coldstream Guards, at Wadi Akarit, is typical of rations at this time:

Breakfast: half a slice of bacon, beans, biscuits, margarine
Tiffin: biscuits, syrup, two slices tinned peach (the latter a special treat)
Supper: bully beef, potatoes, beans, biscuits.

But soldiers are nothing if not great improvisers and immense ingenuity was devoted to the problem of trying to make such fare at least palatable. Biscuits and bully both became the central ingredient of numerous variations upon a theme. Of biscuits, Keith Douglas wrote: 'The issue varied from light and palatable ones by Peak Frean or Jacobs to dry, solid, soapy-tasting slabs made somewhere in Australia.'[6] The latter were often smashed into pieces, dust if possible, and slowly heated together with condensed milk and sugar or treacle to produce a gooey mess generally known as 'burgoo'. The best results were obtained if the powder could be soaked overnight. Roy Farran recalled that 'bully beef was served cold, stewed and fried. Biscuits were crushed to make flour for fritters and even porridge'.[7] Cecil Beaton, in 1943, observing that 'throughout the desert the ingredients are unvarying: bully beef, tinned potatoes and tomato sauce', asserted that 'the clever disguise of bully beef is an incentive to good morale. Tonight it was made into pancakes'.[8] Robert Crisp has described another method of preparing bully in the desperate hope that it might taste like something else:

My crew spent some time discussing plans for lunch. We settled for some bully beef pudding, a precious can of potatoes, tinned pears and condensed milk . . . I watched them making the pastry by crushing up biscuits to a fine powder, adding water and kneading it to a dough. This they wrapped around the unbroken chunk of bully and placed it in one of the desert ovens they were adept at making out of sand and tin.[9]

Keith Douglas, with his Boy Scout's enthusiasm for the adventure of war, was immensely struck by his regiment's culinary improvisation, and his men do indeed seem to have displayed particular talents in this direction. For them 'burgoo' was almost *infra dig*:

From biscuits and jam, cakes and puddings were made, well browned on the outside and doughy in the middle. Sometimes there were currants to add and a sort of duff was made. Biscuits were fried in the fat of American tinned bacon. There were immense stews of tinned meat and vegetable, Worcester sauce, onions, tinned potatoes, fried bully shreds, brown and crisp, with potato chips or crisps, and fried and flavoured rice cakes. If there were a flour issue, we had bully fritters, in batter, or fritters of dried fruit, or batter dumplings . . . Cheese fritters, flapjacks, pancakes, angels on horseback – the triumphs of these menus were endless.[10]

During this period it was officially recognised that the rations generally available at the front were inadequate. Theoretically this was not the case. The Middle East Field Service Ration was supposed to contain at least 3,700 calories and the Battle Ration 3,100. But the constituent parts of these ration scales were often not all available at any one time and chronic deficiencies resulted as well as long periods of subsisting on the same few items. The authorities did make some effort to counteract this. Special issues of lime juice or tinned fruit were made to increase the vitamin intake. Ascorbic acid was issued in tablet form as well as other tablets containing 'B' vitamins. Ground nuts were sometimes added for their protein value and at certain periods the daily salt ration was increased from $\frac{1}{2}$–$\frac{3}{4}$oz. In 1942, the Battle Ration was increased to include oatmeal, margarine and bacon, with *ghee* for the numerous Indian troops.

But the greatest problem was the monotony of the diet which could easily cause men to lose all interest in food, with a consequent deleterious effect on efficiency and morale. To counter this the authorities worked out a completely new ration scale in which the emphasis was upon variety just as much as on dietary efficiency. This was the famous 'compo-ration' which was the main source of food for British troops in Tunisia, Italy and northwest Europe. A 'compo' pack contained the ingredients for the daily meals of fourteen men, though where necessary it might have to provide 1 man with 14 days food, 2 with 7 or whatever combination seemed easiest. The food was all tinned and included such things as bacon, sausages, Irish stew (made in Argentina), steak and kidney pudding, meat and vegetable (known rather pompously as 'macedoine of vegetable'), fruit, puddings, butter, cheese and jam. There were also seven cigarettes per man, matches, a small cooker, some boiled sweets and lavatory paper. Nor were the latter two items the least of the contents. There was a constant shortage of disposable paper on all fronts, and in the desert things had been made even worse by the general lack of grass or leaves. The boiled sweets were particularly valuable for men waiting to go forward, who could not bear the thought of food. Sergeant Green

wrote of the north-west European campaign: 'We went twenty-
four hours at a time on a few biscuits, but the urgency of battle
produces a tightness of the stomach and a dryness of the throat
which rejects all feelings of hunger; bless those boiled sweets with
which we were so abundantly provided.'[11] Front-line troops, particularly during big attacks or amphibious assaults, were sometimes required to live for a short time on 24-hour ration packs, the
successor to the mess-tin ration, which were entirely made up of
items that needed minimal preparation. That for the D-Day landings came in a waxed cardboard container and consisted of two
blocks of pre-cooked dried meat, four oatmeal blocks for porridge,
a few compound blocks of tea, sugar and milk and some biscuits,
salt, sweets, sugar and meat extract.

Generally the 'compo' ration was well received. An officer in
Tunisia was moved to write home that 'our rations are really
excellent [though] all tinned of course'.[12] Even so, they were far
from ideal and if troops had to live on them for any length of time
they began to suffer from vitamin deficiencies. These could be
quite serious. An officer in Europe wrote of being visited in his slit
trench,

> . . . white and sick. [Peter] sat on the rim of the trench looking
> thoughtfully down at me.
> 'You look bad,' he said crisply. 'What's the matter?'
> 'I don't know,' I said. 'I've been sick all night and I think I've got a
> temperature; I'll be all right in a minute.'
> 'Compo-sickness,' said Peter, 'everybody's going down with it;
> you'd better come back to squadron headquarters for twenty-four
> hours; that will put you on your feet again.'[13]

Another soldier in north-west Europe, Corporal D. B. Jones (4th
Shropshire Light Infantry), remembered deciding to 'have something done about a painful boil on the back of my neck, which had
burst . . . but when I saw the Doc surrounded by bodies, I decided
he'd far more important work for the knife . . . Very many men
had these boils in England and in Normandy, so it was probably
something to do with the diet, which was only theoretically and for
propaganda purposes adequate in vitamins'.[14] The rations could
also have uncertain effects on one's bowels, either binding them up
like cement or causing acute diarrhoea. Cures for the latter varied.
According to Captain Cochrane, 'the only cure is to drink brandy
after it has been burnt for some moments . . . My innards sealed

like concrete by this infallible remedy'.[15] A Guards colonel, in Italy, would have thought this most effete. When asked how he had managed to cure himself of a particularly bad case of the 'runs' he maintained it could only be done 'by consuming an entire tin of treacle duff followed instantly by another tin of rice'.[16]

Fortunately, the troops did not have to subsist on such rations all the time. Wherever possible, and this could include the front line itself, they were fed by the company cooks. If the unit was in reserve or rest this would mean being served from the company kitchens, and soldiers actually at the front, whenever humanly possible, would have hot rations sent up in large vacuum containers. The quality of the food obtained in this way varied enormously. Many cooks, particularly in the fighting battalions, took their jobs seriously and laboured hard to maintain a good supply of hot and appetising food. They worked, of course, under severe limitations. The permissible extent of culinary initiative was flatly defined by a War Office manual which stated: 'The various methods of cooking adopted in the Army are roasting, baking, boiling, steaming, stewing and frying.' More limiting were the raw materials they had to work with and the difficulty of buying or 'liberating' additional fresh items. Considerable ingenuity was displayed, however. This anecdote of Captain Cochrane epitomises the spirit of the front-line battalions where everything possible was done for the fighting troops. No baking powder was available to his battalion cooks in Italy but one of them came up with the idea of using Liver Salts instead. His first venture produced a very palatable batch of scones; 'the trick caught on, and there was soon almost theological controversy between the company cookhouses on whether one got a lighter pastry with Andrews or Enos'.[17]

Ironically, many troops further back were not so well served by their unit cooks. Perhaps because there was less moral incentive to supply wholesome food, signallers, artillerymen and such were treated in a rather 'take it or leave it' fashion. Private Melling was a signaller and he came to feel almost hatred for the men in charge of his kitchens. At one point 'we queued for breakfast at 4 a.m. – one small slice of bacon, two biscuits, lumpy unsweetened porridge, and unsweetened tea. I remember cursing that breakfast and hearing others on all sides cursing it, as we ate in the dark. The food had got wicked of late.'[18] Stephen Berlin was an artilleryman and he too remembered many meals served almost with contempt. 'The gunners work well. They are tired but only grumble in the early morning when, after firing all night, they are given for breakfast one slice of spam, one slice of bread, and one mug of tea.'[19]

Nor should it be thought that rations at the front varied only between good and indifferent. Even after the lessons learnt in the Desert it often proved impossible to provide anything but the most meagre supplies, cooked and eaten in appalling conditions. Often rations were cut. During the week before Dunkirk they were reduced by 50 per cent. After the Japanese attack on Rabaul the retreating Australian 8th Division was reduced to a daily diet of a tiny scrap of bully beef, a biscuit, and a few ounces of native food all mashed together and cooked in a tin hat. Even during the Fourteenth Army's victorious push to Rangoon, in 1945, rations were reduced by a half to allow more ammunition to be brought forward. During the great sieges in Burma, in the previous year, things were worse. At Imphal, between May and June, the ration was cut from 3,500 to 2,750 calories. This was done by giving units 6 days' rations that had to last for 7. At Kohima, ration scales were abandoned entirely. According to Captain Hornor (2nd Royal Norfolk Regiment)

> . . . all cooking was in mess tins and the general menu was: breakfast – porridge of crushed biscuits, with a little salt and powdered milk added; and of course char, made with boiling water if possible, and if not, stewed up to some degree of warmth, painfully, and with much blowing and blasphemy. Tiffin would be a biscuit and bit of cheese . . . and for dinner a bully stew with selected leaves to flavour.[20]

As in many other respects, Burma was probably the worst theatre for food. The sobriquet 'Forgotten Army' tended to apply right across the board and bully and biscuit were always more familiar to its members than any of the improved rations that appeared in Europe. The only innovation that did appear, in depressingly large quantities, was the soya-link sausage, an experiment in synthetic foodstuffs that elicited universal abhorrence. Things were not helped much by the almost universal ban on naked lights after dark, because of the fear of surprise attacks, and most meals at the front were eaten cold. Some units discovered that very finely shaved bamboo produced a smokeless fire but this knowledge does not seem to have been widespread. Nor were the generally appalling conditions conducive to eating with relish. This description of a meal on the march, recorded in a company diary of the 9th Royal Sussex Regiment, is as good an example as any of the unremitting privations of the war in the East:

> After four hours marching in the drenching rain, breakfast eventually
> came up in a jeep train . . . [It] consisted of porridge, bacon and beans
> and a slice of bread. None of us will ever forget that breakfast – quite
> the end! The rain filled the mess tins of porridge so fast that, however
> quickly the chaps ate it, it always remained filled, and by the time one
> was ready to eat the bacon and beans, one found the former sunk to the
> bottom and the latter floating on top. A variety of novel expressions
> were heard as . . . ['A'] Company stabbed at the elusive beans and
> dredged for the bacon and bread. We shall leave that, as did most of the
> company.[21]

However, other fronts too had more than a few grim periods as
regards rations. Things could be very bad at the front in Italy, both
because of the climate and the difficulty of getting adequate rations
forwards. Hot food was the greatest problem. The history of the
Royal Scots Fusiliers, referring to the 2nd Battalion, says:

> Physical discomfort became almost an agony after a man had lain all
> night in bitter cold on a wet bank or in a slit trench half-filled with rain.
> The chances of getting a hot meal were often slight; there were times
> when little more could be expected than a lukewarm drink from one
> day's end to another. Matches to light the tommy-cooker or a 'desert
> fire' were often soaked and useless.[22]

The tommy-cookers, tiny personal stoves supposedly to boil up
water or heat the contents of tins, were not up to the rigours of the
Italian weather. The 2nd Duke of Cornwall's Light Infantry, on
Monte Ornito, in February 1944, found that available stocks of
fuel only worked out at $1\frac{1}{2}$ tablets per man per day, just about
enough to warm a mug of tea but not bring it to the boil. In such
circumstances, it took a doughty man to see any humour in the
instructions on the compo-tins – 'simply stand in boiling water for
thirty minutes'. A Grenadier Guardsman of the 3rd Battalion, a
month later, objected on aesthetic grounds as much as any other.
'What I really hate is that every morning we have bits of cold bacon
on the same tin plate as a mess of apricot jam. The jam gets into the
bacon and the bacon gets into the jam.'[23]
Elsewhere, cooking proved somewhat easier, both at individual
and unit level. In the desert, petrol-soaked sand was the usual
standby and water could be brought to the boil or food cooked in a
very short time. Even so, the climate had its drawbacks. Sometimes the weather was so hot that the food cooked itself, in the tin.

Such was the case in Eritrea, where bully beef was the staple item. During the day the tins often became too hot to handle and when opened they spewed out their contents, a revolting oily liquid containing a few strings of gut-like meat. Again the manufacturer's instructions were not without a grim irony, cautioning the diner to 'chill before serving'. In north-west Europe this unfortunate side effect was put to good use and self-heating tins were developed, though in this case the troops themselves decided just when the cooking should be done. As John Foley wrote, when his men were caught

> . . . in a pretty fierce snowstorm . . . But each of us had one of those excellent tins of tomato soup, filled with a centre tube carrying a quick heating element. All that was necessary was to touch a small wick with the lighted end of a cigarette and in a matter of seconds we were drinking hot soup and bringing down blessings on Mr Heinz and the shadowy figures of I.C.I. who were jointly responsible for this salvation.[24]

The British and Americans had very little regard for each other's rations. During the first months of the Tunisian campaign all First Army troops used compo-rations and the GIs were not particularly impressed, missing above all the carbohydrate content of 'real' American food. Yet the British, for their part, felt that their ally's rations lacked anything one could get one's teeth into. William Woodruff, at Anzio, was perpetually hungry, 'surviving on what we can scrounge and Yank pack rations. Dammit, it's a wonder we haven't lost the war eating that Yank stuff. It's all wrapping and bull. When you've swallowed the spearmint and the fags and the glucose candy and dehydrated muck that goes with it, your guts feel empty. Gives you wind it does. It's got nothing on British treacle and duff'.[25]

In fact, British and American experience with rations offers many parallels. What Woodruff was referring to was the 'K' ration, the American equivalent of the mess-tin ration or 24-hour pack. Theoretically it was only to be used at the front and that only for very short periods. It came in three waxed cardboard containers for breakfast, dinner and supper. Each meal contained meat – veal, spam and dried sausage respectively – though American troops continually complained about the lack of bulk. There was also a fruit bar, cellophane-wrapped crackers and chewing gum as well as a bouillon cube and malt-dextrose tablets. The latter were particularly despised and were thrown away almost without exception. The cardboard cartons were unsuitable for storage and especially in the Pacific they deteriorated very quickly. The crackers went rancid and the warm chewing gum permeated its taste into everything else.

The 'K' ration also formed part of the 10-in-1 ration, introduced in late 1944. This was the American equivalent of the compo-pack and was meant to feed 10 men for 1 day.[26] The 'K' ration was meant for the noon meal whilst breakfast and supper were one of several different menus, including a wide range of dehydrated cereals as well as canned or dehydrated meat and vegetable dishes, such as meat-balls and spaghetti, frankfurters and beans, pork and beans, ham and eggs, chicken and vegetable. Like the compo-ration it also included accessory packs of cigarettes, matches, toilet paper, halzone tablets and a can opener. It was generally acknowledged to be an improvement on previous ration scales, though certain items were universally unpopular. Hundreds of tons of Carter's spread (a processed butter), dehydrated tomato juice and, above all, dehydrated cabbage flakes, soon littered the various theatres of war.

The 10-in-1 was the successor to the 'C' ration, the equivalent of the British Field Service Ration in the first years of the war. This came in six round metal cans and consisted of three meat and three 'bread' units. The latter comprised crackers, hard candy, and soluble coffee. Troops in the Pacific theatre were most familiar with 'C' rations because they were the portable ration with the highest calorie content, organised front-line cooking being very difficult during the island campaigns, and because the tins kept better than fresh food or 'K' rations. Even so, they had a short shelf-life. The history of the Quartermaster Corps notes that 'through lengthy exposure to high temperatures the fat in the [meat] components separated from other elements and formed a reddish conglomeration on the ends of the can so distasteful in appearance that soldiers repeatedly threw the whole mass of food away'.[27] Cold weather did not help much either. During the Tunisian winter the meat components became absolutely flavourless and after three days on nothing but 'C' rations men suffered spells of nausea and acute digestive disturbances. In Italy, Fifth Army surgeons maintained that all army rations were deficient in calories. Depending on the weather, the daily deficiency for troops subsisting only on 'C' or 'K' rations was estimated to be between

400 and 1,800 calories. Reports from the soldiers themselves veri-
fied this. Men lost weight, bodily exhaustion increased, body fat
decreased, and there was an upsurge in such complaints as neuritis
and skin lesions, typical symptoms of chronic vitamin deficiency.

Theoretically, of course, no troops were supposed to live for
very long on 'C', 'K' or 10-in-1 rations. It was assumed that they
would have regular contact with their unit kitchens, attached, like
the British, at company level. Here 'B' rations were prepared, a 10-
day cycle of various menus utilising as much fresh meat, vegetables
and dairy produce as possible. Supposedly each man would receive
5lb of food per day. Indeed, 'B' and other prepared kitchen rations
formed the great proportion of all food served in the US army
during World War II. In both north-west Europe and Italy, they
made up 80 per cent of all rations served. But this does not mean
that all men got such food 80 per cent of the time. Most men did get
them most of the time but the odd 20 per cent of 'operational'
rations were consumed by the men in the front line – the very
troops who needed hot food the most being denied it for days and
even weeks at a time. For them 10-in-1 rations were usually the
best that could be hoped for. Otherwise it was 'K' or 'C', sometimes nothing but 'D' rations, stodgy cocoa cakes masquerading
under the name of chocolate bars. In the Central Pacific a special
assault ration was devised, known as the 'candy ration' which
contained only hard candy, a peanut chocolate bar and packs of
chewing gum. This was only supposed to last two days and was
designed to carry men through the period when they were too tense
to take heavy food. This made sense, as has been noted with regard
to boiled sweets, but it left much to be desired when men were cut
off from their kitchens for up to a week at a time.

The combat troops did get kitchen food sometimes, even when
at the front. Ralph Ingersoll has described conditions in Tunisia:

> When the kitchen truck was on hand, a typical day's menu in the line
> would start with either scrambled eggs or wheatcakes for breakfast.
> The eggs would always be scrambled because they came in cans,
> powdered . . . Along with the main breakfast dish, there would be
> canned apricots or prunes and hardtack or crackers and coffee . . . For
> dinner you would get fried spam, canned succotash and – if there had
> been luck with the weather, and the time to bake it – bread . . . For
> supper there would be thin frankfurters split in two and fried, or cut up
> like Tootsie rolls and mixed with some vegetables in a stew.[28]

But this was far from typical and even the kitchen rations could be a lot less appetising than Ingersoll makes them sound. Often they were served in haste, in appalling conditions and with many of the constituents missing. The popularity of unit kitchens reached a low ebb in Italy, in spring 1944, when dehydrated meat and vegetable seemed to be all they ever served. One of the main problems was that the cooks did not bother to rehydrate it properly before slopping it into the mess tins. By October the gross vitamin content of the chow issues was reckoned to be not more than 30mg per man per day, often down to 12 after cooking, and vitamin tablets had to be issued. On many occasions there was no kitchen at all. This was particularly the case in the Pacific and Italy where the Americans consistently fared much worse than the British with regard to hot food. In the Pacific, ten days or more often elapsed before the company cooks were able to land and even then, in the difficult terrain, they often fell behind the forward units or, if exceptionally assiduous, outstripped their own supplies. More-over, neither the Army nor the Marines usually had the facilities to heat the food up in their own foxholes. What was known as 'canned heat' was an official issue, but few men could be bothered to carry it around. Whilst in combat, inadequate, monotonous, cold, sometimes rancid food was the lot of the ordinary soldier. On New Georgia, according to Captain Mathieu, 'men lived on cold rations for days at a time while they were fighting. I talked to some on one occasion who were enjoying hot coffee and doughnuts, the first hot food they had in twelve days. Their food consisted mainly of C rations . . . and the D ration'.[29] On New Guinea an officer related 'that for more than a week the only food he could get on issue was five pounds of rice and a one pound tin of beef per section per day'.[30] On Guadalcanal 'food was so scarce and sweets were so craved that I heard soldiers offer two dollars for another man's chocolate pudding, three dollars for an extra 'K' ration, and two dollars for a sweet roll. Matches were useless in the damp air of the jungle. One dollar cigarette lighters were sold for ten or fifteen dollars'.[31]

In Italy, where the food often rivalled the appalling weather and both quality and quantity often left much to be desired, a survey of four infantry divisions, in April 1945 when the front was fairly stable, asked the question: 'When last on active service did you get as much to eat as you needed? If not why not?' Only 36 per cent said they had had enough to eat, whilst 10 per cent said they didn't feel like eating, 30 per cent didn't like the food they were offered, and 22 per cent simply couldn't get hold of adequate amounts. Bill Mauldin remembered one unit at the front who, 'because they were on K rations . . . had coffee only once a day. The supper ration had a sort of bouillon soup, which was impossible. It takes a lot of water to make it, and a lot more to down the salty thirst that it causes'.[32] Perhaps the saddest point of all was that if troops near the front did manage to get good, hot food they could be pretty sure that it presaged something unpleasant. Lieutenant Bond remembered such a meal overlooking Cassino:

> Two days later we were served steak for dinner, large delicious pieces brought up hot from the kitchens in the rear. When the veterans saw it they knew we would be sent back into the fighting right away . . . During the last four months, whenever there was to be a big attack, they had been served steak, and they dreaded seeing it come.[33]

As with the British, the Americans fared best for rations in the European Theatre of Operations. Greater efforts were made to keep the kitchens close to the front, where they bivouacked 'in the battalion service area. From there hot food was taken forward in . . . insulated containers. Hot drinks were also transported in such containers if available, but a 5-gallon water can wrapped in blankets was an adequate substitute'.[34] Even so, this system could not always operate and the following vignette by Major Johns is perhaps more typical of troops at the front than any organised 'chow line'. Each of his companions

> . . . took turns heating, over the single candle, his little can of meat that came out of the supper K-ration. He did this by opening the lid most of the way with the key that came with the ration, bending it back and holding the can over the candle flame by grasping the bent back lid with a pair of pliers. The meat simmered and the grease melted and spat, but if it was a bit messy it was still the best available way to get a hot meal. The bouillon powder, which nobody ever used to make a soup, made an excellent flavouring agent and with it the meat wasn't bad at all.[35]

Drink and Cigarettes

There were two basic types of drink – the one that went with the food, necessary to keep men alive, and that given as a faint re-

minder of civilian times spent in saloons, bars and pubs. The basis
of the former allotment was water, a simple enough commodity,
but one whose regular supply to forward positions often presented
considerable difficulties. Nowhere was this more so than in the
desert. There men were often limited to $\frac{3}{4}$gal or less per head per
day, and that was for everything; washing, shaving, cooking and
drinking.[36] If a unit was stationary, half this allowance went direct to the cookhouse. The greatest economies were exercised with
regard to the men's ablutions. Washing-up water was often re-
cycled repeatedly by pouring it through a perforated tin full of
sand. In other units

> . . . After the morning wash it was left in your canvas camp basin (or
> the half of a petrol tin if not an officer) all day. For the evening wash the
> soap suds were skimmed off and it was used again. Another skim
> next morning and it was poured into a petrol tin to accumulate for
> washing clothes. Finally, after the sand had been allowed to settle, it
> was carefully decanted into the radiator.[37]

At one point in 1941, according to W. Trebich (21st Royal Horse
Artillery), there was 'an acute shortage of water which later led to
our having to shave in the dregs of our tea'.[38]

This introduces a key point about the water ration; no one
actually drank it as it came, but used it to make either tea in the
British or other associated armies, or coffee in the American and
South African. It would be difficult to overstate the importance of
these beverages to the front-line soldier. Indeed, it can fairly be
stated that at times the regular supply of hot drinks was all that
stood between a resigned acceptance of conditions at the front and
complete demoralisation. To some extent this *penchant* for tea and
coffee was forced upon the men as the water itself was virtually
undrinkable. On the one hand it was heavily chlorinated as well as
being purified with some combination of alum and soda ash. On
the other it was usually brought up to the front in *ad hoc* containers, notably petrol and oil cans. Even in those cases where the
water did not taste of petrol and chlorine, the internal coating of
the cans – paraffin wax or bitumen and benzine – tended to flake off
and add its own unmistakable taste. This was one reason why all
tea and coffee was heavily sugared, in that this tended to minimise
the effect of the chlorination as well as counterbalance the
excessive saltiness of some pipelines.

But the pyschological effect of a hot drink was the crucial factor.

Almost every British memoir and unit history attests to this point.
R. L. Crimp described the collection of rations from a divisional
dump in 1942. First came the fairly liberal allocation of bully and
biscuit, and 'then the distribution of tea, a meticulous business,
almost every leaf counted. "One third of a mug for each section!" is
the sergeant's edict, and he dips in his sack, gauges narrowly,
submits for approval, before relinquishing the precious herb'.[39]
Later he describes a desert brew, a procedure that remained virtually unchanged throughout the war, in whatever theatre:

> These desert brews are an institution, the making being almost a ritual.
> Half a gallon of water is poured into the brewcan and set on the fire.
> The fire . . . usually consists of a cut-down biscuit tin or petrol can,
> gashed in the sides for ventilation with a few inches of neat petrol or
> petrol-soaked sand in the bottom, which burns fiercely for several
> minutes. When the pot is boiling a couple of handfuls of tea are cast
> upon the seething water. Then the pot's removed and the brew allowed
> to strengthen up. Meanwhile the section mugs are marshalled on the
> ground, and spoonfuls of tinned milk and sugar put in each. Then
> they're filled with tea, straight out of the brew can.[40]

Often in fact tea, sugar and dried milk were thrown in the pot
together, and compo-rations presented these items ready mixed.
Those who preferred unsweetened tea were out of luck, though if
tea and sugar were kept and brewed together the tea leaves absorbed much of the sweetness.

Of such rituals Roy Farran wrote: 'Tea was brewed three or four
times a day, and if the supplies had ever failed the morale of the
army would have been reduced more than by a major defeat.'[41]
Another officer was equally emphatic. 'At midday, the sweat pouring off us, char cooled us, while the same char stopped our teeth
chattering at night; char kept the army going through everything.
Any quartermaster knew that whatever the circumstances he had
to get the char ration . . . and the ammunition up front; anything
else could be sacrificed.'[42] An RAMC orderly was once asked to
name the five major principles for the prevention of shock and he
was not being entirely flippant when he answered: 'A cup of tea and
four lumps of sugar.'[43]

Tankmen, too, brewed up at every available opportunity. In
Normandy a common slogan on both soft-skin and armoured
vehicles was 'When in doubt – brew up'. One officer wrote of his
men: 'There are no greater adepts in the world at producing a cup

of hot tea under any conditions than a British tank crew. They will make tea at the receiving end of an artillery bombardment, they will bring a kettle to the boil in the middle of a night-leaguer when even striking a match is a punishable offence. There is a quality of genius in their method and a quality of greatness in their determination.'[44] They even endeavoured to brew up on the move and a common trick in the desert was to tie a can of water to the hot exhaust so the tea could be thrown in as soon as they stopped. Even combat could not always banish thoughts of a brew. One officer noted the 'incredible but not unusual sight . . . [of] some tank crew, temporarily immobile or disengaged, but still under fire, huddled over a stove making tea'.[45]

The authorities certainly realised the crucial importance of hot tea. As has been seen, commanders and quartermasters deemed it second only to ammunition and gave it the highest priority at every stage of the supply line. The government, too, seems to have got the message. From 1942 the British undertook to purchase the world's entire crop and distribute the surplus to the fifty-two members of the United Nations. At any one time there were over 30 million tons of tea stored in England, and when it is realised that 1,000 tons will make about 500 million cups of tea it becomes clear that this was one commodity of which there could be no conceivable shortage.

Tea has never been to the American taste ever since they threw a shipload of it into the harbour at Boston. An American soldier at Salerno gave perhaps the neatest judgement when he was offered a mug by a sergeant-major. He took one sip and announced incredulously: 'Gee! Hot ice-cream.' Coffee was the American alternative, and though it was never quite the magic potion that tea was to the British, it was a very important item, especially in the Tunisian and European winters. Soluble coffee appeared in certain of the combat ration scales, though this was regarded as being barely palatable. Much more popular was the roasted coffee distributed by the unit kitchens, and in the ETO demand rose to an unprecedented height. The Third Army, for example, consumed 212,000lb in November 1944 and 1,075,000lb in the following January. Civilian coffee-roasting establishments in Paris had to be utilised to meet the demand. But even when the coffee was readily available there were still problems for the individual soldiers and their enjoyment was seriously hampered by an elementary design fault in the issue canteen cup. Ernie Pyle explained its 'one big drawback. The rolled-over rim collected so much heat we couldn't put it to our lips without burning them, hence we had to wait until our coffee was lukewarm before we could drink it. A few soldiers, I noticed, had partly solved the problem by cutting the rim off and filing the top smooth'.[46]

The US army also laid great store by cold beverages though these were never very popular with the men and were often ludicrously inappropriate to the weather conditions. The contempt for dehydrated tomato juice has already been mentioned in passing, and though other fruit juices were available these too were generally spurned, even in the Pacific at its hottest. The usual generic term was 'battery acid'. But the most unpopular item of all was lemonade crystals, which were to be dissolved in hot or cold water and were meant to provide the vitamins missing from the canned rations. The intention was laudable but few soldiers could be persuaded to do anything but throw them away. In winter they seemed a calculated insult and even when prepared with boiling water, if you could boil any, a lemon drink seemed a particularly pathetic counter to driving rain or snow. Bill Mauldin wrote caustically of the 'synthetic lemonade – a mixture of carbolic acid and ersatz lemon powder. Try drinking that in a muddy foxhole in freezing weather'.[47] The authorities later admitted that the

> . . . lemon crystals were characterised by a biting acidity which could only be countered by vast amounts of sugar. Cooks were taught a dozen tricks to disguise them or persuade the troops to consume them, but all in vain. The troops detested the synthetic lemonade and all its variants and offsprings. Every observer report from the Mediterranean and European theatre included complaints on this score.[48]

And of course there was Coca Cola. One soldier is reputed to have written home: 'To my mind I am in this damn mess as much to help keep the custom of drinking Cokes as I am to help preserve the million other benefits our country blesses its citizens with.'[49] It was hardly a regular item at the front, but there can have been few soldiers who did not consume it avidly when in reserve or resting. For a firm selling a product that was 99 per cent sugar and water the Coca Cola Company had a remarkably good war. They supplied it to the forces for one nickel a bottle but sewed up 95 per cent of the overseas PX (Post Exchange) soft drink market. In all GIs gulped down 10 billion bottles of the stuff. The government was suitably appreciative: in 1939 the company had only 5 overseas bottling plants; by VJ-Day they had been generously assisted to build a further 59.

As it had been in World War I, the US Army was 'dry', at least insofar as there was no free, official issue of alcohol to either officers or men. The latter were not even allowed to buy spirits though they could purchase bottles of beer when off duty. And even though the officers could buy liquor, for the mess, this was strictly limited to only ½ bottle per officer per month. In July 1945, too late to do any good, Eisenhower also sanctioned a liquor ration for the NCOs' messes in the European Theatre of Operations. For the most part the soldiers were dependent on the occasional goodwill of their commanders – Patton allowed the distribution of a huge cache of captured German booze to the Third Army on Thanksgiving Day, reputedly 7 bottles of wine or cognac per man – or their own ingenuity. In Europe, of course, there were vast amounts of wine to be had, usually purchased from the French and Italians or liberated from the German civilians. When General Richardson was leading a task force to Paderborn in the Ruhr pocket on a very foggy night, his jeep 'was in imminent danger of being run over by the tanks behind him, the drivers of which had found a large champagne warehouse in Brilon and were blind drunk by this time'.[50] Even on the small Anzio beachhead there was wine available for those who knew where to go. The area became honeycombed with underground shelters and dugouts and

> . . . inevitably some of these . . . became 'speakeasy' dens where the local black marketeers sold *vino* to the troops. The Military Police placed them off-limits and kept a strict watch on them, but it was impossible to clean them up altogether. Soldiers found their way past the guards wherever a notice was scrawled on the door which said *Al Ricovero*. True, this simply meant 'To the Air Raid Shelter' . . . but the troops assumed that Al Ricovero was the proprietor of the wine store and a visit to Al's place could procure you a flask of something to forget the present miseries . . . No-one inquired too closely at the mess where he had got it from for a 'slug of the old *vino*' before going to sleep gave a good many people on the Beachhead enough 'catacomb courage' to face the anguish awaiting them next morning.[51]

Booze was rarest of all in the Pacific. Not only did the army not provide it but there was hardly any indigenous production outside of Australia and New Zealand. As Sergeant M. S. Babcock (37th US Division, wrote:

Dipsomaniac soldiers on the South Sea islands lack regular supplies of liquor. In Fiji liquor could be obtained over a bar but rarely could a soldier reach the bar when it was open. He was too far away or in the field. However, Indian bootleggers were intermittently contacted selling a sundry collection of rot-gut at prices ranging from twelve to eighteen dollars a quart. A scant supply of beer is now provided in the New Hebrides.[52]

On Guadalcanal, the first and last issue of beer was on Christmas Eve. Non-drinkers were offered up to $3 a can. There were only two reasonable supplies of liquor for enlisted men in this theatre. One was Air Force and Navy personnel with whom a lively barter trade in souvenirs was established:

The Air Corps men could and would pay higher because it was they who imported the booze . . . [On the regular transport runs] they stuffed every available bit of space with bottles or cases of scotch . . . A silk battle flag, preferably bloodstained, was always worth at least three Imperial quarts. A rifle, on the other hand, would hardly bring a pint . . . A typical, normal 'Samurai sabre' was always worth five Imperial quarts at least and the better grade ones with gold and ivory chasing could bring as high as nine Imperial quarts . . . Men who had [money] but no souvenirs to trade were known to pay as high as fifty dollars for one Imperial quart of scotch.[53]

The only other way to get hold of liquor was to distil it oneself. James Jones recalled

. . . 'raisin jack' or . . . 'swipe', which was a Hawaian word for bootleg liquor . . . In my outfit we got blind asshole drunk every chance we got . . . We made our 'swipe' by stealing a five-gallon tin of canned peaches or plums or pineapple from the nearest ration dump, and putting a double handful of sugar in it to help it ferment, then leaving it out in the sun in the jungle . . . It was the most godawful stuff to drink, sickly sweet and smelling very raunchy, but if you could get enough of it down and keep it down, it carried a wonderful wallop.[54]

Another favourite for fermentation was coconut milk, and Australian troops in the Pacific also used this type of liquor, generally known as 'jungle juice', in large quantities. Sometimes even cruder methods were used. James Jones remembered a PX on Guadalcanal in which only two items were left for the front-line troops, Barbasol shaving cream and Aqua Velva aftershave. The Barbasol remained on the shelves but the Aqua Velva went like hot cakes.

'Mixed with canned grapefruit juice . . . the shaving lotion did not taste at all. Grapefruit juice seemed to cut all the perfume out of it. It made a drink rather like a Tom Collins. Everyone loved it.'[55]

Bootlegging seems to have been rare in other armies, though the troops were prepared to buy illicit booze if it was available. In north-west Europe there was some traffic between American and British forces from the stills that had been set up by the former. Otherwise there was only a small official issue of beer, usually two pint bottles per man per week. Even this modest allocation imposed a considerable strain on shipping resources. In 1941, for example, 80,000 tons of shipping were used to take beer to the Middle East and eventually the authorities began to brew it *in situ*. This experiment was generally successful though some local brews did leave a lot to be desired. A famous one was Egyptian 'Stella' beer 'with its vague and puzzling flavour of onions'.[56] Elsewhere, the experiment was not so successful. The product of an experimental field brewery in India, set up in 1944, was universally condemned as undrinkable. Local products were used in Italy, but when Churchill gave the order that the beer allocation was to be increased to 6 pints per week it proved almost impossible to find the extra shipping necessary to import over 30 million bottles each month. Spirits were not officially issued, though officers were permitted to purchase a certain amount for their messes. This was theoretically the same allowance as that to American officers, but it seems that many considerably increased their intake by private purchase. In one sample of 200 officer psychiatric cases, it was found that excessive consumption of alcohol was a primary cause of breakdown for 38 per cent. About a third of these had been heavy drinkers before the war, but the rest had turned to whisky and gin to help them sleep or as a stimulant to get through the great load of paperwork.

In one respect, however, the British had a great advantage over the Americans in that the hallowed tradition of the rum ration was kept up throughout World War II. There were important qualifications. It could only be issued on the Medical Officer's authorisation, and the amount given to each man was hardly over-generous. When given before an attack, according to one officer, it was intended as a substitute for a hot meal and it 'at least warmed one up, though the tot available was nothing like enough, unfortunately, to launch one forward in stupified oblivion of danger, or to release whatever atavistic instincts may be supposed to lurk in any combatant'.[57] However, whilst it is certainly absurd to think in terms of battalions of drunken beserkers, this officer does tend to understate the importance of rum in action. Another wrote of his experiences in Tunisia:

> When committed to battle our men for the most part ate nothing. I certainly never did, beyond perhaps a nibble of chocolate once in a while. We simply kept going on rum. Realising this our Quartermasters, with the active connivance of the C.O.s, and indeed of our Brigade H.Q., went to enormous pains to indent, borrow, seize or steal immense quantities of the stuff. Eventually it became unthinkable to go into action without it. Rum, and morphia to silence our wounded.[58]

Nor was drunkenness at the front completely unknown. Before an attack in Holland, one of Martin Lindsay's officers 'walked around with a large earthenware jar and everyone got well rummed up, the first time I had seen this happen. They left in a state bordering on hilarity'.[59] Occasionally soldiers waiting to go forward would get drunk on stuff they had appropriated themselves. Lieutenant Mitchell saw this happen in Italy, though the agent this time was a large cache of vermouth. As he walked over to his platoon Mitchell noted that

> . . . a few of them were obviously pretty drunk . . . Sergeant Dempsey, who was sober, saw my aghast expression and said, 'Don't worry, sir. They'll be sick on the way up and then they'll be alright.' And this was how I moved up to battle for the first time, sitting beside the driver of my truck, with some of my platoon vomiting and retching over the tailboard.[60]

But the main purpose of the rum ration was not to make soldiers heedless of danger before an attack. Most issues were not made just before combat but when the men were in the line during bad weather. In Tunisia and Europe, during winter, issue was authorised night after night to try and warm the men up slightly and help them get through the long watches and stand-tos. On the Island, in Holland, the 2nd Cheshire Regiment had a rum issue on every day of its 8-week stay there. In Italy, in December 1943, a rum ration was even authorised at army level, but this seems to have been frowned on in some quarters for it was soon superseded by an extra allowance of tea, sugar and milk.

Rum was the favoured stimulant for front-line troops. Similar needs for those further back were not ignored however, and many rear-echelon troops with demanding jobs, especially those who sometimes had to work days and nights at a stretch, were issued with liberal quantities of amphetamines. The Germans were the first to issue them in large quantities to their troops but the British soon followed suit. A paper by Brigadier Q. V. B. Wallace, the DDMS of X Armoured Corps, records:

> 'Pep' tablets, i.e. benzedrine tablets, were used for the first time in the Middle East on a large scale. 20,000 tablets were issued to the A.D.M.S. of each division . . . who was responsible for their distribution and safe custody. The initial dose was 1½ tablets two hours before the maximum benefit was required, followed six hours later by another tablet, with a further and final tablet for another six hours, if required . . . I consider that 'Pep' tablets may be very useful in certain cases, particularly where long-continued work is required over extended periods, i.e. staff officers, signallers, lorry drivers, transport workers, etc. The tablets must only be used when an extreme state of tiredness has been reached. The tablets have practically no ill-effects, and an ordinary night's sleep restores the individual to his original working capacity.[61]

It seems that the front-line troops also received them from time to time in other theatres. The history of the Scots Guards notes that the 2nd Battalion, near Rochetta, in October 1943, spent 'ten days . . . in terrific feats of mountaineering, with the men desperately tired towards the end, and having to be kept awake with benzedrine tablets'.[62] In north-west Europe, they were issued to certain Canadian armoured units. One sergeant recalled: 'We had been awake for forty-eight hours, fatigue-laden hours; all seasickness had disappeared, but the men were still weak from it; we had been issued "bennies" to keep awake, and the haggard look they gave the men made us appear like "zombies".'[63]

The Americans were far less blasé than Brigadier Wallace about the cumulative effects of amphetamines and a prominent physiologist, Dr Andrew Ivy, ruled that they were too toxic to be issued to the troops. In the event, however, they were simply dispensed to US troops by British medical personnel and it has since been estimated that at least 80 million tablets were distributed from this source as well as a further 100 million that the American medics themselves managed to lay their hands on. At least 10 per cent of all American troops, it has been suggested, took amphetamines at one time or another. How many of these men suffered adverse aftereffects is not known, but it is revealing to note that a study made in

1947 showed that 25 per cent of all men in army stockades were
heavy and chronic users.

One of the few other non-essentials that the armies gave away
with the rations were cigarettes. The Americans were the more
generous; normally their men got between 5 and 7 packs a week,
whilst the standard British ration was only 50 cigarettes. They
were also available in Naafis and PXs where the British paid
around 6d for a pack of 20 and the Americans 5 cents. Supplies did
not always hold up, however – as ever, the 'Forgotten Army' did
not receive the full ration of 50 until the middle of 1944. Both the
British and Americans experienced an acute shortage in December
1943 when only the most obscure brands were available and these
in limited quantities. The Americans went through another crisis
in October 1944, in north-west Europe, caused by the incompetence of Com Z at Supreme Allied Headquarters. The question
of brands was very important. Both the major allies far preferred
such market leaders as Woodbines, Players, Gold Flake, Chester-
field, Lucky Strike and Camel and both resisted more obscure
brands unless there was absolutely no alternative. Americans in
Britain left many thousands of cartons to rot on the shelves of the
PX rather than abandon their favourites; the Quartermaster's
Department was only saved from having to write the whole lot off
by the unlucky Canadians and Australians whose less indulgent
governments agreed to buy 10 million packets. The British army
was forced to foist the most amazing rubbish on its soldiers,
usually locally produced merchandise. In Italy, Africa and Burma,
'V' cigarettes, produced in India, were particularly notorious. The
most damning comment on them was that even the Arabs wouldn't
smoke them, cigarettes being a common means of barter. Another
horror were 'C-to-C' (Cape to Cairo), made in Egypt. In Burma
there were also 'Lions' which provoked the following letter in a
forces newspaper:

> The British Lion greets us with a Lion cigarette. Lions have strength –
> don't we know it! They now have the audacity to issue even worse
> cigarettes than V's to fellows who are doing the scrapping, to fellows
> not within miles of a canteen who cannot even buy other cigarettes. A
> man who is suffering the hardships and privations of the front line
> should be given the best his country can give.[64]

Nor were English profiteers above turning out execrable products.
A brand called 'RAF' were amongst the worst. It was discovered

that they were made from cigarette butts swept up from cinema floors and the manufacturer was eventually sent to prison, though this did not stop them turning up at the front for some months afterwards.

Though cigarettes were theoretically non-essential, the various high commands were sensible of the need to give them a high priority. Many of the men called up had been smokers in civilian life and the effort of trying to stop would have been a severe psychological strain when added to the other tensions of the front line. There cigarettes were a vital buttress to morale and the most stringent black-out regulations could not prevent men from lighting up. As one officer noted: 'Soldiers have a genius for smoking unobtrusively; the fag would be lit, asphyxiatingly, under one's blanket, and then cupped between the hands. I once told the platoon, on parade, to put their hands out, palms up, and apart from those of the few non-smokers, every pair was clearly distinguished by a bright orange patch.'[65] Even those who were non-smokers when inducted, soon picked up the habit, particularly if exposed to combat. Ernie Pyle was always quick to observe the habits of the ordinary GIs and in north-west Europe he talked to a soldier who 'never smoked cigarettes until he landed in France on D-Day, but after that he smoked one after another. He was about the tenth soldier who had told me the same thing. A guy in war has to have some outlet for his nerves, and I guess smoking is as good as anything'.[66] Lieutenant Colonel John Whitfield (2/5th Queen's Regiment) came to pretty much the same conclusion and, after the Salerno landings,

. . . learned that many of the troops were short of cigarettes, having had them ruined by sea-water. Whitfield, a non-smoker, had at one time tried to ban smoking during exercises, but discovering it produced an appalling effect on morale, he determined that the troops would always have a liberal supply. Before leaving North Africa he brought five thousand and loaded them into his jeep.[67]

Unfortunately, when his sergeant went to fetch them, it was found that they had been stolen.

Rest and Leave

All the armies realised that the stress of combat necessitated frequent periods of rest. Even if a spell in the line did not involve an actual attack, the strains of shelling, waiting for enemy raids, and of simply existing in waterlogged slit-trenches were more than men could take for a few days at a stretch. The measures adopted were little different from those of World War I and consisted of two main palliatives. One was leave, where individuals were granted passes, usually for about a week, to travel away from their unit to get really cleaned up and sample the flesh pots; the other was rest, where whole units, usually battalions but sometimes entire divisions, were taken out of the line for a few days and, where possible, sent to special divisional, corps or army rest centres.

Neither system worked as well as might have been hoped. The ideal regarding leave operated during the years of training in America and Great Britain. For troops in their home country this meant roughly 1 week's leave every 3 months, whilst the GIs in Britain got a 1-day pass once every 6 to 7 weeks. In the combat theatres, however, things did not work nearly as well as this. During the first two years of the war in the Middle East the ideal was generally realised but during the rest of the war, for all armies, it was unusual to get leave more than once every 6 to 8 months. This was partly attributable to the obvious difficulties involved in taking a set percentage of men away from fighting units at regular intervals. More important, though, was the often forgotten fact that both the British and American armies were badly short of combat troops throughout the last three years of the war. Even when the army as a whole was expanding, a remarkably small percentage of these men went into the fighting divisions and this proved barely enough to offset the drain of casualties. During 1943, for example, the US army added 2 million men to its rolls but only 365,000 of these were assigned to combat units. Between 1941 and the end of the war the net number of fighting troops had increased by only 100,000 men.[68] In north-west Europe this led to desperate economy measures. The British broke up the 50th Division in December 1944 to try and increase the number of replacements, whilst in October Eisenhower had been forced to make a 5 per cent levy on all rear-echelon troops and rush these up to the front. The situation was never satisfactory, however. The Canadians, for example, had started the campaign expecting that some 48 per cent of a division's casualties would be among the infantry. By mid-August 1944, the actual figure was 76 per cent and there were simply not enough replacements. At this time the 2nd Canadian Division was 1,910 men short of its official establishment, most of them infantry.

These difficulties badly affected the opportunities for rest. The system was based upon the rotation of units and this demanded a surplus of men, a proportion of whom could always be kept out of the line. From an early date this surplus was simply not large enough. In Tunisia, the 1st US Division was in combat for 3 to 5 weeks at a time, and even when it was pulled out for what was supposed to be a week's rest, half of this period was usually spent travelling between the front and the rest area. In the 78th Division, between November 1942 and the following April, none of the battalions had more than 3 days rest *in toto*. In Europe, notably Italy, things were just as bad, but the American authorities coped least well with the situation. Whilst British and Dominion troops were rarely kept at the front for more than a fortnight before being given at least a couple of days' rest, American battalions were usually in the line for 20 to 30 consecutive days, often for 30 to 40 and occasionally for as much as 80.[69] In the ETO some effort was made to improve the situation, and in December 1944 a systematic rotation programme was drawn up. It applied only to individuals however, rather than the whole units, and the Americans found that in effect only one man per company could expect to be pulled out each month. It proved far more realistic simply to hope for the war to end.

In the Far East and the Pacific the situation was no better. American troops had one advantage in that the island campaigns, ferocious though they were, were often quite short so that the periods of rest and refitting in between were much longer than in Europe. Even so, many units did stints in the line that lasted just as long as those of their counterparts in Europe. On Guadalcanal the 1st Marine Division was in unbroken combat for 4 months, and in the Philippines the 7th US Division on Luzon was in the line for 110 consecutive days. Nor was it possible to offer any decent rest facilities on these islands themselves, and units pulled out of the line hardly knew any difference except a certain diminution in noise and nervous tension. Usually units had to travel vast distances to reach organised rest facilities, such as those at Pearl Harbor or in the Marianas. In this respect, the experiences of troops on Iwo Jima and the Anzio beachhead for example, offer a startling contrast. Whilst the latter moved only 5 miles to the rest camp at Caserta, the former had to be flown 3,500 miles. In Burma, the situation was if anything worse. Not only were facilities for rest just as limited, but the troops were as a matter of course held in the line for much longer periods. Even at the very end of the war, when Rangoon was available as a rest centre, an official report on welfare facilities for the Fourteenth Army noted that 'outside the city, in the battle areas, welfare was almost non-existent. In most cases it was impossible, for even cigarettes had to be dropped in water-proof packets to outlying troops by low-flying aircraft'.[70]

Elsewhere rest and leave facilities were somewhat better, though they varied enormously from theatre to theatre and even sector to sector. One thing was consistent however – home leave was virtually unknown. This was not so much because of the time factor, but because of the acute shortage of shipping and aircraft. Once they had embarked, most Eighth Army men never saw England again until the end of the war, and even British troops in north-west Europe were not able to revisit their homes during their leave periods. The absence of home leave was a common complaint of Americans in the Pacific. The following responses to an army survey are typical:

'43 months is a long time to be away from home; even a furlough would help a lot. The Army seems to think we have no feelings.'
'In forty months I have had one three-day pass and I can't go back to Hawaii for a rest leave. Enlisted personnel seldom get a break.'
'I started fighting at Guam, slept on the ground, and the food was no good. Then Leyte. After that rested seven days and then a lot more fighting, then Io Shima and now we are fighting on Okinawa for a hell of a long time. What the hell is fair in that?'[71]

In theatres nearer home, a few desultory efforts were made towards the end of the war to improve the situation, but they never affected more than a lucky few. A scheme introduced by the British army in Italy, in winter 1944, could only accommodate four to five men per battalion every fortnight, which meant that a soldier might have to wait five years until he was guaranteed his turn would come. In December 1944, a similar scheme was adopted in north-west Europe with the same ludicrous odds against one's turn ever coming round. The authorities seemed unable to handle even this miniscule concession. As Lieutenant Colonel Lindsay explained:

We asked ourselves once again why 'A' Branch was always so incompetent. The latest General Routine Order was to the effect that the fighting troops' vacancies for February and March would be greatly cut down 'as it had been found that leave allocation for Lines of Communication formations had been underestimated.' Nobody blamed them for having made a miscalculation, but why publish such a tactless explanation?[72]

For the most part, then, soldiers were dependent on the facilities provided in army rest camps or on the indigenous pleasures available in the larger towns and cities. Once a unit was placed in reserve it did not move off to a rest area as a man; the majority of the troops remained with the battalion and were granted 2- or 3-day passes in rotation. Otherwise they maintained a relaxed military routine, usually drilling and training in the morning and having the afternoon free. Swimming and sunbathing were great favourites in the summer months whilst gambling and reading were the standbys in poor weather. In every unit there was a dedicated group of men for whom gambling was a veritable mania and schools of brag and pontoon in the British army, poker, cassino and craps in the American, kept going for hours, even days on end. Other games were more bizarre. On Anzio there developed a craze for beetle-racing in which certain contests attained the status of race-meetings. Betting was lavish, conducted between individuals as well as through regular bookmakers, and champion beetles exchanged hands for as much as 3,000 lire.[73] Racing colours were painted on the backs of the beetles and they were placed under a glass jar in the middle of a 6ft circle. The jar was then lifted up and the first beetle to crawl out of the circle was the winner.

For many men, however, gambling held few attractions and they were perfectly happy just to lounge around and read. Escapism and a hunger for information were both important factors here. With regard to the latter, newspapers were very important – both local and national papers from home that enabled men to maintain some tenuous link with family and pre-war habits, or the numerous forces newspapers that kept them abreast of the war news. The troops showed a great interest in the latter, particularly news from the Russian Front which was clearly seen as a vital factor affecting the likely duration of the war. These forces papers proliferated as the war went on, ranging from quite lavish productions such as *Parade, Yank* or *Stars and Stripes*, through theatre journals like *SEAC* and *Union Jack*, to tiny cyclostyled productions such as *IAF Over Burma* and regimental magazines. One printing unit in Italy, in 1943, was producing 30,000 daily copies of both *Eighth*

Army News and *Union Jack*, 20,000 *Stars and Stripes* (Italian edition) and 100,000 *Crusaders*. Books, too, were surprisingly popular. Even after the mental anguish of the front many men seem to have found it easy to slough off their day-to-day fears and ghastly memories and immerse themselves in books. The Special Services Division of the American army, for example, sent 4 million books and 10 million magazines overseas each month. The type of literature favoured differed enormously with the educational background of the soldiers. Many officers immersed themselves in classics, poetry, history and travel books. A more reliable guide to mass tastes is given in the following list which names the ten top best-sellers in the ETO of American Pocket Books, one of the first paperback giants: [74]

1 *Pocket Book Dictionary*   6 *Pocket Book of Boners*
2 *Nana*, Emile Zola   7 *The Case of the Curious Bride*
3 *Pocket Book of Cartoons*   8 *Damon Runyon Favourites*
4 *See Here, Private Hargrove*   9 *Ellery Queen*
5 *Pocket Book of Verse*   10 *Lost Horizon*

None of this differs much from Allied experience in World War I when baths, gambling, newspapers and books were equally basic to the all too infrequent rest periods. One important World War I morale-booster that was missing, however, was songs. This was especially true in terms of active entertainment in that the troops do not seem to have gone in much for group singing, either on the march or at rest. To a large extent this simply reflected the cultural trend of the time and the increasing importance of passive, non-participatory entertainment. Particularly noticeable is the almost complete absence of songs, usually corruptions of existing standards, that commented on the soldiers' own situation. [75] The radio, the gramophone and the cinema seem to have killed off that grass roots, sardonic genius that emerged time and again on the Western Front, and few contemporary songs excited the soldiers' imagination. General Auchinleck was so aware of this that he offered a £25 prize to anyone who could compose a new song, for the Eighth Army, of the calibre of 'Tipperary'; not only did no classic emerge, but the competition attracted hardly any entrants. Ironically, the only song that could be uniquely identified with the war was 'Lilli Marlene' which the troops had picked up from German radio broadcasts. [76] For the rest, though songs were in great demand at regimental, ENSA (Entertainments National Service Association) or Special Services concerts, it was almost always the old favourites that were called for. For the Americans, numbers like 'Harvest Moon', 'Home on the Range', 'When Irish Eyes Are Smiling' were the only ones that would induce the audience to join in. The British in Normandy 'took up as a favourite . . . [Blake's 'Jerusalem' which] expressed exactly the depth of their feelings after the first dreadful shock of battle . . . [Others] preferred German or Italian versions of 'Lilli Marlene', and while the official anthem of the 15th Scottish Division was 'Scotland the Brave', the more popular, unofficial tune was 'I'm nae awa' to bide awa'. Two current American numbers did strike a chord, 'My Guy, Come Back' and 'Long Ago and Far Away', though like the other songs they emphasised the nostalgic yearnings of the soldiers and all 'had a red thread running through them; as sung or played, they were nostalgic, deeply melancholy, laments for dead friends, from those about to die'.[77]

The soldiers were not left entirely to their own devices during rest periods or when on leave. Both the British and the Americans made fairly determined efforts to provide some organised entertainment. The British had ENSA and the Americans the United Services Organisation (USO) and Special Services Division. Both did sterling work, often under difficult circumstances. It is a depressing reflection on human organisation, however, that all ran into fierce opposition from rival organisations that could not bear the thought of any responsibilities slipping from their control. ENSA had intermittent struggles with Army Welfare who felt that nothing to do with the troops' well-being should be outside direct military control, whilst USO was sniped at continually by the American Red Cross who asserted that they alone should have full control of forces' entertainment. The latter struggle necessitated the intervention of General Marshall himself who ruled that the Red Cross should be responsible for entertainment within the USA and the USO for all shows overseas. Both overseas organisations concentrated upon music hall/vaudeville shows and films. Their efforts were not inconsiderable. In 1944, in Italy alone, ENSA was running 34 theatres and 131 cinemas whilst after the invasion of Normandy they had 4,000 artistes on their rolls and in one month alone put on 13,500 stage shows and 20,000 films.[78]

The forces fared very well for films, or at least no worse than anybody else, for they often saw them before they opened in their

home cities. Not surprisingly, for troops marooned in the middle
of a sexual wilderness, the great favourites were American musi-
cals featuring the maximum amount of leg or whatever else the
Hays Office might let slip through. The variety shows were more of
an unknown quantity. Top-rate performers did appear regularly
though there were simply not enough to go round the hundreds of
stations that required regular entertainment. Particular favourites
were George Formby, Tommy Trinder, Gracie Fields, Frank
Sinatra, Mickey Rooney and Bob Hope. Such names were not
featured on the average bill, however. Mostly they were un-
knowns, whose talents varied from the competent to the appalling.
Yet again, the Fourteenth Army in Burma and American forces in
the Pacific fared worse than their counterparts in Europe. In the
Far East, ENSA was virtually unknown until 1944, although there
were seventeen companies of the Bengal Entertainment for the
Services Association, the Besa Belles, which toured various army
camps. Even when ENSA did arrive, as Jack Hawkins explained,
organising it 'was a comic and sometimes downright depressing
business. I don't suppose that even the world's most unsuccessful
theatrical agent ever had to handle quite so many dead beat acts as
were sent to me'.[79] But, for most soldiers, almost anything was
some kind of break in the deadening routine of army life and
numerous mediocre acts received far more approbation than they
would have got on English or American provincial circuits, or even
in their own parlour. For the troops' tastes were hardly esoteric. A
British survey revealed that they rated the following as their
favourite turns; soubrettes, accordion players, bands, sing-songs,
ballad singers and women dressed up in 'fancy costumes'.

Fortunately, in many theatres there were amenities other than
those provided by the army itself. In Africa and Europe, particularly, the big cities became little more than leave centres for the
troops, the streets a constant throng of pleasure-seeking servicemen. Cairo, Alexandria, Tripoli, Benghazi, Bombay, Delhi,
Rome, Naples and Brussels all did very well out of the war once the
Allied armies had consolidated their hold there, and a whole
plethora of bars and cafés sprang up to cater for the soldiery.

Even so, the range of things to do was limited and the following
observations on Cairo, in 1942, apply equally to leave centres all
over the world:

The entertainment amenities . . . are limited. If you like drinking or going to the pictures, you're 'quids in'; culture hardly exists . . . [Nor is there] any real point of contact between civilians, or the more desirable sort, and the ordinary squaddy . . . If it weren't for the various service clubs and canteens, he would have a very lean time. Leave, in fact, has already degenerated into more or less continuous eating and drinking within their welcoming doors.[80]

The service clubs and such were also important in that they offered their goods at reasonable prices. In most indigenous commercial establishments, be they in London or Calcutta, prices soared in response to shortages, the fact that men often had several months' pay to 'blow' at one go, and the higher pay of American soldiers.[81] In the Middle East, soldiers got so fed up with what they regarded as the cheating ways of the Egyptians that at Christmas 1943 the 78th Division went on the rampage in Cairo, smashing up bars and beating up the locals. So intense was the feeling that even the Divisional Military Police joined in or assiduously looked the other way. In Europe the Black Market flourished, pushing up prices inordinately. Taking prices in April 1940 as the norm, by late 1944 in Brussels bread had gone up 12 times, sugar 18, chocolate 99, and roasted coffee 107. The army was forced to take over the organisation of rest facilities, and Montgomery requisitioned seventeen of the best hotels in Brussels and brought in Billy Butlin, the holiday-camp magnate, to help run them.

There remains one important aspect of the soldiers' relaxation that is often skirted around, namely sex. All the rest and leave centres named so far contained not only numerous bars and cafés but also large numbers of brothels, the one often being an extension of the other. Official attitudes to these were somewhat ambivalent. On the whole, however, it was at least tacitly admitted that soldiers needed some sort of sexual relief and that it was almost inevitable that they would seek it. The men should be discouraged, certainly, as these notes for a chaplain's training course in England show: 'Creative part of us – makes us divine – can create, like God – also makes us beasts – don't want to be like beasts – use this instinct with reverence and respect – the girl – perfect woman – respect her – religion – emphasise new start – loyalty to regiment.' In the last analysis, however, it was seen as a medical problem. In the training course just cited it was categorically laid down that, though the chaplain had the right to attend the MO's lecture on venereal disease, 'if not in agreement with the M.O. no chaplain will *on any account* raise a general discussion at such lectures'.[82]

In the first years of the war the British army allowed many
brothels to remain open, only insisting that the girls submitted to
regular medical check-ups. In Tripoli certain houses were made
official, open from 1.00 till 6.00pm with a Royal Army Service
Corps NCO in charge. Most of the women were Italian though
there were different houses for coloureds, white ordinary ranks,
NCOs and warrant officers, and officers. One Eighth Army man
wrote:

> The army, with its detailed administrative ability, was able to organise
> brothels in a surprisingly short time and a pavement in Tripoli held a
> long queue of men, four deep, standing in orderly patience to pay their
> money and break the monotony of desert celibacy. The queue was four
> deep because there were only four women in the brothel. The soldiers
> stood like units in a conveyor belt waiting for servicing . . . Brothels
> for officers were opened in another part of town, where a few strolling
> pickets of military police ensured that the honoured ladies were not
> importuned by those who did not have the King's Commission.[83]

The Chaplain General soon intervened, however, and they were
closed down. Montgomery also was responsible for a clamp-down
on brothels. On his arrival in the Middle East he placed the red
light Berka area in Cairo out of bounds, and in north-west Europe
he co-operated with the Canadian and American authorities in
closing down all brothels in the fighting area. In other theatres,
too, known red light districts, such as the Via Roma in Naples or
Grant Street in Bombay were invariably placed out of bounds.
This was not always successful. Private Finch recalls that at one
stage the Via Roma was only labelled as being 'Off Limits' – the
American equivalent – and British soldiers argued that this did not
have any meaning for them. A 'bi-lingual' sign soon appeared.
Even so, most soldiers found it fairly easy to evade these restrictions. Many prostitutes operated outside the brothels, pimped
for by protectors, brothers or mothers. In Naples, in April 1944,
the Bureau of Psychological Warfare estimated that out of 150,000
nubile females in the city, 42,000 of them were part or full-time
prostitutes.[84] Moreover, once a brothel had been closed down it
soon moved to fresh premises and many of them moved on a day-
to-day basis, always keeping one step ahead of the authorities.
Indeed, the whole 'Off Limits' system was somewhat self-
defeating in that the quickest way to find a brothel was to look for a
building with an MP's jeep parked outside.

It was also very short-sighted of the military authorities to pander in this way to the sanctimony of certain religious and other critics. Lieutenant McCallum's observations about the administrative efficiency of the army are very pertinent in that wherever they organised their own brothels they ran them well, offering a cheap and, above all, disease-free service. In Delhi for example the army ran what was known as the regimental brothel, in a building near Hakman's Astoria. The entrance was rather like a cinema with a corporal in a glass booth to whom one gave the last three numbers of one's army number and 5 rupees. He then handed over a chit with a room number on it and one was led there by an Indian *babu* and given condoms.[85] The girls were well paid, in Indian terms at least, and were medically examined once a week by members of the Royal Army Medical Corps. Unfortunately, certain do-gooders in England got to hear about this and raised a storm of protest. The official brothels were quickly shut down, but this merely served to drive the prostitutes on to the streets or into other illicit establishments. 'Within three weeks', according to Corporal John Bratt (RAMC), 'every bed in the previously almost deserted V.D. ward, and every bed that could be crammed onto the verandah outside, was full'.[86]

For the rest of the war, in all theatres, the army fought a continual battle to minimise the incidence of VD. The MO's lecture on venereal disease has already been mentioned, and it was often very forcefully stated. As one soldier wrote: 'We go in search of women. We know the risks. Doc said that we were sticking our pricks where he wouldn't put the heel of his dirty boot. Doc is worried. He says more soldiers fall from V.D. than from bullets. But as one old-timer said: "Which would you rather have, laddie, a dose of V.D. or a packet of shrapnel up your arse?"'[87] These lectures were later supplemented by a film show; a South African effort, *Two Brothers* was generally reckoned to be the most effective of the various hygiene films shown. The Americans also had a film of their own on this subject and it was scheduled to be shown to all troops passing through the embarkation areas prior to D-Day. In the event few saw it because some prim staff officer felt that the mainly female personnel of the command cinema sections should not be allowed to handle it. Indeed, it is doubtful whether the High Command had much faith in the effects of this type of propaganda and their main weapon in the fight against VD was more realistic – the free issue of contraceptives. The American

High Command however was not convinced that the general public would condone condoms, and their issue was played down as
much as possible. John Steinbeck criticised the hypocrisy of the
public who seemed to subscribe to a

> . . . sternly held rule . . . that five million perfectly normal, young,
> energetic and concupiscent men and boys had for the period of the War
> Effort put aside their habitual preoccupation with girls. The fact they
> carried pictures of nude girls, called pin-ups, did not occur to anyone
> as a paradox. The convention was the law. When Army Supply or-
> dered X millions of rubber contraceptive and disease-preventing
> items, it had to be explained that they were used to keep moisture out
> of machine gun barrels – and perhaps they did.[88]

The authorities were certainly right to take stringent precautions, for it is not generally appreciated what a severe drain on
manpower VD was. It has already been noted that disease as a
whole caused more casualties than battle; what should also be
realised is that VD was one of the most common diseases and at
times it alone put more men in hospital than did combat. The
following table tells much of the story:

These figures are for the British army only, but the Americans
were not much different. For example in Tunisia, in the first two
months of 1943, British troops contracted VD at the rate of 21.4
cases per 1,000 men, and white Americans at 33.6 per 1,000. The
rate for black Americans was a staggering 451.3 per 1,000 but it
must be assumed that the bulk of these were men who had already
contracted the disease in the States and been unable or unwilling to
seek medical attention.[89] In Italy, in late 1943, a sample of four US
infantry divisions showed more VD cases than battle casualties. In
the Third US Army, during the north-west European campaign,
the average *monthly* rate per 1,000, for white troops, was 12.41.
Nor did the Canadian troops lag behind in this respect. In April
1945 patients were reporting to north-west European hospitals at
the rate of 54.6 cases per 1,000 per month.

Such figures were extremely disturbing to the authorities. Few
generals gave a hoot about their soldiers' morality; what was un-
acceptable was that the average VD case was spending twenty days
in hospital getting cured, at a time when the acute shortage of
combat soldiers was becoming more and more worrying. It was
this consideration, rather than puritanism, that made the High
Commands apply punitive measures. The British seem to have

Table 10: Incidence of venereal disease in the British army 1941-5 (Cases per annum per thousand ration strength)

	MIDDLE EAST			ITALY			N.W. EUROPE			BURMA[1]		
	V.D.	Battle Casualties	Rating[2]	V.D.	Battle Casualties	Rating	V.D.	Battle Casualties	Rating	V.D.	Battle Casualties	Rating
1941	41.2	35.5	3									
1942	31.4	31.1	4							72.2	4.5	3
1943	21.8	22.5	5	31.3	63.9	6				157.9	13.9	2
1944				49.9	89.6	4	5.9	61.3	7	69.2	101.9	5
1945				68.8	9.8	1	19.3	33.7	5	72.2	73.2	2

[1] British O.R.s only
[2] Indicates nth most numerous disease

been more resigned to the problem and the only sanction upon a
VD patient was that 1s 6d per day was deducted from his pay for
hospital charges. The Americans were tougher. Ernie Pyle visited
a hospital in Tunisia, at the far end of which

> . . . behind an evil-looking barricade of barbed wire, was what . . .
> [was] called 'Casanova Park'. Back there were 150 soldiers with ven-
> ereal disease.
>   'What's the barbed wire for?' I asked. 'They wouldn't try to get out
> anyhow.'
>   'It's just to make them feel like heels,' said the colonel. 'There's no
> damned excuse for a soldier getting caught nowadays unless he just
> doesn't care. When he gets venereal disease he's no good to his country
> and somebody else has to do his work. So I want him to feel
> ashamed.'[90]

In Italy the treatment was sometimes even more brutal. British
soldiers in towns and rest areas were often amazed to see large
stockades with 12ft-high barbed-wire fences behind which were
disconsolate GIs with the letters VD emblazoned across their backs.
MPs patrolled the perimeter and any attempt to throw over cigarettes or chocolate was brusquely pounced upon.

Of course not all sexual activity was of this purely mechanical
nature. Many men fell in love with European and Asian girls and
married them, whilst others had favours freely given by the
womenfolk of countries denuded of their young, male population.
The rise of the VD rate in England by 50 per cent and more during
the war years cannot be attributed solely to the expansion of pros-
titution. Nat Frankel made some interesting remarks on the sexual experiences of troops in Germany where the problems caused
by the shortage of German males were compounded by a pathetic,
and often rather disgusting, eagerness to appease the invading
Allies:

> what then is the reality of love and sex amid the conflagration of an
> entire continent? The average soldier who landed at Utah Beach and
> survived to take Germany, the man who was neither stud nor sissy,
> probably slept with something like twenty-five women during the war
> – and few of them were, I might add, prostitutes. But the sexuality of
> the dogface in Europe was neither flamboyant nor sentimental, nor
> was it callous. There was great desperation in it and considerable
> satisfaction, but, just as it often began with terrible yearning, it often
> finished that way, too; with yearning of a deep and multi-faceted
> character.[91]

And there was immense frustration, not so much because of a lack of outlets for purely physical demands, but because men were cut off from their own kind of women, from any real possibility of a romantic love that matched their civilian preconceptions. Here was one reason for friction between officers and men, because it was the former who were able to monopolise the favours of the more respectable natives and of the numerous female personnel serving overseas. Nothing sums up these tensions so well as concerts in Brussels or Rome where the other ranks, packed into the circle and galleries looking down on the officers and their pert escorts in the stalls, regularly began to float down inflated contraceptives amid a barrage of jeers, catcalls and Bronx cheers.

Thus, the picture painted so far of rest and leave is rather bleak. Granted that the first priority of any army is to fight and that the difficulties of supplying recreational facilities and even basic amenities to so many theatres of war was enormous, it would seem a great deal more could have been done, or done better. But armies are parsimonious organisations, both with money and with their soldiers' time and, moreover, seem to have little real interest in what men might want to do in their rare moments of relaxation. For after all an army devotes much of its energies to making a man forget that he has any right to free time or personal preference. Sometimes it is difficult to say whether the authorities' actions were the result of callousness or plain incompetence; certainly, there were times when the fighting soldier could but think that his needs were the least of the army's concerns. One of his most elementary requirements was that he was able to wash himself now and again, and theoretically the facilities existed, both British and Americans having mobile bath and shower units which could be brought up to the reserve positions. As often as not, however, they were never where they were needed. General Truscott of the 3rd US Division noted that after one year in Africa, Sicily and Italy his men had never once been accorded any bathing facilities and his division was eventually forced to manufacture their own. Of the European experience in general, Bill Mauldin wrote: 'The infantryman bathes wherever he has the opportunity, which is about twice in summer and not quite as often in winter . . . The only consistent thing about his bath is that it is always cold.'[92] When troops actually did get a chance to wash they were usually given a change of clothing, both underwear and outer garments. The luxury of this was often diminished by finding darned-up holes in the new clothes where a bullet or shell fragment had bored into the previous wearer. The soldiers tended to be inordinately sensitive about that sort of thing.

In the Pacific some efforts were made to provide attractive facilities.[93] But because the distances involved made it impossible to pull troops back regularly enough, they were usually left to their own or grossly inadequate official devices on the island on which they had fought. Sport became compulsory tedium, as on one night in June 1944 when 'angry soldiers were piled into trucks and forcibly sent to attend an amateur prize-fight. Probably a *Time* photographer was present to gather pictures appropriate to a magazine article entitled "High Life on Bougainville".'[94] Of the facilities on Leyte, no less a personage than General Eichelberger wrote:

> There was little in the way of recreation even for troops not im-
> mediately in the line . . . In camps and headquarters along the coasts,
> privates and generals alike often sat gladly in pouring rain to watch an
> outdoor movie. There was a recognised technique for a rainy night;
> you adjusted your poncho around yourself and your chair and put a
> helmet liner on your head so the water wouldn't drain down in your
> eyes. Thus, with vision clear, you were a proper and appreciative
> audience for the artistry of Gloria Gumm in *Passion's Darling*.[95]

On many British fronts things were just as bad. During the 'phoney war' one journalist wrote:

> During the whole of the time I was in France, I never met a British
> soldier, outside of the actual town involved, who had discovered the
> whereabouts of . . . [a NAAFI canteen], let alone secured the permis-
> sion or raised the transport to visit it; just as I never met a British
> soldier who possessed more than one blanket, more than the memory
> of English cigarettes or London newspapers, or the hope of a letter
> from home written less than six days previously.[96]

In Eritrea, in 1940

> . . . the amount of relaxation which the gaunt and weary men of 11th
> Brigade could enjoy was strictly limited. A NAAFI depot had been
> opened at Agordat but too often its stocks ran out; limited quantities of
> beer which found their way to Kassala were quickly snapped up but, as
> this was the era before tinned beer made its début, broken bottles often
> reduced the contents of crates to disappointing proportions. Razor
> blades were at a premium.[97]

But such problems were not limited to the first months of the war or to the more obscure fronts. In the Western Desert, in 1942, R. L. Crimp joined his battalion as it was 'resting' 200 miles behind the front, after a three-month spell in the battle zone. His section were living in the open, around their own truck 'with all its gear . . . unloaded around it "to ease the springs". Near by is the "kitchen", a couple of fireplaces built out of cut-down petrol cans on the ground. Just adjacent are the section bed-spaces, with each man's personal kit stacked at the head of his own patch. Everything is absolutely austere and primitive. Fortunately the weather is invariably dry.'[98]

In north-west Europe, many major towns, like Le Havre, Rouen and Paris were placed out of bounds to front-line troops whilst such rest centres as did exist were often woefully inadequate. Forty-eight hours leave in Brussels was not too bad but that came all too infrequently. More common was a spell of rest with hardly any facilities laid on. A battalion commander wished that it

> . . . were possible to arrange more recreation for the men. I feel sure all the rear HQs and people far from the battle-front had plenty of mobile cinemas, concert parties etc. The only pleasure resort [at Ranville] was 'Nobby's Bar' where men could buy chocolate, toothpaste etc., nothing very exciting. I sent parties off to the seaside but there was nothing for them to do there except bathe.[99]

And of course, every year there was Christmas. In rear areas the season of goodwill was celebrated with considerable zest and official backing. At the front, though senior commanders and regimental officers did their best, there was often just not the time for more than the most perfunctory observances. This is how a radio correspondent set the scene for the Canadians' Christmas dinner at Ortona:

> Christmas dinner in the shelled, broken church in Ortona. Candles and white tablecloths . . . not four hundred yards from the enemy, carol singers, the platoons coming in in relays to eat a Christmas dinner – men who hadn't had their clothes off in thirty days coming in and eating their dinners, and carol singers singing 'Silent Night' . . . A carnival of fury.[100]

And yet . . . No one who has not been through the ghastliness of the front line can have any real conception of how sweet, how

downright sybaritic even the most dreary rest area, the most run-
down facilities could seem. Everything is relative, says the cliché,
and that is the real reason why men could gain almost ecstatic
pleasure merely from the absence of mines, mortars, machine
guns, mutilation and death. Almost all soldiers have commented
on this, and these brief moments of peace represent some of their
most vivid memories of the war. Just the pleasure of being clean
was luxury in itself. Wrote an infantryman in Italy:

> We are in the baths at Castellamare. We stand as our mothers made us.
> Only the identity discs hanging round our necks remind us of war . . .
> How blessed the hot water feels. Now we are sprayed; our hair is cut;
> we have new clean clothes; we choose them, they are not thrown at us;
> we feel reborn.[101]

An officer in the desert wrote:

> The bliss of clean clothes after the mummying effect of eight days of
> ever closer, smellier and dirtier confinement has to be experienced to
> be fully appreciated . . . The psychological magic of it moved us right
> out of the desert and its battles into some oasis of the mind in which
> just being able to wash and change our underclothes produced . . . a
> complete metamorphosis.[102]

Another officer, in Tunisia, remembered a spell when his unit was
still in the line itself but had managed to dig deep and for once
make themselves fairly rainproof. Added to the pleasure of being
able to wash their clothes and shave this meant a remarkable
transformation in the men's outlook. 'We find it is only the simple
things in life that matter here, sleep, feeding and remaining dry;
and achieving that, everything is rosy.'[103] A soldier in Italy spent
one period out of the line sleeping in a rickety old house whose only
solid amenities were four walls and a roof.

> An observer regarding our tousled forms in thick army socks, battle-
> dress trousers and woollen jerseys, gazing upon our shaven faces,
> would not perhaps have considered our beds – two blankets spread on
> a tiled floor, a haversack or a bundle of dirty underwear for our pillows
> – the ultimate in luxury. But he would not know. Everything is
> comparative. To sleep in this pleasant unrest, to be dry, to be warm, to
> own a share in a fire, to be freed from duties, to have a roof, to be away
> from filth and death and wretched tiredness – that is luxury. That is an
> infantryman's larger portion of heaven.[104]

Sergeant J. W. Fraser (8th Royal Scots Fusiliers) fought for five days in the notorious Scottish Corridor before being pulled out for a short period of rest. He spoke for every combat soldier when he wrote in a letter home: 'It was unbelievably good to sit quiet. No mud, dust, shell holes, dead cows, smells. It was good to lie back and know you were alive; good to shave, eat, sleep – above all to sleep.'[105]

8
Attitudes

Suddenly, passing the known and unknown
Bowed faces of my company, the sad
And potent outfit of the armed, I see
That we are dead. By stormless Acheron
We stand easy, and the occasional moon
Strikes terribly from steel and bone alike.

. . . I have read that God let Solomon
Stand upright, although dead, until the temple
Should be raised up, that demons forced to the work
Might not revolt before the thing was done.
And the king stood, until a little worm
Had eaten through the stick he leaned upon.

So gentlemen – by greatcoat, cartridge belt
And helmet held together for the time –
In honourably enduring here we seek
The second death. Until the worm shall bite
To betray us, lean each man upon his gun
That the great work not falter but go on.

HOWARD NEMEROV

These apparently rude and brutal natures comforted, encouraged and reconciled each other to fate, with a tenderness and tact which was more moving than anything in life. They had nothing; not even their own bodies, which had become mere implements of warfare. They turned from the misery and wreckage of an empty heaven to the silence of their own hearts. They had been brought to the last extremity of hope, and yet they put their hands on each others' shoulders and said with a passionate conviction that it would be all right, though they had faith in nothing, but in themselves and in each other.

FREDERIC MANNING, 1887–1935

It was better not to remark that the Americans and the English were still fighting. It was better to say nothing; to take it as it was meant. It was happening all along the line from Nijmegen to Basle, but to a smaller degree. The horizon of an infantryman is bounded by his battalion. He may fight for weeks within a mile or two of troops of whom he is unaware. After Woensdrecht the Canadians had become welded together, kindred, a tight community. The truth is that they wanted to feel alone, alone with the sustained and terrible experience which they began to clasp to themselves as something personal, and upon which no one had a right to intrude.

R. W. THOMPSON, 1944

No organisation, except perhaps the most vicious totalitarian régime, can rely purely on force to make people do its will. This applies as much to armies as to any other system. Admittedly armies are especially authoritarian organisms with remarkably wide coercive powers, yet even so they are not capable of holding their men in line, let alone forcing them to continually risk death in attack after attack, unless there is some tacit concensus among the rank-and-file that such things need to be done. Hardly anyone *wants* to do them, because most men are sane, yet most do feel some kind of moral imperative that helps shape their decision. This was certainly the case in World War II, on both sides. It is simply not enough to suggest that disciplinary threats alone could force men to obey orders, for what is the threat of even the ultimate sanction, death, in the face of another kind of death? Moreover in the British army it was known that this sanction was no longer available, and in the American that it would only be used with the greatest reluctance. If men had cared to maximise their chances of survival in a purely rational way the stockades and military prisons would have been full to overflowing. On the other hand, it is groundless to suggest that the personal conviction that men *did* feel had much to do with ideological fervour or crusading zeal. Many of the men for whom such beliefs were a sufficient motivation had been wiped out in Spain, and anyway they are never more than a tiny handful in any conscripted mass army. For the average soldier, once he was in combat, his view became microcosmic, and he lived only from day to day, barely daring to think about the end of the war, increasingly unconscious that life had any meaning beyond the unremitting ghastliness of endless combat. The soldier became increasingly bound up with his tiny fraternity of comrades who shared his suffering and they alone came to represent the real world. In the last analysis, the soldier fought for them and them alone, because they were his friends and because he defined himself only in the light of their respect and needs.

Patriotism, Politics and Boredom

However, it would be going too far to claim that neither patriotism nor politics had any importance to front-line soldiers. Nominally at least, World War II was an overtly ideological struggle, the forces of democracy ranged against the evils of fascism. It is not my concern here to assess the extent to which this was the case, but to try and gauge how far the troops themselves bothered with such concepts. To judge from the accounts they have left behind, the answer is hardly at all. A few might be swept along by high-flown sentiments and volunteer for military service; even conscripts might balance the common good against their personal inconvenience. But once they had got to the front there was simply no place for such generalities. The world became reduced to a company or a troop and the only important thing in life was the chances of preserving one's own. The enemy was bullets, shells, grenades, dugouts and bunkers – occasionally an actual German or Japanese soldier – and the struggle against these was too all-consuming to allow of irrelevant 'flannel' about just wars or the good of humanity. These were irrelevancies in the fullest sense of the word, for they simply had no place on the battlefield. It is not that men would not have cared deeply about such things back home, but simply that modern combat took *everything* out of a man so that his mind was entirely occupied with the problems of eating, drinking, staying awake and staying alive. Three observations by fighting soldiers put the whole thing in a nutshell. A British tank officer went home on leave:

> As he went about, he heard people talking about the war. They talked about what they were fighting for – and it made no sense. Soldiers don't fight for something. War was something that caught them up. After that it was a closed arena, in which you struggled with yourself and your fear. Soon, when the first sensations of homecoming became blunted, he began to feel lost outside this arena. [1]

An American combat veteran was interviewed by the indefatigable army researchers and was asked the question, 'What are we fighting for?' 'Ask any dogface in the line,' he replied, 'you're fighting for your skin on the line. When I enlisted I was patriotic as all hell. There's no patriotism on the line. A boy up there 60 days in the line is in danger every minute. He ain't fighting for patriotism.' [2] Neil McCallum at one stage found himself musing in his diary as to whether he and others were fighting on behalf of such abstract concepts as liberty or mere nationalism. He soon pulled himself up with a jerk, and tried to express his real feelings through a self-consciously bathetic device. 'But this is flapdoodle. These notes are nonsense. The more I waste time with this the less efficient I am as an infantry officer. Let me exercise my freedom of choice by digging a small hole in the bottom of my trench. It is more

comfortable for the hip bone.'[3] A further splendid confirmation
that these were not just individual reactions is given in an official
account of the Okinawa campaign. 'When word of the defeat of
Germany reached the rifle companies [of the 3rd Regiment 1st
Marine Division] they were immediately notified and the most
favoured comment, typical perhaps of the reaction along the entire
front, was "So what?".'[4]

An ancillary point here is that the front-line troops found it
difficult to hate the enemy combat troops, at least in Europe. Even
a limited period at the front soon made one aware that the *Wehrmacht* was going through just the same hell and probably had as
little theoretical commitment to the war as oneself. Each side was
simply doing its job and, to some extent. at least, each felt a
common sense of holding the rough end of the stick. But one
should not over-emphasise the degree to which this affected the
soldiers' actual behaviour. In World War I truces were fairly
common and in many sectors of the front line tacit agreements to
live and let live were honoured by both sides. One reason for this
was that the soldiers were stuck in their respective trenches for
weeks on end, only actually going after the enemy head on during
one of the big offensives. In between times the enemy front-line
soldier contributed little to one's discomfort – this was all done by
the weather and his artillery – and it was possible to sympathise
with him, knowing he was suffering just as much from the climate
and one's own big guns. In World War II, however, the fighting
was much more continuous and front-line weapons, notably mortars, greatly increased one's own misery. The front was rarely
static enough, or quiet enough, for vague notions of mutual torment to develop into real compassion. The ethos of fighting was
different, too. In World War I, though it never really came, the
emphasis was upon the decisive breakthrough, rolling up the line,
cutting communications, mass surrender. In World War II, especially in western Europe and the Far East, it soon became
apparent that every yard of ground would have to be torn from the
enemy and only killing as many men as possible would enable one
to do this. Combat was reduced to its absolute essentials, kill or be
killed.

For all these reasons there are few examples in World War II of
much dialogue, tacit or overt, between the opposing sides. There
were a few truces to collect wounded, and frequent expressions of
respect for the enemy's bravery and tenacity as at Cassino or Caen

for example, but combat itself was characterised by an extreme ferocity. Newcomers to the line might display a vague compunction, as the American private who told an interviewer, 'I'll tell you a man sure feels funny inside the first time he squeezes down on a Kraut.'[5] This was soon dissipated, however, and the ruthless logic of the situation buried any vestige of moral scruple. A British soldier wrote: 'The question of killing does not present itself as a moral problem any more – or as a problem at all – for in such total war death and life are so dovetailed into each other that they don't seem separate or distinct as states of being and non-being.'[6]

This attitude was particularly evident in the treatment of prisoners and it seems clear that any German who surrendered, unless *en masse*, had at best a fifty-fifty chance of not being killed on the spot. During the Battle of Alamein, Sergeant Carnduff (5th Seaforth Highlanders) was approached by a soldier in his company who said:

> 'Sergeant, I think you're passing trenches with folk in them.' I asked him how he made that out and he said: 'Well I'm positive something moved in the last slit we went by.'
> So we went back and found a slit, and there was a man in the bottom of it with his head under a blanket. You could just see him and no more, but you made out that the blanket was shaking a wee bit. We hunted about on that line and found eight more, all the same. Well, the boys had been moaning about having to carry the big anti-tank grenades. So we got rid of them.[7]

Of the campaign in northern France one historian has noted that both sides indulged in so-called 'atrocities' simply because they became carried away by the savage tempo of the fighting, finding it impossible to switch at will between the roles of trained killer and scrupulous umpire. Nor did the circumstances of most German surrenders engender much respect for the Geneva Convention:

> This was the more usual pattern: snipers would pick off two, three or four men of an advancing platoon, then as they came to close quarters, stand up and surrender. The men whose friends had just been shot by him did not always feel inclined to let the killing stop at that point . . . Canadians stated: 'When the Jerries come in with their hands up, shouting "Kamerad", we just bowl them over with bursts of Sten fire.' A witness from the 15 Scottish . . . [said], 'But any German who tries to surrender nowadays is a brave man; we just shoot them there and then with their hands up . . .' L. Uppington of 1 Worcesters . . .

[said], 'I noticed that when the enemy meet us, whoever had the advantage of surprise or position, it was nearly always shoot first, regardless of whether or not a man could be taken prisoner. None of this "Hande hoch" business; see the enemy, and let loose with Spandau, Bren, Sten or Schmeisser; get in first, no matter if the other fellow was a sitting duck or not.'[8]

Yet all such behaviour has to be attributed to the ferocity of prolonged combat rather than to a generalised hatred of the Germans.[9] In the war against Japan, on the other hand, it is possible to speak of a real loathing for the whole race. In part this was due to Japanese military methods and their treatment of prisoners and wounded, but in the last analysis it reflects the cultural gulf between very different societies and the smug rascist contempt that such a divergence usually produces – on both sides. Neither the British, the Indians nor the Americans really regarded the Japanese as human beings. Their fantastic bravery and spirit of self-sacrifice was seen merely as a dangerous form of insanity, and one killed them as one might exterminate a particularly intransigent pest. The American surveys back up this point emphatically. The already mentioned sample of officers who were asked to rank certain factors they felt led to poor performance in combat, gave as one 'Lack of conviction about what we are fighting for'. In the ETO, 22 per cent of officers thought this was a contributory cause, in the Pacific only 8 per cent. The testimony of the 247th Infantry Regiment is even more to the point. The men were asked, while still unassigned in the States, 'How would you feel about killing a German soldier?' A possible answer was 'I would really like to', and 6.6 per cent of the men ticked this box. Where 'Japanese' was substituted for 'German', 44 per cent chose this answer.[10] For the British, a 'small and cruel vignette' illustrates the general point:

> On the banks of the Sittang, a collection of Japanese soldiers, stripped to their shorts, were crammed miserably into what was literally a prisoner of war cage made of bamboo poles. Every now and again . . . [men] came up to stare at them curiously as if they were some rare form of nocturnal animal. Up on the bank was posted a Bren gunner with a slate watching the flooded Sittang roll by. A number of Japanese were trying to cross it and were being swept down, some dead, some floating and playing dead, some clinging to flotsam. Each received a burst, and a resulting cry or a convulsion was recorded with a tick on the slate.[11]

As has been seen, few soldiers had much interest in the ideological aspects of their war. There was however one general topic that did concern most men, at least during those rare moments when they had any chance for reflection. This was the question of what was to be done when the war was over. For this was what men were fighting for, if anything. One of the American opinion surveys asked a sample of troops what positive incentives were most important in helping them to keep going, and by far the most common answer (40 per cent of all replies) was 'Thoughts of getting the war over'. On one level, of course, this was simply a yearning not to be shot at any more, but the very intensity of the wish forced men to speculate upon exactly what should happen when this golden day dawned. It is impossible to generalise about the substantive content of the expectations – they ranged over the whole political spectrum and covered a myriad different topics – but numerous sources have pointed to the general agreement that *something* ought to be done, that pre-war society left much to be desired. The Eighth Army's cynicism about the social and economic situation after World War I and their inability to believe that the authorities would do much better this time has already been referred to. Many men were bitter about the extent to which class still shaped British society and the fact that the same men who had filled the dole queues seemed to be those who had to bear the brunt at the sharp end. Dan Billany summarised such feelings in a speech by an Eighth Army infantryman:

> Sir, this is a fine way for a man to spend his fucking life, isn't it? Have you ever heard of Class Distinction, sir? I'll tell you what it means, it means Vickers-Armstrong booking a profit to look like a loss, and Churchill lighting a new cigar, and the 'Times' explaining Liberty and Democracy, and me sitting on my arse in Libya splashing a fainting man with water out of my steel helmet. It's a very fine thing if only you're in the right class – that's highly important sir, because one class gets the sugar and the other class gets the shit.[12]

However, the radical upheaval in their own lives caused by the war led many soldiers to hope that it might have a similar effect on society at large. In the last two years or so of the war there is some evidence of a burgeoning belief in the actual possibility of social change, even justice. One correspondent noted that many British troops had 'asked me to tell them what I knew of the Beveridge Report of which, on their wireless, they have heard a little. Those who have spoken of it seem to think its acceptance a foregone conclusion, so I have tried to disabuse their minds . . . The men know a lot more than they did when this war began; and they are beginning to learn that there is no need for the grinding poverty from which so many of them came'.[13] Another wrote of discussions he had with the troops and their caution about the high-sounding rhetoric of politicians' speeches, official reports or the Atlantic Charter:

> . . . was it just a lot of catchpenny words? It had better mean something, they added. They were fighting this war because things had been wrong . . . Somehow ordinary people had had a raw deal from the financiers and the politicians. That must not happen again. They would see that it would not happen when they got home. In the meantime, they had to smash the Germans. They would do that, but it would be only the first part of a much larger job.[14]

Similar concerns were prevalent in the American army. John Steinbeck noted this in his own conversations with GIs who, he felt

> . . . know deeply that the destruction of the enemy is not the end of this war. And almost universally you find among the soldiers not a fear of the enemy but a fear of what is going to happen after the war. The collapse of retooled factories, the unemployment of millions due to the increase of automatic machinery, a depression that will make the last one look like a holiday.[15]

Later in the war such general concerns seem to have receded somewhat and the average GI became most anxious about his own particular place in the post-war world. To judge from the pages of *Stars and Stripes* the GI Bill of Rights, which made provision for veterans' education and financial assistance, was their main concern and the correspondence columns are full of letters questioning its actual efficacy.

In the end, the soldiers did not prove a very effective lobby. In Britain, however, there still remains a suspicion that it was the army vote that was responsible for the surprise defeat of Churchill in the 1945 election. It is difficult to ascertain the truth of this though it is known that 60 per cent of the forces did vote in this election – an extraordinarily high number considering the bureaucratic difficulties and passive obstruction of the military authorities. For many officers, the final result quite took the edge off the military victory. In some circles it was felt necessary to apportion blame and a prime whipping-boy was the Army Education Corps which had conducted current affairs seminars and issued its own teaching aid, *The British Way and Purpose* for its hundreds of supposedly left-wing instructors. In fact, it is impossible to judge what the effects of these classes were, though for myself I would eschew any theory so offensively patronising as to suggest that the ordinary soldier was not capable of making up his own mind about issues which became increasingly important to him as the war drew to a close. If one is talking in terms of a left-wing 'conspiracy' by the Education Corps then the following delightful anecdote must also go on record as equally plausible evidence of right-wing nefariousness. According to one regimental history, 56 men of a particular company voted, 37 of them for the Conservatives and 19 for Labour. When the votes were being despatched back to England the company commander found his clerk in a state of great distress. At first he was unable to explain his agitation and then asked for a private interview. After beating about the bush for some minutes he finally managed to spit it out. 'I am sorry to tell you, sir, that nineteen of your Company have voted Socialist. Shall I burn their votes, sir?'[16]

When it comes right down to it, however, all such considerations of ideology, patriotism and politics seem remarkably remote from the real concerns of the front-line soldier, where everything about the front line forced him to look only to his immediate circle for support and understanding, for any meaning in the chaos around him. Soldiers became increasingly alienated from anything that did not reflect directly upon the next attack and their own chances for survival. To think in terms of the war as a whole could only make men feel utterly helpless, aware only of their derisory inadequacy in the face of the material might each nation could deploy. James Jones has written of this sensation of complete powerlessness in discussing a soldier's reactions to an aerial combat, a duel between two expensive machines:

> . . . and that there were men in these expensive machines . . . was unimportant – except for the fact that they were needed to manipulate the machines. The very idea itself, and what it implied struck a blade of terror into . . . [his] essentially defenceless vitals, a terror both of unimportance, and of powerlessness: his powerlessness. He had no control or sayso in any of it. Not even where it concerned himself, who was also a part of it. It was terrifying.[17]

Even the comfort to be had from pondering on the resources one's own army could deploy was a two-edged weapon. Whilst it was at one level reassuring, it also reminded the individual soldier that he, as one single person, was an almost complete irrelevancy to the success or failure of the whole mighty organisation and the question of whether he lived or died was commensurately unimportant. One could not really identify with the army as a whole. Not only did its sheer size emphasise one's own transient triviality, but service therein had absolutely nothing to do with one's choices. From their conscription onwards, soldiers had been told what to do, their autonomy of will completely subordinated to a task they found increasingly odious. One officer of the Eighth Army wrote that it was 'really a "whodunnit" story of involved ritual and procedure. It is a crime story involving the species and not the individual – except that the individual remains, as ever, the victim'.[18]

Moreover, the transition to this new, soulless existence was so abrupt and total that many soldiers were plagued by a continual sense of unreality, unable to reconcile their own personal aspirations with their new status as expendable units. An American officer told how it never ceased to be difficult for him to see his own situation, his own actions as a real extension of his autonomous self:

> Then there was the strange [sic]. I think every soldier must have felt at times that this or that happening fitted into nothing that had gone before; it was incomprehensible, either absurd, mysterious or both . . . We began to feel foreign to our own skins, intruders in the world. More often than at home we would wake up in the night and wonder where we were . . . I suppose this feeling of strangeness came over us so often because of our comrades. Since they were not chosen and usually had no prewar connections with each other or each other's home towns, however dear they had become in military life, they represented discontinuity with all but the present and the immediate past.[19]

An English soldier, Michael Anglo, tried to convey much the same sort of impression in verse. The result is no masterpiece but it reflects very clearly this feeling of unreality, of continually moving in a kind of dream world. The title itself, 'Through Ether', says much about how soldiers felt.

I am not here:
Though I walk in the heat of the day,
And rest through the dark hours of night.
I am not here
But a thousand miles away.
Though I breathe and eat and sleep,
And see and act and speak,
There is no cheer;
I am not here.
A disassociated self
The ether spans,
And lives the life the body bans:
Though I am, I am not:
It is clear,
I am not here.[20]

Another facet of this sense of depersonalisation were the periods of intense boredom that were part and parcel of military life. Numerous soldiers have commented on this. The very nature of military life, the ponderousness of the system was in itself a problem. Bill Mauldin reminded his readers of 'one of the worst things about a war – its monotony. That is the thing that gets everyone . . . the "hurry up and wait" system which seems to prevail in every army (double time to the assembly area and wait two hours for the trucks – drive like hell to the docks and wait two days for the ship – fall out at four in the morning to stand an inspection which doesn't come off until late afternoon), that's one of the things that makes war tough'.[21] Military camps were also terrible places where, outside strictly military tasks, there was absolutely nothing to do except observe the myriad petty regulations that defined all that one could *not* do. None were worse than the replacement depots where men were not even with their own friends but surrounded by hundreds of similarly unattached strangers. An American officer recalled one such depot in Italy: 'Life at the camp was depressing . . . Morale is always low at such places. The officers had little or nothing to do . . . Having no troops to command, many of them were bored with themselves and almost all of them loathed army life . . . [They] held off disgust and ennui, in some cases even despair, by drinking and gambling.'[22] The nature of the theatre also had some bearing; Africa and the Pacific were especially bad, the usual constraints of army life being compounded by an almost complete lack of facilities. An Eighth Army soldier described a particularly enervating bout of

desert weariness. There was the utter featurelessness of the landscape which deprived the mind of any sensory stimulation. 'Then
over and above the physical factors, there's the total lack of change
or relaxation; nothing really certain even to look forward to, that
after a term of such vacuum living, would make it tolerable . . .
Here there's no respite or getting away from it all. For weeks more,
probably months, we shall have to go on bearing an unbroken
succession of empty, ugly, insipid days.'[23] In the Pacific the physical features at least were more than impressive, but for most men it
was not long before the simple lack of anything to do more than
outweighed them. An American sergeant, temporarily based in
Fiji, was amazed that 'a land of such breath-taking beauty can be so
deadly dull. Men are irritable from excessive monotony and
tedium. Tempers are ragged. The expression "blowing your top",
a form of verbal and mental explosion, is a daily occurrence'.[24] A
Marine, D. T. Brown (1st Division) was out of combat for almost
twelve months and he found this period the most trying of his life:

> In the past months I think I have wasted more time doing nothing than
> in all the rest of my life. All this is inevitable. If for a day we disengage
> ourselves from the endless round of military rituals and routine, the
> whole structure might collapse into nothingness. For out here it is
> nothingness, emptiness that men fear. The military treadmill, the
> mission in the offing, is our one tangible proof of reality. The conquest
> of desolation, of sheer ennui is a matter of genuine heroism, as much as
> battle itself.[25]

The intensity of this ennui should not be underestimated. One is
not merely talking of men at a loose end, with a few hours to kill.
The drab landscape, the lack of facilities, the tedium of military
routine were only part of the problem. As soon as a soldier was out
of the line he was overtaken by a soul-destroying emptiness, a
spiritual vacuity which made it difficult to see any point in the
simplest task. The army had dislocated one from one's past, whilst
thoughts of the future prompted only despairing foreboding. Nor
did living for the day have much meaning, not simply because
amenities were almost non-existent, but because the army had
reduced one to a cipher, hedged one's life around with such a mass
of petty constraints that the individual spirit was less and less able
to assert itself. A part of the mind was aware of this, yet it could find
nothing concrete to hang on to to halt the drift from boredom to
torpor to *anomie*. It groped around feebly, unable to assert itself to

do *anything*. R. L. Crimp wrote that his state of mind degenerated into 'extreme mental sluggishness, sheer mental apathy, and a vast aversion to exertion in any form. The most trivial actions . . . seem utterly not worthwhile and require a tremendous effort to perform. It all seems so futile.'[26] A writer who was called up remembered how the army swallowed him up and made everything that had once engaged his interest seem like too much hard work. 'For six years I scarcely wrote a word or read a book and when it was over I came to the surface like a blinded pit pony. Friends . . . found me unintelligent about the war that was over and uncomprehending of the changes in public life. I had been in the Army.'[27] Another officer in Italy, normally interested in everything going on around him, was equally conscious of the dreadful emptiness of the times when he was not actually fighting. In a letter home he worried about

> . . . the cessation of all mental and emotional activity from which I'm suffering . . . When one has to be in the army one can compensate one's loss, if one is advancing or fighting, by all sorts of daydreams about the end being in sight. But nothing is more depressing than the awful waste of sitting still in the army. I don't mean waste of the huge military machine, one doesn't think about that – but personal waste.[28]

Comradeship

For all the disorientating pressures cited so far, there still remained the fundamental truth that armies are made up of men. The horrors of combat, the dreadful soullessness of army life gnawed at a man's basic belief in the integrity of his own destiny and yet, at the end of the day, there still remained certain positive human emotions that actually seemed to flourish amidst the ghastliness. Pride, loyalty, comradeship, selflessness, even love were all basic to the front-line soldiers' dealings with one another and only by understanding this can one put one's finger on just what it was that sustained men in the line. But to avoid charges of sentimentality and skating over the facts, very real divisions between various groups of soldiers must be looked at first.

National rivalries do not seem to have been of great importance, at least as far as the soldier at the front was concerned. Certain generals, however, did their best to undermine any spirit of co-operation, especially in north-west Europe where Patton and

Montgomery let their overblown egos reduce their relations to barely concealed antipathy. This had its effect, and at senior and staff levels Anglo-American relations sank to a very low level. The mutually contemptuous rivalry that sprang up is well summarised by a remark attributed to a Third Army staff officer. During the Battle of the Ardennes the First and Third Armies found it hard to agree who was doing the real fighting, though at one stage a First Army Estimate noted that as long as the Third continued to attack the First had nothing to worry about. When asked by a liaison officer what he made of this remark the American replied

> Well at least he's frank. He admits we are the only Army that's fighting. That's quite a concession coming from them. But you can tell them this. If First Army will stay put, we'll run the Krauts up their ass. And then if Monty will stay put for a few days, we'll run both the Krauts and First Army up his ass, trains first.[29]

But such acrimony was mostly limited to senior officers, intensely jealous of their personal reputations. The ordinary soldier held no strong opinions either way and, if pushed, American, British and Commonwealth troops were usually quite happy to admit that each side fought as well as the others. In fact, they rarely fought together, the only mixture of troops being at Army level in Tunisia and Italy, where British and American divisions were under a common commander. However, American and British battalions did occasionally see one another go into action and all but the most bigoted could appreciate that any units that could endure the same trials that they had been through without breaking must be more than adequate soldiers. Except for some rather supercilious aspersions cast by the British during the Tunisian campaign, there was never any lack of mutual respect amongst the front-line soldiers of the respective nations. This might seem to be contradicted by the incessant brawling that went on in leave centres in Europe, Australia and New Zealand, but this should be seen more as a function of unrelieved battle tensions rather than real animosity between the various Allies. In leave centres most men got into fights simply because, as one soldier recalled, 'it wasn't possible to stop fighting suddenly. All of us were overtense. We drank with a grim determination to get drunk. Then, we fought. There was blood and glass everywhere. In a drunken stupor we slept where we fell'.[30] In such circumstances it was always possible to find group differences as a pretext for a fight – Scots and English, Army and

Navy/Marines/Airforce, front and rear, even different battalions –
and nationality became an issue simply because it was one of the
most conspicuous differences.

A more authentic and insidious division was that of race. The
role of racialism in the British army is difficult to assess. Certainly
it was rarely a burning issue, again because men of different
colours never served in the same units, except as officers and men,
and most white troops were quite prepared to concede that Indian
and West African troops were doughty fighters. They were not
quite so tolerant of native civilians, however. In Egypt the Royal
Army Service Corps had to be forced to supply food to the conscripted local labourers, whilst GHQ Egypt refused to supply a
special hospital for them. At about the same time the NAAFI ruled
that they would serve no natives, in or out of uniform, and all
cinemas were also closed to them.

Relations were not always good, even between the troops themselves, and it was perhaps for the best that they fought in separate
units. At best, British troops had an insufferably patronising attitude to non-white soldiers and one soldier recalled 'an attitude of
racial prejudice that was pervasive in all ranks . . . [It] was expressed in jocular, even quite affectionate terms, but the fact
remains that it was deep-rooted and ubiquitous and behind it lay
an unquestioning assumption of natural superiority . . .'[31] Such
attitudes pervaded even the relations between officers and men in
the Indian army where the former treated the Indians like children, their approach varying between paternalism and offensively
patronising behaviour. It was taken for granted that the Indians'
smiling acceptance of this meant that they indeed revered the
white father, and not as an indication that for most of them the
army only meant some kind of security and that they were perfectly
aware of how to operate within the system. Close relationships
were established in fighting battalions and the following musings
by a British officer, Patrick Davis (3rd Gurkhas), are not mere
sentimentality:

> And perhaps Sarbajit, and Tulbir my runner . . . and Nandalal and
> Jemadar Manbahadur, and all the others, but especially these, form
> the heart of my memory of that time, and of any meaning it has for me.
> As I have said, a man can become what he is expected to be. Our
> Ghurkas expected as much of us as of ourselves. We grew better for
> being with them. Whatever first drove us all to war, it was friendship,
> trust and loyalty to one another that kept us at it long after we might
> have preferred to be elsewhere.[32]

But there was another side, and the faintly patronising tone of the above remarks often became an overt sense of superiority. The Indians were not slow to recognise this and from time to time their complaints were printed in theatre newspapers, notably that for South East Asia Command, where they were present in the greatest numbers.[33] One complained 'I do not enjoy the . . . facilities offered to [the British]. I feel awful at times, particularly in this place where civilisation seems like something left behind . . . Recently the W.V.S. opened a canteen of sorts where one can get a drink and a few eats. Even this canteen is unapproachable to us. There is no place where I can spend a couple of hours enjoying a drink. I did not expect this colour bar from the W.V.S. organisers.' Another commented on the hypocrisy of British propaganda about the Japanese and of those who 'state that the Japs have a racial superiority complex, and that they treat all other people contemptuously and deceive themselves. Many B.O.R.s and British officers treat Indians in the same contemptuous manner . . . We I.O.R.s are working with the B.O.R.s, doing the same job and putting in the same amount of work. Yet what a difference in our pay and privileges.'[34]

Similar problems were apparent in the American army, though again overt conflict was minimised by the general lack of contact between white and black troops, especially at the front. In fact few blacks were actually in combat units, the bulk of them being assigned to the Service Force branches for labouring and driving work. The figures tell their own story. Whereas the Service Forces accounted for 39 per cent of all army personnel, 75 per cent of all black inductees were posted to such units. In 1945, blacks made up only 1.97, 2.45 and 3.05 per cent of the Armor, Artillery and Infantry respectively, an actual decline from the figures for 1942.[35] Even in these latter arms, mainland traditions were maintained and the blacks fought in segregated units, usually divisions,[36] although in north-west Europe, with the acute shortage of replacements, some black platoons were organised within other divisions. Only fifty-three platoons were raised, however, and there was never more than one platoon to a regiment, each being commanded by white officers and sergeants. Once the war was over these units were swiftly broken up and the men, all volunteers, returned to their original outfits. In fact, the army was not effectively desegregated until 1950.

In the first years of the war, particularly, the racial factor was less of a day-to-day problem than that of what might be called 'caste'. By this is meant the friction, notably in the officers' mess, between the regular army and the newcomers from the Territorial Army/National Guard or those who came straight from the officers' training courses. This was especially the case in the British army where long-service regulars felt it was impossible for anyone who hadn't seen at least twenty years service to be a real soldier. Their studied avoidance of 'shop' talk also struck many new-comers as bizarre. One officer wrote of his mess in Cairo, in 1940: 'It all seems so luxuriant and so far removed from what we came to do. The sole topics of conversation are polo and cocktail par-ties . . . One might say they hardly know there is a war on.'[37] But the problem was far from one-sided. Territorial units, notably the Yeomanry cavalry regiments, were often somewhat reactionary organisations for whom tradition and social standing were of much greater import than military expertise. Lieutenant Colonel Lucas Phillips wrote of his appointment to command the Northumber-land Hussars in the Middle East:

> When I was appointed . . . it was clear that a peculiar set of problems were in front of me. The strength of the regimental feeling in the Northumberland Hussars had to be experienced to be believed. They were not merely 'Yeomanry' or 'County', they were 'feudal' . . . Their attitude was that, though the incidents of modern warfare had caused them to be armed with anti-tank guns instead of the sabre, they could never be anything else than Northumberland Hussars, and they dis-owned, insofar as they could, the appellation 102 Anti-Tank Regi-ment. The one has no traditions, the other has something to be proud of.[38]

When Keith Douglas joined the Nottinghamshire Sherwood Rangers Yeomanry he soon

> . . . recognised the unbridgeable gulf between those who had been the original horsed officers, most of whom lived in or near the county from which the regiment took its name, and the 'odds and sods' who came to make up the regiment's officer strength when mechanisation was com-plete . . . These new officers were not gentlemen, in the sense of *gentilhomme*. Very few of them could ride, and very few of them could afford to hunt or shoot, or knew any of the occupations or acquain-tances of 'the boys' . . . The newly joined officers . . . knew their work reasonably well. Yet it was obvious to the cavalrymen that newly joined subalterns could not be allowed to tell the regiment what to do. If they tried, they made themselves more and more disliked and received snub after snub.[39]

Many Territorial units, because of their close links with the county élite, actually felt themselves superior to the regular professionals, presumably on the grounds that one cannot do a thing as a gentleman should if one actually gets paid for it. Major Brodie was posted to the 5th Black Watch, in Normandy, along with another genuine Territorial officer. The colonel greeted the latter 'warmly, but contrived to conceal his delight at getting me. He led Graham into the orchard and, so I believe, asked him what I was like. Graham gave me a good character, and I was then led into the orchard. "As you are here, you may stay for the time being. But I should like to make it quite clear that this is a Territorial battalion and we don't like Regular Officers."'[40]

Amongst the other ranks such distinctions were far less important, partly because of their innate common sense and partly because the continuous influx of replacements soon made them virtually meaningless. Only in the first two years or so of the war was it possible to discern any real division between regulars, part-timers or conscripts or any noticeable coldness of one group to another. In late 1941, R. L. Crimp was always aware of the clique of pre-war soldiers in his own battalion:

> Amongst themselves they're pretty clannish, a sort of closed-shop trade union attitude . . . There's a tendency for stress to be put on 'Service', the implication of which is that the Old Soldier having already over many a long year supported the outpost pillars of the Empire . . . is now entitled to rest on his laurels and give the conscripts the chance to do their bit. The conscripts, on the other hand, incline to the view that it's up to the veterans to bear the brunt, or at least set an example by their military prowess.[41]

In the American army friction between regulars and others was most noticeable around the time of Pearl Harbor when the first Selective Service draftees began to appear after their training. These draftees had very firm ideas about their inborn superiority to mere regulars and were especially contemptuous of their non-coms whom they regarded as overbearing cretins. The Army Research Branch picked up this tension in one of their questionnaires and two of the responses they received sum up the situation. A draftee ventured the cocksure 'advice to run an IQ test and let the men who have the most knowledge be the bosses'. A regular grumbled, 'Selectees have been allowed to wise off too much. Many of them are too smart for their own good.'[42] In the Aus-

tralian army the peculiarities of the conscription system created a
slightly different sort of tension. In effect the army was divided
into three types of soldier, the AIF, the Chockos and the Rainbows. The first were all volunteers, mainly Militiamen (the
equivalent of the Territorials or National Guard) who had opted to
be transferred before the end of 1942. Rainbows were Militiamen
who were transferred compulsorily after this date and who were
almost invariably retained in the militia units. The Chockos, or
Chocolate Soldiers, were those who had declined to transfer to the
AIF and had made their service contingent upon only being called
to fight if Australia was invaded. Relations between the AIF and
the other two groups, notably the Chockos, were acrimonious and
the ensuing slanging matches, brawls and near riots were known in
some quarters as the Chocko War.

With this last distinction we begin to get nearer to the really
important features of the combat soldiers' attitudes to those
around them. For to a large extent the Chocko War was a conflict
between those who felt they were doing the fighting and the rest.
This distinction was keenly appreciated in all the Allied armies,
though the dividing line was usually that between the fighting
troops in the battalions and regiments and the millions of men who
operated in the rear. The disparity between their living conditions
was extremely marked and the troops at the front were keenly
aware of it. Nor was it simply that the combat soldiers led a more
precarious existence than those in the bases or on the lines of
communication. This might have been quietly accepted, with
some pride, as a natural concomitant of the job. What particularly
rankled was that the natural inertia of the distribution network
meant that whilst those in the rear were well-supplied with food,
blankets, clothing, entertainment and miscellaneous comforts,
hardly any of these actually got to the front to the troops who really
needed them. In north-west Europe, for example, the Second
Army launched a vigorous campaign to supply all fighting troops
with two battledresses and a third blanket. These were vital to
allow the troops a change of clothes when they got wet and to
permit them to sleep in a minimum of comfort. In fact the order
was never fulfilled and though an airlift of 50,000 battledresses was
supposedly arranged, only 15,000 pairs of trousers ever reached
the front. Yet throughout the war most men at base had three
battle-dresses each and at least five blankets.

For the troops shivering in the dykes and polders none of this

came as much of a surprise. Over two years previously an Eighth
Army man had made a bitter entry in his diary about just this same
disparity between the front and rear, and the latter's callous
indifference to the plight of the former. In April 1942 his unit
received a 'special issue of cigarettes today – two packets per man –
gifts from the schoolchildren of Kilgussie, Scotland, bless their
bonny hearts and ha'pence! Fancy buckshees reaching as far forward as this! Are the base-wallahs losing their nerve?'[43] American
forces had identical, equally justified complaints and these featured prominently in various army surveys. The Quartermaster
Corps history, referring to the supply of food in the ETO, notes
that 'frequent and outspoken criticism was aimed at the dump
personnel, who were accused of retaining the popular II and IV
menus for themselves, leaving the three less popular menus for the
combat troops.'[44] The Research Branch questionnaires revealed
similar antagonisms and the comment of one soldier about the
progress of PX rations to the front is typical and terse: 'PX rations
by the time they have reached a rifle company have been picked
over all down the line. It has ended up with shower slippers for
riflemen.'[45]

American surveys also emphasise the point that the combat
troops' hostility was not simply based upon envy that those in the
rear were in much less danger. In one sample only 20 per cent of
responses were in this general vein, and only 9 per cent asserted
that all troops should be required to fight. Most men at the front
recognised that someone had to man the lines of communication,
and the bulk of their complaints were about specific inefficiencies,
reflecting a general feeling of being let down. In the survey just
cited complaints were distributed as follows:

	%		%
Food	31	Transport	3
Clothing, ammunition		Mail	2
and equipment	9	Other	3
PX rations	8	General	
Water	5	inefficiency	17

The surveys revealed another not entirely surprising fact, that the
combat soldiers' attitudes to those in the rear were not fully appreciated by the service troops themselves. The question was

posed a little obliquely, asking 'How many soldiers in combat units do you think feel resentful about troops who have rear area jobs?' The sample units answered as follows:

	Most %	Quite a few %	Don't know %	Not many %	Hardly any %
Ground combat units	50	35	3	9	3
Army and Corps Service units	23	41	5	24	7
Service units in rear bases	33	36	3	22	6

The point is clearly made that most service troops tended to understate the positive resentment felt by the men at the front. In fact, numerous sources give evidence of their bitter feelings about the contrast in life styles, although it is fair to say that rear-echelon colonels and above, as well as staff officers, were the main butt rather than the ordinary private and NCO. During the nadir of British fortunes in the Middle East, according to one tank commander, 'we heard of the panic in headquarters and supply areas and were unpatriotically delighted at the thought of generals and staff officers fleeing for Alexandria or wetting themselves in slit trenches. It was the universal, if unmerited, reaction of the front line troops at the thought of any form of disaster befalling the immunity of the rear areas'.[47] Even generals could vent their spleen on such types. General F. Tuker, an authentic fighting general commanding 4th Indian Division, was contemptuous of the

> . . . bolt-hole beetles who always cluster about the base . . . the queer little people who, when the war is done, re-emerge fresh and whole to figure so prominently in our organs of publicity, arrogantly, avidly and spitefully trying to drag others down to their deplorable level . . . There is much more 'flap' in the back areas of the Army where mischievous tatlers mouth each others' rumours and vent their malice, than up front; after all, up front all a man has to lose is his life, while way behind he can easily lose all his luggage. That prospect can be most worrying.[48]

Such feelings were common in most theatres throughout the war. They were often more than justified. The troops battling it out at Kohima were far from amused to receive demands from GHQ that showed total obliviousness of reality. Some of the more gross included queries from the Pay Office asking by what authority a brigade had paid wet sweepers 25 rupees a month at Galunche in 1943, from No 83 Sub-area wanting to know what the brigade had done with three tables on loan at Mahableshwar in October 1942, and from the Railway Accounts Branch demanding the refund of 57 rupees and 8 annas in respect of a journey by Sergeant Jones whose travel warrant was not marked 'by the quickest route'. Feelings could be intense in Europe too, and the following outburst by an infantryman speaks volumes about the depth of their antipathy:

> I'll tell you what hurts most of all – *they* call themselves soldiers . . . They talk about their long service, whine about going home. Service! Why, God damn me! It's one long picnic for them. Bloody little small town nobodies doing the big-shot act all over Italy, it makes you cry . . . And when you talk to 'em, they don't look you in the eye, most of 'em. But you know what they're thinking; oh yes, you know all right: 'Here's another of the bloody fools, one of the thick-head tribe that wasn't clever enough to get a soft job like me!' . . . Do you get it? That's what those pimps think. That every one of us has tried for a safe job but we all missed, because we weren't as clever as they are. How d'you like it? We're no better than they are, but *they've* got brains and we haven't. That's what those base boys think of you.[49]

All this brings us nearer to the major theme of this chapter, in that such attitudes created a fierce sense of pride among front-line soldiers about their ability to hang on in conditions inconceivable to those further back. Out of this pride there arose a sense of exclusivity, of apartness, that in turn blossomed into a deep compassion for and loyalty towards other members of the same élite brotherhood. Pride was a shared emotion, in which *mutual* esteem, a sense of common suffering, dominated over any tendency to selfish individualism.

Yet there were hints of the latter, and these must be mentioned before concentrating upon the prevailing spirit of comradeship. A tendency towards a more personal pride, almost selfishness, was more overt in the American army, a reflection no doubt of the fact that the ethic of individualism and self-sufficiency is almost written into the Constitution. A veteran interviewed in hospital in 1944 summed it up admirably when he proclaimed: 'A real soldier is a guy – he'll drink and swear – but he relies on himself; a guy that can

take care of himself.'[50] James Jones brought out the selfish aspects
of such an attitude when he explained how the veteran's experience
and expertise forced him to try and blot out any thoughts of his
fellows and concentrate purely on assessing and maximising his
own chances of survival:

> He knew by the sound of incoming shells whether they would land
> near enough to be dangerous. He knew by the arc of falling aeriel
> bombs if they would land nearby or farther out. He had learned that
> when fire was being delivered, being thirty yards away could mean
> safety, and that fifty or a hundred yards could be pure heaven. He had
> learned that when the other guy was getting it a couple of hundred
> yards away, it had nothing to do with him; and that conversely when he
> was getting it, the other guy two hundred yards away wanted nothing
> to do with him, either.[51]

The one group at the front who did sometimes suffer from these
potentially callous attitudes were the replacements, especially
those who had arrived in a unit only a few days or even hours before
being thrown into combat. In such circumstances the novices from
replacement centres, or 'repple depples' as the Americans called
them, had no time in which to get to know their fellow soldiers in
the platoons and squads, and this lack of personal contact, as well
as the rookies' often infuriating ignorance, sometimes tempted the
veterans and their officers to use them almost as cannon fodder. A
survey of returning American veterans put forward the prop-
osition, 'When a replacement comes into an outfit during combat,
the veterans usually try to help him all they can', and 88 per cent of
the interviewees agreed. Other sources, however, are more honest.
James Jones recalled a conversation with an American sergeant
who had been at Anzio:

> One day . . . we got eight new replacements into my platoon. We were
> supposed to make a little feeling attack that same day. Well, by next
> day, all eight of them replacements were dead, buddy. But none of us
> old guys were. We weren't going to send our own guys out on point in a
> damnfool situation like that. We knew nothing would happen. We
> were sewed up tight. And we'd been together through Africa, and
> Sicily, and Salerno. We sent the replacements out ahead.[52]

Another American was even more blunt, recalling a sense of contempt for the gaucheness of the hapless rookies, 'a contempt with
which even the gentlest of us viewed these unqualified victims of

tactical necessity. It was a contempt that was certainly mixed with pity, but I think there's always something disgusting about victims. You can't help it . . . We called them poor sons of bitches, and we almost smiled when we said it'.[53]

In many cases, however, the fast turnover in replacements simply meant that no other troops had been available. In the later stages of the European and Pacific campaigns, casualties were so high that raw soldiers had to be sent out immediately on tough assignments because there was simply no one else to do the job. But their inexperience exacted a terrible toll. During the battle for St Lô, according to an officer of the 30th US Division

> . . . in two weeks . . . there must have been at least a 75 or 80 per cent turnover in the [rifle] platoons . . . In order to fill the ranks, the replacements were sent up to their squads without any satisfactory pre-battle orientation. The squads never had a chance to get really organised and worked into a reasonable team. Casualties among these raw recruits were relatively high. From the viewpoint of these boys, things were really rather dismal, and had a natural tendency to discourage that dash and self-sacrificing spirit which one sees in the movies and picture books.[54]

Sergeant Junkin (77th US Division) wrote to his commanding officer about his recent experiences on Okinawa and told of raw replacements who froze with their fingers on the trigger when they saw a Japanese, who shouted for other men to kill a plainly visible enemy soldier while their own rifle was in their hand, or who desperately tried to loose off their guns without realising they had emptied the magazine. He went on:

> Sir, I mean no disrespect by the above comments . . . but I deplore the necessity of taking green recruits, who hardly know how to load a rifle, into combat . . . I know that you have the interests of the men of our battalion at heart, and I believe that you will agree that these teen-age youngsters fight with great courage, but are just too green and inexperienced to do the job.[55]

The problem was just as serious in other theatres. In a sample from four American divisions in Italy in April 1945 (line companies only), only 34 per cent of the men had been with their outfit when it landed in that country. All the rest were replacements, over 50 per cent of whom had gone into combat within 2 days of joining their unit, and a further 20 per cent within less than a week. In a typical

chronically understrength Canadian regiment in north-west
Europe, less than half of its 379 combat soldiers had more than 3
months' training, of any kind, while 174 of them had received only
1 month or less.

In such circumstances there was really little the few remaining
veterans could do. They had to use the newcomers in combat
almost immediately and could only leave them to their own devices, to sink or swim. Circumstances were almost always too
pressing for any thought of a gradual introduction to combat. As a
tank commander wrote, when even rear-area non-combatants
were being rushed forward to help plug the line in north-west
Europe:

> I remember one man – he must have been thirty-five if he was a day –
> who wet his pants and then wept in shame. And all the while we had to
> teach these men how to fight. There were long hours in the turret when
> I was literally showing men how to feed bullets to the gun. Could they
> shoot straight? They couldn't even hold the gun right! In the midst of
> the toughest fighting of the Third Army's campaign . . . I was teach-
> ing men what I had learned in basic training.[56]

Similar conditions prevailed in the infantry divisions. Private
Morris Sussman, who found himself assigned to a rifle company in
the 4th US Division was a typical example. He trained at the Cook
and Bakers' School but was suddenly given a further 17 weeks
basic infantry instruction and shipped overseas where he was
dumped in the middle of the Hürtgen forest. An interview with
Sussman tells the rest of the story. After being relieved by some
veterans of what he was told was 'excess equipment' he

> . . . and several other men 'walked about a mile to some dugouts'. At
> the dugouts the men received company assignments, and their names
> and serial numbers were taken down. A guide then led them towards
> the front line. On the way they were shelled and saw a number of . . .
> dead scattered throughout the forest. Private Sussman said he was
> 'horrified' at the sight of the dead, but not as much as he might have
> been because 'everything appeared as if it were in a dream'. At a front-
> line company his company commander asked him if he knew how to
> operate a radio. Sussman said, 'No'. Handing him the radio the captain
> told him: 'You're going to learn.' Learning consisted of carrying the
> radio on his back and calling the captain whenever he heard the
> captain's name mentioned over the radio. For all his ignorance of
> radios, Sussman felt good. Being a radio operator meant he would stay
> with the captain and back in the States he had heard that captains

stayed 'in the rear'. Subsequently, Private Sussman said, he 'found out different'.[57]

The absorption of such rookies was a particular problem for the NCOs. Sergeant L. Pingatore, of the same division, stated: 'When I get new men in the heat of battle all I have time to do is . . . impress them that they have to remember their platoon number, and tell them to get into the nearest hole and to move out when the rest of us move out.'[58] In fact, many of these replacements were knocked out so quickly that in the evacuation stations they could not say to which platoon or even battalion they belonged. Those that survived might find themselves starting off an attack as ordinary riflemen and completing it as acting squad leaders. Many couldn't take it all. In the Pacific the demand for replacements was just as heavy as elsewhere and a sergeant on Bougainville recalled that 'under fire at night in pillboxes rookie soldiers became hysterical – laughing insanely, weeping or shrieking. Psychoneurosis and other forms of insanity resulted in numerous evacuations'.[59]

But rookies only remained such for a very short time. Either they were hit or they soon acquired the instinctive caution of the other veterans. Then they were absorbed into the fraternity of the front line and began increasingly to share the comradeship, the mutual respect and regard that typified the sharp end of battle. The tensions and antipathies that existed within the armies have been described at some length, for it would be poor homage to sentimentalise the experience of the fighting soldier. Nevertheless it cannot be emphasised too strongly that such animosity is in no way typical of army life at the most basic level, that of the squadron or the section. In the stress of battle there emerged a poignant combination of sympathy and respect to be found amongst men in hardly any other situation. As one American officer wrote: 'This sense of comradeship is an ecstacy . . . In most of us there is a genuine longing for community with our human species, and at the same time an awkwardness and helplessness about finding the way to achieve it. Some extreme experience – mortal danger or the threat of destruction – is necessary to bring us fully together with our comrades . . .'[60] For those so exposed the presence of others was of crucial importance, both for their explicit attempts to comfort and reassure, and for their tacit proof that they were suffering as grievously as oneself and that they seemed to be able to take it. Military psychiatrists were not slow to recognise the importance of small-group solidarity in enabling soldiers to keep going. American observers noted that the vital precipitating factor in most soldiers' breakdowns was not so much a particular military encounter as

> . . . some event which necessitated a sudden change in the . . . soldier's group relationship. He had been able to carry on with his pattern. The precipitating event shattered this pattern. The soldier lost his group relationship and . . . forfeited all the strengths and comforts with which it had sustained him. As a member of the team he would have been able to take it; alone he was overwhelmed and became disorganised.[61]

A British doctor, Lieutenant Colonel T. F. Main, wrote: 'The sense of separation from home, from its security and comforting permanence and its familiar reassurance of one's personal status, is a permanent stress. A camaraderie is the only human recompense for a threatening sense of impotence in the face of death and the waywardness of elemental forces and the decisions of the mighty who use soldiers like pawns.'[62] The Second Army psychiatrist, in Normandy, was even more to the point. In July 1944 he averred: 'The emotional ties among the men, and between the men and their officers . . . is the single most potent factor in preventing breakdown.'[63]

Other observers were equally emphatic about the vital role of such ties within the platoons and squads. An American general, S. L. A. Marshall, who devoted himself to a study of the ordinary soldiers' reactions to modern combat was quite unequivocal on this point: 'I hold it to be one of the simplest truths of war that the thing which enables an infantry soldier to keep going with his weapons is the near presence or presumed presence of a comrade . . . He must have at least some feeling of spiritual unity with him . . . He is sustained by his fellows primarily and by his weapons secondarily.'[64] J. Glenn Gray, who was attached to various infantry divisions in Italy and southern France, felt that this sense of comradeship was more than merely supportive, and actually provided an emotional uplift that sometimes allowed men to transcend the ghastliness around them:

> Many veterans who are honest with themselves will admit, I believe, that the experience of communal effort in battle, even under the altered conditions of modern war, has been a high point in their lives. Despite

the horror, the weariness, the grime, and the hatred, participation with others in the chances of battle had its unforgettable side, which they would not want to have missed. For anyone who has not experienced it himself, the feeling is hard to comprehend and, for the participant, hard to explain to anyone else. Probably the feeling of liberation is nearly basic. It is this feeling that explains the curious combination of earnestness and lightheartedness so often noted in men in battle.[65]

It was not only observers who commented on the vital importance of emotional ties among the men. Almost all participants' accounts mention it and often regret that this sense of comradeship had no real equivalent in peacetime. It operated at many levels. In the more far-flung theatres whole armies were bound together by shared sufferings and privations. Major Paddy Boden of the Rifle Brigade wrote of the desert war:

A large body of men sharing a common experience over a period of months and even years, isolated from all contact with their home country, developed a set of customs, habits and even jargon of their own. We felt different from, and by reason of our longer experience and of the flattering accounts of our exploits which appeared in the press, superior to the [First Army] men from England, sometimes mockingly referred to as 'those bloody Inglese'.[66]

For other soldiers the battalion was held to be the crucial unit, holding men together by a mixture of earned respect for the officers and regimental pride. Certainly such a spirit burned strongly in some regular and territorial battalions in the first years of the war. An extreme example is that of the 1st Duke of Cornwall's Light Infantry, smashed in battle in June 1942. A cadre was returned to England, around which to rebuild the battalion, and the rest of the survivors were amalgamated with the 1st South Wales Borderers and the 1st Royal Regiment. This decision was badly received. Captain Sir C. Derman says:

There is little doubt that the decision to amalgamate the remnants of the regular battalions into one was a personal disaster for many. Loyalty to their regiment was imprinted very deep and perhaps carried with it feelings of antagonism for other regiments. In the early days of the . . . [new unit] the discord between the three elements was carried to extreme limits . . . which had to be dealt with drastically.[67]

However, as the war dragged on and the battalions were increasingly made up of heterogeneous collections of replacements, it ceased to be realistic to claim that loyalty to a mere organisation was sufficient to keep men going. Bill Mauldin got to the heart of the matter in the following observation about American troops in Europe. He was referring to the large number of soldiers who went straight back into the line once they had been discharged from hospital, making no attempt to take convalescent leave. What motivated them was not loyalty to the unit as such. 'A lot of guys don't know the name of their regimental commander. They went back because their companies were very short-handed, and they were sure that if somebody else in their own squad or section were in their own shoes, and the situation were reversed, those friends would come back to make the load lighter on *them*.'[68] Another American soldier, interviewed by army researchers, emphasised the fact that it was at squad level that the front-line soldier found most support from his fellows:

> The men in my squad were my special friends. My best friend was the sergeant of the squad. We bunked together, slept together, fought together, told each other where our money was pinned in our shirts. We write to each other now. Expect to get together when the war is over . . . If one man gets a letter from home over there, the whole company reads it. Whatever belongs to me belongs to the whole outfit.[69]

But this is not to say that the troops were unconcerned with the sufferings of those in other units. An important component of their attitude towards the war was their sense of exclusivity, of being members of a unique brotherhood of the damned which embraced all front-line soldiers. The very term 'the sharp end' was their own, highlighting the absolute distinction between those who put their lives on the line and the vast majority who only catered to their needs. There was something almost of arrogance in this feeling. Lieutenant Colonel Mulgan wrote of

> . . . a Brigadier who offered bottles of beer for prisoners brought back on a raid; the men who were going on the raid swore quietly among themselves, feeling that the raid and their lives were something more important than a game of darts. Only afterwards, coming back from the raid, they might talk about it as a game, and then only among themselves. Their actions in war were not thrown open to outsiders for comment.[70]

A British soldier in the communication lines in north-west Europe knew of the gulf between the fighting troops and the rest:

And then there were the fighting troops who lived in a different world of which most of us knew nothing. When we met them while they were resting out of the line, we noticed how they kept together and seem to regard the life we led as being cut off from a greater reality . . . They were quite friendly, but they made us feel that there were secrets which could only be known to those who shared their existence. As we looked at them from the comfort of our soft vehicles and clean clothing, their eyes returned our glance and said, 'We don't hold it against you that you're not here with us, it's all a matter of how you're posted and it might have happened to you. But since it hasn't, don't try to understand what you can't.'[71]

Bill Mauldin was equally aware of this sense of exclusivity and wrote vividly about it in his paeon to the 'dogface':

While men in combat kid each other around, they have a sort of family complex about it. No outsiders may join in . . . If a stranger comes up to a group when they are bulling, they ignore him. If he takes it upon himself to laugh at something funny they have said, they freeze their expressions, turn slowly around, stare at him until his stature has shrunk to about four inches, and he slinks away, and then they go back to their kidding again . . . Combat soldiers are an exclusive set, and if they want to be that way, it is their privilege.[72]

On many fronts this sense of apartness was compounded with a cynical, fatalistic, fey almost, pride in their utter isolation from the normal world. Such was the case with the Fourteenth Army in Burma. Their self-appointed sobriquet, 'the Forgotten Army', expresses their feelings perfectly, and though these sometimes led to periods of deep despondency, at others they had a curiously uplifting effect, welding the victims together in a doomed band of brothers. A particularly striking example of this is cited by a historian of the Kohima battle who notes:

The curious thing was, though, that despite its horrors . . . Kohima Ridge still seemed to hold a fascination. Troops coming back from dirty, flea-bitten rest camps in Dinapur would smile, even laugh, as they trudged up Garrison Hill again and saw the familiar sights. Life as it existed before the battle now seemed very, very far away, and in some perverted manner the Ridge had become the nearest thing to home.[73]

So it was too in the Pacific. During the first disastrous Philippines campaign the retreating Americans felt an increasing hopelessness about being rescued and the following song was more and more to be heard:

> We're the battling bastards of Bataan;
> No mama, no papa, no Uncle Sam,
> No aunts, no uncles, no cousins, no nieces,
> No pills, no planes, no artillery pieces,
> . . . And nobody gives a damn.

A soldier who fought in later campaigns noticed no appreciable change of sentiments in the months that followed. June 1943 to the following June was perhaps the worst period which even 'that great Shakespearian actor General MacArthur . . . himself called . . . sourly "the stony broke war". The ground troops who fought it, even more sourly amongst themselves, referred to it as this fucking poor man's war".'[74]

In the Middle East, particularly during the see-saw campaigns of 1941 and 1942, such affected bitterness was very much the order of the day. When the British found themselves fighting alone, in mid-1941, a popular catchphrase was that 'we're in the final now', the point being that everyone else had scratched rather than we who fought our way through the qualifiers. Some months later it was widely asserted that the letters MEF (Middle East Force) stood for 'Men England Forgot'. An American correspondent recalled these same soldiers singing a song about the folks back home that included the chorus

> Poor guys are dying
> For bastards like you.

Italy, too, from mid-1944 to the end of the war, seemed another forgotten theatre and the soldiers reacted in characteristic fashion. After D-Day had been trumpeted around the world, Eighth and Fifth Army men would ask each other with mock seriousness, 'Which D-Day? Sicily, Salerno, Anzio?' They picked gleefully upon a notably crass remark by Lady Docker who felt, in her infinite military wisdom, that the men in Italy were just sun-tanned malingerers or 'D-Day Dodgers' as she called them. A song was soon current:

> We're the D-Day Dodgers out in Italy,
> Always drinking vino and always on the spree.
> Eighth Army shirkers and the Yanks,
> We live in Rome and dodge the tanks –
> We are the D-Day Dodgers,
> The boys whom D-Day dodged.

If you look round the mountains and through mud and rain,
You'll see the rows of crosses, some which bear no name.
Heartbreak and toils and suffering gone,
The boys beneath they linger on –
They were some of the D-Day Dodgers
And they're still in Italy.

But even those on whom this D-Day spotlight was turned were not immune to similar feelings. In north-west Europe, a war correspondent with the Canadian troops noted a similar perverse pride amongst the front-line troops enduring the hardships of the appalling Dutch winter. He was driven to try and analyse the mood of the troops and ask himself why they carried on in conditions that almost beggared description. This mood he found

> . . . profoundly interesting. How they put up with it – or don't put up with it. Why they put up with it. How they digest the horrors, assimilate sights and experiences for which all their upbringing, all the life they have known previously, has given them no experience . . . [In fact] the Canadians were not really unhappy, or if they were they had a curious pleasure in it, like men stubbing sore toes . . . A peculiar sense of isolation had been growing in them up from the Seine . . . They had felt that the main strength of the war had turned away, and that they were increasingly forgotten. They heard the triumphant echoes of the armoured thrusts, the tears, laughter, flowers and champagne of the liberations . . . Their own experiences had been in a lower key. They began to take a pride in that, a provincial pride, the pride of the unsung, the unappreciated, and with an underlying bitterness, a derision . . . The Canadians had become welded together, kindred, a tight community. The truth is that they wanted to feel alone, alone with the sustained and terrible experience which they had begun to clasp to themselves as something personal, and upon which no one had a right to intrude.[75]

This last quote, however, comes near to implying self-pity and that would be a travesty of the truth. Certainly the troops at the front were often preoccupied with their role in the war, and the contrast between their day-to-day existence and that of the soldiers further back, but they never became preoccupied with their *personal* suffering, never immersed themselves in their *individual* anguish. Out of their sufferings there emerged a real sense of selflessness and equality and it is these that ultimately characterise this exclusive fraternity. An officer in north-west Europe recalled a visit to the front: 'It was a tonic to find oneself again in the free air of good comradeship, co-operation and good-humoured stoicism of the front line after months of jealousies and petty rivalries so rampant farther back.'[76] A tankman made an interesting observation on front line *mores* that show how a man's standing in the world back home was deemed irrelevant, how he was only to be judged in terms of his day-to-day behaviour within the unit. A new tank commander

> . . . soon learned the unwritten rules: the abuse was kept within carefully understood limits – a man's honour, courage, honesty, truthfulness or morals could be torn to shreds with impunity, it was permissible to accuse another man of always avoiding work, to maintain that he would run like a rabbit at the sound of a pop-gun, to accuse him of lying, cheating or stealing and no offence would be taken; but nothing could be said that reflected upon his social status, his ability to pay his share, his personal cleanliness, or his family.[77]

An artilleryman stressed the egalitarianism that soon becomes a marked feature of the front line, attributing it to

> . . . one's insignificance at the front, where everyone's personality is negated in the great struggle for life: only basic things matter there; a man finds that, in spite of the many defences and pretences used to get through daily life, he is in fact very little different, fundamentally, from his fellows. Battle strips you bare; you are known and seen for what you are.[78]

It is this egalitarianism, this sense of common identity that overrode any tendency to individual self-pity. At the front the troops nearly always tried to make the best of their situation and concentrated upon doing everything possible to help each other through. In every theatre and unit one finds repeated evidence of a loving concern and respect for one's fellows. Of British troops in Germany, in early 1945, R. W. Thompson wrote:

> No rewards of peace could have induced men to this patience, to this readiness for incessant effort, to labour until they dropped, to live in mud, and to often sleep in it, to feed upon biscuit and bully beef and mugs of 'char' . . . Above all to die, to crawl over wire and mines to drag back some person previously unknown, or to share a last cigarette. It was – it is – a miracle impossible for me to define, a platitude of war which must be stated, a phenomenon, perhaps of human perversity, perhaps a pointer to the possibility of human greatness. All men who have known this experience must hunger for it, a vision as unattainable as the Holy Grail, proving what might be.[79]

Gordon Amos (2nd Canadian Anti-Tank Regiment) made just the same point about his own feelings to his comrades during the Normandy fighting:

> It was never too much trouble, and I don't think it bothered them too much to crawl out to the wounded and get them in even if it was rough. I pulled a wounded man out of a burning truck filled with gas and ammo one night. At the time he needed help; I never thought at the time of being hit or hurt, but I got him out. After, I thought I might have been killed or wounded, but somebody else would have helped both of us. At times like that, you don't think; or if you do, it's the other fellow you think of.[80]

An American who had seen action on many fronts was equally convinced that the sheer ubiquity of such a spirit of self-sacrifice was one of the abiding lessons of the war:

> Who in war has not felt and seen what a world of difference there is between the brutal indifference . . . in the rear lines and the brotherhood and sympathy of the soldiers in the combat zone? It is just those men whose lives are most miserable, the very toughest soldiers, those whose job is to kill, maim and destroy, it is just those men who are the most gentle, considerate and moved by feelings of sympathy for others . . . War binds men more tightly together than almost any other branch of human activity. To share your last crumb of bread with another, to warm your enfeebled body against another's in the bleak and barren mystery of the night, to undergo shame, fear and death with scores of others of your age and mental colouring – who, indeed, would trade these comrades of the battlefield for friends made in time of peace?[81]

The campaigns in the Far East threw men together in circumstances even more extreme than those elsewhere, and there too men bonded their souls together to buttress themselves against their growing hopelessness. A Marine wrote: 'I cannot say too much for the men – "Semper Fidelis" is too grave a motto here. It is noble but too bare. I have seen a spirit of brotherhood, more evident in the most tattered companies, that goes with one foot here amid the friends we see, and the other we see no longer, and one foot is as steady as the other.'[82] An officer of the 1st Royal Scots, in Arakan, wrote:

> The most striking change that came over the individual after he had entered the active zone, and knew that the Jap was just around the

corner, was the way in which *self* disappeared. Money had no longer any value, for you could buy nothing. It was share and share alike with everything you had. No thought of getting anything in exchange . . . At Battalion H.Q. they heard that a platoon was out of cigarettes. All there gave something to a pool and two men set off to take the cigarettes back to the platoon – and in broad daylight along a route that was dangerous . . . These two men had no thought of their own skins – they were just impelled by the spirit that pervaded the whole Battalion.[83]

A further rebuttal to any suggestions of self-pity is the fierce pride that men had in their own achievements, not so much their personal exploits as the joint achievements of their tank crew, platoon or whatever. A sergeant in north-west Europe wrote home saying that he thought the fighting in Normandy must surely have been the most savage of the campaign. 'And if I'm proud of the Regiment, Brigade or Division, can you blame me? They gave so much. They did so much and through it all I've had a charmed life.'[84] Even as the men were fighting in particularly desperate circumstances such pride could help weld them together and keep them going when even survival seemed impossible. Captain Laurence Critchell was at Bastogne during the great siege in December 1944. The nucleus of the defence was the 101st Airborne Division though other assorted units were also caught up. As the German ring tightened

> . . . a curious, very subtle change took place in the atmosphere . . . The stray units and fragments of units which had stayed to fight with us were not accepted just as additional firepower. By their free decision to remain and fight they were raised to the level of airborne troops; were given, so to speak, honorary membership in the division. There were no strangers in Bastogne during the siege. Only after the siege had been lifted, and sad-faced, weary infantrymen of the relieving units filed by the hundreds through the ruined streets, did our men, and those who had fought with us, realise what had come to us for a little while and gone, and would never come again.[85]

Rank was of little significance in this respect. Front-line officers were usually respected by their men whilst they themselves took an enormous pride in their men's achievements. Most realised quite clearly that at the end of the day neither discipline nor military tradition were anywhere near as important as the sheer guts of the ordinary soldier. This applied to every army and theatre but this comment by Donald Easton of the 5th Indian Division in Burma, part of perhaps the most self-conscious of all the armies, makes the point emphatically:

> But the greatest honours are due to Tommy Atkins. He had fought for six months in Arakan, they had flown him to Dinapur, marched him up to Kohima, marched him back again. Then once more back to Kohima, where he was shot at as he got out of his trucks. He fought hand-to-hand battles practically every night, and his pals were shot down all around him. If he was wounded he had no hope of evacuation. Day after day he was promised relief which never came; and his platoon, or section, or just 'gang' got smaller and smaller. My own company finished up just twenty-five strong; one platoon consisted of a single grinning private, who asked if he could put a pip up. And Tommy Atkins did all that on half a mug of liquid every twenty-four hours.[86]

This mutual sense of pride helps to explain the selflessness of the front line soldier in that, as a man looked at what his comrades seemed able to endure, he set for himself enormously high standards and became almost obsessed with the fear of letting them down, of acting in a way that might seem to sully their achievements. At this level concepts today regarded as being almost pompous did have a very real meaning. One British officer wrote: 'In the good unit – and trust and cohesion grow from and create a good unit – the assumption is, of course, that actions will be governed by those never mentioned concepts, duty and honour.[87] It is this concern that lies behind the following oft-repeated conversation between a tank commander and one of his crew who seemed likely to lose a leg:

> We sat alongside the stretcher chatting about everything except that leg. He was a good chap, that gunner, and a good gunner. I was sad at losing him.
> He said to me with a tight smile: 'Did I do all right, Bob?'
> It's funny how many of them will ask you that – the good ones who have done all right but want to be quite sure about it, as something very important to themselves and their whole future.[88]

The sergeant in north-west Europe, quoted before, stated:

> The boys marvel about my apparent lack of nerve. Some say, 'He'll get it yet.' Others refer to me as mad, while I myself – well, if only they knew how really scared I am, how I've had to fight it, how I've had to

bluff it, to carry on to be able to say, 'I've not let them down.' Frankly, every day that passes I feel less able to meet the responsibilities thrown on me, but with boys like I've just told you about I just cannot let them down. If they can stick it – I can stick it. But how, oh how, I would welcome the finish of it all.[89]

Even now one has not said it all. Selflessness, pride, mutual respect are still not adequate concepts to fully describe the front-line soldiers' feelings towards one another. In the last analysis one is speaking of an identification with and a concern for one's fellows so all-consuming that one can only speak in terms of love. How else could one characterise the feelings of this officer returning to his unit after a spell in hospital?

> Being wounded had now ended. It had been an interlude of unre-ality . . . Now he wanted impatiently to get back to the Battalion. For better or for worse that was where his war was, where he had grown used to its being. Not that he wanted to fight again: he wasn't thirsty for action. It was simply that it seemed the most natural thing to do: to go back where he belonged. It was his whole existence. He wanted badly now to be back there with those of whom he had become so much a part and who had become so much a part of him. For him there could only be the Battalion. Now it was tugging at him umbilically, and he was glad.[90]

Another officer spoke of the moments when constant awareness of shared dangers and privations blossomed into an almost ecstatic feeling of oneness with his fellows:

> The system of mutual reliance, almost of love, which held men to-gether in small fighting units during the war could be felt on a wider scale, but never consistently and never for long. It was a feeling not to be relied on but only to recognise with gratitude in its occasional glimpses . . . a feeling that never came from words or speeches, but only at definite times and in the presence of material things, and probably cannot now be recaptured with words alone . . . Honest men know that war is to be fought and destroyed for the suffering and pain and crime that go with it. But honest men will also admit that they themselves as individuals have been happy in war-time and some of them have tried to find the same things in peace and have always failed.[91]

A tank commander felt not so much that this love itself only blossomed occasionally but that there were few times when he had the leisure or indeed the honesty to examine the real nature of his relationship with his crew. One such occasion was on his return from leave when he began to feel

. . . a growing sense of excitement at the thought that tomorrow he would be with the troop. He tried to imagine how he would greet them, and what they would say. He had never realised the depth of his love for them, a love which sprang so unaccountably from mundane things, which in his absence he had almost forgotten – the shared meal, the silent preparation for battle, the closeness of their bodies in the smoke-filled turret, the jokes and obscenities with which they hid their fear.[92]

A private soldier was equally emphatic about the real nature of his feelings towards his comrades and the unique sense of solidarity that characterised the sharp end. As one got nearer the front the whole atmosphere gradually changed until you could

. . . taste, like the elusive flavour of an essence that has been put into a cake, the friendly helpfulness and almost gaiety that increases until it is an almost unbelievably tangible and incongruous thing as you get nearer to the front. A cousin writing to me recently . . . said 'Men are never so loving or so lovable as they are in action.' That is not only true, it is the beginning and end of the matter.[93]

Nothing else so well encapsulates the depth of this love, whilst at the same time describing the soldiers' almost embarrassed recognition of it and their poignantly inadequate ways of giving it full expression, than the following account of a unit finally coming out of the line on the Anzio beachhead. As they march down the road they pass another unit who have just taken up their positions:

What's this mob by the side of the road clapping their hands for? Well, that's really something. That's the first time in four years in action that you've seen one group of British soldiers clap another group on the battlefield. Didn't think you'd done much did you? They do. What will soldiers do next? Kiss each other? You should clap for them, poor bastards. They're staying . . . Bit embarrassing marching past this shower with all this clapping going on. Makes you feel you want to blush. Why don't they turn it in and get back to their digging? Not decent this clapping. What's this? Thanks, mate. That was a good swig of tea the bloke gave you wasn't it? Right out of his own mug too. He didn't say a word but you saw the bloke's eyes. Stirred it with his heart, he did. Must have meant it. No 'bullshit'. They can't have much tea to throw away. Well, perhaps they're not a shower after all; call 'em a mob. Not much further to go now. Wonder why those blokes clapped you so much. Perhaps they thought you looked damned weary. You are.[94]

Reticent the soldiers may have been about expressing their feelings fully, yet a deep love was there and for those who shared it the memory will never fail. It was something not given to most men to experience and in that respect, at least, they were privileged. Many years after the battle an American officer went to visit the cemetery at Cassino:

> The monument itself, I was grateful to find, is extremely simple. In a central courtyard stands a statue of two soldiers, one with his arm on the shoulders of the other, both men stripped to the waist. They seem to be walking forward, as if they had a job to do and are going to do it together . . . My family considerately left me alone for some time as I wandered out into the paths, stopping now at this grave, now at another, hoping that by reading the inscriptions, by busying my mind, I could control my emotions. But I could not keep back the tears, even when with one desperate effort I recalled the great ode of Catullus, who two thousand years ago had come to the tomb of his brother to pay honor to his memory . . . Yet groping for words helped me to discipline myself to say hail and farewell in a dignified way to men who had been my brothers years ago in a common struggle. The struggle is now half forgotten, and perhaps finally, in the larger perspective of history, it was unimportant. But it was for these men that this story was written . . .
>
>> nunc tamen interea haec prisco quae more parentum
>> tradita sunt tristi munere ad inferias,
>> accipe fraterno multum manantia fletu,
>> atque in perpetuum, frater, ave atque vale. [95]

When all else has been forgotten this must be the abiding lesson of combat in World War II. In the midst of seeming chaos it was the love of individuals, one for another, that enabled them to carry on. The fighting soldiers were sustained by a regard for others in which self-respect and mutual esteem were so inextricably intertwined that courage was a commonplace, self-sacrifice the norm. Without this bedrock of genuine human love there would have been no combat divisions, and not a billion cheery exhortations, a million sergeant-majors or a thousand scaffolds could have made a jot of difference. At the last extreme of the human spirit men turn to those nearest to them for reassurance as to their own plight and of the continued existence of common humanity. At the sharp end few men turned in vain.

9
Postscript

One of the most gratifying aspects of the reissue of this book was to discover that, even after ten years, two such eminent authorities as General Sir John Hackett and John Keegan still felt able to be complimentary about the book's accuracy and continued relevance. Frankly, I have come across little in recent literature about the Second World War to prompt me to revise my conception of life at the sharp end in any significant way – and that literature has been substantial. Throughout the 1980s, with military history having been given a kick-start by John Keegan's *The Face of War*, we have enjoyed a whole stream of Second World War titles that dwelt much more closely on the ordinary soldier's experience. The memoirs of individual soldiers have been especially prolific, as can be seen in the extended bibliography; but many of the campaign and battle studies have also been revivified by this more intimate approach, with the best of the new ones, particularly those dealing with North-West Europe 1944–45, taking full account of the dreadful sufferings of the ordinary fighting soldier.

As these sufferings were one of the main themes of the original text, it will be realised that this chapter can have little to say that is dramatically new. But that does not, I trust, make it redundant. As in the earlier chapters, this one relies utterly on the testimony of men who were actually at the front, most of it in their own words. All these are culled from books of which I was unaware, or were unpublished when I was first writing – these are in no way 'reserve' or 'second string' quotations. Had I been aware of them almost all of them would have appeared in the original text, many making their points even more trenchantly than anything cited before. A stern critic might, I suppose, dismiss these extra pages as simply more of the same, but they definitely merit attention when the 'same' are such stark accounts of human suffering and extremes of experience, and when such suffering and extremes are still likely to be the parameters of any warfare short of a nuclear holocaust.

Before moving on to these new accounts from the sharp end, however, there are two omissions from the original edition that I would like to rectify. From its very inception the book was only intended to cover ground combat in the Second World War, and that only as experienced by British, American, Empire and Commonwealth soldiers. Simply for reasons of space it was deemed impossible to include coverage of the war in the air or at sea. I have never regretted this decision; but I do now feel that it was not signposted properly, so that the omission of the airmen and sailors seems almost casual, as though the author knew little of their experiences and cared less. I would like to take this opportunity, therefore, to stress that, both in the air and at sea, actual combat could be quite as horrific as that on land. The battles of the Atlantic and Arctic, for example, still have to find a chronicler who can play down the technical niceties of anti-submarine warfare, and properly highlight the drudgery, gnawing anxiety and occasional terror of life on a tramp steamer or a corvette. Equally grim was the war in the Pacific where, despite the US Navy's eventual enormous material preponderance, the issue was at times extremely close and always fought to the bitterest conclusion. Of the naval battles around Guatalcanal in 1942 the most eminent naval historian wrote: 'So reader, if this tale has seemed repetitive with blood and gore, exploding magazines, burning and sinking ships and plummeting planes – that is simply how it was.'[1]

But just as hard was the war in the air, notably for aircrew in France and Britain in 1940, in the Mediterranean in 1941 and 1942, in the Pacific in 1942 and 1943 and, most notoriously of all, for bomber crews flying over Europe for most of the war. In RAF Bomber Command, for example, the proportion of aircrew killed throughout the war was 47.5 per cent and, if one considers only the period up to the Normandy landings in June 1944, it was probably more like 65 per cent.

The other major omission in the original text was the lack of recognition given to the Russian contribution to victory. Once again, the dictates of space made it quite logical not to deal at any length with the Soviet experience, but I should like to have made at least some acknowledgement of the enormous sacrifices made by the Russian people and the absolutely decisive nature of their contribution. It is a sad fact that, even today, some politicians who should know better prattle on in a way that shows they think that the Red Army merely tied down a few German divisions while the real war was being won in Africa and North-West Europe. Let it be noted, therefore, that between 1941 and 1945 some 20 million Russians died. In that period 4,900,000 German soldiers were killed or wounded on the Eastern Front as opposed to 580,000 in Africa, Italy and North-West Europe. If one divides the total amount of time spent by all German combat divisions on all fronts into units called 'divisional combat months', it is found that the Army and SS spent 7,146 divisional combat months on the Eastern Front and 1,121 in Africa, Italy and North-West Europe. It is with great satisfaction that I have taken this opportunity to point out these facts.

Returning to a review of some of the individual chapters of the original text, I find that I have had little cause to revise my comments on the nature of preliminary training in the armed forces. The comments of Sergeant William Manchester (29 US Marine Regiment) offer a particularly chilling re-statement of rationale and method. At 'boot camp'

> ... the Corps begins its job of building men by destroying the identity they brought with them. Their heads are shaved. They are assigned numbers. The DI is their god. He treats them with utter contempt. I am told that corporal punishment has since been banned ... but in my day it was quite common to see a DI bloody a man's nose, and some boots were gravely injured, though I know of none who actually died.[2]

Such open brutality was perhaps not the norm, being more likely to occur, ironically, in a corps made up of volunteers, who were less likely to complain. But there were more subtle ways to impose the tyranny of rank, mainly the constant imposition of mindless rules and petty regulations to rub the conscripts' noses in the dirt of their own unimportance and impotence. In the US Army this was known as 'chickenshit', a concept best described by Lieutenant Paul Fussell of 103 US Infantry Division:

> Chickenshit is so called ... because it is small-minded and ignoble and takes the trivial seriously. Chickenshit can be recognised instantly because it never has anything to do with winning the war. If you are an enlisted man, you'll know you've been the victim of chickenshit if your sergeant assigns you to K.P. not because it's your turn but because you disagreed with him on a question of taste a few evenings ago. Or you might find your pass to town cancelled at the last moment

because, you finally remember, a few days ago you asked a question during the sergeant's lecture on map reading that he couldn't answer ... It is chickenshit that requires that brass and leather care occupy so important a part of the service day, that saddle soap and leather polish, Brasso and the Glad Rag become such indispensable elements of bellicose equipment.

Frequent unnecessary inspections – of personal appearance, barracks, weapons, vehicles, kit – remain the commonest ways of indulging in chickenshit. As a way of 'keeping the men on their toes' the barracks inspection on Saturday morning, when passes can be withheld at the last moment and plans for good times frustrated, is effective. For its victims it has its own serial psychological structure generating maximum anxiety over matters of minimum significance.[3]

As Fussell reminds us, Private Louis Simpson (101 US Airborne Division) went so far as to claim that 'the aim of military thinking is not just to prepare men for battle, but to make them long for it. Inspections are one way to achieve this.'[4] Nor did chickenshit disappear when training was finished. Corporal Wes Burrows (Royal Hamilton Light Infantry) was sent back to Canada having completed five years in the Army, the last months as a stretcher-bearer when he had carried upward of 200 men back to safety. On the ship home a rifle drill was held 'and Burrows, clumsily wrestling with the gun bolt, was hauled up by an English sergeant major: "What do you think you're doing! Hold you head up! What a pitiful sight you are." '[5]

Training could also be a sore physical travail. The 43rd (Wessex) Division trained for three winters in Kent at Stone Street, north of Folkestone. According to the divisional historian it was 'undoubtedly the coldest place in the British Isles ... A midwinter spent in the open there is calculated to leave no man in doubt as to the reason why the Scandinavian concept of eternal punishment was ... linked with extreme cold and not excessive heat. In real war some shelter from the elements can usually be found. This was not the case with Stone Street. The philosopher who asserted that eternity is beyond human conception never trained with the 43rd Division, otherwise he would have been less dogmatic.'[6]

The divisional historian's assertion that conditions at the front were never as bad as this should, however be treated with some caution, for a dominant theme of almost all war memoirs is still the emphasis upon the frequent awfulness of life in the line, in whatever theatre. Chapter Two has already dealt with this topic

in some detail, and everything I have read since has only served
to underline the conviction that life in the slit-trenches, dugouts
and foxholes of the Second World War was frequently just as
grim as that of the troglodytes of the Great War. New quotations
abound and here I must content myself with only a few from some
of the major theatres.

In the Western Desert heat and dust were an obvious problem,
but even worse were the ancillary plagues of flies. These have
already been mentioned but it was only recently that I came across
a description that did full justice to the utter loathsomeness and
fanatical pertinacity of these creatures. The chronicler was Peter
Llewelyn of 2 New Zealand Division:

> The foul and dismaying thing about the Alamein flies was their
> oneness. None was separate from its fellows any more than the wave
> is separate from the ocean, the tentacle from the octopus. As one fly,
> one dark and horrible force guided by one mind, ubiquitous and
> enormously powerful, they addressed themselves to the one task,
> which was to destroy us body and soul. It was useless to kill them, for
> they despised death and made no attempt to avoid it ... We slew them
> in mounds with our bare hands until the crunch of minute frames and
> the squish of microscopic viscera, felt rather than heard, became a
> nightmare. But what was the use? Their ranks closed at once and they
> went on with the all-important task of driving us out of our minds.
>
> Flies crave moisture, and you knew from watching your friends –
> and the knowledge was disproportionately humiliating and dis-
> gusting – that you too were walking around with half a hundred
> miniature old-men-of-the-sea clinging dourly to the back of your
> damp shirt. And when you shut your eyes – this is the plain truth –
> flies tried to open them, mad for the delectable fluid.
>
> We couldn't always be killing them, but we had to keep on brushing
> them away, otherwise even breathing would have been difficult. Our
> arms ached from the exercise, but still they fastened on our food and
> accompanied it into our mouths and down our throats, scorning death
> when there was an advantage to be gained. They drowned themselves
> in our tea and in our soup. They attended us with awful relish on our
> most intimate occasions.[7]

But the Eighth Army was also sorely tried in Italy, although the
greatest problem, and biggest surprise, was the dreadful climate
there, especially in winter. The first months of 1944 were spent
below Monte Cassino, the lynch-pin of the German Gustav Line,
and there soldiers endured a grim period of static warfare as
bad as anything in Flanders 30 years before. Major Shore (1/2
Gurkhas) wrote home to his father:

Bad weather has made life almost unbearable at times. For weeks on end we have sat on a draughty mountain top in heavy snow and rain, with one's clothing and blankets soaked through in the first five minutes. Behind the line one can always make a hole in the ground and rainproof it with a tent or bivouac. But in the forward positions one's hole or sangar can either be anti-German-counterattack or rainproof – not both.[8]

The 2nd Coldstream Guards occupied positions on another mountain ridge that were constantly buffeted by 'icy wind and rain ... Blankets and greatcoats were soaked through by day and frozen hard by night.' Some leather jerkins, clean socks, tents and a rum ration were sent forward but 'it was not so much these things that made life possible as the sheer exhaustion which, from day to day, enabled men to sleep in spite of soaking blankets and driving sleet. There was some respite from enemy fire, but the cold, which at night froze water solid in the water-bottles, was constant and merciless.'[9] Such conditions were an enormous strain on the troops' morale and simple endurance became a major achievement. According to Captain Fred Majdalanay (2 Lancashire Fusiliers) one came to believe that 'there was no past, present or future. There was only *now*. We'd always been here and always would be ... It was just a passive state of sustained awfulness.'[10] Alan Moorehead, one of the best British war correspondents, described men who had been exposed on yet another Italian mountainside and who had

... for two days and nights slept waist-deep in water. In utter weariness they lost all sense of time and place and even perhaps the sense of hope. Only the sense of pain remained, of constantly reiterated pain that invaded sleep and waited for the end of sleep to increase. For these soldiers the risk of war had passed out of consciousness and was replaced by the misery and discomfort of war, which in the end is worse than anything.[11]

But North-West Europe, particularly during the winter of 1944–45, which was one of the worst on record, was no better. Frank Mead (102 US Infantry Division) went into the line around Geilenkirchen in October 1944, and even by then 'the weather was terrible ... The constant rain and overcast skies seemed to prevent any evaporation. The earth was just plain mud. Our foxholes were virtual wells and the anti-tank ditches stagnant canals. No matter how careful we were, our weapons became constantly clogged and jammed, by the mud. It was combat under the worst possible conditions.'[12] Conditions in Holland were, if anything, even worse, though it has to be admitted that the original text dealt rather cursorily with the mainly Canadian effort in this sector. Happily some recent publications by Canadian authors (see W. D. & S. Whitaker and J. Williams in the Bibliography) have highlighted the rigours of campaigning on the left flank of the slow Allied advance across Europe, and this Postscript can in turn give it due prominence. Some British troops fought with the First Canadian Army, and a regimental history recently brought to my attention was moved to rare eloquence in its description of conditions between the Rivers Roer and Maas:

> What is difficult to describe is the physical agony of the infantryman when fighting forward against two enemies at once: men and their lethal weapons, and vile weather ... The days and nights were wet. The November rain seemed piercingly cold. After exertion when the body warmed, the cold air and the wet seemed to penetrate the very marrow of every bone in the body, so that the whole shook as with ague, and then after shaking would come the numbness of hand and leg and mind, and a feeling of surrender to forces of nature far greater in strength than any enemy might impose.[13]

The worst terrain of all was the network of polders, or dykes, that protected those large, bleak expanses of land that had been reclaimed from the sea, and it was among these that the Canadians languished for months on end. Conditions were uniformly ghastly, as the War Diary of the Toronto Scottish testified: 'Living conditions at the front are not cosy. Water and soil make mud. Mud sticks to everything. Boots weigh pounds more. Rifles and Brens operate sluggishly. Ammunition becomes wet. Slit trenches allow one to get below ground level but also contain several inches of thick water. Matches and cigarettes are wet and unusable.'[14] A Canadian officer who fought there, Lieutenant W. D. Whitaker (Royal Hamilton Light Infantry), was even more trenchant, noting that any attack against a fortified dyke would be bad enough 'but when it had to be done in cold, driving rain, through ankle-deep mud, with little hope of a change of dry clothes or a warm place to sleep, not knowing from one moment to the next whether you would be dead or alive, it was a new form of hell. This was polder warfare.'[15]

Another theatre where physical conditions virtually beggared description was the Pacific and, though my original text dealt at some length with the agonies of surviving among coral reefs and rain forest, several books have since been published which offer some particularly graphic first-hand accounts. One of the best is William Manchester's *Goodbye Darkness*, a record of a journey through the theatre where he had suffered so grievously over 30 years before. He remembers New Guinea, where US soldiers 'aged rapidly and came to look more like tramps than soldiers. Their helmets had rusted red. Their dashing, broad-brimmed felt hats were caked with mud. Sores erupted on their genitalia. Their uniforms rotted on their backs. The flesh on their feet, swollen by endless slogging, peeled away when they removed their socks.' He tells also of Guadalcanal where

> ... the typical Marine ... ran a fever, wore stinking dungarees, loathed twilight, and wondered whether the US Navy still existed. He ate mouldy rations and quinine. He alternatively shivered and sweated. If he was bivouacked near Henderson, he spent his morning filling in craters left by enemy bombers the night before. If he was on his way back to the line, he struggled through shattered, stunted cocoanut trees, scraggy bushes, and putrescent jungle, clawing up and down slopes ankle-deep in mud, hoping he could catch a few hours of uninterrupted sleep in his foxhole. Usually he was disappointed.

And most graphically of all he tells us of Okinawa, the only island where he himself actually saw combat, with a horrendous two months in the line. Most of it was spent in the wet. The rain was falling, it seemed,

> ... most of the time ... You were fully exposed to it, and helpless in deluges. By the time you had a hole dug, a couple of inches of rain had already gathered in it. Tossing shrubs in didn't help; their branches jabbed you. You wrapped yourself in your poncho or shelter half, but the water always seeped through. You lapsed into a coma of exhaustion and wakened in a drippy, misty dawn with your head fuzzy and a terrible taste in your mouth resembling, Rip once said, 'a Greek wrestler's jockstrap'.

On Okinawa, according to Manchester, conditions were made even worse by the concentrated nature of the fighting. In the Machinato Line 300,000 soldiers were crammed into an area of only a few thousand square yards. 'In the densest combats of World War I, battalion frontage had been approximately eight hundred yards. Here it was less than six hundred yards. The sewage, of course, was appalling. You could smell the front line long before you saw it; it was one vast cesspool.'[16]

Simply existing in these conditions was bad enough, but when one also had to go forward against a well entrenched enemy they became almost unendurable. Another outstanding Pacific memoir is that by Eugene B. Sledge, who fought with 5 US Marine Regiment on Pelelieu and Okinawa. Of conditions on the former island he wrote:

> The struggle for survival went on day after weary day, night after terrifying night … time lost all meaning. A lull of hours or days seemed but a fleeting instant of heaven-sent tranquility. Lying in a foxhole sweating out an enemy artillery or mortar barrage or waiting to dash across open ground under machine gun or artillery fire defied any concept of time.
>
> To the non-combatants and those on the periphery of action the war meant only boredom or occasional excitement; but to those who entered the meat-grinder itself the war was a nether world of horror from which escape seemed less and less likely as casualties mounted and the fighting dragged on and on. Time had no meaning; life had no meaning. The fierce struggle for survival in the abyss of Pelelieu eroded the veneer of civilisation and made savages of us all. We existed in an environment totally incomprehensible to men behind the lines.

On Okinawa Sledge fought below Sugar Loaf Hill, where conditions on the ridge held by his company were always grim:

> When enemy artillery shells exploded in the area, the eruptions of soil and mud uncovered previously buried Japanese dead and scattered chunks of corpses. Like the area around our gun pits, the ridge was a stinking compost pile.
>
> If a Marine slipped and slid down the back slope of the muddy ridge, he was apt to reach the bottom vomiting. I saw more than one man lose his footing and slip and slide all the way to the bottom only to stand up horror-stricken as he watched in disbelief while fat maggots tumbled out of his muddy dungaree pockets, cartridge belt, legging lacings, and the like. Then he and a buddy would shake or scrape them away with a piece of ammo box or knife blade.
>
> We didn't talk about such things. They were too horrible and obscene even for hardened veterans. The conditions taxed the toughest I knew almost to the point of screaming. Nor do authors normally write about such vileness; unless they have seen it with their own eyes, it is too preposterous to think that men could actually live and fight for days and nights on end under such terrible conditions and not be driven insane. But I saw much of it there on Okinawa and to me the war was insanity.[17]

Experiences such as these undoubtedly represent the furthest extremes of human suffering at the front. Nevertheless, they should not be thought wholly untypical of the combat soldier's life in any other major theatre. The mass of new and rediscovered front-line memoirs makes it abundantly clear that the PBI of the Second World War everywhere faced much the same physical and mental anguish as their forebears. The 'Face of War' might have changed in certain details, but it was still a countenance that few could look in the eye for long.

In Italy, for example, the shock of the harsh climate and terrain was compounded by a mode of fighting characterised mainly by unremitting brutality. River crossings against formidable German fortifications were commonplace, as on the Rapido in 1944, where, according to Sergeant Kirby (36 US Infantry Division):

> We were under constant fire. I saw boats being hit all around me, and guys falling out and swimming. I never knew whether they made it or not ... When we got to the other side it was the only scene that I'd seen in the war that lived up to what you see in the movies. I'd never seen so many bodies – our own guys. I remember this kid being hit by a machine gun; the bullets hitting him pushed his body along like a tin-can ... Just about everybody was hit. I didn't have a single good friend in the company who wasn't killed or wounded.[18]

Natural obstacles dictated the fighting methods in Italy, slowing advances to a snail's pace where successive defensive positions behind river and mountain lines had to be wrested from the Germans in bitter slugging matches. This description of the French attack on Monna Casale, in the Gustav Line, could equally well be part of some desperate assault at Verdun 30 years earlier. It was

> ... a battle of grenades ... in which the enemy occupying the heights threw or rolled down grenades on to the Tirailleurs. The latter had to crawl up the slopes ... to reach a position where they could reach the enemy with their grenades ... The Germans ... had to be attacked each time with bayonets and grenades. If they were overwhelmed they counter-attacked at once. The summit was taken and retaken four times. Each time bayonets and grenades were decisive ... More than a thousand grenades were thrown by the two assaulting companies.[19]

But purely man-made obstacles were an equal handicap, and images of the First World War are again conjured up by the experiences of a soldier in the 48th Highlanders of Canada, whose

battalion ran into dense barbed wire entanglements during an
attack on the Hitler Line:

> That was the fearful thing. If you fight with barbwire it only gets
> worse. You must ignore the machine gun bullets plucking at your
> sleeves and quietly take out the barbs ... one ... by ... bloody ...
> one. Try counting them. Or you can keep from panic if you hum
> *Mother Machree*. At least I did. But I heard the Corporal screaming,
> and a new man was raving; he was thrashing and fighting with the
> wire like a man gone insane. The bullets started socking into him, and
> he jerked and kicked with each hit. Then he crumpled beside me.
> Nothing was very bad in the war after that.[20]

In North-West Europe natural and man-made obstacles presented a whole array of hazards, not least of them the polders of
Holland. The problems of day-to-day existence in this waterlogged wilderness have already been dealt with; if these were a
sore trial, then actually trying to fight there was a nightmare.
Every assault was a model of tactical insanity, for the dykes that
bisected the polders were

> ... dead straight, ten or twelve feet in height ... ready-made defensive
> lines for the Germans. For the attacking Canadians the only other
> approach was across the sunken fields between the dykes, 'flat as the
> local beer' as one artillery punster put it. There was really no protection
> at all. It was a battleground heavily weighted on the side of the
> defender, who could dig in his troops and guns along the sides of the
> dykes and at their intersections, and set up a crossfire that would
> destroy any foe approaching up the dykes or across the polders. Strug-
> gling through flooded fields at times up to two metres deep, totally
> vulnerable to enemy fire, the Canadians fought hard under near-
> impossible conditions against a well-entrenched opposition.

Often the fields were completely impassable, and then the infantry was faced with the yet more daunting task, if that were possible,
of attacking 'straight up a dyke ... on a one-man front, dyke by
wretched dyke, without respite.'[21] One such attack, on a rather
grander scale than usual, was along the so-called Causeway linking
Walcheren and South Beveland. According to the historian of
52 Infantry Division (like all unit historians, normally a very
phlegmatic author), one attack by the Glasgow Highlanders took
'the battalion into hell. That conventional phrase does not exag-
gerate the horrific situation. The Germans had the Causeway
completely taped and plastered ... To move a foot in daylight was

nearly impossible; to advance a yard in the darkness was an adventurous success.'[22]

Clearly, then, whatever criticisms might be levelled at the original edition of this book, no-one could convincingly claim that its emphasis upon the agony of the infantryman's war was in any way hyperbolic. This second edition can also call a most distinguished witness, of whose testimony I was unaware the first time around. In December 1944 General Eisenhower wrote to Ernie Pyle, the famous US war correspondent, stating:

> I get so eternally tired of the general lack of understanding of what the infantry soldier endures that I have come to the conclusion that education along this one simple line might do a lot toward promoting future reluctance to engage in war. I get so fighting mad because of the general lack of appreciation of real heroism – which is the uncomplaining acceptance of unendurable conditions – that I become completely inarticulate.[23]

The soldiers were often inarticulate themselves, unable to convey to outsiders the reality of these 'unendurable conditions'. Captain C. B. MacDonald (23 US Infantry Regiment) remembered one of his men, Private Coteau, being asked by a newspaperman who had actually got up to the front 'what he would like best from the States about now'. Coteau at first declined to answer but, when pressed, said:

> 'O.K. .... I've got something to say. Tell them it's too damned serious over here to be talking about hot dogs and baked beans and things we're missing. Tell them it's hell and tell them there're men getting killed and wounded every minute, and they're miserable and they're suffering. Tell them it's a matter more serious than they'll ever be able to understand. Spread it on thick and leave off the sweet syrup that all the others write about' ... there was a choking sob in his voice ... 'Tell 'em it's rough as hell. Tell 'em it's rough. Tell 'em it's rough, serious business. That's all. That's all.'[24]

Judging from previous reviews, there may still be those who prefer to regard the picture of combat that I've tried to paint in this book, and to reinforce in this Postscript, as something of a distortion. By concentrating so much on subjective impressions of ordinary soldiers I have missed out on the tactical dimension, on the actual military rationale and method that shaped any attack. Most soldiers were probably unaware that there was any method in the madness, as they saw it, but this does not mean that it was not at least supposed to be there. In the interests of historical balance, therefore, I include the following rather more detached analyses of infantry combat, analyses that are of particular value in that they represent the stripped-down tactical wisdom of soldiers who had actually fought at the sharp end. The first comes from the battalion orders of 2 Cameronians prior to an attack across the River Garigliano in January 1944:

Warn all ranks
a) No-one except a stretcher-bearer or a wounded man helps a wounded man out of action . . .
c) Silence is vital. Noise will cost lives. No coughs. Tools and equipment padded. No light. No smoking.
d) German tactics are to evacuate positions and then put in immediate counter-attack with grenades and tommy guns.
e) It is fatal to halt when mortared. Once you are in among his troops he will stop mortaring.
f) Dig or die.[25]

A second summary comes from a Canadian officer in Holland who was suddenly faced with the task of absorbing some replacements who had had no training as infantrymen.[26] The officer endeavoured to do in a couple of hours what should have been the work of months.

The first thing I stressed was that all tactics were based on the principle of fire and movement: in other words, infantrymen should move in attack only when supported by fire of sufficient volume to keep the heads of the enemy down. I emphasised the importance of keeping close to our artillery fire in the attack so as to close with the enemy at the earliest possible moment when the fire lifted. They were introduced to the all-important trenching tool. Most of all, I advised them to rely on help from the old sweats.
    I described how they should hug the ground for the greatest protection, how to use 'dead' ground out of sight of the enemy. I stressed a few truths, such as that the enemy shell that they could hear for a long time was safe enough; you only heard the dangerously close ones for a couple of seconds – and if you didn't hear them at all, it was game over.[27]

A similar situation confronted William Manchester on Okinawa. Although his 'repples' had gone through basic infantry training, it was clear that none of them had much idea of what

actually lay ahead of them, and they were keen to hear it from the
lips of a veteran.

> I told them how to learn about shell-fire on the job, and the tricks of
> Jap snipers, and booby traps, and how doubt is more fatal than slowed
> reflexes, and where they might avoid being enfiladed on the line ...
> Their boondockers [boots], I said, were their best friends; they should
> dry them whenever possible. If they were overrun by a Jap charge
> they should play dead, affecting a grotesque pose of death ... They
> should be alert for the sharp click of steel on steel, which probably
> meant trouble, because that was how Japs armed grenades. If they
> heard it, they should move fast ... To be avoided, and if necessary
> ignored, were gung-ho platoon leaders who drew enemy fire by order-
> ing spectacular charges. Ground wasn't gained that way; it was won
> by small groups of men, five or six in a cluster, who moved warily
> forward in a kind of autohypnosis, advancing in mysterious concert
> with similar groups on their flanks.[28]

My final distillation of tactical wisdom comes from a slightly
more academic source, although written by an infantry officer.
This was a paper prepared for HQ French Expeditionary Corps
in Italy in which the author attempted to sum up his experiences
of combat in the last months, and to put forward tactical rec-
ommendations. Certain of his conclusions give a remarkably
concise description of infantry combat, as well as making it clear
that, in essence, such combat has changed very little over the
centuries:[29]

> ... as far as infantry fighting is concerned, I am more than ever
> convinced that the standard infantry action consists of a body of
> attackers seeking hand-to-hand combat. Bear in mind that all advances
> in armament over the centuries have only aimed at one thing: to fire
> from as far away as possible to avoid this hand-to-hand combat, which
> men fear. The job of the infantry is to break through the enemy lines;
> to do that they must get in among those lines. In an attack, no matter
> how powerful the artillery and the heavy weapons, there comes the
> moment when the infantryman gets close to the enemy lines, all
> support ceases, and he must mount the charge that is his last argument,
> his sole *raison d'être*. Such is the infantryman's war ... [and] the object
> of his training should be to prepare him for what one might call 'the
> battle of the last hundred metres'.[30]

Another thing that had changed little over the centuries was
that it was the infantry who bore the brunt of the casualties. The

point is examined in detail in the original text, mainly illustrated with British examples, but it is worth counterpointing these with American and Canadian figures. In North–West Europe, for example, American infantry divisions suffered heavily, as is clearly shown in the following table, which shows total casualties in the division and percentage casualties in the rifle companies, which suffered up to 90 per cent of total casualties. Only those divisions that served for nine months or more are included, where such figures exist.

Div.	Months in Europe	Total casualties		Percentage	
		Dead	Wounded	Dead	Wounded
4	11	4,834	17,371	18.1	65.1
29	11	3,786	15,541	15.9	56.3
30	11	3,516	13,376	16.5	62.7
79	11	2,943	10,971	16.1	59.8
83	11	3,620	11,807	19.2	62.5
90	11	3,930	14,386	17.3	63.2
5	10	2,656	9,549	15.9	60.3
8	10	2,820	10,057	16.3	45.3
35	10	2,947	11,526	15.6	61.0
28	9	2,683	9,609	16.1	57.7
80	9	3,480	12,484	17.0	61.1

The Canadian figures below again refer to North-West Europe and are a comparison of certain units' casualties there with Canadian casualty rates in the First World War. The battles compared are that on the Scheldt in October and November 1944, and Passchendaele almost exactly 27 years before. At Passchendaele

... in 29 days the four Canadian divisions lost 15,654 men killed, wounded or missing, 3,914 per division. On the Scheldt the 2nd Canadian Division lost 3,650 in 33 days.

But in the First World War each division had twelve battalions, in the Second only nine (in both cases disregarding machine gun units which were similar in size). At Passchendaele the average loss per batallion was 326 men. On the Scheldt the losses of the 2nd Division were 405 per batallion in much the same length of time.[31]

Even a vague awareness of casualty rates like these did not give the fighting soldier too much faith in his commander's absolute commitment to conserve lives. A staff officer in 5 Canadian Armoured Brigade in Italy wrote of one series of battles in 1944:

As for the main obstacle of the German tanks ... the only reason why
it was possible to make headway against their qualitative superiority
was by weight of numbers ... General Leese [has been cited] as saying
that in his offensive he was prepared to lose 1000 tanks. As he had
1900 at his disposal, the Panther stood a fair chance of becoming an
extinct species among the fauna of Southern Italy. On our side losses
had to be taken and replacements thrown in. Being somewhat up
against it, the tankmen were compelled to improvise and make the
most of what they had.[32]

The US Marine E. B. Sledge finally got the message while
settling into a muddy foxhole on Pelelieu:

Slowly the reality of it all formed in my mind: we were expendable.
It was difficult to accept. We come from a nation and a culture that
values life and the individual. To find oneself in a situation where
your life seems of little value is the ultimate in loneliness. It is a
humbling experience. Most of the combat veterans had already grap-
pled with this realisation on Guadalcanal or Gloucester, but it struck
me out in that swamp.[33]

A particularly futile activity for an author is to bother too much
about reviews although, with the original edition of this book, I
was lucky enough to receive a very flattering press. However, one
reviewer, himself a battalion commander in the war, did rather
surprise me when he asserted that my argument, that what kept
men going was their comradely love for one another, more than
duty or loyalty to the cause, was mistaken. Not overdone or
exaggerated, just plain wrong. The point I had completely missed,
it seems, was that 'it is leadership ... which keeps men going in
battle ... Alexander, Montgomery and Slim ... these men were
all leaders. Their soldiers ... followed them without question,
because they knew beyond doubt that, by their commanders'
professional knowledge and skill, their lives were as safe as possible
in battle conditions.'
I still find it difficult to believe that a fighting officer could
seriously claim that this was the whole and sufficient reason for
the generally superb performance of the Allied armies in the
Second World War. All I can do is draw his attention to the
evidence – not to my arguments, which are as fallible as anyone's,
but to the copious and explicit evidence of serving soldiers –
assembled on the last 13 pages of the original text and now
buttressed by these further statements by men who served at the

sharp end. An American war correspondent, for example, never ceased to marvel at the riflemen's 'grim purpose, selflessness, and a spirit of exaltation in the mutual high endeavour'.[34] An officer of the Lancashire Fusiliers watched his men coming down from a tour of duty on the Cassino massif, and, as he saw them wearily heave themselves into the trucks, he 'was conscious of the feeling of high comradeship which binds a man with fierce intensity to those with whom a profound and fearful mission has been shared. It is something which can only be known through the moral and emotional purge of battle. It is the fighting man's reward.'[35] A sergeant in 88 US Infantry Division asked himself:

Why do I fight? ... I don't know, unless it's because I feel I must because I'm expected to. If I should fail to do what is asked of me, I would betray the trust of the men fighting with me. And if I betrayed this trust ... in my own eyes I believe I would become so despicable that no longer would I feel worthy of the comradeship of men ... It seems that there is an urge inside me that compels me to go with my buddies when they attack and sweat it out with them in defence and ... to endure seemingly useless privations, all to what may be a useless end.[36]

Finally, here is the testimony of two US Marines, not men given to sentimentality. E. B. Sledge wrote: 'War is brutish, inglorious and a terrible waste ... The only redeeming factors were my comrades' incredible bravery and their devotion to each other. Marine Corps training taught us to kill effectively and to try and survive. But it also taught us loyalty to each other – and love. That ésprit de corps sustained us.'[37] William Manchester was wounded on Okinawa but soon discharged himself from hospital to return to his unit. The reason was simple:

It was an act of love. Those men on the line were my family, my home. They were closer to me than I can say, closer than any friends had been or ever would be. They had never let me down, and I couldn't do it to them. I had to be with them, rather than let them die and me live with the knowledge that I might have saved them. Men, I now knew, do not fight for flag or country, for the Marine Corps or glory or any other abstraction. They fight for one another.

Notes and References

Full details of sources are given in the bibliography under authors

Chapter 1 (*Induction and Training*)

1 It should be emphasised, however, that this was not an attempt to produce an army of supermen who would never crack up. In the end, as is shown in Chapter 6, any soldier will break under the strain of prolonged combat. The army recognised this, though somewhat reluctantly, and at the induction stage were only trying to cull those who were obviously completely inadequate to the pressures of the front line
2 Quoted in E. Ginzberg *et al*, p38
3 Quoted in E. H. Rhodes-Wood, *A War History of the Royal Pioneer Corps*, Gale & Polden, Aldershot, 1960, p212. Men deemed too old for 'active' service were also posted to the Pioneer Corps
4 Non-military considerations, such as general improvements in health and education, are also obviously of relevance here
5 R. R. Palmer *et al*, p6
6 J. Lucas, p9
7 H. Brotz and E. Wilson, 'Characteristics of Military Society', *American Journal of Sociology*, vol 51, 1946, p374
8 A. B. Hollingshead, 'Adjustment to Military Life', *American Journal of Sociology*, vol 51, 1946, p441
9 A. Cotterell, *Oh, It's Nice . . .*, p8
10 R. Croft-Cooke, p35
11 J. Guest, p24
12 J. Jones, *WWII*, pp42-3
13 D. T. Brown, p19
14 Quoted in C. W. Valentine, pp36-8
15 Brotz and Wilson, *op cit*, p372
16 A. Wilson, pp19-20
17 R. Ingersoll, *The Battle is . . .*, p137
18 R. L. Eichelberger, p142
19 Jones, *op cit*, p136
20 Quoted in J. Strawson, p101

Chapter 2 (*The Physical Setting*)

1 A. Bowlby, p180

371

2 Quoted in L. F. Ellis, *Welsh Guards at War*, Gale & Polden, Aldershot, 1946, p247

3 H. L. Bond, pp122–3

4 J. D'Arcy Dawson, pp227–8

5 C. B. MacDonald, *The Siegfried . . .*, p444

6 L. Farago, p480

7 A. Gibbs, p86

8 J. Horsfall, p34

9 Quoted in R. F. Johnson, *Regimental Fire*, private publication, 1958, p189

10 Ellis, *loc cit*

11 A. Muir, *The First of Foot*, private publication, Edinburgh, 1961, p233

12 J. Guest, pp199–200

13 Quoted in D. Orgill, pp184–5

14 N. Nicholson, *The Grenadier Guards*, Gale & Polden, Aldershot, 1949 (2 vols), p153

15 B. Mauldin, p35

16 G. Cox, p32

17 Quoted in I. M. Stewart, p77

18 G. Talbot, p36

19 I. G. Cameron, *The History of the 7th Argylls, From El Alamein to Germany*, Nelson, 1946, p58

20 R. L. Crimp, p29

21 *Ibid*, p23

22 B. B. Kennett and J. A. Tatman, *Craftsmen of the Army*, Leo Cooper, 1970, p64

23 P. Cochrane, p66

24 R. L. Crimp, p24

25 Quoted in R. Grant, p61

26 Quoted in D. C. Quilter (ed), p199

27 D. Grant, p97

28 US War Department, *Makin*, p108

29 C. H. Metcalf, pp479–80

30 The average annual rainfall in England is 35in. In New York it is 39.3in and in California 23.9in

31 E. McKelvie, p272

32 Quoted in D. S. Daniell, *Cap of Honour*, Harrap, 1951, p312

33 H. Buggy, p145

34 C. A. Willoughby and J. Chamberlain, *MacArthur 1941–51*, Heinemann, 1956, p5

35 Quoted in G. H. Johnston, p170

36 Quoted in M. Myers, *Ours to Hold it High*, Infantry Journal Press, Washington, 1947, p84

37 R. L. Eichelberger, p64

38 F. Hough, p241

39 *Ibid*, p164

40 J. Jones, *The Thin Red Line*, pp54–5

41 The nature of enemy defences is dealt with in Chapter 3
42 Quoted in A. R. Buchanan (ed), p94
43 Myers, *op cit*, p167
44 R. L. Eichelberger, p267
45 H. Buggy, p20
46 A. Swinson, pp121–2
47 W. Miles, *The Gordon Highlanders 1939–45*, Aberdeen University Press, Aberdeen, 1961, p35
48 The Transvaal Scottish, quoted in J. A. Agar–Hamilton, pp129–30
49 D. Billany, p207
50 Quoted in J. Sym (ed), *Seaforth Highlanders*, Gale & Polden, Aldershot, 1962, p246
51 N. McCallum, p51
52 A. B. Austin, pp31–2
53 A. Bryant, *Jackets of Green*, p425
54 J. Guest, p201
55 E. D. Smith, *The Battles for Cassino*, p99
56 Quoted in M. Blumenson, *Bloody River*, p29
57 Quoted in D. C. Quilter (ed), p195
58 W. Vaughan-Thomas, p208
59 Quoted in C. B. MacDonald, *The Mighty Endeavour*, pp125–6
60 H. L. Bond, pp84–7
61 P. Cochrane, pp118–19
62 G. Wilson, p135
63 Smith, *op cit*, p138
64 B. Mauldin, pp143–4
65 Quoted in A. McKee, *Caen . . .*, p198
66 *Ibid*, p320
67 J. Watney, p169
68 Quoted in McKee, *op cit*, p253
69 Sergeant Mack Morris, quoted in D. Congdon (ed), *Combat: European Theatre*, p246
70 Quoted in D. Hawkins, pp266–7
71 A. Swinson, p103
72 *Ibid*, p139
73 Quoted in H. Maule, *Spearhead General*, p288
74 Quoted in P. A. Crowl, p397
75 Quoted in C. S. Nichols and H. I. Shaw, p202
76 Quoted in Myers, *op cit*, p107
77 Quoted in C. O. West *et al*, *Second to None*, Infantry Journal Press, Washington, 1949, p113
78 Quoted in A. R. Buchanan (ed), p77

Chapter 3 (*Combat: Infantry*)

1   Chapter 5 includes a numerical analysis of this point, whilst Chapter 8 has something to say about the attitudes of combat soldiers to those in the rear

2 R. Grant, p13

3 Quoted in D. S. Daniell, *Cap of Honour*, Harrap, 1951, p246

4 G. Wilson, p7

5 Quoted in A. Bryant, *Jackets of Green*, p426

6 Quoted in R. Grant, p111

7 D. Grant, pp204–6

8 In 1944 putting a division ashore required 500 ships and craft from 100 to 15,000 tons

9 Known to the Americans as Auxiliary Assault Ships (ASAs). Both carried 1,000 men and 87 officers

10 W. Robson, p18

11 Quoted in M. Howard, *The Coldstream Guards*, Oxford University Press, 1951, p108

12 N. Mailer, *The Naked and the Dead*, Allen Wingate, 1949, p24

13 J. Belden, p252

14 Quoted in A. McKee, *Caen . . .*, p11

15 E. Pyle, *Brave Men*, pp357–8

16 Quoted in W. F. Ross and C. F. Romanus, p55

17 M. Myers, *Ours to Hold it High*, Infantry Journal Press, Washington, 1947, p69

18 P. Bowman, p13

19 E. L. Jones, quoted in M. J. Weiss (ed), *Man and War*, Dell, New York, 1963, pp158–9

20 P. O'Sheel and G. Cook, p90

21 Quoted in A. R. Buchanan (ed), p77

22 Quoted in J. E. Mrazek, p179. This was not just a human problem. During the lift of the 5th Indian Division to Imphal, in March 1944, several aircraft were endangered because the mules on board urinated on the floor and shorted the wiring that ran underneath

23 L. Mayo, p112

24 R. Ingersoll, *The Battle is . . .*, p135

25 J. Binkoski and A. Plant, *The 115th Infantry Regiment in World War Two*, Infantry Journal Press, Washington, 1948, pp292–3

26 Quoted in J. Sym (ed), *Seaforth Highlanders*, Gale & Polden, Aldershot, 1962, pp257–8

27 E. D. Smith, *The Battles for Cassino*, p162

28 G. Cox, pp73–4

29 L. Simpson, p114

30 Quoted in D. Erskine, *The Scots Guards 1919–55*, W. Clowes, 1956, pp143–4

31 G. Wilson, p13

32 S. Bagnall, p184

33 Quoted in D. C. Quilter (ed), p222

34 Smith, *op cit*, p103

35 M. J. P. M. Corbally, *The Royal Ulster Rifles*, private publication, nd, p157

36 Quoted in J. L. Moulton, *The Battle for Antwerp*, p90

37 D. C. Quilter (ed), p146

38 R. L. Crimp, p197
39 Quoted in A. Muir, *The First of Foot*, private publication, 1961, pp313–14
40 Binkowski and Plant, *op cit*, p166
41 Quoted in C. Whiting, *Bloody Aachen*, p43
42 Quoted in D. Congdon (ed), *Combat: European Theatre*, p247
43 Quoted in P. A. Crowl, p258
44 Quoted in L. Mayo, p198
45 H. Buggy, p198
46 Captain C. Matthieu Jr, quoted in C. H. Metcalf (ed), p515
47 Quoted in P. O'Sheel and G. Cook, pp36–7
48 Quoted in US War Department, *Makin*, pp72–3
49 Quoted in P. O'Sheel and G. Cook, p76
50 *Ibid*, p97
51 *Ibid*, p94
52 Quoted in C. S. Nichols and H. I. Shaw, p237
53 M. Myers, *op cit*, p301
54 S. Bidwell, p218
55 Tanks and artillery were also widely used and this is dealt with in Chapter 4
56 K. W. Cooper, pp12–13
57 No mean task. For the invasion of Sicily, the 45th US Division took along 83 tons of maps
58 G. Cox, p39
59 Quoted in Whiting, *op cit*, p43
60 Quoted in S. L. Falk, *The Liberation . . .*, p129
61 C. B. MacDonald, *The Siegfried . . .*, p262
62 J. D'Arcy Dawson, *Tunisian Battle*, p60
63 A. B. Austin, p54
64 P. Cochrane, p57
65 Quoted in K. Douglas and W. A. B. Greenhous, p215
66 Quoted in A. McKee, *Caen . . .*, p185
67 Quoted in D. Congdon, *op cit*, p347
68 Quoted in E. Belfield and H. Essame, pp123–4. The mention of pistols here justifies a few remarks on Allied weapons. Artillery, mortars and machine guns were just as effective in their hands as in those of the enemy, but certain other weapons, especially those that tend to feature prominently in Hollywood's version of World War II, left much to be desired. Of no weapon was this more true than the officer's pistol. A wounded officer in Normandy, Captain H. H. T. Hudson (9th Parachute Battalion) thought '[I] ought to do something to help before I died, so I got out my revolver and wavering it at the nearest emplacement, I managed after a physical effort to pull the trigger. In fiction, of course, the bullet would have gone through the heart of the German battery commander: in real life it went straight through my right foot'. (Quoted in McKee, *op cit*, pp40–1.) According to an authority on small arms, one general has said that in the whole war 'he was present when precisely thirty men were

wounded or killed by pistol fire. Sadly, twenty-nine were of his own side, and were the victims of accidental discharges, or neglect of safety precautions'. (J. Weeks, p22.) Whilst grenades were definitely much more effective, and very widely used, an American soldier has reminded us that they could not be handled with the gay abandon of a John Wayne or an Errol Flynn. 'Grenades were one of the most fearfully respected and accident-prone tricky instruments an infantryman had to deal with. They were often as likely to hurt your own people or yourself as the enemy. Usually we spread the cotter pins so wide that it took a strong arm to pull the pin out; teeth wouldn't do it. And if we wore them hanging by their rings under our pocket flaps, we made damn sure the spoon levers were taped to the grenade body with the tape from the cylinders the grenades came in. You didn't let the spoon fly off and ignite the fuse in your hand, because many grenades, though they were supposed to have three-second fuses, had fuses of two seconds, one second, and a lethal few had half-second fuses. A lady fuse-cutter at the grenade factory defence plant with a hangover could wreak real havoc with a box of grenades.' (J. Jones, WW II, p110.) Finally, that great American favourite, the Thompson gun, was rarely used with the casual ruthlessness of the cinematic soldier. It used a very large bullet and was an extremely difficult weapon to control, invariably firing high and to the right unless gripped very securely

69 Quoted in K. Douglas and W. A. B. Greenhous, p215
70 Quoted in Moulton, op cit, p31
71 Quoted in R. Grant, p121
72 Quoted in D. Hawkins (ed), pp263–4
73 Artillery barrages, however, were infrequent. The largest, on the Kyaukmeyaung bridgehead over the Irrawaddy in 1945, utilised only fifty guns
74 Quoted in US War Department, op cit, p70
75 M. Smeeton, p63
76 G. S. Johns, pp106, 154–5
77 Quoted in K. Ayling, p128
78 C. H. Metcalf, pp501–9; also P. O'Sheel and G. Cook, pp311–16
79 C. H. Metcalf, pp515–16
80 M. Myers, op cit, p78
81 A. J. Barker, The March on Delhi, p111
82 H. Maule, Spearhead General, p225
83 Quoted in M. Carver, El Alamein, p110
84 L. Atwell, p168
85 Quoted in K. Douglas and W. A. B. Greenhous, p134
86 S. Berlin, p61
87 K. Douglas and W. A. B. Greenhous, p142
88 This could create considerable problems for the Quartermaster Corps, for it was often not feasible to reclaim the gear left behind or get it forward again to its owners. As General Littlejohn wrote, of those European theatres where 'local actions . . . consisted of a life

and death race across a 50yd space. The American soldier skinned down to the clothes he had on, his rifle, his ammunition belt . . ., and one day's ration. The blankets, shoulder pack, overshoes were left in a dugout which he had made for himself. Raincoat and blanket were usually at the bottom. The shelter half was staked down on top of the hole and covered with about two feet of dirt. The items left behind . . . were scavenged by the natives. Another important thing in the high consumption of clothing and equipage was mud. If one dropped his knife, fork, spoon or mess kit at night it disappeared in the mud and had to be replaced. At the close of the Battle of Normandy it was necessary for me to . . . re-equip approximately 1,000,000 American soldiers almost as if they were completely naked'. (Quoted in W. F. Ross and C. F. Romanus, pp573–4)

89 J. Belden, pp12–13
90 K. Douglas, p5
91 R. Crisp, *Brazen Chariots*, p31
92 N. McCallum, p13
93 *Ibid*, pp88–9
94 Quoted in P. O'Sheel and G. Cook, pp101–2
95 N. Frankel and L. Smith, pp20, 14
96 See S. A. Stouffer *et al*, vol 2, p71
97 J. Jones, *WW II*, p39
98 In this instance, one suspects this to be the case with the officers, whose consciousness of the responsibilities of leadership and the need to set an example probably greatly influenced their answers
99 G. Wilson, p93
100 S. A. Stouffer *et al*, vol 2, p202
101 *Ibid*, p201
102 A. Baron, *From the City* . . ., p110
103 P. Bowman, p12
104 Quoted in W. Richardson, pp88–90
105 Quoted in P. O'Sheel and G. Cook, p88
106 T. Carew, *The Longest Retreat*, p130
107 J. Belden, p15
108 S. A. Stouffer *et al*, vol 2, p186
109 *Ibid*, pp174–5
110 J. Steinbeck, p122
111 L. H. Bartemeier *et al*, p368
112 A. Wilson, p66
113 R. Crisp, *The Gods* . . ., p12
114 Quoted in R. Grant, p129
115 J. Watney, p192
116 P. Cochrane, pp173–4
117 K. Douglas, pp23–4
118 N. McCallum, p52
119 R. Crisp, *op cit*, p55
120 Quoted in R. Grant, p117
121 J. G. Gray, p102

122 *Battle*, articles from *Saturday Evening Post*, Whiting & Wheadon, 1966, p200
123 H. Pond, p67
124 J. Steinbeck, p124
125 P. O'Sheel and G. Cook, p86
126 J. Lucas, p189
127 Quoted in R. Grant, p21
128 A. Wilson, p115
129 R. Ingersoll, *The Battle is . . .*, p158
130 E. Sevareid, *Not So Wild a Dream*, Knopf, New York, 1946, p182
131 C. Mitchell, p52
132 N. Frankel and L. Smith, p74
133 Quoted in J. Sym (ed), *Seaforth Highlanders*, Gale & Polden, Aldershot, 1962, p246
134 Quoted in N. McCallum, p50
135 Quoted in G. H. Johnston, p122
136 O. White, p283
137 Quoted in K. Douglas and W. A. B. Greenhous, pp107–8
138 Quoted in C. Whiting, *op cit*, p32
139 Quoted in P. O'Sheel and G. Cook, p38
140 Ingersoll, *op cit*, p184
141 F. Nauheim, p39
142 S. Berlin, p93
143 G. S. Johns, p180
144 P. Elstob, *Warriors . . .*, p105
145 M. Lindsay, p52
146 Quoted in R. Grant, p115
147 R. Crisp, *The Gods . . .*, pp191–2
148 R. L. Crimp, p114
149 Sergeant L. R. Gariepy (6th Canadian Armoured Regiment) quoted in A. McKee, *Caen . . .*, p103
150 Quoted in E. Belfield and H. Essame, p240

Chapter 4 (*Combat: Artillery and Armour*)

1 The peak British artillery strength on the Western Front, in World War I, was 8,760 pieces
2 In Tunisia, however, such concentrations were rare. One unit history has commented: '[Because the armour was used in penny packets] their artillery, their normal partners in tank warfare, rushed up and down the so-called "line" in detached batteries and troops, supporting improvised forces against unexpected attacks.' (R. F. Johnson, *Regimental Fire*, private publication, 1958, p186)
3 E. Linklater, pp143–4
4 1,050 pieces as compared with 1,481 available to the Fourth Army prior to the Somme offensive in July 1916
5 Quoted in A. McKee, *Caen . . .*, p355

6 However, on the few occasions where the terrain was suitable, guns were used in large numbers. On Okinawa, between 1 April and 22 June 1945, field guns loosed off 1,766,352 rounds

7 Quoted in I. V. Hogg, p133. In every theatre the material and moral effect of artillery hardly ever caused units to crack *en masse*. The only known case in north-west Europe was at Bauchem in November 1944, where the 150 entrenched German defenders offered absolutely no resistance when the infantry assault finally went in

8 Quoted in W. E. Duncan, pp134-5

9 Quoted in H. Maule, *Spearhead General*, p225

10 Quoted in W. E. Duncan, pp110-11. This use of field and anti-tank guns in small groups for bunker-blasting was one of the commonest roles for artillery in the Far East and the Pacific and it will be discussed further in the next section of this chapter, as this was also the main function of armour in these theatres

11 Though not completely. On the Salerno beachhead, the 189th US Artillery Battalion was almost overrun in a German armoured thrust. The action gave rise to a famous Texan war cry, for when the battalion commander was asked for orders as the tanks reached the very edges of the gun-pits he simply said, 'Put out local security, and if necessary fight with the rammer staff'

12 E. Pyle, *Brave Men*, pp100-1

13 J. Guest, p199

14 S. Berlin, p177

15 A. Wilson, p47

16 By the end of the war Britain and the USA had produced 113,213 tanks as against 24,360 manufactured in Germany

17 R. Farran, p37

18 L. F. Ellis, *Welsh Guards at War*, Gale & Polden, Aldershot, 1946, p201

19 R. Crisp, *Brazen Chariots*, p39

20 The Yeomanry were territorial regiments raised in the nineteenth century. A few of them actually fought on horseback in Syria, in 1941. Many of them became tankmen, though thirty-two regiments were converted to artillery

21 Crisp, *op cit*, p96

22 Quoted in K. J. Macksey, *Tank Force*, p79

23 An armoured regiment or tank battalion had a theoretical establishment of 670 officers and men and 61 tanks

24 B. Liddell Hart, *The Tanks*, p226

25 Quoted in C. N. Barclay, *History of the 16/5th Queen's Royal Lancers*, Gale & Polden, Aldershot, 1963, p91

26 Macksey, *op cit*, p96

27 R. Ingersoll, *The Battle is . . .*, p188

28 R. L. V. B. ffrench-Blake, *History of the 17/21st Lancers 1922-59*, Macmillan, 1962, p153

29 R. M. P. Carver, *Second to None*, private publication, nd, pp105-6

30 S. Bagnall, p201

31 Quoted in A. Brett-James, *Ball of Fire*, Gale & Polden, Aldershot, 1951, p192

32 P. Jordan, p249

33 G. L. Verney, *The Desert Rats*, Hutchinson, 1954, p141

34 Quoted in J. Bright (ed), *The 9th Queen's Royal Lancers 1936–45*, Gale & Polden, Aldershot, 1951, pp168–9

35 Quoted in C. Ryan, *The Last Battle*, p92

36 Quoted in D. Erskine, *The Scots Guards 1919–45*, W. Clowes, Edinburgh, 1956, pp345–6

37 R. J. B. Sellar, *The Fife and Forfar Yeomanry 1919–56*, Blackwood, Edinburgh, 1960, pp227–8

38 *Ibid*, pp226–7

39 G. L. Verney, *op cit*, p271

40 A. Graham, *Sharpshooters at War*, Regimental Association, 1964, p237

41 J. D. P. Stirling, *The First and the Last*, Art and Educational Publishers, 1946, p65

42 P. Elstob, *Warriors . . .*, p275

43 J. Foley, pp180–1

44 Quoted in US War Department *St. Lô*, p22

45 Quoted in Erskine, *op cit*, p366

46 Quoted in D. Orgill, pp178–9

47 Quoted in Sellar, *op cit*, p172

48 Quoted in McKee, *op cit*, p363

49 Quoted in B. Perrett, *Tank Tracks . . .*, p109

50 M. Myers, *Ours to Hold it High*, Infantry Journal Press, Washington, 1947, p108

51 Quoted in *ibid*, pp328–9

52 Quoted in Perrett, *op cit*, p162

53 J. Foley, p148

54 R. Farran, p34

55 A Sherman crew consisted of 5 men: the commander who stood in the turret all the time, the gunner who sat on a small seat in the turret peering through a small periscope about 6in by 2in, and also in the turret the operator-loader who loaded the breech, worked the machine gun and operated the wireless. In the actual hull, at the front, were the driver, who was also in charge of maintenance, and the co-driver who was usually appointed cook as he had the least to do

56 Elstob, *op cit*, p23

57 Quoted in B. Perrett, *Through Mud . . .*, p163

58 Macksey, *op cit*, pp130–1

59 Crisp, *op cit*, p57

60 Quoted in Liddell Hart, *op cit*, p30

61 Quoted in O. Fitzroy, *Men of Valor*, private publication, Liverpool, 1961, vol 3, p160

62 An armoured box. A defensive position of tanks and infantry or tanks alone in which the armour was drawn up in a defensive perimeter, not unlike a circle of American pioneers' covered wagons

63 Quoted in Liddell Hart, *op cit*, pp210–11
64 Quoted in I. Halstead, p117
65 Replenishment with fuel might involve up to 100 gallons, all of which came in jerrycans, and all of which had to be manhandled and poured into the petrol tank
66 Quoted in Erskine, *op cit*, pp366–7
67 N. Frankel and L. Smith, p94
68 J. Foley, p66
69 F. Nauheim, p14
70 Quoted in R. Sherrod, p107
71 D. Orgill, pp112–13
72 Elstob, *op cit*, p23
73 M. Blumenson, *Rommel's* . . ., pp65–6
74 A. Wilson, p48
75 N. Frankel and L. Smith, pp136–7
76 N. Lewis, *Naples 44*, Collins, 1978, p21
77 Bagnall, *loc cit*

Chapter 5 (*Casualties*)

1 See Appendix for a breakdown of casualties by country. It should be borne in mind that the exactitude of most of these figures is spurious. Any attempt to reconcile different sets of casualty figures inevitably ends in confusion, and they should only be regarded as approximate guides. In many instances figures simply do not exist and some of my estimates for numbers serving overseas are only informed inferences. Readers who instinctively feel that the figures for the US forces are too low should bear in mind that the Army Air Force, a vast organisation, is not included
2 W. S. Churchill, *The Second World War*, Cassells, 1948, vol 2, pp619–21
3 A further indication of the need for this sort of adjustment is given in the casualty rates for those countries that were not able to supply much of a supportive tail of their own, and which are much higher than those for either Britain or America. New Zealand is a prime example here. If the total number of dead and wounded are expressed as a percentage of the total number who served overseas, the figures for the UK and USA are 13.88 and 16.9 respectively, whilst the New Zealand rate is over 20 per cent. The high proportion of Canadian dead and wounded in Europe, almost 22 per cent of the peak number serving there, is another example of battle casualty figures relatively undistorted by the presence of a large but inactive tail
4 41,296 POWs and missing at Dunkirk, 113,451 at Singapore, 9,713 in Greece and Crete, and 32,220 at Tobruk
5 M. Lindsay, p249
6 Though they of course proliferate at senior levels. Officers made up

almost 6 per cent of American divisions and, by 1945, 10.8 per cent of the total army. The reader is also referred to Table 4

7 S. A. Stouffer *et al*, vol 2, p102

8 In the following section it will be useful to bear in mind that the theoretical strength of a British and American infantry battalion was about 36 officers and 800 men. Only about 370 of these were actual riflemen

9 Montgomery has been accused of being a somewhat ponderous and unimaginative general. Casualty figures as low as these seem to be a powerful vindication. The 143 battalions that attacked on the first day of the Somme suffered 50 per cent casualties

10 G. W. Beebe and M. E. de Bakey, pp48–57

11 It must be noted, at least in passing, that Japanese casualties were staggering. The kill ratio in some battles must be amongst the highest in the history of war. On Leyte-Samar the 1st Cavalry Division killed 5,937 Japanese for the loss of 241 men, on Luzon the ratio was 14,114 for 680

12 Quoted in Vaughan-Thomas, p141

13 Expressed as a percentage of their original strength

14 This point is best illustrated by certain British figures. Two battalions recorded the following battle casualties in north-west Europe:

	1944							1945				
	Jun	Jul	Aug	Sep	Oct	Nov	Dec	Jan	Feb	Mar	Apr	May
5th Coldstream	11	32	47	50	7	3	1	1	17	21	36	0
5th K.S.L.I.	10	49	45	44	27	4	2	3	9	15˙	49	2

15 Quoted in US War Department, *St. Lô*, p126

16 Quoted in C. Whiting, *Bloody Aachen*, pp60–1

17 C. B. MacDonald, *The Siegfried . . .*, pp470–1

18 M. Lindsay, p150

19 Venereal disease is dealt with in Chapter 7

20 Though even in these circumstances inexperience could create problems. During the Tarawa battle, empty LVTs were used to ferry back the wounded. One convoy of fifteen boats had been so badly shot about during the approach to the beaches that all of them, loaded with casualties, sank on the return journey

21 This process of selection was known as 'triage'

22 O. White, pp189–90

23 A battalion's own stretcher bearers were recruited from the regimental bandsmen

24 Considerable numbers of medical personnel were needed. In 1945 the Royal Army Medical Corps numbered 11,421 doctors, and there were another 5,482 in the Indian Army Medical Corps; 83,000 other ranks also served. The US Medical Corps utilised the services of 45,000 doctors, the same number of nurses and half a million enlisted men. As regards doctors, this meant that the Americans called

40 per cent of their practising doctors to serve only 8 per cent of the nation's manpower

25 44 per cent of died-of-wounds cases were in north-west Europe
26 Many more men survived such wounds than might be expected. Whilst US figures show that 47 per cent of all fatal wounds were in the head, those who were not killed instantly had a good chance of surviving – around 80 per cent
27 Many samples give much lower figures but these generally also contain a high proportion of (unspecified) multiple wounds
28 Neither sample adds up to 100 per cent because both include a proportion of multiple wounds
29 Indian troops were also significantly more immune to dysentery, sandfly fever and several other diseases. The importance of this can be gauged from the fact that, between November 1944 and May 1945, the average strength of the 14th Army included 127,000 Indian troops and only 47,000 British
30 J. Dos Passos, p19
31 F. A. E. Crew (ed), vol 4, p422
32 *Ibid*, vol 1, p249
33 *Ibid*, vol 5, p640
34 Whiting, *op cit*, p61
35 Letter to the *Sunday Times*, 11 June 1978

Chapter 6 (*Discipline and Morale*)

1 The US category 'sergeant' includes those in the British army who would be referred to as 'warrant officers'
2 A few men were commissioned directly from the ranks whilst on active service, but in the US army such commissions were only 5.5 per cent of the total
3 D. Erskine, *The Scots Guards 1919–45*, W. Clowes, Edinburgh, 1956, p81
4 R. L. Crimp, p154
5 J. A. I. Agar-Hamilton, p154
6 A. B. Austin, p93
7 W. Vaughan-Thomas, p217
8 Quoted in R. Grant, p129
9 F. Majdalany, *Patrol*, p19
10 Though not to the Guards, who retained the traditional system
11 S. A. Stouffer *et al*, vol 1, pp366–7; vol 2, p121
12 J. Mulgan, pp49–50
13 Quoted in S. A. Stouffer *et al*, vol 2, pp117 and 124
14 P. Jordan, p96
15 Quoted in R. L. Eichelberger, p49
16 A. Wilson, p127
17 Quoted in S. A. Stouffer *et al*, vol 1, p389

18 H. Brotz and E. Wilson, 'Characteristics of Military Society', American Journal of Sociology', vol 51, 1946, p373

19 Ralph Lewis, an American officer cadet was drilling a platoon when his instructor intervened and said '[I] needed more force and abruptness in my commands. "If you want men to follow your commands," he said, "you will have to shout at them as you do at an animal; for instance, when you shout 'Come here!' to your dog."' (R. Lewis, 'Officer-Enlisted Men's Relationships', *American Journal of Sociology*, vol 51, 1946, p413)

20 Quoted in S. A. Stouffer *et al*, vol 1, pp213–15

21 A. Wilson, p96

22 K. Douglas and W. A. B. Greenhous, p109

23 Quoted in M. Anglo, pp79–80

24 Quoted in J. Vader, *Anzac*, p107

25 See *Report of the Army and Air Force Court Martial Committee*, Cmd 7608, 1949, p15

26 See S. Crozier, *A History of the Corps of Military Police*, Gale & Polden, Aldershot, p121

27 M. R. McCallum, 'The Study of the Delinquent in the Army', *American Journal of Sociology*, vol 51, 1946, p481. Though General Harmon's qualification on this point should be noted. 'Very little of the pillaging was done by combat troops; their discipline was higher, they had no way to transport booty, and perhaps most important, they were too busy fighting . . .' (Quoted in C. Whiting, *Bloody Aachen*, p76)

28 R. L. Crimp, p120

29 McCallum, *op cit*, p482. This officer relates that at one point 6 officers and 182 men of a railroad battalion were court martialled for the systematic appropriation of whole wagon-loads of army supplies

30 Quoted in R. Grant, p29

31 Quoted in M. Cunliffe, *The Royal Irish Fusiliers 1793–1950*, Oxford University Press, 1952, p390

32 J. Verney, p97

33 G. Malcolm, *The Argyllshire Highlanders*, Halberd Press, Glasgow, nd, p130

34 J. Belden, pp24–5

35 L. J. Thompson, 'Operational Strains: Psychological Casualties in the Field', in Royal Society of Medicine, *Inter-Allied Conferences on War Medicine*, Staples Press, 1947, p240

36 S. A. Stouffer *et al*, vol 2, p78

37 J. Steinbeck, pp123–4

38 *History of the East Lancashire Regiment in the War*, Rawson & Co, Manchester, 1953, p213

39 B. Mauldin, pp144–7

40 Quoted in A. McKee, *Caen* . . ., p338

41 Quoted in N. Nicholson, *The Grenadier Guards*, Gale & Polden, Aldershot, 1949 (2 vols), p153

42 Quoted in C. Wilmot, p409

43 Quoted in R. Ingersoll, *Top Secret*, p185
44 Quoted in E. Belfield and H. Essame, p147
45 Quoted in A. Graham, *Sharpshooters at War*, Regimental Associ-
    ation, 1964, p9
46 N. McCallum, p69
47 Quoted in H. Maule, *Spearhead General*, pp221–2
48 W. Woodruff, p130
49 J. Jones, *WW II*, p41
50 S. A. Stouffer *et al*, vol 2, p88
51 Quoted in *ibid*, p90
52 P. Jordan, p68
53 O. White, pp204–5
54 P. Cochrane, pp138–9
55 Conversation with the author
56 S. A. Stouffer *et al*, vol 2, p88
57 *Ibid*, p90
58 N. Frankel and L. Smith, p81
59 In the British army, the death penalty for desertion had been abol-
    ished in April 1930
60 Private M. Slovik (28th US Division). Sentenced, European
    Theatre of Operations, 11 November 1944
61 R. H. Ahrenfeldt, p273
62 Jones, *op cit*, p139
63 M. Lindsay, p241
64 J. Horsfall, p89
65 H. L. Bond, p92. The problems were not insuperable, however, and
    quite a few hard cases managed to vanish from the ken of authority,
    mainly by organising themselves into large gangs. There were sev-
    eral of these preying upon the base areas in the Middle East, with
    names like the Dead End Kids and the British Free Corps. In Crete,
    numbers of men from the abortive Greek expedition took to the hills
    and remained there until the end of the war. In Italy there were
    many blood-curdling tales about units of Moroccan *goums* who had
    vanished into the mountains and taken over whole villages, whilst
    many roads were subject to harassment by bands of British and
    American deserters. On New Guinea, an Australian company of the
    39th Battalion won a fortnight's home leave in a brigade competition
    for the best camouflaged defence post. On reaching Australia they
    went AWOL to a man. In Brussels one group of deserters set
    themselves up as the so-called 'Field Corps Police' with their own
    unit sign, number and workshop where they repaired and sold a
    succession of stolen vehicles
66 Roughly 80 per cent of soldiers suffering from battle exhaustion
    were returned to some kind of duty, around 30 per cent back to their
    combat units. Most of these groups were back with their units within
    a week
67 L. H. Bartemeier *et al*, p367
68 Quoted in *ibid*, p368

69 Quoted in S. K. Weinberg, 'The Combat Neuroses', *American Journal of Sociology*, vol 51, 1946, p471

70 J. W. Appel and G. W. Beebe, 'Preventive Psychiatry: An Epidemiological Approach', *Journal of the American Medical Association*, 131 (1946), p1470

71 As no soldier fights all the time, 10 combat days were assumed to be spread over 17 calendar days

72 A. J. Liebling, *Normandy Revisited*, Gollancz, 1959, p107

73 Quoted in K. Douglas and W. A. B. Greenhous, p215

74 R. L. Swank and W. E. Marchand, pp238–41

75 Jones, *op cit*, p86

76 E. Pyle, *Brave Men*, p270

77 Ingersoll, *op cit*, p185

78 N. Frankel and L. Smith, p89

79 Quoted in Weinberg, *op cit*, p472

80 B. Mauldin, p39

81 S. Bagnall, p160

82 P. Davies, pp252–3

83 Majdalaney, *op cit*, pp106–7

84 H. L. Bond, pp130–1

85 G. Wilson, pp90–1

86 Quoted in P. M. Ross, p96

87 F. A. E. Crew (ed), vol 2, p507

88 Major General E. Weston quoted in J. H. Spenser, p61

89 R. Crisp, *The Gods . . .*, p143. At a much later date, however, inexperienced troops were still likely to panic in the face of sustained bombing. In December 1942, certain First Army units around Tebourba, in Tunisia, had to be removed from the line because they were so unsettled by German aerial attacks

90 Quoted in S. L. Falk, *Seventy Days . . .*, p126

91 Quoted in *ibid*, p141

92 Quoted in M. Howard, *The Coldstream Guards*, Oxford University Press, 1951, pp44–5

93 E. T. C. Gordine, p157

94 L. Farago, p197

95 P. Jordan, p233

96 R. McKelvie, p260

97 R. L. V. B. ffrench-Blake, *History of the 17/21st Lancers 1922–59*, Macmillan, 1962, p209

98 Euphemism is a major feature of official and semi-official pronouncements upon this topic. Of an infantry attack in November 1944 an armoured regimental history chides: 'There were those who thought that, without straining themselves, the infantry might have advanced with slightly less deliberation.' (Graham, *op cit*, p230)

99 J. D. P. Stirling, *The First and the Last*, Art and Educational Publishers, 1946, p91

100 R. Crisp, *Brazen Chariots*, p195; see also p156

101 Quoted in Vader, *op cit*, p104

102 The strike was purely nominal in that the Canadians were fed by fellow members of their division, the 9th British Paratroop Battalion
103 It is worth noting, however, that with regard to the Vietnam war the authorities admitted to numerous cases of 'fragging': 96 in 1969 and 209 in the following year
104 See H. Pond, pp208ff
105 Cunliffe, *op cit*, p390
106 P. Knightley, *The First Casualty*, Harvest Books, New York, 1975, p232. All his details come from R. Collier, pp41, 123–4, 177–9, 233. See also pp76 and 156
107 See Collier, *op cit, passim*, as well as D. Divine, *The Nine Days . . .*, or R. Jackson, *Dunkirk*
108 Quoted in Falk, *op cit*, p231
109 Quoted in C. Bateson, p133
110 Quoted in T. Carew, *The Longest Retreat*, p73
111 G. C. Kenny, *General Kenney Reports*, Duell, Sloan & Pearce, New York, 1948, pp154–7
112 R. L. Eichelberger, p180
113 Quoted in H. Essame, *Patton . . .*, p68
114 Quoted in Maule, *op cit*, p142
115 R. H. Ahrenfeldt, pp183–4
116 R. Lewis, pp16 and 18. See also J. Belden, pp61 and 151–2. The latter notes that on 12 September '1st Battalion 142nd Infantry [45th US Division] retreated in disorder, some of the troops in a panic, and were not stopped until they reached the gun lines . . .' (p152)
117 Quoted in H. Pond, p109
118 Liebling, *op cit*, pp24–5
119 Richardson, *op cit*, p109
120 McKee, *op cit*, p248
121 Quoted in E. Belfield and H. Essame, p184
122 C. B. MacDonald, *The Siegfried . . .*, pp54–5
123 *Ibid*, pp364–5
124 C. B. MacDonald, *The Last Offensive*, p78

Chapter 7 (*Relaxation*)

1 G. L. Verney, *The Desert Rats*, Hutchinson, 1954, p23
2 I. Halstead, p117
3 R. L. Crimp, p90
4 N. McCallum, p75
5 E. T. C. Gordine, p37
6 K. Douglas, p111
7 R. Farran, p38
8 C. Beaton, p71
9 R. Crisp, *Brazen Chariots*, p114
10 K. Douglas, p111

11 Quoted in A. McKee, *Caen . . .*, p199
12 J. Horsfall, p35
13 J. Watney, p190
14 Quoted in McKee, *op cit*, p256
15 P. Cochrane, p127
16 Quoted in R. Braddon, p199
17 P. Cochrane, p150
18 L. Melling, p68
19 S. Berlin, p122
20 Quoted in A. Swinson, p123
21 Quoted in E. D. Martineau, *A History of the Royal Sussex Regiment*, Moore & Tillyer, Chichester, nd, p289
22 A. Muir, *The First of Foot*, private publication, Edinburgh, 1961, p233
23 Quoted in N. Nicholson, *The Grenadier Guards*, Gale & Polden, Aldershot, 1949 (2 vols), p419
24 J. Foley, p155
25 W. Woodruff, p74
26 A day's menu contained, in theory at least, 3,668 calories
27 A. P. Stauffer, pp3–4–5
28 R. Ingersoll, *The Battle is . . .*, p77
29 C. H. Metcalf (ed), p516
30 O. White, p48
31 M. S. Babcock, p98
32 B. Mauldin, pp168–9
33 H. L. Bond, p64
34 W. F. Ross and C. F. Romanus, p527
35 G. S. Johns, p90. From early June 1944, four 10in candles had been included in the 10-in-1 ration. There were also small, one-burner Coleman stoves but these were never available in sufficient quantities
36 In other theatres, the ration was more plentiful. Even in Sicily US forces were receiving around 2gal each per day, though it is worth bearing in mind that the *per capita* consumption in Las Vegas, for example, at this time was 100gal per day
37 C. R. Lucas-Phillips, *Alamein*, p24
38 W. Trebich, p63
39 R. L. Crimp, p14
40 *Ibid*, p33
41 R. Farran, p38
42 P. Cochrane, p8
43 Quoted in F. G. Richardson, p42
44 R. Crisp, *The Gods . . .*, p71
45 Crisp, *op cit*, p29
46 E. Pyle, *Brave Men*, p243
47 B. Mauldin, p169
48 W. F. Ross and C. F. Romanus, p214
49 Quoted in E. J. Kahn, *The Big Drink*, Max Reinhardt, 1960, p12

50 C. Whiting, *Battle of . . .*, p46
51 W. Vaughan-Thomas, p154
52 M. S. Babcock, p57
53 J. Jones, *The Thin . . .*, pp330–1
54 J. Jones, *WW II*, p94
55 J. Jones, *The Thin . . .*, p95
56 R. Crisp, *The Gods . . .*, p15
57 P. Cochrane, p172
58 J. Horsfall, p35
59 M. Lindsay, p122
60 C. Mitchell, p44
61 Q. V. B. Wallace, The Battle of Alamein and the Campaign in Libya, in Royal Society of Medicine, *Inter-Allied Conference on War Medicine*, Staples Press, 1947, p316
62 D. Erskine, *The Scots Guards 1919–55*, W. Clowes, 1956, p179
63 McKee, *op cit*, p86
64 Quoted in M. Anglo, p72
65 P. Cochrane, p7
66 E. Pyle, *op cit*, p447
67 H. Pond, p92
68 In fact, only 300,000 more combat troops than were available in 1918
69 In the British army there was an additional opportunity for a brief rest period under the LOB (Left Out of Battle) system. This had evolved in Tunisia and meant that the commanding officer or his second-in-command in each sub-unit was left out of a large-scale attack to form a cadre in the event of severe casualties. In many units this procedure was extended and a 'system of resting the more responsible, and therefore generally the most tired officers, warrant officers and indeed any other rank, was often practised in addition to the LOB arrangements . . .' (*History of the East Lancashire Regiment in the War*, Rawson & Co, Manchester, 1953, p38)
70 R. McKelvie, p273
71 Quoted in S. A. Stouffer *et al*, vol 1, p216
72 M. Lindsay, p150
73 In 1944 £1 = $4 = 500 lire = 66 piastres = 100 francs = 15 rupees
74 *Stars and Stripes*, 5 April 1945, p3. Altogether 280 Pocket titles were available. At the risk of sounding supercilious, it is likely that the popularity of the Zola work derived from its reputation, in those days, for being a 'dirty book'
75 As in such World War I favourites as 'When This Lousy War Is Over' and 'They Were Only Playing Leapfrog'
76 Though it was not really a contemporary number. The words were written in 1922 and the tune in 1938 and first sung by a Swedish girl, Elli Anderson, in that year in a Hamburg nightclub. It caught on among German troops in 1941 when it was played over the radio in Yugoslavia. Miss Anderson profited little; she ended up in a concentration camp

77 McKee, *op cit*, p154
78 In all ENSA spent £14,877,000. NAAFI, under whose umbrella they operated, had even more impressive outgoings. Their annual turnover rose from £8m in 1939 to £182m in 1945 and their trading establishments from 1,350 to 10,000. Even so these things should be kept in perspective; Britain's total defence expenditure in these 6 years was £22,174,800,000
79 Quoted in P. Nicholson, 'A Matter of Morale', *Sunday Times*, 17 February 1974, p42
80 R. L. Crimp, pp79–80
81 This latter point was a source of considerable bitterness. Of American troops in England it was said that there were three main problems – they were 'overpaid, oversexed and over here'. US overseas troops received $60 a month, though much of this was in fact sent back home, up to 73 per cent at one point in the ETO; Canadians got $1.50 a day, Australians 6s per day (plus 1s deferred until discharge), the British got 14s per week, less 2s compulsorily deducted for barrack-room damages and 7s family allotment
82 A. Cotterell, *Oh, It's Nice . . .*, p55
83 N. McCallum, p75
84 See R. Lewis, p115. This fact is not presented censoriously. Starvation was usually the only alternative
85 The officers' brothel was in Thompson Road and cost 75 rupees. Most of the women there were white, some of them the wives of absent officers keen to make a little pin money
86 In conversation with the author
87 W. Woodruff, p112
88 J. Steinbeck, p9
89 In this respect it is worth noting that whilst British other ranks in Burma, between 1942 and 1945, suffered an average of 92.9 cases per 1,000 men, the comparable figure for Indian troops was only 46.7
90 E. Pyle, *Here Is . . .*, p68
91 N. Frankel and L. Smith, p75
92 B. Mauldin, p162
93 On the Marianas, in 1945, there were 233 outdoor cinemas, 65 theatre stages, 3,500 radios, 95 soft-ball and 35 regular diamonds, 225 volley-ball and 30 basket-ball courts, as well as 35 boxing arenas
94 M. S. Babcock, p118
95 R. L. Eichelberger, p206
96 A. Gibbs, p134
97 A. J. Barker, *Eritrea, 1941*, p126
98 R. L. Crimp, p13
99 M. Lindsay, p31
100 Quoted in K. Douglas and W. A. B. Greenhous, p136
101 W. Woodruff, p109
102 R. Crisp, *Brazen Chariots*, pp112–13
103 J. Horsfall, p33
104 G. Wilson, p13
105 Quoted in Muir, *op cit*, pp299–300

Chapter 8 (*Attitudes*)

1 A. Wilson, p143
2 S. A. Stouffer *et al*, vol 2, p169
3 N. McCallum, p96
4 C. S. Nichols and H. I. Shaw, p154
5 Quoted in S. A. Stouffer *et al*, vol 2, p87
6 S. Berlin, p75
7 Quoted in J. Sym (ed), *Seaforth Highlanders*, Gale & Polden, Aldershot, 1962, p250
8 A. McKee, *Caen* . . ., pp215–16
9 In this respect it is significant that the authorities consistently felt it necessary to issue strict orders about non-fraternisation with either enemy POWs or, from 1945, German civilians. Under the terms of a directive from Eisenhower there was to be no 'mingling with Germans upon terms of friendliness, familiarity or intimacy, individually or in groups, in official dealings'. In the words of one official history, however, 'the policy soon broke down . . . [and] strict enforcement of such a rule, particularly in regard to children and women, proved impossible'. (C. B. MacDonald, *The Last Offensive*, p330)
10 S. A. Stouffer *et al*, vol 2, pp89 and 68
11 S. Bidwell, pp228–9
12 D. Billany, p294
13 P. Jordan, p79
14 H. Marshall, p58
15 J. Steinbeck, p55
16 Quoted in R. Verdin, *The Cheshire Yeomanry*, private publication, 1971, pp440–1
17 J. Jones, *The Thin* . . ., p47
18 N. McCallum, p55
19 J. G. Gray, p15
20 M. Anglo, p97. In terms of the sentiment expressed this poem is remarkably close to 'Back' by the World War I poet, W. W. Gibson
21 B. Mauldin, p46
22 H. L. Bond, pp16–17
23 R. L. Crimp, pp23–4
24 M. S. Babcock, p6
25 D. T. Brown, p64
26 Crimp, *loc cit*
27 R. Croft-Cooke, p35
28 J. Guest, pp160–1
29 Quoted in R. S. Allen, p193
30 W. Woodruff, p112
31 V. Scannel, p43
32 P. Davies, p258
33 The average strength of Fourteenth Army, between November 1944 and the following May comprised 47,142 British troops, 15,710

NOTES AND REFERENCES

Africans and 127,299 Indians. Five Indian Divisions, 4th, 5th, 6th, 8th and 10th, also fought in Africa and Italy

34 Both quoted in M. Anglo, pp76–7
35 Blacks only accounted for a maximum 8.62 per cent of the whole army whereas, in 1940, they comprised 10.1 per cent of the population
36 The 92nd and 93rd Infantry and 2nd Cavalry Divisions
37 Lieutenant K. Watt (3rd Royal Horse Artillery) quoted in H. Maule, *Spearhead General*, p118
38 Quoted in H. Tegner, *The Story of a Regiment*, F. Graham, Newcastle, 1969, pp84–5
39 K. Douglas, pp98–9
40 Quoted in R. Grant, p109
41 R. L. Crimp, p27
42 Quoted in S. A. Stouffer *et al*, vol 2, p296
43 R. L. Crimp, p93
44 W. F. Ross and C. F. Romanus, p236
45 S. A. Stouffer *et al*, vol 2, p296
46 *Ibid*, p302
47 R. Crisp, *Brazen Chariots*, p101
48 F. Tuker, pp141–2
49 G. Wilson, pp202–4
50 Quoted in S. A. Stouffer *et al*, vol 2, p131
51 J. Jones, *W W II*, p57
52 *Ibid*, p186
53 N. Frankel and L. Smith, p87
54 US War Department, *St. Lô*, p72
55 Quoted in M. Myers, *Ours to Hold it High*, Infantry Journal Press, Washington, 1947, p346
56 N. Frankel and L. Smith, p85
57 C. B. MacDonald, *The Siegfried . . .*, p470
58 *Ibid*, p469
59 M. S. Babcock, p118
60 J. G. Gray, p45
61 L. H. Bartemeier *et al*, p370
62 Quoted in R. H. Ahrenfeldt, p166
63 Quoted in F. A. E. Crew (ed), vol 4, p209
64 S. L. A. Marshall, *Men Against Fire*, pp42–3
65 J. G. Gray, p44
66 Quoted in A. Bryant, *Jackets of Green*, p411
67 Quoted in E. G. Godfrey, *op cit*, p119 (footnote)
68 B. Mauldin, p60
69 S. A. Stouffer *et al*, vol 2, p99
70 J. Mulgan, p76
71 C. MacInnes, *To The Victor . . .*, pp20–1
72 B. Mauldin, p58
73 A. Swinson, p184
74 J. Jones, *WWII*, p76

75 R. W. Thompson, *85 Days*, pp126–7
76 Quoted in H. Essame, *The Battle . . .*, p175
77 P. Elstob, pp57–8
78 S. Berlin, p71
79 R. W. Thompson, *Battle For . . .*, p156
80 Quoted in McKee, *op cit*, p317
81 J. Belden, p27
82 D. T. Brown, p66
83 Quoted in A. Muir, *The First of Foot*, private publication, Edinburgh, 1961, pp143–4
84 Quoted in R. Grant, p105
85 L. Critchell, p184
86 Quoted in A. Brett-James, p321
87 P. Cochrane, p174
88 R. Crisp, *op cit*, p167
89 Quoted in R. Grant, p105
90 F. Majdaleney, *Patrol*, p96
91 J. Mulgan, p77
92 A. Wilson, p146
93 S. Bagnall, p21
94 W. Woodruff, p107
95 H. L. Bond, pp242–3. He renders the ode as follows:

Even so, accept this tribute handed down
According to the old parental custom,
Moist with a brother's tears.
And, forever, brother, hail and farewell.

Chapter 9 (*Postscript*)

1 S. E. Morison, *History of United States Naval Operations in World War II*, Oxford University Press, 1948–62, vol 5, p315
2 W. Manchester, *Goodbye Darkness: A Memoir of the Pacific War*, Little Brown, Boston, 1980, p120
3 P. Fussell, *Wartime: Understanding and Behaviour in the Second World War*, Oxford University Press, 1989, pp80–81
4 L. Simpson, *Air With Armed Men*, London Magazine Editions, 1972, p101
5 W. D. & S. Whitaker, *The Battle of the Scheldt*, Souvenir Press, 1985, p252
6 H. Essame, *The 43rd Wessex Division at War*, Clowes, 1952, p56
7 Quoted in J. L. S. Scoullar, *Battle for Egypt: the Summer of 1942* (Official History of New Zealand in the Second World War 1939–45), Oxford University Press, 1955, p372
8 G. R. Stevens, *The History of the 2nd Gurkha Rifles*, Gale and Polden, Aldershot, 1952, vol 3, p106
9 M. Howard and G. Sparrow, *The Coldstream Guards 1920–46*, Oxford University Press, 1951, p212

NOTES AND REFERENCES

10 F. Majdalanay, *The Monastery*, John Lane, 1946, pp51, 56
11 A. Moorehead, *Eclipse*, Sphere Books, 1967, p58
12 Quoted in K. Ford, *Assault on Germany: the Battle for Geilenkirchen*, David and Charles, Newton Abbot, 1989, p32
13 E. G. Godfrey, *History of the Duke of Cornwall's Light Infantry 1939–45*, pvte pub, Aldershot, 1966, p340
14 Quoted in Whitaker & Whitaker, *op cit*, p276
15 *ibid*, p250
16 Manchester, *op cit*, pp113–14, 182, 258 and 359
17 E. B. Sledge, *With the Old Breed at Peleliu and Okinawa*, Presidio, Novato (Cal.), 1981, pp120–21 and 260. This book, rightly highlighted by Paul Fussell and John Keegan as one of the outstanding memoirs of any war, urgently deserves a British publisher
18 Quoted in R. Wallace, *The Italian Campaign*, Time–Life Books, Alexandria (Va.), 1978, pp116–17
19 Quoted in J. Ellis, *Cassino: the Hollow Victory*, Andre Deutsch, 1984, p59
20 Quoted in K. Beattie, *Dileas: the History of the 48th Highlanders of Canada*, pvte pub. Toronto, 1957, p566
21 Whitaker & Whitaker, *op cit*, pp168–9 and 250
22 G. Blake, *Mountain and Flood: the History of the 52nd (Lowland) Division 1939–46*, Glasgow University Press (Jackson & Son), Glasgow, 1950, p92
23 D. Chandler *et al* (eds), *The Papers of Dwight David Eisenhower*, John Hopkins Press, Baltimore, 1970, vol 4, p2349
24 C. B. MacDonald, *Company Commander*, Bantam, New York, 1978 (first pub 1947), p66
25 Quoted in Ellis, *op cit*, p73
26 This scandalous state of affairs was very common in the Canadian Army in winter 1944–5 when untrained rear echelon troops were drafted into rifle companies to make up for the unexpectedly heavy casualties. All this time, some 70,000 fully trained infantrymen who had not volunteered for service overseas remained in Canada. None were sent to Europe until January 1945, when more than three-quarters of them deserted or went AWOL. See Whitaker & Whitaker, *op cit* pp201–34
27 Whitaker & Whitaker, *op cit*, p219
28 Manchester, *op cit*, pp367–8
29 Lack of space has not permitted me to include any further details on armoured combat. Nevertheless, mention must be made here of three new books that between them give a very full picture of day-to-day life in a tank, with especially vivid descriptions of the cramped and fetid conditions inside and the terrible strain of being constantly alert for enemy tanks and anti-tank weapons. See G. Forty (ed.), *Tanks Across the Desert: the War Diary of Jake Wardrop*; N. Smith, *Tank Soldier: the Fight to Liberate Europe 1944*; and K. Tout, *Tank! 40 Hours of Battle, August 1944*
30 Quoted in Ellis, *op cit*, p64

31 J. Williams, *The Long Left Flank: The Hard Fought Way to the Reich 1944–45*, Leo Cooper, 1988, p164
32 Quoted in Ellis, *op cit*, p407
33 Sledge, *op cit*, p100
34 E. Sevareid, *Not So Wild A Dream*, Knopf, New York, 1946, p378
35 Majdalanay, *op cit*, p77
36 Quoted in J. P. Delaney, *The Blue Devils in Italy*, Infantry Journal Press, Washington, 1947, pxiv
37 Sledge, *op cit*, p315
38 Manchester, *op cit*, p391

Appendix

Army Battle Casualties by Country

	POPULATION	Served in Army	Served Overseas		Killed		
		% Population	% Pop	% Army	% Pop	% Army	O
U.S.A.	134,000,000	7,500,000 *	4,950,000		202,434		
		5.6	5.4	66.6	0.15	2.7	4
U.K.	47,000,000	3,788,000	2,640,000		126,734		
		8.0	5.62	69.69	0.3	3.3	4
CANADA	11,300,000	691,300	371,000		17,683		
		6.1	3.29	53.67	0.16	2.5	4
AUSTRALIA	7,100,000	726,543	396,661		10,694		
		10.2	5.6	54.5	0.15	1.47	2
N.Z.	1,700,000	138,000	105,000		5,414		
		8.12	6.17	76.0	0.3	3.92	5
S. AFRICA	2,400,000 †	132,194	?		3,378		
		5.51	?	?	0.14	2.55	
INDIA	339,000,000	3,698,000	398,613		24,338		
		1.09	0.12	10.78	0.007	0.66	6

* Includes Army and Marines but excludes Army Air Force
† Whites only
≠ All arms

396

Wounded			Missing & P.O.W.			Total Killed & Wounded			Total Casualties			Dead as % of Dead & Wounded
%op	% Army	% O/seas	% Pop	% Army	% O/seas	% Pop	% Army	% O/seas	% Pop	% Army	% O/seas	P.O.W. as % of Total Casualties
	641,013			103,918			843,447			947,365		24.0
.48	8.5	12.8	0.07	1.4	2.1	0.62	11.2	16.9	0.71	12.6	18.9	10.9
	239,575			203,192			366,509			569,501		34.57
.5	6.3	9.07	0.4	5.4	7.69	0.78	9.67	13.88	1.21	15.03	21.57	35.6
	51,660			6,432			69,343			75,775		25.50
.45	7.47	13.92	0.05	0.93	1.73	0.61	10.03	18.69	0.67	10.96	20.42	8.49
	22,116			30,117			32,810			62,927		32.59
.31	3.04	5.57	0.42	4.14	7.59	0.46	4.51	8.27	0.89	8.66	15.86	47.86
	16,270			10,686 ≠			21,684			32,370		24.97
.95	11.79	15.49	0.63	7.74	10.17	1.27	15.71	20.6	1.9	23.4	30.83	33.0
	7,236			12,271			10,614			22,885		31.82
.30	5.47	?	0.51	9.28	?	0.44	8.03	?	0.95	17.31	?	53.62
	64,354			91,243			88,692			179,935		27.44
.02	1.74	16.14	0.02	2.47	22.89	0.03	2.39	22.25	0.05	4.86	45.14	50.70

Extended Bibliography

I have not included in this Bibliography the dozens of unit histories
consulted. Generally their usefulness for this type of book is at best
sporadic. Those that have been of some help are cited in the Notes and
References. All books are published in London unless otherwise stated.

General Works

Bidwell, S. and Graham, D., *Fire-power: British Army Weapons and
  Theories of War*, Allen and Unwin, 1982
Bugler, W., *The Story of 114*, W. Bugler, Eastbourne, 1984
van. Creveld, M., *Fighting Power: German and U.S. Army Performance
  1939–45*, Arms and Armour Press, 1983
Crosskill, W. E., *The Thousand Mile War*, Robert Hale, 1980
Dank, M., *The Glider Gang: an Eyewitness History of World War II
  Glider Combat*, Cassell, 1977
Dear, I., *Ten Commando 1942–45*, Leo Cooper, 1987
Devlin, G. M., *Paratrooper! The Saga of Parachute and Glider Combat
  Troops During World War II*, Robson, 1979
Dintar, E., *Hero or Coward: Pressures Facing the Soldier in Battle*, Cass,
  1985
Ellis, J., *Cassino: the Hollow Victory*, André Deutsch, 1985
Englander, D. and Mason, T., *The British Soldier in World War II*,
  Centre for Social History, University of Warwick, Coventry, 1984
Fawkes, R., *Fighting for a Laugh: Entertaining the British and American
  Armed Forces 1939–46*, Macdonald and Janes, 1978
Ford, K., *Assault Crossing: the River Seine 1944*, David and Charles,
  Newton Abbot, 1988
——. *Assault on Germany: the Battle for Geilenkirchen*, David and
  Charles, Newton Abbot, 1989
Forty, G., *Fifth Army at War*, Ian Allen, Shepperton, 1980
——. *XIV Army at War*, Ian Allen, Shepperton, 1982
Fraser, D., *And We Shall Shock Them: the British Army in the Second
  World War*, Hodder and Stoughton, 1983
Frost, J., *A Drop Too Many*, Buchan and Enright, 1982 (2nd ed.)
Fussell, P., *Wartime: Understanding and Behaviour in the Second World
  War*, OUP, 1989
Golley, J., *The Big Drop: the Guns of Merville June 1944*, Janes, 1982
Griffith, P., *Forward into Battle: Fighting Tactics from Waterloo to
  Vietnam*, Antony Bird, 1981

Hargrove, H. B., *Buffalo Soldiers in Italy: Black Americans in World War II*, McFarland, 1985

Holmes, R., *Firing Line*, Jonathan Cape, 1985

Jefferson, A., *Assault on the Guns of Merville*, John Murray, 1987

Kellett, A., *Combat Motivation*, Kluwer-Nijheff, Boston (Mass.), 1982

Lewin, R., *Man of Armour: Lt-Gen Vyvan Pope and the Development of Armoured Warfare*, Leo Cooper, 1976

Lovell-Knight, A. V., *The Story of the Royal Military Police*, Leo Cooper, 1977

Marshall, S. L. A., *Island Victory: the Battle for Kwajalein in World War II*, (first pub. 1945), Zenger, Washington D.C., 1982

Martin, R. G., *The G.I. War 1941–45*, Little Brown, Boston, 1967

McDonough, J. L. and Gardner, R. S., *Sky Riders: History of the 327/401 Glider Infantry*, Battery Press, Nashville (Tenn.), 1980

McDougall, M. C., *Swiftly They Struck: the Story of No. 4 Commando*, Arms and Armour Press, 1986

Miller, H., *Service to the Services: the Story of NAAFI*, Newman Neame, 1971

Riordan, T. M. J., *7th Field Company R.E. 1939–46*, Riordan, York, 1984

Robertson, G. W., *The Rose and the Arrow: a Life Story of 136th Field Regiment R.A., 1939–46*, Old Comrades Association, Reigate, 1988

Smith, G., *When Jim Crow Met John Bull: Black American Soldiers in World War II in Britain*, I. B. Tauris, 1987

Smithers, A. J., *Rude Mechanicals: an Account of Tank Maturity During the Second World War*, Leo Cooper, 1987

Terkel, S., '*The Good War': an Oral History of World War Two*, Hamish Hamilton, 1982

Turnbull, P., *Battle of the Box*, Ian Allen, Shepperton, 1979

Vinie, A. A., *The Pompadours: 2 Battalion the Essex Regiment, D-Day to VE-Day in North-West Europe*, Royal Anglian Regiment, 1987

Whettan, J. T., *Z Location or Survey in War: the Story of the 4th Durham Survey Regiment R.T.A.*, R. H. Ogden, Bolton, 1982

Whitaker, W. D. and S., *The Battle of the Scheldt*, Souvenir Press, 1985

——. *Rhineland: the Battle to End the War*, Leo Cooper, 1989

Whiting, C. *Poor Bloody Infantry*, Stanley Paul, 1987

Williams, J., *The Long Left Flank: the Hard Fought Way to the Reich 1944–45*, Leo Cooper, 1988

Williamson, H., *104 Field Battery Royal Artillery: 3 September 1939 to 3 September 1945: an Informal History*, H. Williamson, Oxford, 1985, (2nd ed.)

Willis, L., *None Had Lances: the Story of the 24th Lancers*, Old Comrades Association, Old Coulsden, 1985

Zimmerman, J. L., *The Guadalcanal Campaign*, Historical Division USMC, Washington, 1949

Eye-Witness Accounts

Anderson, D., *Three Cheers for the Next Man to Die*, Hale, 1983

Atkins, D., *The Forgotten Major*, Toat, Pulborough, 1989

Aylett, S., *Surgeon at War*, New Horizon, Bognor Regis, 1979

Barrington-Whyte, J., *The Great Tribulation*, New Horizon, Bognor Regis, 1983

Bateman, G. C., *Diary of a Temporary Soldier*, G. C. Bateman, Guildford, 1986

Baty, J. A., *Surgeon in the Jungle War*, Kimber, 1979

Beach, G. R., *The Task Supreme*, New Horizon, Bognor Regis, 1983

Belchem, D., *All in the Day's March*, Collins, 1978

Bell, G., *Sideshow*, Muller, 1953

Blythe, J., *Soldiering on: A Soldier's War in Africa and Italy*, Tri-Service Press, Shrewsbury, 1989

Boel, G., *The Normandy Nobodies*, Blandford, 1988

Bowman, J. E., *Three Stripes and a Gun: a Young Man's Journey Towards Maturity*, Merlin, Braunton, 1987

Bracken, P. J. P., *2,500 Dangerous Days: a Gunner's Travels 1939–46*, Merlin, Braunton, 1988

Bright, P., *Life in our Hands*, MacGibbon and Kee, 1955

Burgett, D., *Currahee! A Paratrooper's Account of the Normandy Invasion*, Hutchinson, 1967

Byrne, J. V., *The General Salutes a Soldier*, Hale, 1986

Carfrae, C., *Chindit Column*, Kimber, 1985

Carnegie, S., *Noble Purpose*, Peter Davies, 1954

Carver, M., *Out of Step: Memoirs of a Field-Marshal*, Hutchinson, 1989

Cheetham, A. M., *Ubique*, Freshfield, Formby, 1987

Chettle, M. E., *The Road from Normandy*, Titus Wilson, Kendal, 1946

Cole, D., *Rough Road to Rome*, Kimber, 1983

Collister, P., *Then a Soldier*, Churchman, Worthing, 1985

Cooper, R., *B Company*, Dobson, 1978

Cox, G., *A Tale of Two Battles: a Personal memoir of Crete and the Western Desert 1941*, Kimber, 1987

Craig, N., *The Broken Plume: a Platoon Commander's Story 1940–45*, Imperial War Museum, 1982

Currey, C. B., *Follow Me and Die: the Destruction of an American Division in World War II*, Military Heritage Press, New York, 1984

Daniel, J., *The Siege*, Allison Busby, 1974

Davis, R., *Marine at War*, Little Brown, Boston, 1961

Denholm-Young, C. P. S., *Men of Alamein*, (first pub. 1943), Spa/Tom Donovan, 1987

Ding, D. F., *One of Many, or, A Soldier's Journal*, Ding, Prince's Risborough, 1989

Douglas, N., *And No Glory*, Corgi, 1958

Edgar, D., *The Day of Reckoning*, John Clare, n.d.

England, D., *The Great Turnabout: Being the Saga of a Young Officer*

During the Final Throes of the Second World War, Pallant, Havant, 1983

Finnerty, J. T., *All Quiet on the Irrawaddy*, New Horizon, Bognor Regis, 1979

Franklin, F. K., *Road Inland*, Hutchinson, 1958

Frost, C. S., *Once a Patricia: Memoirs of a Junior Officer in World War II*, Tri-Service Press, Shrewsbury, 1988

Fuller, S., *The Big Red One*, Corgi, 1980

Gallant, T. G., *The Friendly Dead*, Doubleday, New York, 1964

——.   *On Valor's Side*, Doubleday, New York, 1963

Galloway, S., *With the Irish Against Rommel*, Langley (Brit. Col.), 1984

Gander, M., *After These Many Quests*, Macdonald, 1949

George, J., *Shots Fired in Anger*, National Rifle Association, Washington, 1981, (2nd ed.)

Gilchrist, D., *Don't Cry For Me: the Commandos: D-Day and After*, Hale, 1982

Gilroy, F. D., *Private*, Harcourt Brace Jovanovich, New York, 1970

Glassop, L., *We Were the Rats*, Angus and Robertson, Melbourne, 1944

Golden, L., *Echoes From Arnhem*, Kimber, 1984

Goldstein, W., *Farewell Screw Gun*, The Book Guild, Lewes, 1986

Gruber, R. J., *No Room For Heroes*, Vantage Press, New York, 1972

Gullett, H., *Not As a Duty Only: an Infantryman's War*, (first pub. 1976), Melbourne U.P., Carleton, 1984

Hale, E. R. W. and Turner, J. F., *The Yanks Are Coming*, Midas, Tunbridge Wells, 1983

Hall, J., *A Soldier of the Second World War*, J. Hall, Bournemouth, 1986

Hall, P. *What a Way to Win a War*, Midas, Tunbridge Wells, 1978

Hammond, E., *1941–43: the War Diary of Edward Hammond*, Ixworth Association, Ixworth, 1980

Harpur, B., *The Impossible Victory: a Personal Account of the Battle for the River Po*, Kimber, 1980

Heading, J., *Ten Thousand Lines Across Europe*, Book Guild, Lewes, 1986

Henslow, J., *A Sapper With the Forgotten Army*, J. Henslow, Petersfield, 1986

Holbrook, D., *Flesh Wounds*, Methuen, 1966

Holding, R., *Since I Bore Arms*, R. Holding, Cirencester, 1987

Holman, G., *Stand By to Beach!*, Hodder and Stoughton, 1944

Horsfall, J., *Fling Our Banner to the Wind*, Roundwood Press, Kineton, 1978

——.   *Say Not the Struggle*, Roundwood Press, Kineton, 1977

How, J. J., *Hill 112: Cornerstone of the Normandy Campaign*, Kimber, 1984

——.   *Normandy: the British Breakout*, Kimber, 1981

Howarth, H., *Where Fate Leads*, Ross Anderson, Bolton, 1983

Howarth, P., *My God, Soldiers: From Alamein to Vienna*, Hutchinson, 1989

James, R. R., *Chindit*, John Murray, 1980

Johnson, G. and Dunphie, C., *Brightly Shone the Dawn: Some Experiences of the Invasion of Normandy*, Frederick Warne, 1980

Johnston, D., *Nine Rivers from Jordan*, Derek Verschoyle, 1953

Joseph, M. K., *I'll Soldier No More*, Gollancz, 1958

Josephy, A. M. Jr., *The Long and the Short and the Tall: the Story of a Marine Combat Unit in the Pacific* (first pub. 1946), Zenger, Washington, 1979

Kelly, A. J., *There's a Goddam Bullet for Everyone*, Tyoweronh, Paris (Ontario), 1979

Kent, R., *First In: Parachute Pathfinder Company*, Batsford, 1979

Kitching, A. F., *Men England Forgot*, Chivers, Bath, 1984

Knappett, F., *The Mad Recce*, Merlin, Braunton, 1984

Legg, F., *War Correspondent*, Angus and Robertson, 1965

Lewis, G., *Dear Courtney, or Why I Never Won the DSO*, Redcliffe, Bristol, 1985

Longhurst, H., *I Wouldn't Have Missed It*, Dent, 1945

Lovat, Lord, *March Past*, Weidenfeld and Nicholson, 1979

Lyell, A., *Memoirs of an Air Observation Post Officer*, Picton, Chippenham, 1985

Manchester, W., *Goodbye, Darkness: a Memoir of the Pacific War*, Little Brown, Boston, 1980

Mawson, S. R., *Arnhem Doctor*, Orbis, 1981

McBryde, B., *A Nurse's War*, Chatto and Windus, 1979

McGivern, W. P., *Soldiers of '44*, Collins, 1979

McGuire, P., *Taps for Jim Crow: Letters from Black Soldiers in World War II*, ABC-Clio, 1983

McKie, R., *Echoes from Forgotten Wars*, Collins, 1980

Meads, R. J., *A Reservist's War and the 252*, Merlin, Braunton, 1988

Melville, A., *First Tide*, Skeffington, n.d.

Mennell, K. H., *Death Trap*, Digit, n.d.

Merritt, M., *Eighth Army Driver*, Midas, Tunbridge Wells, 1981

Mills, M., *Tempt Not the Stars*, Harrap, 1958

Monks, J. Jr., *A Ribbon and a Star: the Third Marines at Bougainville*, Holt, Rinehart and Winston, New York, 1945

Moore, M., *Battalion at War: Singapore 1942*, Glidden, Norwich, 1988

Morgan, I. E., et al, *The Reminiscences of Four Members of C Squadron, 3 Carabiniers: Burma Campaign 1943-45*, pvte. pub. 1989

Mowat, F., *And No Birds Sang*, Cassell, 1980

Oliver, F. R., *Our Colonels Are Methodist*, Merlin, Braunton, 1987

Oliver, K., *A Man Amongst Men*, Angel, East Wittering, 1986

Owens, H. A., *Nightmare Towards the Path*, H. A. Owens, Stockport, 1985

Petty, G. F., *Mad Gerry: Welsh Wartime Medical Officer: a True Story by a Major in the RAMC*, Starling, Newport, 1982

Phibbs, B., *The Other Side of Time: a Combat Surgeon in World War II*, Hale, 1989

Potter, F. E., *Tebessa? Wherever's That?*, Merlin, Braunton, 1987

Price, B., *What Did You Do in the War, Grandpa?*, Watermill Press, Woolhampton, 1989

Ramsey, G., *One Continent Redeemed*, Harrap, 1943

Richardson, C., *Flashback: a Soldier's Story*, Kimber, 1985

Riley, N., *One Jump Ahead*, Clare, 1984

Roach, P., *The 8.15 to War: Memoirs of a Desert Rat*, Leo Cooper, 1982

Roberts, C. P. B., *From the Desert to the Baltic*, Kimber, 1987

Ryder, P., *Guns Have Eyes: One Man's Story of the Normandy Landings*, Hale, 1984

Samuel, I., *Doctor at War*, Autolycus, 1985

Scannel, V., *Arguments of Kings*, Robson, 1987

——.   *The Tiger and the Rose*, Robson, 1971

Selby, D., *Hell and High Fever*, Currawong, Sydney, 1956

Semmler, C., (ed.), *The War Diaries of Kenneth Slessor, Official War Correspondent 1940–44*, University of Queensland Press, St Lucia, 1985

Shaw, I., *The Young Lions*, Jonathan Cape, 1949

Shaw, J., *Special Force: a Chindit's Story*, Alan Sutton, Gloucester, 1986

Sheil-Small, D., *Green Shadows: a Gurkha Story*, Kimber, 1982

Sire, G., *The Deathmakers*, Muller, 1960

Sledge, E. B., *With the Old Breed At Peleliu and Okinawa*, Presidio, Novato (Cal.), 1981

Small, B., *The Reluctant Gunner*, Aberdeen U.P., Aberdeen, 1983

Smith, N., *Tank Soldier: the Fight to Liberate Europe 1944*, Book Guild, Lewes, 1989

Steward, H. D., *Recollections of a Regimental Medical Officer*, Melbourne U.P., Carleton, 1983

Stockman, J., *Seaforth Highlanders: a Fighting Soldier Remembers (1939–45)*, Crecy, Somerton, 1987

Stokoe, E. G., *Lower the Ramps: Experiences with the 43rd Royal Marine Commando in Yugoslavia*, Chivers, Bath, 1988

Sutherland, D., *Sutherland's War: an English Gentleman Goes into Battle*, Leo Cooper, 1984

Tapert, A. (ed.), *Lines of Battle: Letters from American Servicemen 1941–45*, Time Books, New York, 1987

Taplin, A. E., *The Day Thou Gavest*, Merlin, Braunton, 1988

Tennant, C., *My War, My Mules, and Me*, Albyn, Edinburgh, 1987

Thornburn, N. (ed.), *First into Antwerp*, Castle Museum Trust, Shrewsbury, 1987

Tout, K., *Tank! 40 Hours of Battle, August 1944*, Hale, 1985

——.   *Tanks Advance: Normandy to the Netherlands 1944*, Hale, 1987

Turnbull, P., *The Forgotten Battalion*, Hurst and Blackett, 1956

Turner, P. W. and Haigh, R. H., *The Great Stand at 'Snipe'*, Dept. Political Studies, Sheffield Polytechnic, 1983

Tyler, H., *One of the D-Day Dodgers*, Regency Press, 1986

Wagner, G., *The Sands of Valour*, Cassell, 1967

Wardrop, J. (ed. G. Forty), *Tanks Across the Desert*, Kimber, 1981

West, K. J., *An' it's Called a Tam-o'-Shanter*, Merlin, Braunton, 1985

Willis, D., *Eggshells and Tea-leaves: Memoirs of an Ordinary Man*, Dugdale, Oxford, 1981

Witte, J. H., *The One That Didn't Get Away*, New Horizon, Bognor Regis, 1983

Woods, R., *One Man's Desert: the Story of Captain Pip Gardner, VC MC*, pvte. pub., 1986

Yindrich, J., *Fortress Tobruk*, Benn, 1951

Index

acrimony, among Allies, 327
airborne forces, unpopularity, 64
airborne landings, casualties, 63
air, combat casualties, 354
air-strikes, Far East, 120
Alamein, 28, 67–8, 73, 75, 97, 111
All Quiet on the Western Front, 42
Allied forces, aims, 57
amphibious operations, 57 *et seq*;
    Anzio, Guam, Normandy, N
    Africa, Okinawa, Salerno, 61;
    casualties, 63; hazards, 62; losses at,
    61; ordeal of, 59; overburdening at,
    61; *see also* seasickness
Anglo-American relations, lowered by
    generals, 327
anti-tank weapons, 139; German
    superiority, 128; German, Allied,
    129
anxiety, normal reactions, 248
Anzio, compared with Passchendaele,
    73; communicating trenches at, 42;
    described by W. Vaughan-Thomas,
    42; stalemate at, 42
Arakan, conditions in, 30; Japanese
    defence of, 83
armoured warfare, 125–54; bear brunt
    of attack, 136; cooperation with
    infantry, 137; D-Day doctrine, 140;
    fighting, US in N Africa, 133;
    Liddell Hart on, 132; losses before
    Alamein, 131; rate of progress, 137;
    suspected by infantry, 135; troops
    as infantry, 41; unlike cavalry, 129;
    vehicles, limitations, 125; *see also*
    Ingersoll, tankmen, tanks
army, soldiers' attitude to, 13–16; US
    soldiers' attitude to, 230
Army Education Corps, 322
artillery, 118–25; discomfort in gun-
    pits, 124–5; domination in WWI,
    118; effects of Allied and enemy, 68–
    9; effects on troops, 67 *et seq*; high
    casualty rate at Alamein, 165; as
    infantry, 41, 121–2; 'last stands'
    against tanks, 122–3; lesser role in
    Far East, 120–1; no soft life in
    Europe, 124; prelude to assault,
    118; rate of fire, 68; rounds fired,

WWI, 118; rounds fired, WWII,
    119, 120; *sine qua non*, 119; 25 pdr
    against tanks, 122; use of *en masse*,
    123; in WWI & II, 118–19
Assam front, fighting in, 35, 84
assault, airborne, confusions, 63;
    infantry, typical, 93–4; landing
    craft, 58
Atlantic Wall, 74
attack, the, 72–96; frontal, against
    entrenchments, 75; hand-to-hand
    fighting, 73; Japanese at night, 95–
    6; Japanese suicidal, 78;
    preparation for, 57; reactions to
    enemy fire, 97; under enemy fire,
    72–3
Australian Army, 'class' tensions, 332

Baron, Alexander, describes battle
    reaction, 103
barbed wire, 363
barrage effects, at Alamein, 67–8
bathing facilities, 309
battle, approach to, 57–67; reaction to,
    103; a slaughterhouse, 116;
    uncertainty, 99–100
beer, shipped to Middle East, 291
Bernhard Line, 42
beverages, cold for US, 288
Bismarck Archipelago, 33
Blitzkrieg, psychological in 1940, 125–
    6
boils, recurrence of in England and
    Normandy, 276
bombardment, 67–72; description of,
    70–1; mental strain of, 69; physical
    effects, 69–70; reactions to, 70;
    shelling own troops, 71
bombing, air support, hitting own
    troops, 71; crew casualties, 354
boredom, 324–6
Box, Admin, 49; Knightsbridge, 38;
    ineffective as defence, 37–8
Breskens Pocket, 73
Brest, strong points eliminated, 76
brewing up, 286–7
brothels, attitudes to, 303–5
brotherhood, spirit of, 347–8
Bruce, Gen, 50